Socio-cultural Dynamics

Socio-cultural Dynamics

An Introduction to Social Change

Francis R. Allen

THE MACMILLAN COMPANY . NEW YORK
COLLIER-MACMILLAN LIMITED . LONDON

THE MACMILLAN COMPANY
866 THIRD AVENUE, NEW YORK, NEW YORK 10022

COLLIER-MACMILLAN CANADA, LTD., TORONTO, ONTARIO
Library of Congress catalog card number: 70–134884

First Printing

To Gertrude

Preface

This book includes what this writer thinks should be the basic
knowledge for the college or university student in the field of social
change at this fast-moving and tumultuous time. The aims and
scope here are, thus, broad. The field of social change is itself of a
panoramic nature. Because this area of sociology is currently receiving major attention, and because important (perhaps outstanding)
developments may lie ahead, one objective is to point out the various types of contributions that are being made. The latter include
advances in theory, methodology and measurement, processes (such
as innovation, diffusion, and resistances to innovation), and special
substantive areas (such as the study of developing nations). Theoretical and methodological advances include contributions in cybernetics, systems theory, information theory, game theory, and simulation
as they apply to social change, as well as endeavors relating to the
continued study of social trends, social indicators, and social accounting. Regarding substantive areas, special attention is paid to the current emphasis on the activist perspective, which is regarded as a
significant development. A notable characteristic of the present period,
indeed, is the widespread interest in actively seeking to direct social
change for the benefit of man—to determine major social objectives
and then put forth continued efforts in the hope of attaining them.
However, this volume, it must be said, is not concerned with specific
problems or programs, but rather with more general and perhaps
more fundamental aspects of social change; the latter may of course
have specific applications. Nevertheless, whether the student has a
general interest in this fascinating field or intends sooner or later
to make active contributions or applications, he would do well to
inform himself of the existing knowledge. The new often grows out
of, and should be an improvement on, the old. To attempt to add
to a field can be perilous if one is unfamiliar with what has already
been accomplished. This includes profiting from past mistakes. To
make specific application without knowledge of the theoretical ideas
and processes involved can sometimes bring desired results; but it is
to toil without awareness of and guidance from the broader design.
This writer, then, has attempted a general stocktaking of the field

of social change, with special regard for what is conceived to be its more enduring and worthwhile elements and its directions of activity on the current scene.

I am grateful to a number of people for various kinds of aid received: Sincere appreciation is extended to Mr. Charles E. Smith, sociology editor at The Macmillan Company, for astute guidance at many points, for numerous helpful suggestions, and for general encouragement; and to students in my undergraduate classes and graduate seminars in social change who, in the usual give-and-take of the classroom experience, have stimulated the development of ideas and conclusions more than they may realize. To my former teachers collectively, but especially to Professor Rupert B. Vance (director of my dissertation) and to the late Professors William F. Ogburn and Robert M. MacIver, deep appreciation is expressed. Professor Vance, as sociologist, demographer, and friend, has been a major inspiration. It was a great privilege to have received instruction regarding social change from Professors Ogburn and MacIver; as a colleague, co-author, and friend of Professor Ogburn during his later years, I am conscious of a special debt. I would also like to express very sincere appreciation for the many years of association and much intellectual stimulation from the late Dr. Meyer F. Nimkoff. To my present colleagues at Florida State University and to other contemporary sociologists I am very grateful for aid in the form of reactions and criticisms to parts of the manuscript, namely to: Professors Leland J. Axelson, T. Stanton Dietrich, James M. Fendrich, Robert M. French, Charles M. Grigg, Robert E. Herriott, Charles B. Nam, Ronald M. Pavalko, A. Lewis Rhodes, Lee Sloan, Donald D. Smith, and J. Timothy Sprehe; Professor T. Lynn Smith of the University of Florida, Gainesville; Professor Lewis M. Killian of the University of Massachusetts; Professor Bernard Phillips of Boston University; Professor Benjamin J. Hodgkins of the University of Manitoba; also Professor Charles E. Rockwood, Department of Economics, Florida State, and Dr. Myron R. Blee, Director, Associated Consultants in Education, Inc., Tallahassee, Florida. For aid relative to a specific point I wish to thank Professor Abbott L. Ferriss, Chairman of the Department of Sociology and Anthropology, Emory University (formerly with the Russell Sage Foundation). Despite this plentiful help, I bear sole responsibility for the final product. For expert typing and superb cooperation I am indebted to Mrs. Bernice Quick. Finally, on the personal front, there is no question as to where the debt lies. In dedicating this volume to my wife, an all-important sustaining force over the years, I trust that the gratitude felt is communicated.

F. R. A.

Contents

Socio-cultural Dynamics

1 The World Changes

THE REALITY OF CHANGE

Of one thing we can be sure: All the world changes. Life in our many societies is on the move. We are not always certain *how* societies will change or *how rapidly*—or that we shall like the changes. We do not say that all elements of a society will change during a given time period. Later we shall consider relatively constant factors in an otherwise changing milieu. It is clear, furthermore, that all societies or other defined areas do not change at the same rate of speed. Man's situation is similar to that of being on a huge moving stage or platform; ongoing society has been viewed as, indeed, an equilibrium the nature of which is constantly changing.[1] As people gradually grow older and accumulate ideas and experiences, society also matures and is modified by innovations, diffused ideas or objects, unique historical events, and other occurrences. Society and its institutions develop partly from within (according to their natures) as well as in response to external influences. The internal unfolding element means that change in human affairs is virtually guaranteed even if the external environment were somehow to remain static—which it cannot do. We know that in varying degrees climate, resources, and other geographical elements change. We know also that in one decade people will be ten years older, even if other population factors such as birth rates, death rates, and migrations experience no fluctuations—a highly unlikely prospect. If a stagnant, "dead-center" operation seemed to exist in some location, it would be an unexpected condition that would need explanation. People may choose to resist the coming of certain developments; later (in Chapter 11) we shall discuss resistances to innovations and events. But once a change has been made, man (if rational) has to accept the fact of change itself, whatever his personal viewpoint toward it. One can return to earlier times or "the good old days" only in memories,

[1] Robert M. MacIver, *Social Causation* (New York: Ginn and Co., 1942; Harper Torchbook Edition, 1964), p. 173.

dreams, history books, literature, art forms, and recordings. Sometimes, of course, something resembling a change back may take place. In general, however, the community, neighborhood, or family environment that we knew well a few years back is different today. A pertinent question always is, *how great* has been the change? [2]

Change has been so great in modern times that the examination of this phenomenon has become a major and pressing enterprise. But before we attempt to analyze alleged changes or suggest causes, let us review, however briefly and sketchily, changes in selected areas, keeping in mind that we shall *later* attempt explanations. Descriptive comment will first document the reality and the immensity of change.

Let us begin by observing the onward surge of change in the American socio-cultural environment. We propose to do this by comparing the socio-cultural conditions of approximately one century ago (dating this base period as approximately the year 1870; we see no need to go all the way back to America's beginnings) with conditions of approximately two generations ago (which we shall date at about the year 1910), with circumstances of approximately one generation ago (dating this at about 1940), and with present-day conditions. Even though this comparison of the American socio-cultural environment of these different points in time will be general in nature, it will be sufficient to vividly indicate the vast changes that have taken place in this nation.[3]

One Century Ago. At the year 1870—which marks a time only a few years after the ending of the Civil War—the American socio-cultural environment was populated by less than one fifth of its numbers today. The total national population as recorded in the Census of 1870 was only about 39,905,000. The West was largely a frontier, although the Western States were growing rapidly at this time.

---

[2] As Herskovits declares, no living culture is static. Melville J. Herskovits, "The Processes of Cultural Change," in Ralph Linton (ed.), *The Science of Man in the World Crisis* (New York: Columbia University Press, 1945), p. 143.

[3] Because these descriptions essentially comprise a sketch (which is all we are trying to do), we shall not document all factual statements here. When such statements are not cited, the reader can assume that figures are usually derived from the *Statistical Abstract of the United States* or the U. S. Bureau of the Census, *Historical Statistics of the United States, Colonial Times to 1957* (Washington, D. C., 1960), and its "Continuation to 1962" (Washington, D. C., 1965). Also, selected works in American History have been consulted such as Allan Nevins and Henry Steele Commager, *The Pocket History of the United States,* new enlarged edition (New York: Pocket Books, Inc., 1956); Harold U. Faulkner, *American Political and Social History,* 5th ed. (New York: Appleton-Century-Crofts, 1948); and Harvey Wish, *Society and Thought in Modern America* (New York: Longmans, Green and Co., 1952). At the conclusion of these descriptive sketches we summarize selected factual data in a table; sources *are* given here.

If one pushes the clock back to 1850, it is significant that no population at all is listed in the *Historical Statistics of the United States* for the Dakotas, Nebraska, Kansas, Montana, Idaho, Wyoming, Colorado, Arizona, and Nevada. The number of settlers rose notably in Kansas, Nebraska, Colorado, and North Dakota after that. The great bulk of foreign immigrants, incidentally, had not reached American shores. Railroads were being built in the eastern half of the nation, although the major coast-to-coast expansion was yet to come. The tempo of the (roughly Civil War) times is indicated by the speed of the railroads that were then operating—which was about thirty miles per hour.[4] Horse-drawn streetcars were operated in the eastern cities; covered wagons and stage coaches were used out West. Steamboats plied the Mississippi and other waterways. American life in these simple times was, of course, predominately rural (in 1870 slightly more than 28 million people lived in rural territory, not quite ten million in urban areas).[5]

Manufacturing was growing rapidly in the East and Middle West,[6] but, like other developments, it was a "toddling infant" compared to a century later. The nation's first department store had been established by Alexander T. Stewart in New York in 1848. Although something of an event at the time, this store would be dwarfed by such present-day enterprises as Macy's or Marshall Field's, much as the factories of a century ago would be dwarfed by comparison with today's General Electric, DuPont, or IBM plants. The same, of course, would follow for banks, insurance companies, and other business enterprises. Large fortunes were being made during the 1870s; however, in those laissez-faire times, cries and charges were frequently made declaring gross fraud and corruption.[7] Government, similarily, was in a stage of relative underdevelopment. The Federal Government had close to 51,000 civilian employees in 1871, with total expenditures of $309 million (1870). This was partly a result of little being expected of it under the prevailing laissez-faire emphasis (it was supposed to keep its hands off business and other activities); it was also due to the comparatively small national population and the essentially uncomplicated life of this period.

The condition of education, again, was in its veritable infancy. Cultural expectations, in the first place, did not even require high school graduation for the average person. Those who attended college almost

[4] Arthur Charles Cole, *The Irrepressible Conflict, 1850–1865.* (New York: The Macmillan Company, 1934), pp. 14–20.
[5] *Historical Statistics*, p. 14 (Series A 195–209).
[6] Cole, *op. cit.*, pp. 24–26.
[7] *Ibid.*, pp. 28–30.

always intended to enter one of the professions. Harvard seems to have been the leader at this time. Yale granted its first doctor of philosophy degree in 1861; in fact, this was the first such degree to be granted in the United States. Technical schools were established at Columbia, Dartmouth, Lehigh, and other places. Medical schools were function-ing in all parts of the nation, some dental schools had been established, and law schools were developing fast.[8] However, regarding both quality and quantity, education was undeveloped. The stock of knowledge was so small as to make low quality inevitable, and the quantity factor can be illustrated by the fact that at this time both Columbia and New York University each had approximately 150 students.[9]

A few colleges admitted women students at approximately this time: Elmira, Oberlin, Antioch (founded by Horace Mann in 1852), and Vassar (founded in 1861). The woman's rights movement was gathering force under the leadership of Elizabeth Cady Stanton and others. Family life was patriarchal. The life of a woman was tied to the home. The notion of employed mothers did not fit these times; divorces were rare. Another factor of this period was that the state of public health was elemental: the desire to establish a community water supply was developing, and major concerns related to epidemics of smallpox, yel-low fever, and cholera (not at all controlled, needless to say). The average expectation of life at birth in the United States was about forty years—certainly not high enough to warrant concern over such de-generative diseases as heart disease, cancer, and strokes.

Meager and sketchy as is this picture of the socio-cultural environ-ment of about 1870, it suggests the simple, slowly changing, nondif-ferentiated activities and institutions of the time. This was the mostly rural, primarily isolated, horse-and-buggy, "gas-lit home scene" type of living—with frontier conditions in the West. Sociology, of course, would not have been studied in the existing colleges. Sociology had not yet been added to the educational curriculum of American colleges, but Comte had established the field with his worthy endeavors in France; Spencer had issued his *First Principles* in 1862 in England (and his *Principles of Sociology* was soon to appear, in 1876); and Lester F. Ward in the United States would before long (1883) make a major

---

[8] *Ibid.,* pp. 211–213.

[9] See, for example, Horace Coon, *Columbia, Colossus on the Hudson* (New York: E. P. Dutton & Co., 1947), pp. 75–76. Not only was Columbia's enrollment low, considering the fact that it was located in a leading metropolis and had been operating for a century, but its faculty consisted of six professors. Reflection on the early years of great bureaucracies suggests the theme of "great oaks from little acorns grow." A century later Columbia's student enrollment was close to 16,000, with its faculty numbering about 3,200; a century later NYU's enrollment was about 39,000, with its faculty roster comprising about 3,900.

contribution for those times with his *Dynamic Sociology*. However, we must appreciate that many currently prominent colleges and universities in the western half of the United States (and some in the East), where such works might be studied, were not even in existence in 1870.

Two Generations Ago. America's population two generations ago—which means approximately the year 1910—numbered more than 92,407,000. Less than one half of the total (45.7 per cent) lived in urban communities. Negroes constituted 10.7 per cent of the total population, and the vast number at this time lived in the South; it was after this, indeed, that the exodus to the North and West began. The social setting of 1910 emphasized an increasing industrialization (although its amount at the time was small compared with later generations); the formation of large business combinations such as United States Steel and General Motors; an increasingly active Federal Government (reflecting in large part an expansion of the powers of the presidency under Theodore Roosevelt, which was mostly maintained by his successor, William Howard Taft); reform as indicated by the passage of the Pure Food and Drug Act and the Meat Inspection Act, life insurance reforms, and reforms in municipal politics; and the quest for social justice with special reference to women working in industry (who had often been exploited in wages and hours of work) and child labor (many states passed child labor laws between 1900 and 1915). Agitation for woman suffrage occurred at this time, and the Woman Suffrage Amendment to the Constitution of the United States was passed in 1919 and was ratified in 1920. Finally, agitation grew for urban improvement. Problems of housing, backward sanitation, overcrowding, filth, disease, and vice were pronounced in 1910—although these were not necessarily the equivalent of the "crime in the streets" and the urban ghetto problems of the 1960s and 1970s because of markedly differing contexts. The problem of assimilating immigrants was a considerable one (over one million immigrants had entered the United States in the one year 1907); many of the immigrants lived in the urban slums.

Health and education were in rudimentary condition. Tuberculosis was a leading cause of death, and Edward L. Trudeau and others were inaugurating the sanitarium movement. Vaccination against typhoid and smallpox was gradually developing despite some problems and some public resistance. The final yellow fever epidemic to occur in the United States had raged a few years before (1906). The infant mortality rate, using the figures of the state of Massachusetts, was a high 116.7 per 1,000 live births; the total expectation of life at birth in 1910 was precisely fifty years. Other interests of this time were the hookworm disease eradication campaign in the South, which was notably successful, and nutritional discoveries such as vitamin research, which offered much social benefit, conducted by the scientists L. B. Mendel, Henry C. Sherman, and E. V. McCollum. Educationally, the American nation was moving slowly. In 1910 a mere 8.8 per cent of Americans of age 17 were graduates of high school; the major secondary education movement in the nation had not yet occurred. The enrollment in higher education was no more impressive. A total of 5.1 per cent of Americans of the ages 18–21 were enrolled in institutions of higher learning; many of these were headed for the professions. A very small number were female or Negro.

Concerning transportation, this was the heyday of the railroad—and of course shipping. The railroad had been America's first large-scale industry developing from an invention. A total of more than 32 million passenger miles of railroad traffic was recorded for 1910, which is one of the few items numerically greater at this time than one and two generations later. The automobile age was in its early stage in 1910, although nearly a half-million registrations were recorded; the mass production of the motor vehicle, led by Henry Ford and others, would begin in 1913. Auto travel expanded rapidly after that, and roads were gradually improved. Then, the Wright Brothers made their first plane flight in 1903—another important milestone. However, aviation developed slowly during the following decade or two. We shall observe the acceleration of interest after that.

Other inventions of note include the high-speed power press and the linotype, which were important for newspapers. These inventions, and also the typewriter and telephone, had appeared before 1900, but their full influence was felt after that time. Moreover, the motion picture had been invented by Thomas Edison and was gradually developing as an entertainment and educational source.

Finally, America in 1910 was rapidly becoming a world power.

One Generation Ago. If, again, a few bold strokes can be used to describe the essential socio-cultural conditions of a time in the development of the American nation, let us turn to the period of one generation ago—by which we mean the society of approximately the year 1940. The over-all social climate of this period was vastly different from the preceding one, being dominated by (1) the political activities of Franklin D. Roosevelt and his New Deal program and (2) the ominously gathering clouds of major war in both Europe and Asia. Although we know from hindsight that Hitler did attack Czechoslovakia, Poland, France, and other countries and the Japanese did bomb Pearl Harbor (thus starting the Second World War), these occurrences are wide of our immediate interest. It may be well to add, needless to say, that had not the Allied side been victorious in that war, the nature and condition of American society *today* would undoubtedly be immensely different.

America as of the year 1940 had a population of more than 132 million; Hawaii and Alaska were not members of the union at that time. The population was steadily becoming more urban (it was 56.5 per cent urban and 43.5 per cent rural in 1940). The Negro population comprised about 10 per cent of the total (the actual figure was 9.8 per cent). Negro migration from rural South to urban North and West continued: A total of 347,500 Negro Americans had migrated between 1930 and 1940; 749,000 between 1920 and 1930; and 454,300 between 1910 and 1920.[10] The index of domestic productivity (all around) had jumped to 124.0 based on a 1929 figure of 100 (the 1940 figure was twice that of the generation before), and the value of factory production (expressed as the value added by manufacture) had risen to over $24 billion or about three times that of the preceding generation; this high industrial productivity would be invaluable in the war effort. Americans were becoming increasingly educated: In 1940 more than one half of those of age 17 (male and female) were graduates of high school, which was more than five times the figure of the preceding generation; and more than 15 per cent of the population of the ages 18–21 were enrolled in institutions of higher learning, which was roughly three times that of the preceding generation. The health of the people was also improving: The total expectation of life at birth in 1940 was 62.9 years (it had been 50.0 years in 1910); the infant mortality rate was rapidly declining (it was 34.3 in 1940, or approximately one quarter of the rate in 1910); control of communicable diseases had especially been advanced. With regard to transportation, railroad travel was significant but was nevertheless declining as compared with earlier years, whereas motor vehicle travel had virtually skyrocketed as compared with one generation before, and air travel was moving up fast (and giving increased competition for the railroads and steamship lines). The automobile age, in particular, had now come into its own: The figure of more than 32 million auto registrations in 1940 as compared with a mere 468 *thousand* in 1910 reflects the great popularity of automobiles with Americans; it also shows the influence of the production of better cars, the important gain in total population, a constantly advancing economy (so that many could afford to purchase a car), the wide open spaces of the American nation, and other factors. However, there is little wish to minimize aviation in

10 Philip M. Hauser, "Demographic Factors in the Integration of the Negro," *Daedalus* (Fall, 1965), "The Negro American," Vol. 1, especially 851.

this quarter. In 1940 more than a billion passenger miles were flown in scheduled airline operations, which was roughly nine times the number flown only eight years before; aviation was developing that rapidly. Also, aircraft production had become big business. Incidentally, many of these factors had war relevance, and United States air power in particular was *one* of the decisive factors in the Second World War.

Concerning the field of communications, the radio age was at its zenith. Roosevelt's fireside chats were famous. However, television had been unveiled at the New York World's Fair of 1938–1939, and *its* spectacular rise was to take place with the ending of the war. Nuclear energy was also poised for a dramatic development. The year 1940 would be generally considered as pre-atomic age, but Harold C. Urey and others were experimenting with "heavy water"; Enrico Fermi had discovered that bombarding uranium with neutrons makes it radioactive; the German scientists Hahn and Strassmann had split the uranium nucleus (1939); and Niels Bohr of Denmark had made the finding (on a theoretical basis at least) that the bombardment of a small amount of pure isotope of 235 uranium would start a chain reaction whereby a great atomic explosion would occur. All of this had as a basis Einstein's theoretical formula of 1906 that mass and energy are interchangeable ($E = mc^2$). To actually make an atom bomb was the next goal. Development of the first A-bomb was rushed as a (United States) military project. The objective was successfully achieved, and the first detonation took place during July, 1945. The second and third bombs were dropped on Hiroshima and Nagasaki several weeks later to end the Pacific part of the Second World War. Peacetime applications of nuclear energy, especially in industry and in medicine, would be made gradually. Accomplishments with regard to developing the electronic computer and space travel were taking place, but the major events were yet to come.

It is clear that governmental expansion had to occur, with activities such as the preceding requiring regulation. Also, New Deal philosophy included extending governmental supervision and control over the economic life of the nation in order to "make Capitalism work." [11] Critics contended that Roosevelt was breaking down free enterprise and bringing socialism. In any event, the Washington bureaucracy grew considerably during the New Deal years. Civilian employees of

[11] This is not to say that F. D. Roosevelt was the first to extend governmental regulations. In fact, his predecessor, Herbert Hoover, who often extolled "rugged individualism," instituted various important controls. Actually, controls go back to the Interstate Commerce Act of 1887, the Sherman Antitrust Act of 1890, and even earlier. Yet the New Deal did mark a conspicuous acceleration in the decline of laissez faire.

the Federal Government numbered more than one million in 1940, nearly three times the figure of one generation before. Total expenditures of the Federal Government in 1940 exceeded $9 billion (1940 was, moreover, *not* a war year); one generation before the total expenditures had amounted to $693 million.

    Present-Day America. A glimpse at the socio-culture environment of today reveals initially that this nation is inhabited by a large population (a steadily increasing number of more than two hundred million). The people live more and more in and around metropolitan centers (especially "around")—Negro Americans and other minority groups tend to concentrate in the centers, white people in the suburbs. The Negro population, comprising about 11 per cent of the national total, has steadily migrated out of the South to the urban North and West, especially to the states of New York, Pennsylvania, Ohio, Michigan, Illinois, and California; a total of 2,701,700 Negroes are estimated to have migrated out of the South between 1940 and 1960.[12] However, this out-migration seems to have declined between 1960 and 1969.[13] A large number of the American labor force is employed in business, industrial, and service occupations, an increasingly smaller percentage are employed in agriculture (the latter now comprising roughly 6 per cent of the labor force). Business and industrial activities are increasingly dominated by large corporations, with small businesses and family firms now much less characteristic of the economy. An increasingly automated industry has made the American economy exceedingly productive, often the envy of other nations; the Gross National Product has in fact soared: in 1969 it attained the very high figure of $932.3 billion in current dollars.[14] This productivity, coupled with an abundant purchasing power, has brought the highest standard of living found in the world. Business and industrial enterprises (large and small) are currently subject to a considerable amount of governmental regulation; a regulated economy, in short, has replaced the earlier free market. The governmental structure, for its part, has become huge ("big government"); the federal bureaucracy, with its many departments, bureaus, and agencies, currently employs close to three million

12 Hauser, *loc. cit.*

13 A joint report prepared by the Bureau of the Census and the Bureau of Labor Statistics declares that the annual out-migration from the South declined to 88,000 in the 1960s (it had averaged 146,000 during the 1950s, and 159.7 during the 1940s). See *The Social and Economic Status of Negroes in the United States, 1969,* BLS Report No. 375 and *Current Population Reports,* Series P–23, No. 29 (Washington, D. C.: Government Printing Office, 1970), p. 5.

14 This is the figure given by President Nixon's Council of Economic Advisers in its Annual Report (see *The New York Times,* January 31, 1970). This figure is computed at 1969 price levels.

civilians. Governmental functions have greatly expanded during the last half century for a variety of reasons: (1) the increasing complexity of modern life, due partly to population growth itself and partly to the transition from rural to urban living, in which increased governmental controls are needed to replace the earlier informal controls; (2) the need to deal with pressing problems and crises (such as health and sanitation problems, business depressions, strikes, financial speculation, air and water pollution, educational problems, crime and delinquency); and (3) the need to supervise institutions in their normal functioning, resulting from the value change from a laissez-faire to government-intervention emphasis (increasingly the government was expected to have an interest in business and other matters, instead of maintaining the aloof, "hands-off" view, and currently may be looked upon as a general overseer and regulator of society).

Education has similarly grown into a big business. Nearly two million teachers are employed at the primary and secondary levels and an additional half million in higher education; more than 15 million young Americans now attend high school as well as upward of six million enrolled in colleges; and the vast enterprise is characterized by a marked proliferation of activities and curricula. The median amount of schooling completed by the "average American" now exceeds the second year of high school. College attendance is increasingly desired both for occupational and general social preparation on the part of both sexes and all races. Blacks lag in educational attainment, although their situation shows improvement. High school and college students, especially the latter, increasingly demand a voice in the decision making that affects their activities and concerns. Avoiding further detail we can observe that, just as government may be increasingly looked upon as the general overseer of society, education (formal and informal) becomes a more important vehicle of socialization and preparation; long related to skills and choice of occupations (skilled, semi-skilled, unskilled, professional), it bears a significant relationship to the perspectives of people and their range of interests. And because the total society has become highly complicated, education has had to increase its content; its value to people would seem to be greater in modern times. Science has become an essential part of education as well as constituting a significant national influence in itself. Research has expanded impressively (research and development funds in the United States have increased more than threefold during the past decade). Not only do scientific discoveries often form the basis for technological inventions, but both importantly affect medicine, family life, and other departments of living. The impact of science and technology upon medicine has been enormous (too great to permit citing of details here). It is clear that they have increased the effectiveness in conquering disease (especially communicable disease); they have made the practice of medicine more specialized; and they have brought the frequent use of machines to the practice. Family life has been much affected by findings of biological and social science and by techno-logical inventions (especially in the contraceptive realm with current emphasis on the pill). The Industrial Revolution, with other influ-ences, set forces in motion that undercut the patriarchal family, and equalitarian, joint-rule family structure is the dominant one in this nation. Companionship, sex fulfillment, and the rearing of children are the main functions presently of the American family. The em-ployment of mothers is common, which is linked with a rise of nur-series; moreover, the family ideal is increasingly one of having wanted children and spacing births. The scientific influence on religion has been indirect: It appears to have brought some decline in the net influence of religion (although church going remains high), and it has caused religion to be more secularized.[15] Leisure-time and recrea-tional activities have been affected by the increasing use of machines in industry and elsewhere. The extension of automation makes the prospects for further increases in leisure realistic. Some workers, how-ever, have resisted the "leisure-time ethic," preferring to use free time by taking a second job (or occasionally even a third one) and so swell-ing personal or family income. It appears that the force of the Protes-tant ethic has not entirely been dissipated.

The various conditions that have been described are not held to be ideal. Problems relate to most of them. Nevertheless many of the accomplishments in the economic, industrial, educational, scientific, and medical areas—and others doubtless—show a vast improvement over past years, and they can be viewed as impressive indeed. The mobility of the nation's people, moreover, resulting especially from automobile and air travel, is notable; also worthy of special attention is our elabo-rate communications system, with the emphasis on television—although again it is acknowledged that problems exist in these areas. The space age has had a spectacular and successful beginning period. Many mile-stones were passed in the orbital flights of NASA's Mercury, Gemini, and Apollo programs, culminating in man's epic landing on the moon on July 20, 1969—a tremendous industrial-technological-organizational triumph. For man to go to the moon, land there, and return home, was only several decades back regarded as symbolic of the impossible. Never-theless the total (United States) range of achievements, from the

15 See, for example, Harvey G. Cox, *The Secular City* (New York: The Macmillan Company, 1965); and Howard Becker, *Through Values to Social Interpretation* (Durham, N. C.: Duke University Press, 1950), p. 248.

economic and political to space, have made this nation a leading world power, even a super power in many respects. With its rapid rate of change still continuing and probably accelerating, the United States seems headed toward a postindustrial society in which educational, research, and service institutions will more and more be dominant rather than the business and industrial institutions as was true in the past.[16] Some sizeable problems, however, cloud the contemporary scene and threaten society's onward march.

The major problem areas of present-day American society center around the persistence of important pockets of poverty amid the affluence of the many, continued racial injustice, and a generalized revolt on the part of various youth and other groups against "the establishment." To some extent these problem areas are interrelated. Some Negroes have significantly raised their income and status, many others have not; a considerable gap between the latter and the white population is still found. Prejudice and injustice with respect to Negroes and other minority groups, moreover, are erased slowly in many cases. Protests and riots against poverty conditions in ghettoes as well as alleged injustices are prominent on the American scene: demonstrations, confrontations, sit-ins, and militant takeovers of office or campus buildings occur. American college students who, only a few years ago, were quite apathetic have often become active rebels for varied reasons. Indeed the battleground has many times shifted to college campuses. Sympathy toward the racial protests and especially objections to the Vietnam War have been prominent inciters, although protesters have been a mixed army of idealists, dissidents, revolutionaries (the Students for a Democratic Society), and general nihilists. Many ardent protesters have not been able to point to any goal or specific ideas that they wish would replace the current establishment (or ideas held by the latter), hence they have been called "rebels without a cause."

Most of the problem areas are complex in nature. For instance, the trend of average income of American families during recent decades is impressively upward and it would seem to constitute no problem at all. Herman P. Miller points out that the increase in incomes has been widespread throughout the population,[17] granting that the aged, uneducated, and unskilled have not moved ahead as rapidly as the others.

16 Daniel Bell, "Notes on the Post-Industrial Society (I) and (II)," *The Public Interest,* No. 6 (Winter, 1967), 24–35, and No. 7 (Spring, 1967), 102–118.

17 Miller, *Rich Man Poor Man* (New York: Thomas Y. Crowell Co., 1964), p. 46. Miller's figures show that in 1929, 51 per cent of American families had an annual income under $3,000; in 1962, only 21 per cent were in this needy category. At the other end of the scale, in 1929 5 per cent of families had an annual income of $10,000 and more, whereas in 1962, 19 per cent (nearly one fifth) were in this grouping. (See Table III–2, p. 47.)

Moreover, this increase in family income continued on to the end of the 1960s.[18] Gratifying as is this trend in the *amount* of income, have rich and poor *shared* about equally in the increase? Unfortunately, Miller's answer here is in the negative. Has the income gap between white and nonwhite workers narrowed with the passage of years? Again, his answer is "No" (his figures relate to the period between 1947 and 1962). More recent figures comparing the median income of white and nonwhite families show some narrowing of the gap between 1965 and 1968; in 1965 the median income of Negro families constituted 54 per cent of that of the white families, whereas in 1968 the former comprised 60 per cent of the latter.[19] With much of the white-nonwhite income gap remaining, then, and with the differential in rich-poor sharing continuing, some might say: If the poor now receive substantially *more* income than a few decades ago, isn't that enough? However, as Miller declares,[20] many who have pondered the question regard the *share* as a key element. If, furthermore, discriminations and handicaps are factors in the situation, feelings of dissatisfaction are even more likely to develop.

What is more, reactions toward and even *consciousness of* such matters may change in time. Perhaps people were not so aware of such differences in *share* of income in earlier years as they are today. As Duncan declares,[21] ". . . today we recognize as forms of inequality, or manifestations of discrimination, social patterns that were accepted only a few years ago—not because they were then deemed just, but simply because they were still unidentified." Moreover, as Duncan makes clear, the handicaps of the Negro American (for example) unfortunately build on each other; that is to say, inadequacies relative to family background affect the young Negro's schooling, inadequacies concerning schooling then affect the job obtained, the latter in turn affects family income, and the amount of income affects life satisfactions and morale.[22] Frustrations and handicaps, in short, are often cumulative. And surely people are more articulate today concerning dissatisfactions than ever before.[23]

---

[18] Median income steadily rose, reaching the figure of $8,937 for whites in 1968 and of $5,590 for Negroes in that year. See *The Social and Economic Status of Negroes in the United States, 1969,* Bureau of Labor Statistics Report No. 375 and *Current Population Reports,* Series P–23, No. 29 (Washington, D. C.: Government Printing Office, 1970), p. 16.

[19] *Ibid.,* p. 14.

[20] Miller, *op. cit.,* p. 55.

[21] Otis Dudley Duncan, "Discrimination Against Negroes," in *The Annals of the American Academy of Political and Social Science,* Vol. 371 (May, 1967), "Social Goals and Indicators for American Society: Vol. I," 86.

[22] *Ibid.,* pp. 87–88.

[23] On the subject of income, poverty, and inequality, see also S. M. Miller, Martin

It cannot be said with certainty whether militant protests would cease if racial injustices, income deprivations, and relative deprivations could somehow be totally eliminated and if the Vietnam War were brought to a sudden halt. Indeed we doubt that—because the world always seems to be well stocked with problems. Protest has already turned in part to the pollution problem. This is another example of a gradually developing problem that suddenly becomes a central point of national attention, even of anguish. Our main comment here is that the pollution problem focuses on the negative features of our industrial, technological civilization. Americans have valued the positive aspects; they must now reckon with the negative, which have in truth befouled the air, polluted rivers and lakes, and affected wildlife. Man must assess what has happened ecologically to the total environment as his society has developed. "His industrial dominance has resulted in a high standard of material well-being," declares Krutilla, "but the ecological consequences may not yet be understood fully nor the ultimate cost appreciated." [24] Just as many of the problems were, it seems, technologically or industrially caused, many will be technologically and/or industrially remedied; [25] air pollution from the automobile, a leading source, can be controlled by devising a new engine design (as a low-compression engine) for which unleaded gasoline can be used or by using cars powered by gas turbines, electricity, or steam. At any rate, one hopes that man will plan his society with the ecological perspective (among others) in mind. Human beings need fresh air and clean water, space and beauty; [26] Americans are rightly giving close attention to the *quality of life* at this time. They need to make peace with nature and to begin making reparations for the damage done to the air, to the land, and to the water.

But problems generally are dealt with in society's no-doubt imper-

---

Rein, Pamela Roby, and Bertram M. Gross, "Poverty, Inequality, and Conflict," in *The Annals of the American Academy of Political and Social Science,* Vol. 373 (September, 1967), "Social Goals and Indicators for American Society: Vol. II," 16–52.

[24] John V. Krutilla, "Some Environmental Effects of Economic Development," *Daedalus* (Fall, 1967), especially p. 1069.

[25] An excellent government report of 1966 made suggestions on this point. See "Report of the National Commission on Technology, Automation, and Economic Progress," *Technology and the American Economy,* Vol. I (Washington, D. C.: Government Printing Office, 1966), Part III, chap. 7, "Applying Technology to Community Needs."

[26] The health factor alone is worth considering. It seems that there is some evidence (but no actual proof) that general air pollution is associated with various respiratory ailments, namely: chronic bronchitis, chronic constrictive ventilatory disease, pulmonary emphysema, bronchial asthma, and lung cancer. For a discussion, see Azriel Teller, "Air-Pollution Abatement: Economic Rationality and Reality," *Daedalus* (Fall, 1967), 1082–1098.

fect ways. One may observe at this point that issues and problems often come to a head quickly in our modern, fast-changing society. The mass media (especially television) are undoubtedly responsible for this. When alleged problems receive public attention in one locality, public demonstrations or strikes may result. Other areas having similar situations become the scene of further demonstrations; that is, strikes in one city often lead to similar strikes in others. Sometimes sympathy strikes may follow. These events become infectious. Although the media cannot be blamed for the objective imparting of the daily news (rather this is their duty and responsibility), nevertheless disruptions often become multiplied. As a consequence modern society tends to become more *disorganization prone.*

The possibilities of social disorganization are especially likely to be increased if force (including radicalized force) is increasingly used. Even though most present-day activists and demonstrators are young people, militant radicals appear to constitute at this time only a small percentage of the total. A key issue with respect to the possibility of future disorganization, then, would appear to lie in the extent to which total youth is generally sympathetic toward, or is disenchanted with, current conditions (including the goals of the establishment). Related to this, undoubtedly, would be the reactions of the broad masses of youth toward the ideas and behavior of the dissidents. Whether the numbers of the latter group will grow or whether they will remain only a relatively small but vocal contingent who make the most of the laws of the free speech (and who may be overemphasized in newspaper headlines and on the TV screen) is something that the coming years will tell us. American society, with its open discussion, often seems to be more disrupted than it really is. (Its experiences with the protestations of Huey Long and Father Coughlin, the radio priest, during the 1930s [27] and Senator McCarthy of Wisconsin during the 1950s,[28] suggest, too, that tumult may sometimes characterize the public scene more than actual disruption.) Totalitarian or other nations may have just as severe (or greater) problems that are more repressed by the leadership. If the American people are more open with their problems, it still may be difficult to tell as one gets down to cases whether some pressing dilemma is gradually being worked out through discussion (and some action) or whether a first-order crisis (some momentous showdown) is indeed at hand. At any rate, we shall return to the social-change-disorganization theme later.

[27] Isabel Leighton (ed.), *The Aspirin Age, 1919–1941* (New York: Simon and Schuster, 1949; paper edition, 1963), pp. 232–257, 339–363.

[28] For some sage comments, see Elmer Davis, *But We Were Born Free* (Indianapolis, Ind.: Bobbs-Merrill, 1954; Permabook paper edition, 1956), Chap. I.

Table I / Selected Indicators of Change in the United States: 1870, 1910, 1940, Present

Indicator of Change:	1870	1910	1940	1970s (or as close as possible thereto)
Estimated total population of U. S.[1]	39,905,000	92,407,000	132,122,000	204,765,770 (Apr. 1970)
Expectation of life at birth, total[2]	n. a.	50.0 years	62.9 years	70.5 years (1967)
Infant mortality rate for Massachusetts[3] (per 1,000 live births)	146.3	116.7	34.3	Wh. 19.2; Nonwhite 34.6 (1967)
Per cent of population that is urban	24.9%	45.7%	56.5%	69.9% (1960)
High school graduates as per cent of population age 17[4]	2%	8.8%	50.8%	79.5% (1970)
Enrollment in institutions of higher education as per cent of population ages 18–21[5]	1.7%	5.1%	15.7%	36.0% (1969)[16]
Value added by manufacture ($1,000)[6]	$4,646,981 (1899)	$8,160,075 (1909)	$24,487,304 (1939)	$285,000,000 (1968)
Total capital expenditure for structures[7] and equipment (in 1947 dollars)	n. a.	$1,000,000,000 (1915)	$3,500,000,000	$20,896,000,000 (1968)
Total passenger miles of railroad traffic[8]	11,848 millions (1890)	32,338 millions	23,816 millions	13,164 millions (1968)
Total miles of travel by motor vehicles[9] (in vehicle miles)		55,027 millions (1921)	302,188 millions	1,016,000 millions (1968)
Total motor-vehicle registrations[10]	8,000 (1900)	468,500	32,453,233	105,000,000 (1969)
Aviation: Revenue passenger miles flown:[11] Domestic (in millions)			1,052	95,946 (1969)
International (in millions)			100	29,468 (1969)
Productivity: Index of the real gross private domestic product (1929 = 100)[12]	43.6 (1889)	64.4	124.0	
Total number patents issued for inventions[13]	6,088	35,141	42,238	71,229 (1969)
Total paid civilian employment of the Federal government[14] (all employees)	51,020 (1871)	388,708	1,042,420	3,100,000 (1969)
Total expenditures of the Federal government[15] (in $1,000)	$309,654	$693,617	$9,062,032	$185,000,000 (1969)

NOTE: Data for 1870, 1910, and 1940 have been taken from the U. S. Bureau of the Census, *Historical Statistics of the United States, Colonial Times to 1957* (Washington, D. C., 1960); the source of data for the 1970s is the U. S. Bureau of the Census, *Statistical Abstract of the United States: 1970.* 91st ed. (Washington, D. C., 1970), supplemented by 1970 Census figures.

Specific references for footnotes 1–15 in the *Historical Statistics* are as follows: [1] p. 7; [2] p. 25; [3] p. 26; [4] p. 207; [5] pp. 210–211; [6] p. 409; [7] p. 410; [8] p. 430; [9] p. 463; [10] p. 462; [11] p. 467; [12] p. 599; [13] pp. 607–608; [14] p. 710; [15] p. 718; [16] Dr. Abbott L. Ferriss, Russell Sage Foundation, 1969.

In Table I the extent of development of some of the factors that have been mentioned as existing in 1870, 1910, and 1940, and as they are today are summarized in order that the enormous changes can be seen readily. The most important *caution* to take concerning this table is that the figures, although they are as accurate as the United States Census Bureau staff and consulted experts could make them, nevertheless represent only a relatively small number of selected indicators of change out of a large stock of quantifiable information collected by the Census Bureau and other organizations. Furthermore, the many *non*quantitative types of change are not represented, such as that involving new meanings or new degrees of significance in various parent-offspring, physician-patient, teacher-student, or other relationships and, importantly, the entire realm of value changes. The true accounting of change is indeed complex and multifaceted. We remind the reader again that we have submitted some sketches only.[29]

In addition changes could be cited with reference to subsystems: industry, government, education, church activities, and family life. Then, too, communities, large and small, often show notable changes in number and composition of the people, and in districts or neighborhoods, and typical problems. The world scene exhibits tremendous ferment, especially in Africa and Asia; here the dynamism probably equals if it does not surpass that found in the United States. Herskovits [30] declares that the Africa of 1930—in its politics, economics, urban centers, and in the aspirations of its people—was worlds apart from the Africa of three decades later. The awakening in Asia, with its emphasis on aggressive Communist China and an India in quest of industrialization and urbanization, is another tremendous event of the past generation and the present. Mankind has, furthermore, witnessed a fast-changing Europe (affected by wars, changes of government, programs of various leaders, and other influences). Decisive changes have occurred in South America and in the Caribbean (including Cuba). Whatever we may say about the modern world, surely a major motif is *change*.

Indeed man now lives in a revolutionary age. As one author expresses it, "We are in fact living with ten or twenty such revolutions— all changing our ways of life, our ways of looking at things, changing

[29] We have ignored, moreover, personality or character alterations that have resulted from socio-cultural changes. See, for instance, David Riesman and coauthors, *The Lonely Crowd* (New Haven: Yale University Press, 1950; Doubleday Anchor edition, 1956). See also, "National Character in the Perspective of the Social Sciences," *Annals of the American Academy of Political and Social Science,* Vol. 370 (March, 1967).

[30] Melville J. Herskovits, *The Human Factor in Changing Africa* (New York: Alfred A. Knopf, 1962), Preface.

everything out of recognition and changing it fast." [31] It seems unnecessary to belabor the point or (for our purposes) to specify details
of revolutionary changes that have occurred in industry, biology, education, sex, communications, the military, and in other realms. Sometimes one invention such as the computer can bring significant changes
in various fields. One incident or event can symbolize vast change in
some cases: The first airplane flight on the part of the Wright Brothers
(1903); the first detonation of an atom bomb (1945); the first Sputnik
satellite launching (1957); and the first manned circumnavigation of
the moon (December, 1968), leading to man's first setting foot on the
surface of the moon (July, 1969). These were all extraordinary events
that, in most cases, opened up new epochs for mankind. Although
the feat of walking on the moon as achieved by astronauts Armstrong,
Aldrin, and Collins during July, 1969 did not inaugurate an era (Sputnik had done that), it did bring forth vast eventual probabilities of a
prime order: namely, that with the passage of some years *many* human
feet would walk on the moon, on the planets, and perhaps (in the
more distant future) on other solar systems. But this discussion may
seem to concentrate unduly on the spectacular. Sometimes, on the
earth as we know it, very important changes are seen in modest or
simple situations: A Negro man and his wife calmly eating a meal in
a hitherto segregated restaurant or attending a movie in a hitherto
white theatre.[32] Little incidents in life may speak volumes. Sometimes
an action (such as passage of a law) is insufficient to bring desired
changes, and further measures and struggles are required. Nevertheless
it seems that the entirety of change in American society and in the
world today has been impressive. Scientific and technological advances,
population and community alterations, mobility between social classes,
changes in occupational categories and roles (and accompanying statuses), changes in educational content and in student and faculty
attitudes, political realignments, public opinion and legal changes, the
occurrence of wars and revolutions, and many other developments,
and their repercussions, have made change a dominant characteristic
of man's life. Moreover, man's habitual dynamism (certainly in the
twentieth century) seems to underscore the need for further alteration

31 Barbara Ward, *The Rich Nations and the Poor Nations* (New York: W. W.
Norton & Co., 1962), p. 13. See also Max Lerner, "Six Revolutions in American Life,"
in Thomas R. Ford (ed.), *The Revolutionary Theme in Contemporary America*
(Lexington: University of Kentucky Press, 1965), pp. 1–20.

32 Also, of course, leaders may develop major ideas amid simple or unimpressive
surroundings. Holding to the race subject, many would point to Martin Luther
King, Jr.'s "Letter From Birmingham Jail," which was published as Chapter 5 in
King, *Why We Can't Wait* (New York: Harper & Row, 1963; Signet paper edition,
1964).

in areas of man's life that still demand attention: Perhaps, for one thing, continued advances will bring problems with them as they often have during the past; man, besides, is almost sure to develop new perceptions of need and new awarenesses concerning older problems.

THE STUDY OF SOCIAL CHANGE

If all social and cultural elements may manifest some degree of change from time to time—which makes the study of social change a most comprehensive one—it can be added that individual social scientists have usually been impressed by some particular factor (or type of alteration). In the main they have concentrated on and explored the influence of that one factor. Because, however, social scientists have had diverse interests (as might be expected), many avenues to change have been investigated and the total field has benefited. Two kinds of diversity in the study can be noted here: First, various broad approaches have been followed, which we shall discuss presently; indeed a brief account of the successive areas of interest on the part of students of social change serves to introduce these broad perspectives. Secondly, various "schools" have been in existence for some time emphasizing the economic, technological, demographic, political, religious, and other factors. These more specific approaches are discussed in Chapters 3 and 4. In pursuing these matters and in developing ideas and formulations social scientists have necessarily been affected by dominant events, the stock of available knowledge, and the available research techniques of their time.

Broad Perspectives

Several broad perspectives regarding social change have successively been adopted by sociologists and other social scientists, if one surveys developments in a relatively long-term manner. If one discusses these viewpoints in their chronological order of appearance, the first is the *evolutionary* one that was prominent during the last half of the nineteenth century. Herbert Spencer (1820–1903) was mainly responsible for introducing the concept of evolution into social thought, although the perspective was also maintained by Edward B. Tylor (1832–1917), a British anthropologist, and Lewis Henry Morgan (1818–1881), an American anthropologist, and others. Comte, Marx, and Durkheim followed this perspective in their writings, but they are not usually linked with evolutionism as a viewpoint as much as the first three. General declarations of the idea were, at any rate, that social evolution *had* occurred; that society and its institutions "evolved" steadily from the uniform to the multiform; and that simple societies consisting of families were unified into clans, clans into tribes, and that tribes often joined to form a nation. With an increase in size came structural and functional differentiation. Spencer further stressed the transition from a military to an industrial society. There is doubt, however, that he held the view often attributed to him that societies *had* to pass through identical stages of evolution; [33] on the contrary, he explained that various disturbances interfered with the straight line of evolution. Morgan's view of social evolution emphasized the technological factor. He divided cultural advance into the savagery, barbarism, and civilization stages, of which the first two had three substages. Each stage and substage was declared to have been initiated by a major technological invention, and each was associated with a characteristic development in religion, family life, political organization, and property system.

Because these comments with respect to the evolutionary view are being made a full century after the publication of Spencer's *First Principles* and it is nearly that long since the publication of Morgan's *Ancient Society,* it is evident that the passage of time may have brought forth developments that would affect the theory. Advancing knowledge may verify or prove mistaken (or require modification for) a theory, totally or in part. Unfortunately, accumulating anthropological and sociological evidence more and more made evolutionary theory untenable as expressed by these writers. Although the achievements of Spencer and Morgan were considerable (perhaps notable) in view of the state of knowledge of the 1860–1880 period, nevertheless one has to record that this early evolutionary thinking was generally discredited by the 1920s. And this occurred despite the efforts of such "neoevolutionists" as Albert G. Keller and Leonard T. Hobhouse to make the theory more scientific. In Chapter 3 we shall discuss the evolutionary view further, and will indicate some of the problems with the early theory. However, during recent years evolutionary thinking has been revived. This does not mean a return to the ideas of Spencer and the other nineteenth-century writers. One may conclude, then, that the evolutionary outlook itself is not dead (perhaps far from it), even though the particular brand espoused by Spencer and the others doubtless is.

[33] Evidence indicates that Morgan held this view of the inevitable passing through the various stages, not Spencer. See Nicholas Timasheff, *Sociological Theory,* rev. ed. (New York: Random House, 1957), pp. 38–39 and 49–50. See also, Lewis A. Coser and Bernard Rosenberg, *Sociological Theory* (New York: The Macmillan Company, 1969), pp. 670–677; and Harry E. Barnes (ed.), *An Introduction to the History of Sociology* (Chicago: University of Chicago Press, 1948), Chaps. 4 (on Spencer) and 5 (on Lewis H. Morgan).

The Cultural Perspective. The biological emphasis had been prominent during the pioneering years of sociology, having developed in part as a reaction to Darwinism. During the early 1920s the cultural perspective was introduced; it swept as a tide over the entire field of sociology. William Graham Sumner and other pioneers had much to do with the ascendency of this perspective. (Sumner's *Folkways* having appeared before this time played a considerable role.) The sociologists who emphasized it in their accountings of social change were especially William F. Ogburn, Hornell Hart, F. Stuart Chapin, and (during the 1930s) Pitirim A. Sorokin. One should add that the anthropologists have maintained a continuing interest in *cultural change* over the long period. Ogburn, Hart, and Chapin stressed the influence of invention, diffusion, resistances to innovation (resulting from habits, traditions, vested interests, social pressures, and cultural incompatibilities), accumulation, and adjustment as major processes of cultural change. However, Ogburn pointed to invention as the *central* process. Many sociologists and anthropologists recognized the importance of diffusion (this has been consistently espoused by anthropologists), although many examples of independent, more-or-less simultaneous invention have also been noted. The present-day study of the influence of diffusion has flourished—with some sociologists making broad assessments of the adoption process or of diffusion generally (Rogers, LaPiere); [34] some concentrating on the spread of medical innovations (Katz, Coleman, Menzel, Levin, and others); [35] some specializing on farm or agricultural innovations (Lionberger, Wilkening, Marsh, L. Coleman, and others); [36] some focussing attention on the "personal influence" factor in the diffusion of ideas (Katz and Lazarsfeld); [37] and at least one

[34] Everett M. Rogers, *Diffusion of Innovations* (New York: The Free Press of Glencoe, Division of The Macmillan Co., 1962); Richard T. LaPiere, *Social Change* (New York: McGraw-Hill Book Co., 1965).

[35] See, for example, James S. Coleman, E. Katz, and H. Menzel, "The Diffusion of an Innovation Among Physicians," *Sociometry*, Vol. 20 (December, 1957), 253–270; H. Menzel, "Innovation, Integration, and Marginality: A Survey of Physicians," *American Sociological Review*, Vol. 25, No. 5 (October, 1960), 704–713; E. Katz, "The Social Itinerary of Technical Change," *Human Organization*, Vol. 20 (1961), 70–82; and J. S. Coleman, E. Katz, and H. Menzel, *Medical Innovation: A Diffusion Study* (Indianapolis, Ind.: Bobbs-Merrill, 1966).

[36] As samples of this literature see H. F. Lionberger, *Adoption of New Ideas and Practices* (Ames: Iowa State University Press, 1960); Bryce Ryan and Neal C. Gross, "The Diffusion of Hybrid Seed Corn in Two Iowa Communities," *Rural Sociology*, Vol. 8 (1943), 15–24; Eugene A. Wilkening, "Change in Farm Technology As Related to Familism, Family Decision Making, and Family Integration," *American Sociological Review*, Vol. 19 (1954), 29–37; C. Paul Marsh and Lee Coleman, "Group Influences and Agricultural Innovations," *American Journal of Sociology*, Vol. 61 (1956), 588–594.

[37] Elihu Katz and Paul F. Lazarsfeld, *Personal Influence* (New York: The Free Press of Glencoe, Division of The Macmillan Company, 1955; paper edition, 1964).

(Bell) [38] drawing attention to the diffusion of privileges as well as of techniques or ideas. What the few have today, Bell declares, the many will want tomorrow. The wish to attend college, for instance, has diffused just as has the use of the computer or the contraceptive pill. Furthermore, the notion of disrupting college campuses as a means of attaining ends has diffused. And one may comment that the diffusion of ideas, technological objects, privileges, and even disruptive techniques has, doubtless, increased on the world scene due to the modern, closely knit interactions in a global society. The modern communications and transportation inventions have without doubt endowed diffusion with much increased importance as a source of change. The cultural vista with respect to change remains, at any rate, a basic and exceedingly consequential, even vital, one. It has experienced no decline or out-of-favor periods as did evolutionism. At this time the importance of cultural values and norms is particularly underlined. Williams,[39] Lipset,[40] and others have done much to clarify and explain the influence of values on the American scene. In the meantime the influence of inventions and diffusion in an automatizing, TV-viewing, and space-orbiting world seems as great, or greater, than ever.

The Social-System Perspective. Emphasis on the social system has come to the fore during the present era; the onset can be dated as roughly 1940. Led by Talcott Parsons, this viewpoint has swept through the field of sociology much as the cultural view did earlier. Indeed, current sociological theory is undoubtedly dominated by social-system thinking linked with the use of the structural-functional approach. It is true that Parsons has concentrated on the study of the social structure. He has occasionally been taken to task for a relative neglect of the subject of social change, although he has made some investigations of changing systems on the basis of Durkheim's social-differentiation theory (as will be indicated later). The Parsonian social-system emphasis does not neglect culture. Cultural values (as noted in the pattern variables scheme, for instance), norms, and other elements have an important place in the analysis.

If Parsons has not devoted major attention to social change, some of his former students have tended to fill in the gap. Wilbert E. Moore,

38 Bell, *op. cit.*, especially "Notes (II)," *The Public Interest*, No. 7 (Spring, 1967), 111–112; also see Commission on the Year 2000, American Academy of Arts and Sciences, "Toward the Year 2000: Work in Progress," *Daedalus* (Summer, 1967), 643. (Bell is chairman of the Commission.)

39 Robin M. Williams, Jr., *American Society*, 3rd ed. (New York: Alfred A. Knopf, 1969); see also, Williams, "Individual and Group Values," *Annals of the American Academy of Political and Social Science*, Vol. 371 (May, 1967), 20–37.

40 Seymour M. Lipset, *The First New Nation* (New York: Basic Books, Inc., 1963).

Neil J. Smelser, Charles P. Loomis, and others—who were in most cases students of both Parsons and Sorokin at Harvard—have taken the lead in this way. Their contributions will be reviewed later. All have maintained the social-system view while suggesting modifications that they deemed advisable as a result of their empirical investigations. Many social systems have been examined in any case: bureaucracies and small organizations and health, educational, religious, and other systems. This most recent perspective has gained considerable momentum at the present time, shows little sign of any diminution, and further contributions are anticipated. Social-system ideas and emphases are applied to modernizing as well as advanced societies.[41] Levy has compared in some detail both the typical structures and problems of relatively modernized and relatively nonmodernized societies.[42] One may point out, moreover, that the planning view—that social groups are likely to more and more plan their own futures, selecting from alternatives—is essentially congenial to the social-system perspective. Then, if leaders steer the ongoing course using feedback in the decision-making process, this perspective becomes linked with the tenets of cybernetics.

Combining Perspectives

The preceding perspectives have been described separately in their chronological order of development, but it should be made clear that most sociologists have not restricted their use to only one in their theory and research. Parsons, as already mentioned, is prominently identified with the social-system view, yet he has abundantly emphasized values, norms, belief systems, reward systems, and other cultural phenomena as has been stated; what is more, he is a leader in the recent renaissance of the evolutionary perspective.[43] Moore, Smelser, and others similarly adhere to the social-system emphasis but, again, are fully cognizant of the importance of the cultural. Those who have paid much attention to inventions and diffusion and their impacts, on the other hand, do not generally underrate the social-system view either. And *all*, we would venture to declare at the present time, are fully aware of the vast intertwining and interinfluencing of social and cultural factors. It is probably correct to say that the vast

[41] Bert F. Hoselitz and Wilbert E. Moore (eds.), *Industrialization and Society*, UNESCO (The Hague: Mouton & Co., 1963), especially Chaps. 1–2; Hoselitz, *Sociological Aspects of Economic Growth* (Glencoe, Ill.: The Free Press, Inc., 1960).

[42] Marion J. Levy, Jr., *Modernization and the Structure of Societies*, 2 vols. (Princeton, N. J.: Princeton University Press, 1966).

[43] Talcott Parsons, *Societies: Evolutionary and Comparative Perspectives* (Englewood Cliffs, N. J.: Prentice-Hall, Inc., 1966).

number do consider both social-system and cultural factors in their theoretical orientations and research, and that Parsons and perhaps no small number of others are also attracted to the evolutionary view. However, if one does state this, some additional comments become necessary. First, divergencies do exist in addition to the commonalities, and some of the divergencies may represent more than nuances of meaning. It is clear that one may stress both social and cultural factors (let us neglect the evolutionary view for the moment) but not emphasize them equally. One can tilt the scales in various ways and to differing degrees. Secondly, semantic problems may confuse true conceptualizations, and here we must be careful. On the one hand, sociologists professing one view will introduce the other in their analyses (yet the study will be known as one involving the changing social system or cultural change); and, on the other, some studies or textbooks will bear the same title—often it will be "Social Change"—but the content will be vastly different. This has indeed happened in the past. Because clear-cut conceptualization concerning this matter is needed and because hope is held that such semantic confusions will not be carried into the future, we endeavor to discuss the conceptualization with especial clarity in Chapter 2. Our point, in any case, is that the *language* that people use in describing their viewpoint must sometimes be scrutinized closely.[44] Thirdly, sociologists or others may pay attention to the various factors in special ways; no error of any kind may be involved in this, yet we will do well to take note of such distinctive features. Sorokin's vast work is an example. Sorokin labels his viewpoint socio-cultural. A prominent feature of his magnum opus is the broad ideational-to-sensate (cultural) transition over a period of approximately 2,500 years in Western and Graeco-Roman civilizations—although he also contributes the explanatory principles of immanent change and the theory of limits (concerning which the social system is more in evidence). He thinks of his unit of study as the socio-cultural system. In actual content, then, one feature of his theory is strongly cultural, whereas the explanatory principles can be described as socio-cultural.[45] To take another example, Robert M. MacIver was comprehensive in his views; he amply considered the social and cultural

44 Because of confusion in the use of the terms *society* and *culture* themselves, Professors Talcott Parsons and the late A. L. Kroeber issued their clarifying statement with respect to these terms. This statement has been very helpful, in our judgment. See Kroeber and Parsons, "The Concepts of Culture and of Social System," *American Sociological Review*, Vol. 23, No. 5 (October, 1958), 582–583.

45 Sorokin observes that his sensitivity to cultural change was at least partly caused by his residential moves from Russia to Minnesota to Massachusetts. Pitirim A. Sorokin, "Sociology of My Mental Life," in Philip J. Allen (ed.), *Pitirim A. Sorokin in Review* (Durham, N. C.: Duke University Press, 1963), p. 24.

orders, also including much evolutionary thinking in his analysis. Perhaps a distinctive characteristic of MacIver's view of change was his ordering of the ways in which causal factors (social, cultural, and psychological) interrelate. He placed emphasis on the "inner" (often psychological) and "outer" (usually social and cultural) factors in the change process and pointed to the *dynamic assessment* of a situation as a primary organizing principle in social causation.[46] Such differing interpretations and explanations of the change process provide alternatives for consideration as well as fascination and spice in the intellectual bill of fare.

Other Current Interests

The field of social change is at the moment bursting forth in many directions, partly because the total discipline of sociology is doing precisely that.[47] We propose to identify these new directions of social-change interest, some of which may gain force and become crucial developments while others no doubt will decline sooner or later and fade from the scene. These current interests and activities are described here. (1) The study of socio-cultural change on the world scene— namely, the subject of modernizing nations—is still one of high and widespread interest. (2) The interest in the *theory* of change remains much alive; this includes modifications of earlier theories as well as the exploration of newer conceptions such as general-systems theory, cybernetics, and information theory. (3) The interest in the *methodology* of studying change similarly persists, including as it does the measurement of change and social trends and the development of social indicators; it also encompasses such subjects as methodological contributions to systems theory, cybernetics, and simulation. (4) The interest in specific subject areas of change (such as population or community) continues, even though the focus tends to be broader than that of the specialist in each subject—it generally links changing areas to other areas or to the total evolving society; thus population and economic, technological, and other changes might be related to race relations or to pollution or crime problems. In short, this kind of study would emphasize relationships between changing social patterns (or institutions) or between parts and the whole (in the manner of systems theory) in time perspective. (5) A substantial number of sociologists (sometimes, although not necessarily activists) are interested in proc-

[46] MacIver, *op. cit.*, Chap. 11.
[47] Professor Neil Smelser expressed it at a panel of the behavioral and social sciences that, "Sociology is going in different directions all at once." *The New York Times* (January 5, 1970).

esses and methods of bringing changes to pass; in this context they may study collective behavior, cooperation and conflict processes, social planning, and other processes or methods involved in making changes. (6) Interest continues in technological and social inventions as causes of change, with current emphasis often placed on such inventions as the computer and television. (7) Interest persists in diffusion as a source of change, with special attention to human interactions in the process (including the role of "influentials"), to new types of diffusion (such as that of privileges within a nation), and to new items or products being diffused (such as the contraceptive pill or the use of drugs). (8) Many sociologists are interested in the activist perspective as a philosophy of change; younger sociologists, who often espouse activism, may want to use sociological knowledge in order to improve society; they press for change itself, demanding relevant information concerning problems and usually showing impatience with neutral and objective study; interest in such cases may often be related to (5) here. (9) Many sociologists continue to be interested in changing values and norms, which may underlie some of the previously mentioned alterations. (10) Many sociologists are interested in studies of the future, and may cultivate, perhaps with exuberance, anticipations of social life in 1985 or 2000; or they may limit their attention to some one subject or institution such as the university of the future, the city of the future, the future family, or technological forecasting. Some of these subjects have considerable vogue at this time.

This list is not intended to be exhaustive. In any case, we shall not extend discussion of these current interests here; many of them will find their place in coming chapters. In general, the sociological study of change is now experiencing a revitalization. In some respects we live in an "age of sociology." The total field is in the limelight much as psychology, physics, and other fields have been during past years. Activists and demonstrators have of course urged *change* in relation to race, ghetto, and other problems. College and university students often see the need of changes on their own campus. Apart from these matters, interest in change itself on the world scene—in developing nations—has provoked an extra zest for social dynamics. Technological advances such as automation, nuclear developments, and space travel have contributed to the same result: namely, the study of social change has itself taken on a new importance.[48]

48 Mr. Max Ways, editor of *Fortune* magazine, declares that, "so swift is the acceleration (of change) that trying to 'make sense' of change will come to be our basic industry. Change has always been part of the human condition. What is different now is the pace of change, and the prospect that it will come faster and faster, affecting every part of life, including personal values, morality, and religion." Ways, "The Era of Radical Change," *Fortune* (May, 1965), 113–115, 210, and 215.

VIEWPOINT OF THIS TEXTBOOK

Let us consider the distinctive perspectives or features of this text. It may be desirable for this writer to frankly discuss basic perspectives and more specific viewpoints that will be followed in this book. Is the emphasis, for example, to be placed largely or even solely on the changing social system or on changing culture or upon both? Or will it be upon something different still? Or, because most sociologists seem to include the social and cultural orders in some fashion, what sort of "mix" do we propose here? We simply declare that both of these orders comprise legitimate interests in this study and should be emphasized equally. The perspective of this textbook holds, then, that consideration of "changing America," "the changing Middle West," "changing New England," "changing China," or "changing Nigeria" involves both the social system and ways of living emphasized about equally. The current sociological vogue appears to give prominence to the social system (discussing cultural factors as they impinge upon, or have relevance for, the ongoing social system). Changing social systems—universities, corporations, governmental structures, medical systems and subsystems, families—are indeed of major interest. Nevertheless, granting the manifold effects of cultural inventions, diffusion, industrialization, urbanization, and other processes, it seems clear that changing culture itself is of considerable interest to large numbers of social scientists. The literature issuing from many social scientists, including Ogburn and Sorokin in sociology as well as many others, is indeed abundant. Just as cultural factors as values surely relate to the changing social system, so social-system influences affect the changing way of life. To neglect either social or cultural order is to fall short of fully discussing the changing human environment. As to the evolutionary perspective, we are congenial to it provided that its formulations are consistent with relevant empirical data. This viewpoint may not receive marked emphasis in the present treatment, although, on the other hand, it will be used where applicable and useful.

We do, then, stress a socio-cultural perspective in which the two factors are given what we conceive to be relatively equal emphasis. Such a perspective is admittedly broad. We see no harm in dividing up the total subject for analytical purposes if and when this suits the interests of some sociologists or anthropologists; if they prefer to concentrate largely on the social system or on culture, that is their privilege. This has been done in the past; such a division of labor is probably helpful, and, considering the complexities of the modern period, it may be wise and sometimes even necessary. There is indeed work enough for all. We would only add that, in the end, neither subject should be neglected; and, furthermore, sooner or later the various analyses need to be integrated so that they will compose a whole (because social system and culture are so highly interrelated).

The elaborate and intricate intertwining of social system and culture is in fact of considerable interest. Even though we shall comment on this interinfluencing in certain respects in the next chapter, we wish to call attention here to one aspect of the interplay that has not received much emphasis: the use of inventions (as accepted in the culture) to form systems of business enterprise (social systems). After an invention has been made, the inventor or others who sense public interest in its use may accumulate capital and establish a firm for manufacturing the article. In the United States, as more and more people have wanted telephone service, an automobile, a camera, a TV set, and the like, the companies producing these goods and services (usually small in the beginning) have thrived. Because population in this increasingly affluent society has grown impressively, the volume of business in these enterprises has become huge. Such giant organizations as American Telephone and Telegraph Company, General Motors Corporation, Eastman Kodak, and Radio Corporation of America are the result. Indeed a roster of prominent corporations based on earlier cultural inventions reads like a "Who's Who" of American business structures. Eleven of the leading twenty industrial corporations at this time are business related to the invention of the motor vehicle alone; they either produce autos and trucks or the gas and oil or tires for their operation.[49] Since one other corporation produces steel, which is abundantly used in automobile manufacture, this is eloquent testimony to the significance of the automobile invention for American corporate life. Two others of the leading twenty are aircraft producers, one a radio-TV manufacturer, and one a computer manufacturer (which also produces typewriters and other office machines). Not only have various inventions often formed the basis for business structures but the latter, in turn, have frequently developed large-scale research organizations in order to make further inventions. Thus innovations for cars are created at General Motors laboratories, new chemical products are developed at DuPont, and new kinds and compositions of glass are invented at Corning. These new inventions often bring a need for additional plants and sometimes for the formation

[49] A recent ranking of industrial corporations based on sales shows that the leading twenty are as follows (in descending order): General Motors Corporation, Standard Oil of New Jersey, Ford Motor Company, General Electric, International Business Machines (IBM), Chrysler, Mobil Oil, Texaco, International Telephone & Telegraph, Gulf Oil, Western Electric, U. S. Steel, Standard Oil of California, Ling-Temco-Vought, DuPont (E. I.) de Nemours, Shell Oil, Westinghouse Electric, Boeing, Standard Oil of Indiana, and Goodyear Tire & Rubber. *Fortune* (May, 1970), 184.

of new divisions in the corporate structure.[50] We suggest that in other areas, too, the social-system-culture interplay is both of interest and of consequence and warrants further exploration.

Viewpoint Regarding Specific Approaches (Schools)

As stated earlier, various schools have been in existence for some time, stressing the economic, technological, demographic, or other influences in the *change* process. What leanings do we maintain here toward some of these emphases toward the subject that presumably may be supported by empirical evidence? It is axiomatic that the significance of different variables in change bear relation to the type of social structure and its dominant values. Change is always related to the existent structure. If we follow Parsons' [51] typology of social structures in relation to the predominance of different values, we may find that social system X emphasizes the universalistic-achievement pattern, social system Y stresses the particularistic-ascriptive pattern, and so on. Relating this discussion to *American* society—which we now attempt to do—it is clear that this social system is of the industrial type wherein universalistic achievement values are stressed. Major factors in change will, then, often relate to, or be consistent with, these predominant value emphases, although some subemphases do exist. We may remind ourselves, furthermore, that American society today is relatively large, well-populated, and advanced; many activities and alternatives in relation to different spheres of living will be found. Institutions are rather fully differentiated. It is likely that many significant factors of change can be enumerated in such a society, and this is what we tend to find. We shall not be able to restrict significant change factors to a mere three or four variables. The following are of extra prominence or carry extra weight as this sociologist sees it: [52]

1. The economic factor. American society is still business-oriented to a marked extent; it veers toward service activities. We do not main-

---

[50] Examples of this corporation-cultural invention new social-system sequence that come to mind are (1) RCA and television: plants were expanded for TV production; (2) IBM and the new System/360 electronic computer (also the IBM electric typewriter): plants were expanded and new ones created; and (3) Corning Glass Works and the invention of pyroceram: new plants were established. Many other examples could be cited. For an "inside account" of RCA's fostering of the television invention, which was made by Dr. Vladimir Zworykin, told from the viewpoint of Mr. David Sarnoff, at the time a top RCA executive, see Eugene Lyons, *David Sarnoff* (New York: Harper & Row, 1966), Chaps. 15 and 20.

[51] Talcott Parsons, *The Social System* (Glencoe, Ill.: The Free Press, Inc., 1951), Chap. V.

[52] We include some brief comments in listing these factors; further discussion is found in Chapters 3 and 4.

tain (with Marx) that the economic factor is *the* key variable in this capitalistic society, but hold that it nevertheless constitutes one of the important ones.

2. The influence of science and technology. Although the latter (technology) is now significantly based on the former (science), the two together exert a strong influence on American society (including, needless to say, economic institutions and productivity).

3. The demographic influence. The changing number and composition of the population have much to do with subsequent changes (dependent variables) in communities, institutions, and national affairs. It is acknowledged that the demographic influence itself is much affected by economic, scientific, technological, and other influences.

4. Value changes relating to categories of the population (for instance, youth or occupational groups). Such value alterations may indeed bring widespread repercussions. Sometimes certain social changes are desired, but value alterations are necessary if the objectives are to be attained.

5. Ideological factors. These are often associated with values, and may relate to social classes, occupations, or other groupings. They may provide the basic assumptions, central beliefs, and the "spark" from which new enterprises for change will grow.

6. The leadership factor. Whether this relates to political, business, educational, or other activities; whether it applies to national, state, or local groups; or whether it represents the establishment or dissident organizations this influence is regarded as of key importance.

7. The political factor. This is currently of great importance, and this influence is likely to be markedly extended in the future. One may simply declare that government constitutes the most important regulator of other institutions and of the total society at this time.

8. The educational influence. This has assumed increasing importance as an independent or intervening variable. The "educational revolution" wherein millions of youth now attend colleges and universities has had many repercussions on leadership, public opinion, and other social forces and institutions (including the economy and government).

9. The mass media (with an emphasis on television). These media bring a sharp impact on many influences and institutions such as those mentioned in (8); modern society is still trying to fully assess the influence of media use.

10. The activist or "self-determination" influence has risen during the past decade. To actively seek out one's wants for the future and vigorously pursue the attainment of them—which is a far cry from man's traditional acceptance of change—is a view that has risen fast.

This deliberate effort to anticipate and direct change may be, as Bell declares,[53] "the most important social change of our time." In short, the attitude toward change has itself been altered by many people.

11. The influence of conflict on the domestic scene has also risen rapidly. To seek goals through the processes of conflict and confrontation is currently in vogue. One grants that if goals are actively and vigorously pursued, such behavior may clash with the actions of others who may have different goals. Hence, one may conclude with reason that the activist orientation tends to promote conflict; certainly this is often likely to occur. One may also note that the conflict behavior in various cases may have been adopted because prior espousal of co-operation has not borne fruit.

12. Social movements. This form of collective behavior appears to have increased in importance. Again, we observe that it bears relation to other influences such as values and ideologies, leadership, the political influence, the mass media, the self-determination view, and conflict.

13. External world influences. Here we refer not only to the diffusion of ideas or material objects from without but also to the effects of economic, educational, political, and even health developments occurring in other world areas; this external influence has clearly increased since the communication and transportation inventions have stepped-up international contacts. Sometimes foreign tensions have developed into wars, and this society has had many transformations that have resulted from participating in wars (as witness the Second World War, Korea, and Vietnam); if one's nation should participate in and *lose* a war, the social changes deriving from *without* might be overwhelming.

Finally, we mention two factors in the change process that are probably not major at this time but that are growing in importance:

14. The increasing use of "feedback" in many social situations. This is helpful in determining courses of action, and its further use is a logical prospect. Whether, and if so how soon, such operations may be assumed to comprise a cybernetic control of social data remains to be seen. Increasing use of the computer in the social sciences is itself to be expected. On the other hand, many obstacles in the path of cybernetic accomplishments regarding social behavior appear to remain. It would seem as if the social sciences can only persevere and expand

---

[53] Bell, *op. cit.,* especially No. 6, 25. On the other hand, it appears that neither this nation nor any other has attained what might be called an active society, meaning that it is master of itself, as of this time. See the discussion in Amitai Etzioni, *The Active Society* (New York: The Free Press, Division of The Macmillan Company, 1968), Preface and Chap. I.

their efforts in this study of communication and control as applied to social phenomena, attempting to meet the various challenges. The subject does at least bear promise.[54]

15. The increasing development and use of social planning. In a complex and fast-changing world, planning is more and more needed in order to reach objectives. Increasingly change becomes planned change. Planning for the growth of the entire society as well as for specific social institutions is becoming more the rule than the exception. Much planning may be made for the university, the corporation, or the urban environment of twenty years hence or for American society as of the year 2000. This view may be coupled with that of self-determination. "Where do we want change to take us?" is the question today. And "What methods will best get us there?"

We think that there is some value in calling attention to the preceding influences. It is clear that many of them are interrelated. Moreover, we shall of course extend our ideas relating to them in the remaining chapters.

Plan of the Book

In the next chapter, as already mentioned, we shall turn to the discussion of the fundamentals of social and cultural change; we shall try to be especially clear in our definitions. In Chapters 3 and 4 we outline the various approaches to this study, some emphasizing social factors, some cultural. Then we shall discuss major theories—that of immanent change in Chapter 5, differentiation and functional theories in Chapter 6, economic and technological theories in Chapter 7, and historical and ideological theories in Chapter 8. We shall then explore the measurement of change in Chapter 9, a subject that is currently on the sociological frontier. In addition to measurement itself we shall be interested in the development of social indicators that will enable us to assess progress in relation to values and goals.

We shall then turn to important *processes* of change. We select the following for discussion: the process of innovation (Chapter 10), resistance to innovation (Chapter 11), and diffusion (Chapter 12). These are time-honored subjects that also have, however, modern significance and implications. In Chapter 13 we focus attention on activism, which has become a most important process of the contemporary scene. Because the activist influence is frequently linked with the mass media,

---

[54] For a helpful discussion see Karl W. Deutsch, *The Nerves of Government* (New York: The Free Press of Glencoe, 1963; Free Press paperback edition, 1966), especially Part II; Etzioni, *op. cit.*, Part Two; and Walter Buckley, *Sociology and Modern Systems Theory* (Englewood Cliffs, N. J.: Prentice-Hall, Inc., 1967).

we shall briefly examine the characteristics of television and other media as significantly relevant phenomena.

In Chapter 14 the sphere of interest is extended to the world scene, and attention is focused on the distinctive types of change found in developing societies. It is clear that once an underdeveloped nation has embarked on the modernization course, certain occurrences are likely—indeed some are necessary—acknowledging that the individual factors of each society will bring variations. In Chapter 15 we conclude with some observations concerning social change and social disorganization. We shall face the issue of whether our fast-changing society has a good chance of becoming markedly disorganized. Social disorganization, after all, occurs as a matter of degree. All inventions cause some disorganization; conflicts disorganize in part (and today confrontation is an "in" process); also, militant radicals seek to disrupt existing society. Yet various forces also favor the ongoing system. Without being able to anticipate future problems or society's answers to them, we nevertheless hold that concluding remarks relative to social disorganization are neither out-of-bounds nor fanciful. Serious disorganization is a continuing concern of modern, tumultous society. At times, indeed, the subject of social disorganization seems *uncomfortably* germane.

ANNOTATED BIBLIOGRAPHY

Allen, Frederick L., *The Big Change, 1900–1950* (New York: Harper & Row; Bantam paper edition, 1961).
> Exceedingly well-written social history. Gives the spirit of change in America during the first half of the twentieth century.

Bell, Daniel, "Notes on the Post-Industrial Society (I) and (II)," *The Public Interest,* No. 6 (Winter, 1967), 24–35, and No. 7 (Spring, 1967), 102–118.
> Unusually perceptive and valuable observations on the present (industrial) and coming (postindustrial) societies.

Etzioni, Amitai, and Etzioni, Eva (eds.), *Social Change* (New York: Basic Books, Inc., 1964).
> A superior reader. Selections are generally well chosen. The editors provide brief but helpful commentary.

Herskovits, Melville J., *The Human Factor in Changing Africa* (New York: Alfred A. Knopf, 1962).
> Well-done study of recent change in an area of ferment. The author was a leading anthropological specialist in Africa.

Lipset, Seymour M., *The First New Nation* (New York: Basic Books, Inc., 1963).
> A historical study of American society, emphasizing the values of equality and achievement and making comparisons with other English-speaking democracies. Superior scholarship.

Moore, Wilbert E., *Social Change* (Englewood Cliffs, N. J.: Prentice-Hall, Inc., 1963).

> An ably written, brief analysis of the changing social system. Society is seen as a tension-management system rather than as a self-equilibrating one. The perceived contrast between actual and ideal behavior or institutional functioning is accented as a motivation for change.

Smelser, Neil J., "Social Change," Part IV in Smelser (ed.), *Sociology: An Introduction* (New York: John Wiley & Sons, Inc., 1967).

> A generally helpful and highly competent introduction to the study of social change.

Ward (Jackson), Barbara, *The Rich Nations and the Poor Nations* (New York: W. W. Norton & Co., 1962).

> Underscores the many revolutions occurring on the modern world scene. Easily read; worthwhile.

Williams, Robin M., Jr., *American Society*, 3rd ed. (New York: Alfred A. Knopf, 1969), especially Chap. XI; also see Williams, "Individual and Group Values," *The Annals of the American Academy of Political and Social Science,* Vol. 371 (May, 1967), 20–37.

> Excellent statements on American values and value changes.

Zollschan, George K. and Hirsch, Walter (eds.), *Explorations in Social Change* (Boston: Houghton Mifflin Co., 1964).

> A stimulating symposium with a wide range of subject matter: a miscellany. Some variation in quality, but "gold nuggets" are to be found.

Fundamentals in the
Sociological Study of Change

The main objective of this chapter is to formulate a conceptual and semantic base for the further consideration of changing human phenomena. This base will largely reflect a consensus of modern sociological thinking; in dealing with cases of disagreement, the writer will follow the course of presenting different viewpoints, then formulating his own conception accompanied by statements of reasons therefor. A conspicuous point of disagreement, it must be said, occurs right at the beginning. This involves the meaning of the bedrock terms *social change* and *cultural change*. One is forced to admit that to some extent eminent sociologists and anthropologists (as well as others) have used these terms differently and sometimes, by implication at least, interchangeably. What is more confusing—and embarrassing—is that some sociologists have discussed the subject of social change in a manner that mostly emphasizes cultural change. These conceptual and semantic tangles must be faced and resolved in as satisfactory a manner as possible.[1] An attempt will be made to bring conceptual order by citing some ten definitions each of social change and cultural change, after which similarities and differences will be observed. A decision will then be made as to the conceptualization and precise definition to be used in the present volume. This initial task, knotty as it is in some respects, is made much easier by the joint statement made by Talcott Parsons and the late A. L. Kroeber entitled, "The Concepts of Culture and of Social System."[2] After clear-cut definitions of these two terms have been adopted, one needs to face the further issue of whether in studying changes in some locality one should emphasize social changes (as defined), cultural changes (as defined), or the *combination*. This discussion is needed because sociologists have in the past maintained different points of emphasis, as was mentioned in the preceding chapter.

[1] Edward A. Shils has stated, for instance, that clarification of ambiguous terms constitutes the first item on the agenda for the entire subject of sociological theory. Social change, it seems, constitutes only one example of a fairly common difficulty. Shils, "The Calling of Sociology," in Talcott Parsons, *et al.* (eds.), *Theories of Society*, Vol. II (New York: The Free Press of Glencoe, Inc., 1961), p. 1442.

[2] *American Sociological Review*, Vol. 23, No. 5 (October, 1958), 582–583.

These conceptual and semantic difficulties should not be exaggerated, however. To accept the picture of a subject in almost total conceptual disorder would be as erroneous as to imagine that the vast number of sociologists must end up with widely divergent views concerning the predominance of these major perspectives. More basic unity is present than one might suspect. It is just that scientists (as other observers) see things differently to some extent, and hence maintain differing interpretations and sometimes definitions. Nothing could be more normal; it is even beneficial for the study in the long run. Despite these (sometimes) varying definitions in the present instance, the vast number of sociologists do *not* maintain widely divergent views concerning the predominance of, say, social or cultural influences. However, the different usages of terms and the varying "mixes" of emphasizing social system or culture or something else, do merit some discussion. The reader should realize not only that varying interpretations do exist but also the nature of the variation.[3]

A high degree of consensus appears to exist with regard to most of the other fundamentals of the study of social change: varying dimensions of change; evolution and revolution; change and progress; levels of conceptualizing change; stability and social persistence; institutionalized sources of change (such as science, research, and development); values that tend to promote change; and the observation that changes may be planned or unplanned.

Defining Social Change and Cultural Change

That the semantic horizon is a bit foggy is evident as we consider the following ten definitions of social change and cultural change that have been formulated by well-known sociologists and anthropologists.

1. The definition of social change as given in the Fairchild, *et al.*, *Dictionary of Sociology* is as follows:

    Social changes are variations or modifications in any aspect of social process, pattern, or form. (It is) a comprehensive term designating the result of every variety of social movement. Social change may be progressive or regressive, permanent or temporary, planned or unplanned, uni-directional or multi-directional, beneficial or harmful.[4]

2. Another general definition—at once compact and comprehensive—is stated by Lundberg, Schrag, and Larsen:

---

3 This is similar to five or six physicians or psychiatrists diagnosing some physical ailment or behavioral problem in somewhat different terms or theoretical reference yet coming to the same essential conclusion as to the nature of the problem.

4 Henry Pratt Fairchild (ed.), *Dictionary of Sociology* (Ames, Iowa: Littlefield, Adams & Co., 1955), p. 277.

Social change represents any observable difference in any social phenomena over any period of time.[5]

3. Kingsley Davis defines social change in a concrete way that differentiates it from cultural change:

> By "social change" is meant only such alterations as occur in social organization—that is, the structure and functions of society. Social change thus forms only a part of what is essentially a broader category called "cultural change." The latter embraces all changes occurring in any branch of culture, as art, science, technology, philosophy, etc., as well as changes in the forms and rules of social organization.[6]

4. Leopold von Wiese also distinguishes between social and cultural change. His meaning is similar, if differently stated, to that of Davis:

> Social change denotes alterations in man-man relationships, while "cultural change" should refer to variations in man-matter connections. Culture is concerned with the products of inter-human activities, society with the producers themselves.[7]

5. Robert M. MacIver and Charles H. Page express the following (which would seem to be close to the meaning of von Wiese):

> By social change is meant changes in social relationships . . . the changing ways in which human beings relate themselves to one another.[8]

6. Another statement is made by Morris Ginsberg as follows:

> By social change I understand a change in social structure, for example, the size of a society, the composition or balance of its parts or the type of its organization. Examples of such changes are the contraction in the size of the family, . . . the breaking up of the domainal economy with the rise of cities, the transition from "estates" to social classes. . . . The term social change must also include changes in attitudes or beliefs, insofar as they sustain institutions and change with them.[9]

7. Finally, there are several recent definitions that tend to emphasize the structural-functional view. It is noted that Wilbert

[5] George A. Lundberg, Clarence C. Schrag, and Otto N. Larsen, *Sociology*, 2nd ed. (New York: Harper & Row, 1958), p. 694.

[6] Kingsley Davis, *Human Society* (New York: The Macmillan Company, 1949), p. 622.

[7] "The Sociological Study of Social Change," *Transactions of the Third World Congress of Sociology* (Amsterdam: International Sociological Association, 1956), p. 7.

[8] *Society, An Introductory Analysis* (New York: Rinehart and Co., 1949), p. 511.

[9] "Social Change," *British Journal of Sociology*, Vol. 9, No. 3 (September, 1958), 205.

E. Moore prefers to include cultural phenomena under social change, a matter to which we shall refer later. Moore's definition is that

> *"Social change is the significant alteration of social structures (that is, of patterns of social action and interaction), including consequences and manifestations of such structures embodied in norms (rules of conduct), values, and cultural products and symbols."* [10]

8. And from Alvin Boskoff there is a view that bears the structural-functional emphasis of Davis and Moore. It specifies that the change must be "significant," which means "significant for the social system." [11] Some difference of opinion could exist as to whether a given alteration is significant. Might subjectivities be involved in such a decision?

> *Social change is the intelligible process in which we can discover significant alterations in the structure and functioning of determinate social systems.*[12]

9. Harry M. Johnson states the following:

> *. . . Social change is change in the structure of a social system; what has been stable or relatively unchanging changes. Moreover, of structural changes the most important are those that have consequences for the functioning of the system—for attaining its goals more (or less) efficiently or for fulfilling more (or less) efficiently the conditions that must be met if the system is to survive at all.*

10. Under "institutional change" we mean to include change in all more definite structures, such as forms of organization, roles, and role content. A change from a polygynous to a

---

[10] Wilbert E. Moore, "Social Change," an article in the *International Encyclopaedia of the Social Sciences*, Vol. 14 (New York: The Macmillan Company, and The Free Press, Inc., 1968), pp. 3–4. (*Note:* This article is also reprinted as Chapter I in Moore, *Order and Change* (New York: John Wiley & Sons, Inc., 1967).

[11] Similarly Moore suggests that sociologists should distinguish between "mere sequences of small actions, that in sum essentially comprise the pattern, the system, and changes in the system itself, in the magnitude or the boundaries, in the prescriptions for action, ..." Moore, *Social Change* (Englewood Cliffs, N. J.: Prentice-Hall, 1963), pp. 5–6. It seems desirable to this writer to discriminate between major structural changes, for example, and small, minor alterations; yet the latter *are* changes.

[12] Alvin Boskoff, in Howard Becker and Alvin Boskoff (eds.), *Modern Sociological Theory* (New York: Dryden Press, 1957), p. 263. Later (1964) Boskoff defined social change as "significant variations from processual and developmental patterns," but he adhered to the social-system emphasis. Boskoff, "Functional Analysis As a Source of a Theoretical Repertory and Research Tasks in the Study of Social Change," Chapter 8 in George Zollschan and Walter Hirsch (eds.), *Explorations in Social Change* (Boston: Houghton Mifflin Co., 1964), p. 216.

monogamous system, from an absolute monarchy to a democracy, from private enterprise to socialism—these are examples of society-wide institutional changes.[13]

The preceding statement does not specify that changes must be fairly large-scale; changes in roles or role content might be small. Johnson does maintain that changes having consequence for the functioning of the system will be of greater importance.

Perhaps a sufficient number of definitions have been reviewed to present various conceptions of social change held by sociologists. Some of the definitions have differed only in verbal expression (not meaning) from others; some have filled in more details than others; and some have had different interpretations and emphases from others. At any rate, the major elements in most of the definitions are approximately as follows (at this point we keep apart Moore's definition): That social change denotes (1) alterations in man-man and/or group relationships—the ways in which people relate themselves to other people; (2) alterations in either structures, functions, or processes of such relationships; and (3) alterations as they take place over any period of time, large or small. The following specific definition, embodying the preceding, is proposed for use in the present text: *Social change comprises modifications in social systems or subsystems in structure, functioning, or process over some period of time.* Such modifications in man-man (group) relationships may relate to community, state, regional, or national structures or functioning or process, or to subsystems (as industry, government, schools, churches, or family life).

But only our first definition has been stated. Cultural change is interrelated with social change, and needs to be distinguished from it. This is so whether or not Moore and perhaps other sociologists elect to include this phenomena within the rubric social change (one has to know what is being included). Moreover, some sociologists and probably many anthropologists may choose to concentrate largely on cultural change; and at least one anthropologist, Leslie White, maintains the "culturology" view that culture needs to be "considered as a process sui generis, quite apart from its human carriers." [14] Distinctions between cultural change and social change as made by Kingsley Davis, Leopold von Wiese, and others, have already been noted. Ac-

[13] Harry M. Johnson, *Sociology* (New York: Harcourt, Brace, 1960), pp. 626 and 628.

[14] Leslie A. White, "Culturology," an article in Julius Gould and William L. Kolb (eds.), *A Dictionary of the Social Sciences* (New York: The Free Press of Glencoe, Inc., 1964), pp. 174–175. Therefore, says White, "Culturology is the scientific study and interpretation of cultural phenomena per se."

tually many definitions of culture have been made (Kroeber and Kluckhohn analyzed 160).[15] For our purposes we begin with the simple statement of Ralph Linton and Melville Herskovits that "culture is the way of life of a people." They contrast this from *society,* which is defined as "the organized aggregate of individuals who follow a given way of life." [16]

A more extended and clearer distinction between society and culture is found in the previously mentioned statement issued by the late Professor A. L. Kroeber and Professor Talcott Parsons. After deploring past confusion among sociologists and anthropologists concerning the use of these terms, they declared the following:

> *We suggest that it is useful to define the concept* culture *for most usages more narrowly than has been generally the case in the American anthropological tradition, restricting its reference to transmitted and created content and patterns of values, ideas, and other symbolic-meaning systems as factors in the shaping of human behavior and the artifacts produced through behavior. On the other hand, we suggest that the term* society—*or more generally,* social system—*be used to designate the specifically relational system of interaction among individuals and collectivities. To speak of a "member of a culture" should be understood as an ellipsis meaning a "member of the society of culture X."*

Kroeber and Parsons further emphasized the fact that society and culture constitute two independent systems. They wrote:

> *They are distinct systems in that they abstract or select two analytically distinct sets of components from the other concrete phenomena. Statements made about relationships within a cultural pattern are thus of a different order from those within a system of societal relationships.*[17]

For the purposes of this volume we shall use the term *culture* as defined by Kroeber and Parsons, which we interpret to be essentially the same as that stated by Linton, Herskovits, and others; we think, furthermore, that most sociologists and anthropologists will find this definition satisfactory. Cultural change will refer, then, to modifications in such "transmitted and created content and patterns of values, ideas, and other symbolic-meaningful systems as factors in the shaping of human behavior and the artifacts produced through behavior" or (more simply) in their "way of life."

[15] Clyde Kluckhohn, "Culture," an article in *ibid.,* pp. 165–168.
[16] Ralph Linton, *The Cultural Background of Personality* (New York: D. Appleton-Century, 1945), Chap. 1; Melville J. Herskovits, *Man and His Works* (New York: Alfred A. Knopf, 1948), p. 29.
[17] Kroeber and Parsons, *loc. cit.*

It may be useful to cite some illustrations. Among many social changes that have occurred one might point to changes in the class structure of a nation, such as an increase in the number of families in the middle class during a given time period or the decrease in number of those in the lower class. Or one might refer to changes in the structure of race relations, such as the recent rise in the status of Negroes in the United States. Or changes in family life might be cited, such as the rise in the status of women in the United States during the past several generations and (partly related to the preceding) role changes of women due to millions of them having gainful employment. Moreover, the size of many subsystems (such as corporations, universities, and governments) has expanded greatly. The General Motors Corporation, DuPont, and IBM have many more employees than they had a generation ago, just as many American universities have far more students and the United States Government (and state governments) employs a much larger number of workers. Large-scale organization—bureaucracy—now characterizes many of these social systems.

Cultural changes, on the other hand, may be illustrated by modifications in folkways or mores, laws, religion, artifacts, and other elements in the way of life (especially values). Much cultural change is brought about by inventions and diffusion. Among illustrations of cultural change one observes the increasingly held belief in secularized religion in the United States; the increased acceptance of family decision making by husband and wife jointly and of the notion that family size should be regulated by contraceptive practices; the increasing acceptance of the idea that young people (male and female) should attend college; the increasing acceptance of the idea that racial discriminations should be abolished; the increasing adoption of the habits of automobile driving, air travel, and TV viewing; the alteration of business, health, sanitary, educational, and other practices brought about by legislation; [18] the increased participation of women with regard to cigarette smoking during the past generation (although reconsideration of the habit by both sexes in the light of health hazards is called for); the spectacular advent of space travel; and the effects, large and small, on the way of life brought by hundreds of other inventions (from recently developed military weapons to wonder drugs to the computer) and by diffused ideas and practices.

The distinction between social and cultural change seems, at any

[18] American values gradually changed from a laissez-faire emphasis (which prevailed around 1880–1900) to one favoring governmental intervention (which was evident after the First World War and became marked with the F. D. Roosevelt regime during the 1930s). As a result social legislation became a subject of much significance.

rate, to be reasonably clear-cut.[19] But a further issue needs to be decided. It is granted that cultural changes affect social systems and the reverse: [20] that changing cultural values, for instance, which favor college attendance, bring a marked increase the size of the institutions themselves (social systems). The invention of the computer ushered in the automation era, which has led to major changes in many factories and offices. As was noted in the preceding chapter, several cultural inventions (telephone, auto, motion picture, radio, TV, airplane, computer) have formed the basis for many of America's leading corporations (vast social systems). The reverse influence is similarly in evidence. Modern industrial society grants an economic primacy over other considerations; its legal systems embody the principles of *universalism* and of *specificity*.[21] Growth in the size of social organizations may bring important effects on ways of interacting and the like.

In granting this socio-cultural entangling one is nevertheless faced with a remaining issue: As one contemplates changing America (or England or Brazil), should one place the emphasis on social change (as it has been defined), on cultural change (as defined), or on both? What is to be the main focus of study? It is clear that one *may* properly concentrate on social change (as previously defined, although with cultural factors influencing the changes), or cultural change (with social factors having effects), or the combination; it is up to the person making the study. Care should be exercised with respect to conceptualizations and semantics lest these differing studies be given the same label (or otherwise be confused with each other). Such confusions have occurred during the past.

In this writer's judgment semantic order can be obtained if two practices are followed: *First,* because a reasonable consensus does appear to exist concerning the meaning of social change and cultural change, sociologists need to be more careful in their use of these terms. The Parsons-Kroeber statement has been valuable in this regard. *Secondly,* sociologists who emphasize one or the other or the combination of these terms (using the widely accepted definitions) should make clear their point of emphasis. This suggestion, which has been made be-

---

[19] The reader must understand here that we mean that the *analysis* seems reasonably clear-cut. It is conceded that different behavioral scientists will still prefer special definitions of terms as they have during the past (some, of course, will not choose to follow the definitions suggested here).

[20] For an able discussion of this subject see Talcott Parsons, "Introduction" to Part IV, "Culture and the Social System," in Parsons, *et al.* (eds.), *Theories of Society,* Vol. II (New York: The Free Press of Glencoe, Inc., The Macmillan Company, 1961), pp. 970 and 977.

[21] Talcott Parsons, *Structure and Process in Modern Societies* (Glencoe, Ill.: The Free Press, Inc., 1960), Chap. 4.

fore,[22] is important in order that perspectives may be better understood. Sociologists will almost certainly continue to stress different aspects of changing phenomena—and this is doubtless needed. In discussing approaches and theories of change those having the social, cultural, or combined emphases should all, of course, be studied.

The need for conceptual clarification notwithstanding, the viewpoint taken in this volume is that change in human affairs is best approached through a combination of social *and* cultural change. Beginning at this point, then, we shall use the phrase *socio-cultural change* (or *dynamics*). In considering changing America or the changing Middle West we shall assume generally equal emphasis on social and cultural change during some specified period of time. This combined emphasis is held, we believe, by many people. In any case the close interweaving of the two systems—even if they may be separated for analytical purposes—is such that they are best considered in combination. As Kroeber expresses it:

> They [*society and culture*] *are counterparts, like the two faces of a sheet of paper. To each distinctive culture there corresponds necessarily and automatically, a particular society: to Hottentot culture, the Hottentot nationality, to Chinese civilization, the Chinese people. It is rather futile to discuss which of the two phases or aspects is primary.*[23]

The combined socio-cultural focus is needed if one expects to have a full, all-around analysis of change in an area. It is required for a complete assessment. Not only do the two orders influence each other but the relationship is extremely complicated. A broadening of the scope of study to include these two perspectives toward change is needed at this time.[24]

The viewpoint of Wilbert E. Moore is here assumed to be one varia-

22 von Wiese expresses it as follows: "To sum up, there are different uses of the concept 'social change.' Every author should make clear, both to himself and to his readers, what he means by the concept, which is apparently so simple but is in reality so complex." von Wiese, "The Sociological Study of Social Change," *Transactions of the Third World Congress of Sociology* (Amsterdam: August, 1956), International Sociological Association, 1956, Vol. 1, p. 9. See also Bryce Ryan, "The Resuscitation of Social Change," *Social Forces*, Vol. 44, No. 1 (September, 1965), 3.

23 A. L. Kroeber, *Anthropology*, rev. ed. (New York: Harcourt, Brace, 1948), pp. 267–268.

24 Because of this close interweaving of culture and social system one could correctly use the term *society-culture* (thus "the society-culture of America" or "the society-culture of Japan"). This, however, is cumbersome. It is nevertheless proper in the same sense that one may speak of "status-role," as Parsons declares (*The Social System*, p. 25 and elsewhere). Our main contention, in any event, is that generally equal emphasis on the factors of social system and culture is needed in studying change.

tion of this combined focus. Regarding his inclusion of cultural factors with the social, some question may exist as to the emphasis placed on the two. It would seem from his writings [25] that emphasis is placed on the social system, but we shall not pursue this. Even more importantly, if social and cultural factors are both duly considered, one may wonder if semantic clarity is served by calling such a study one in social change. Moore recognizes that his emphasis "cuts across conventional distinctions between the social and the cultural." [26] He calls attention to the fact that cultural change requires social actors as agents. Nevertheless some anthropologists may include both factors and yet place the major stress on the cultural (not minimizing the social actors as White's culturology seems to do). In any case the student should be aware of these varying usages maintained by different sociologists and anthropologists.

OTHER FUNDAMENTALS

The remainder of this discussion of the fundamentals of the *change* process relates to matters that are more traditional and standard. These considerations include (1) dimensions of change, (2) specifying what has changed, (3) changes and their significance in relation to the social structure, (4) levels of conceptualizing change, (5) forces of change versus stability in individual situations, (6) the over-all inevitability of change, (7) the existence of constant factors amid fast-changing social systems, (8) differential change, (9) evolution and revolution, (10) the science complex in relation to rapid change, (11) change and progress, and (12) planned and unplanned change. Because major issues do not seem to be present with reference to these topics, the treatment will be relatively brief.

Dimensions of Change

In studying any alleged socio-cultural change it is necessary to specify the spatial and temporal dimensions. The scope of the investigation

[25] Wilbert E. Moore, "Social Change," an article in the *International Encyclopaedia of the Social Sciences, loc. cit.* Also see Moore, *Social Change* (Englewood Cliffs, N. J.: Prentice-Hall, Inc., 1963).

[26] "Social Change," an article in the *International Encyclopaedia of the Social Sciences, loc. cit.* This subsumption of the cultural influence under the social itself seems to deemphasize the former, although we cannot be sure that Moore means to do this. An important reason for proposing relatively equal prominence of the two terms, on the other hand, is that the cultural influence is so very important in *human* behavior (owing to the significance of learning for humans). (It is for this reason that von Bertalanffy and Buckley, in explaining systems theory, emphasize the cultural factor in social systems—as we shall see in Chapter 3.) Cultural change in an area is by no means a secondary subject. However, as we have said, social scientists have their preferences regarding use of these terms.

may have wide or narrow limits as regards space and time. One may contemplate changes involving civilizations over the time span of many centuries in the manner of a Toynbee, or consider the fluctuations in systems of art or of truth or ethics as portrayed by a Sorokin. Or one might investigate changes in the United States, England, or Russia during a century or half century. Or, one might be interested in changes in some state (New York, Illinois, California, or another) during the past twenty years. Or perhaps one's interest will be in a county, a city, or neighborhood of a city—possibly showing the effects of an urban renewal or other program—during a particular five years. Or one may wish to investigate socio-cultural changes in a college or university subsystem, in a church, in an industrial corporation or in a family subsystem over some period of years. Others may be intent on studying the effects of one institution on another, as, in Weberian manner, the effects of a religious change on the economic system. Still others may prefer to concentrate on the effects of population change on an educational system or a community. A recent study has concerned the effects of advancing science on state governments in American society. Or one might explore the changing American high school during a stated period of time. Many will be interested in role changes, as the changing role of the physician or of the college student or of the factory worker or foreman (for example, under the impact of automation) in this nation. All of these possibilities constitute legitimate interests. Indeed all have been done. Studies, in short, may be macroscopic, intermediate, or microscopic. A first task of the researcher, then, is to set the spatial and temporal limits of the investigation that he intends to make.

What Has Changed?

Secondly, one must specify precisely *what* has changed. Is it a patterned regularity of behavior associated with an institution? Is it a change in role expectations or role content—or in functions? Is it a change in mores? Is a new type of socio-cultural behavior evident—as flying or space orbiting—that did not exist before? Has governmental structure changed—as China turning Communist or India or the Congo becoming free? In short, just what has changed? What is *the unit of change*—a role, an institution, a process, a population, a society, a civilization, or what?

As Sorokin has said:

> *Without the* unit *or the logical subject, no process, no dynamic state generally, is observable, thinkable, or describable. . . . The unit may be a thing; it may be a certain dynamic state, for instance, a process of integration, of disintegration, of growth, of degeneration,*

of expansion, etc. But some unit, as a logical subject, change, or modification of which we assert, must be given.[27]

Specify, we must, this focus of interest: *What* has changed?

Changes in Relation to the Social Structure

A cardinal point is that changes and their significance need to be assessed in relation to the existing social structure. Besides knowing *what* has changed, we are equally interested in the relevant conditions of the socio-cultural situation at the beginning of the time period. The fundamental value emphases of the society make a logical point of departure. Has the change occurred in an industrial-type society wherein the values emphasize achievement, universalism, science and secular rationality, efficiency and practicality, and similar attributes? Or are ascriptive, particularistic, or other values emphasized in the social setting? Then, with the specifics of the change in mind, we would like to know which people are concerned. Is it an entire population, an institutional group, an age group, a racial group? What authority structures and leadership factors are present? What "publics" and public-opinion factors are involved? What internal factors of the relevant groups and what external influences bear upon the change? If, for instance, the alteration relates to a college campus, was it initiated by students, faculty, the administration, the overseers or regents, others? Are the alumni, townspeople, public officials, business or other interests related? What, in short, is the *total base situation* from which the change arose? What cultural factors aside from the over-all values have had an effect (mores, laws, other norms, other cultural items)? Some might infer that such a statement of the *relevant structural essentials* would involve a lengthy treatise. We would caution against this; on the contrary, we would say that for most instances of change the important elements of the situation may be stated quite concisely.[28] It is granted that the scope of study and the nature of the change will affect the length of such a statement. Study of the relevant social structure is also worthwhile for a different kind of problem. In various social situations one wonders why a certain possible change has *not* occurred. Some of the factors mentioned here or the power balance between different groups often account for cases of failure to change.

[27] Pitirim A. Sorokin, *Social and Cultural Dynamics,* 1 vol. (Boston: Porter Sargent, 1957), p. 53.

[28] See Smelser's helpful description of the relevant social structure of a New England coastal town in which a commonplace type of change occurred. Neil Smelser (ed.), *Sociology* (New York: John Wiley & Sons, Inc., 1967), Part IV, "Social Change," p. 674 ff.

It must be conceded, furthermore, that in the same social setting some changes may be most important or significant, others much less so. The decision may be made for a previously male (or previously female) college to become coeducational. Perhaps the overseers, regents, or trustees have decided to double or treble the size of the institution. Or, perhaps a minor curriculum change is made. A total society (as India) may change from colonial to independent status; or perhaps some detailed statistic of Hindu life has increased or decreased by one point. Socio-cultural modifications thus may range from gross, overwhelming matters (such as the beginning of a world war) to some slight, barely perceptible fluctuation in a small department of living. Sometimes the importance of a change may be difficult to decide; individuals may disagree as to its importance. Occasionally developments that appear to be important are completely taken in stride, or the reverse may occur: what at first looks to be a minuscule item turns out to be crucial. At any rate, the significance of a change (or failure to change) is importantly related to the existing social structure.

The socio-cultural emphasis maintained in this book provides some clues by which the importance of an alteration may be estimated. Using the social-system approach, Parsons and others have underscored the approach of viewing changes in relation to their effects on the social system. Do they aid the functioning of the system—its survival, persistence, integration, or stability? Or do the modifications undermine or make difficult that functioning—in a word, is the change dysfunctional for the system? More specifically, do the alterations affect the reward system (how?), the belief system (how?), other systems? Do *manifest* or *latent* consequences for the system affect a given change? Sometimes an organization is abolished because an avowed and recognized (manifest) function has led to undesirable results; the members and other affected people have finally become determined to get rid of it. Yet the structure may have unintended (latent) functions that are important and needed. Unless some alternative structure is provided to take care of the latter functions, the change (ending of the organization) is likely to be doomed to failure. As Merton expresses it, "to seek social change, without due recognition of the manifest and latent functions performed by the social organization undergoing change, is to indulge in social ritual rather than social engineering." [29] Changes, then, have to be interpreted in relation to the relevant system and its functioning. If major effects are produced on the ongoing system, the change is to be regarded as important.

Culture has to be considered too. If a change affects the behavior of

[29] R. K. Merton, *Social Theory and Social Structure,* revised and enlarged edition (Glencoe, Ill.: The Free Press, Inc., 1957), p. 81.

virtually all the people of a society (called a universal by Ralph Linton),[30] the sheer numbers affected is likely to mean that the matter is of some consequence. The change may relate, however, to some specialty (as the practice of medicine or the operation of motels) or to an "alternative" (choice situation) in the culture. The change may be qualitatively important in the case of specialties and alternatives, which may make it significant even if the masses of people are not directly affected.

Moreover, the importance of a change bears relation to the system level and to the level of generality of the culture pattern; this is quite apart from the *participation* factor mentioned by Linton. However, the subject of levels of conceptualizing change deserves a separate heading of its own.

Levels of Conceptualizing Change

Any socio-cultural change needs to be viewed in terms of the system level concerned. That is to say, a given change may relate to the entire social system (American society, French society, Chinese society); a change may relate to a subsystem (Negro society within the United States, a regional subsystem, an educational or medical subsystem); or a change may relate to a sub-subsystem (some division of a racial, regional, or institutional subsystem). These are called system levels.

Changes may, furthermore, relate to the level of generality achieved by cultural patterns, as, for example, comparing values, norms, collectivities, and roles. Modifications in over-all societal values have the highest level of generality; then come modifications in norms; then follow modifications in behavior of groups (collectivities); finally, changes in role behavior have the lowest level of generality. Changes may be visualized at any level, and one must specify the level at which he is conceptualizing the phenomenon. Changes in the occurrence of divorces, to take an illustration, may be conceptualized in terms of over-all values; they may be viewed in the light of changing family norms; they may be conceptualized from the standpoint of certain religious or other groups; or the increasing number of divorces may be seen in relation to the changing husband or wife role or perhaps some occupational role. Similarly, changes occurring in a developing (that is, industrializing) nation may be conceptualized in terms of over-all values; the changes may be seen in their effects on various norms, which would be at the next lower level; the changes may affect various groups; and, lastly, the changes due to industrializ-

30 *The Study of Man* (New York: D. Appleton-Century Co., 1936), Chap. 16.

ing will affect specific roles, which would be at the lowest level of generality. Discussion of these matters has been brief, but it is apparent that the significance of socio-cultural changes may be assessed in relation to these various perspectives. Changes in over-all values—which have the highest level of generality—tend to have the greatest manifest importance. Changes in role behavior may be exceedingly important in detail situations, but their level of generality—and over-all importance—would be far less than that of values.[31]

Forces of Change Versus Those of Stability

In any given social situation it is likely that some forces will tend to promote change while others will promote stability or persistence. This is often seen in community situations. Some community interests will favor civic improvement (urban renewal programs and the like); others will fight for the status quo, fearing higher taxes, objecting to the specific plans, or fancying that they will "lose out" in some way if the change is made. Many changes of this kind involve a tug of war between the proponents of the idea and the resisters, and will be decided on the basis of the influence brought to bear on the electorate (if a referendum is held) or on the decision maker. Still, there are certain factors with regard to social systems that tend to give rise to change. These are (1) inherent tendencies to deviate from the existing system, (2) imperfections of the integration of value orientations, and (3) positively institutionalized sources of change in the system (as the commitment to and institutionalization of science or technological research.)[32] Forces impelling toward stability or persistence, on the other hand, include the entire major social processes of socialization and social control.

Various kinds of innovation may be made; scientific achievements that are translated into technological invention are but one. This

---

[31] A good example of this concerns the family revolution in China (beginning with the Republican revolution of 1911 and extended further by the coming of the Communists to power in 1949). The traditional high-prestige, powerful role of the father received a considerable downgrading. The status of women, on the other hand, experienced a rapid rise. Children in turn no longer showed the absolute obedience and devotion characteristic of earlier times; under the Communist regime they could even sternly rebuke their father. But all this was one element of a broader value change in which the State had replaced the family as the center of loyalty. See C. K. Yang, *The Chinese Family in the Communist Revolution* (Cambridge, Mass.: The MIT Press, 1959; paper edition published under the title *Chinese Communist Society: The Family and the Village*, 1965), Chaps. 1, 5–6 and 9; see also, Marion Levy, Jr., *The Family Revolution in Modern China* (Cambridge, Mass.: Harvard University Press, 1949; Octagon Books edition, 1963).

[32] Talcott Parsons, *The Social System* (New York: The Free Press of Glencoe, Inc., 1951), Chap. XI.

subject will be discussed in more detail in Chapter 10. However, it is clear that the values of some cultures favor innovations more than others. Resistances to innovations may also be based on values. If the forces favoring change in a situation are not powerful enough to overcome the forces of resistance, it is clear that the change will not be made.[33] This has sometimes happened with reference to programs seeking to introduce fluoridation of community water supplies, plans to establish nuclear power installations, and others. The subject of resistances to innovation will be discussed in Chapter 11.

The Inevitability of Some Changes

Despite such tug of war situations involving pro and con forces, the occurrence of *some* changes is inevitable. Even if every new proposal or innovation were somehow heavily resisted or totally opposed (which, practically speaking, would not occur because many developments would facilitate the attainment of generally accepted goals and values), the people would be growing older; resources would be gradually depleted; institutions would be changing immanently in the light of their characteristics and potentialities; people would be thinking up new ideas; and needs might provoke the formation of social movements that, if successful, would culminate in the passage of new laws or the establishment of institutions *de novo*. Change, at any rate, is the normal and expected condition. No society can be completely static, although a stationary society can be depicted for theoretical purposes; it can be viewed as an abstraction. Some social scientists, notably Robert Redfield,[34] have pictured this condition most successfully; Redfield drew his conception of the stationary society from empirical studies of relatively slow-to-change ones. The stationary society is one in complete equilibrium. Even though this is an abstraction or fiction, reflection of the conditions of the slow-to-change society may be valuable in providing a contrast from the modern, fast-changing one. Not only is the normal condition one of change, but the important question for any society is, "How fast is the rate of change in comparison with other societies? And what has made it that way?"

Constant Factors Amid General Conditions of Change

It is also to be observed that constant factors may be present in an otherwise fast-changing society. Indeed it is instructive to consider why stationary elements in the dynamic society have remained that way.

[33] As Parsons expresses it, ". . . change is never just 'alteration of pattern' but alteration by the overcoming of resistance." *Ibid.*, p. 491.

[34] "The Folk Society," *American Journal of Sociology*, Vol. LII (1947), 293–308.

Often major values will be relatively unchanging: belief in democracy, in free speech, in freedom of religion, and the like. Values may require restatement from time to time in the light of new conditions. Sometimes people will hold fast to values, sometimes the latter will change; it is important to realize why each has occurred.[35]

Seymour M. Lipset [36] has interpreted trends of American society in the light of the assumption that two values, *democratic equalitarianism* and *strong achievement orientation,* have remained constant. He traces the effects of these values on social mobility, education, religion, family life, bureaucracies, and other institutions. One may also consider the behavior associated with a social institution from the standpoints of what has changed and what factors have remained constant. Marvin R. Koller [37] takes this approach in his study of courtship behavior in three generations of Ohio women. He found that, among the changes made, the couples had more dates per week before engagement in recent times; a decline in chaperonage has occurred; the women have given an increasing number of gifts to the men during courtship during recent times; and that there is an increasing tendency of the parents of the girl to disapprove of the boy (coupled with a decreasing tendency of the girl to yield to her parents' wishes in such cases). On the other hand, constant factors found with regard to the Ohio women were that most of the women in each generation had seriously considered only one man, the one that they eventually married; the mean age at the first date with the man that they later married was about the same—close to 19 in all cases; and that the man financed the dating costs in nearly all cases in all generations. This type of approach, citing changing and constant factors, is fruitful with reference to other socio-cultural subsystems.

Special groups, furthermore, may seek to hold fast to their individual values and customs—to form an "island of constancy"—amid the larger, fast-changing society. Probably the Amish people, living in rural Pennsylvania, Ohio, Indiana, Iowa, and Ontario, are among the more famous of such groups. With strong religious convictions, a distinctive language and dress, and strong patriarchal authority, the Amish have largely preserved their way of life in the United States for more than two centuries.[38] They are taught not to conform to the outer world; they are encouraged to limit their close personal relationships to, and

[35] Robin M. Williams, Jr., *American Society,* 3rd ed. (New York: Alfred A. Knopf, 1969), Chap. XI.

[36] *The First New Nation: The United States in Historical and Comparative Perspective* (New York: Basic Books, Inc., 1963), Chap. 3.

[37] "Some Changes in Courtship Behavior in Three Generations of Ohio Women," *American Sociological Review,* Vol. 16, No. 3 (June, 1951), 366–370.

[38] John A. Hostetler, *Amish Society* (Baltimore, Md.: The Johns Hopkins Press, 1963), pp. 3–4.

certainly to marry, an Amish person. The most universal of Amish norms in the United States and Canada, declares Hostetler,[39] prohibits the use of electricity, telephones, central heating systems, and automobiles. Education beyond the elementary grades is frowned on, and state public education laws requiring school attendance to a certain year constitute a crucial and prime source of conflict between states and the Amish. The Amish seek to maintain, in short, an isolated, religiously oriented, stable, rural culture—a "folk society" or "little community" in the Redfield sense—within fast-moving, modern urban-industrial America. Some erosion of this culture has been indicated.

Differential Change

On this matter we wish to make only one basic, undisputable (in our opinion) point: socio-cultural systems and subsystems vary in their rates of change. This is manifest in two ways: (1) two parts of the same social system may vary in their rate of change, as the religious subsystem may change at a slower rate than the economic subsystem; and (2) the same system or subsystem may vary its rate of change over time.[40] It is not our need in this chapter to expatiate on the "why?". Nor are we interested in trying to maintain that any special system or subsystem consistently has a higher rate of change than some other system or subsystem. Nor are we concerned at this point in relationships that may exist between changing subsystems. Our observation is merely that socio-cultural systems and subsystems do change at different rates of speed—for whatever reasons.

Evolution and Revolution

A familiar distinction between two polar types of socio-cultural change is still useful. *Evolution* refers to alterations in society or culture that are lawful, orderly, and gradual; an unfolding of forces actually or potentially present is implied.[41] *Revolution* connotes a sudden and

39 *Ibid.*, p. 61. For a social-system view of Amish society, see Charles P. Loomis, *Social Systems* (Princeton, N. J.: D. Van Nostrand Co., 1960), Essay 5, "The Old Order Amish As a Social System," pp. 212–248.

40 Notable illustrations of this may be found in India and China where the rate of change was extremely slow for many centuries, but where in recent decades the rate has markedly accelerated. To broaden the example, as all "underdeveloped" nations modernize, the rate of change tends to increase. The history of the United States, of course, illustrates this theme of an accelerating rate of change.

41 See "Evolutionary Change" and "Evolution" in Fairchild (ed.), *op. cit.*, p. 110; see also, Joseph Needham, "Evolution," an article in the *Encyclopaedia of the Social Sciences*, Vols. V–VI (New York: The Macmillan Company, 1931).

far-reaching change from the usual social and/or cultural ongoing. The latter implies a major break in the continuity of development, which often is contrary to the official law. Revolution and violence are frequently connected in the instance of *political* revolutions, but other social or cultural revolutions may involve no violence whatever. A recasting of the social order, or some important part of it, is more characteristic of revolutions than the use of violence as a method of attaining ends. As another example of the distinction, institutions may evolve in an orderly and gradual manner from a condition of simplicity to one of complexity, or groups from a condition of homogeneity to one of heterogeneity. Stages of development, indeed, may be recognized. The over-all modification may be considerable; this is not the crucial point. If, however, it proceeds according to the official law of the group and is, in general, continuous and gradual, we may designate it as evolution.[42] On the other hand, an abrupt modification —a major break in the usual development—warrants the designation of revolution.

Political revolutions involve a sudden and major change in political power, which may range from a comparatively limited overthrow of some governmental organization to a drastic transformation of the ruling class and the entire government (such as occurred in modern Russia, China, or Cuba). Economic revolutions (such as the original Industrial Revolution) may bring a considerable recasting of the industrial order, of places of work, and of conditions of work. Religious changes, as exemplified by the struggles of the Reformation, may similarly be far-reaching and drastic in nature. Abrupt changes may also occur in race relations, in the familial and marriage system, or in other realms.[43]

Distinguishing between evolution and revolution in practical cases is, in the main, not difficult. The rise in the standard of living in the

[42] Thus, "long-term, fundamental changes in the technological, economic, religious or social structure, and any other deep-seated change in systems of thought and habit, if transpiring gradually and without violence, are evolutionary rather than revolutionary." From the article "Revolutionary Change" in Fairchild (ed.), *op. cit.*, p. 260. We would emphasize the gradual versus abrupt recasting of the social order (or one of its major elements), playing down the factor of violence as the main consideration.

[43] Sorokin also distinguishes between such revolutions as have been mentioned in this paragraph and what he calls a total revolution. The latter would be a revolutionary change that attempts to transform the entire body of official law and all important institutions of the group (political, economic, religious, ethical, and so on). He cites the Communist revolution in Russia and the Taborite revolution in Bohemia as examples of this over-all type. Pitirim A. Sorokin, *Society, Culture, and Personality* (New York: Harper & Bros., 1947), p. 482; see also Sorokin, *Sociology of Revolution* (Philadelphia, Pa.: Lippincott, 1925).

United States during the first half of the twentieth century—it approximately doubled [44] is clearly evolutionary. The increase in marriages in the United States and Canada during the early 1960s over the decade before [45] and the increase in the median years of schooling completed by Americans of age 25 and over from 1910–1960 [46] are also evolutionary changes. The increasing mobility of the American people is again clearly evolutionary. On the other hand, the assumption of political control by Castro in Cuba and by the Communists in Russia and in China is *revolutionary*. But situations are not always so clearcut. People may have differing viewpoints in certain marginal conditions (the grey areas), and semantic arguments may then begin. For example, a volume describing the American New Deal government of Franklin D. Roosevelt is entitled "The Roosevelt Revolution." [47] Was the New Deal a *revolution*? The author, Lindley (a conservative), thought so. To many others (including Mr. Roosevelt himself) it was evolutionary. Again, modern automation has been called by various people [48] the second Industrial *Revolution*. Does automation bring abrupt, discontinuous change or does it essentially involve an extension of earlier mechanization? (Is it thus evolutionary?) Those who think of it as a revolution emphasize that the control of machines by other machines (computers) brings a vastly important qualitative difference from simple mechanization. Finally, did the pill (contraceptive) bring about a revolutionary change in birth control since its introduction in about 1960? Did an abrupt change occur with this innovation? Many would reply in the affirmative. However, arguments may rage concerning these and other changes. Nevertheless the distinction between (1) lawful, orderly, and gradual change and (2) sudden, drastic change

44 J. Frederic Dewhurst and Associates, *America's Needs and Resources,* A New Survey (New York: Twentieth Century Fund, 1955), p. 835; William F. Ogburn, "Technology and the Standard of Living in the United States," *American Journal of Sociology,* Vol. LX (January, 1955), 380–386. Per capita income is generally taken as a measure of standard of living.

45 "Marriage Increase in the United States and Canada," *Statistical Bulletin of Metropolitan Life Insurance Company,* Vol. 45 (May, 1964), 1–4.

46 U. S. Bureau of the Census, *Education of the American Population,* by John K. Folger and Charles B. Nam (a 1960 Census Monograph). U. S. Government Printing Office (Washington, D. C., 1967), Table V–1, p. 132. The median school years completed was 8.1 (estimated) in 1910, 10.5 in 1960.

47 Ernest K. Lindley, *The Roosevelt Revolution* (New York: The Viking Press, 1933).

48 See contrasting views in John Diebold, "Automation As a Management Problem," Chap. 26 in H. Jacobson and J. Roucek (eds.), *Automation and Society* (New York: Philosophical Library, 1959); Frederick Pollock, *Automation: A Study of its Economic and Social Consequences* (New York: Praeger, 1957), especially pp. 38–39; and James R. Bright, *Automation and Management* (Boston: Graduate School of Business Administration, Harvard University, 1958), especially Chap. 2.

that constitutes a major break in continuous development, is worth-while and useful.

The Science Complex and Rapid Change

Institutionalized cultural configurations may sometimes constitute a notable source of change—both gradual and revolutionary. An eminent example of this in modern Western civilization is the institutionalization of scientific investigation. Science is universalistic in its orientation and, particularly as allied with emphasis on the *achievement* motivation, it produces a high rate of socio-cultural change. Because the spirit of science is to question and examine, to search for new facts and principles, to unearth new knowledge concerning all subjects that can be investigated by its type of approach, it leads to the new—and is linked with change—virtually by definition. This tends to be true on one condition: That social values be receptive to the scientific influence and its findings. In modern Western society, moreover, scientific results will often lead to technological application. In the present era science provides the basis for virtually all technological products and advances. Indeed it is sometimes difficult at present to draw a sharp line between the supposedly pure scientific endeavors (namely, the scientist is making no effort to think of applications) and the avowedly applied work of the technologist.[49] Certainly it may be difficult for the nonspecialist to tell where science leaves off and where technological application begins. Furthermore, the time gap between acquiring new scientific knowledge and making technological application is being steadily reduced.[50] Because scientific achievements tend to give rise to new types of thinking (as witness the consequences of evolution) and technological inventions bring forth many social affects,[51] it is clear that the science-technology influence is highly dynamic.

[49] Walter A. Rosenblith, "On Some Social Consequences of Scientific and Technological Change," *Daedalus,* Vol. 90, No. 3 (Summer, 1961), 502–503.

[50] Thomas J. Watson, Jr., Chairman of the Board of the IBM Corporation illustrates this. He declares: "The principle of the vacuum tube was understood around the turn of the century, but it was not used in any major way until after World War I. On the other hand, the transistor was discovered in 1948. Within five years, it was being widely used in many types of equipment. The solar battery was hardly born before it was flying in our satellites." "Technological Change," Chap. 8 in *Goals for Americans,* Report of the President's Commission on National Goals (Englewood Cliffs, N. J.: Prentice-Hall, Inc., 1960), p. 195.

[51] For a recent assessment of the over-all effects of technological change, see Report of the National Commission on Technology, Automation, and Economic Progress, *Technology and the American Economy,* Vol. 1 and five Appendix Volumes (Washington, D. C.: U. S. Government Printing Office, 1966); for a discussion of the effects of specific inventions such as the automobile, airplane, television, and nuclear energy, see F. R. Allen, H. Hart, D. C. Miller, W. F. Ogburn, and M. F. Nimkoff, *Technology and Social Change* (New York: Appleton-Century-Crofts, 1957).

Barber expresses it as follows:

> One of the chief internal sources of social change in modern so-
> ciety is science and its extensive applications in industrial and social
> technology. By our approval of science, by the way in which we pro-
> vide such large opportunities for those who want to work at science,
> there has been introduced into the very heart of our society a funda-
> mentally and continually dynamic element, an element which must
> remain the fount of unending social consequences, for both "good"
> and "bad."
> We face a new condition in human society. The simple truth is
> that we must learn to live with social change because we value very
> highly that which cannot do otherwise than cause change. . . . We
> cannot . . . have both science and complete social stability.
> [Thus] behind the technological and social innovations lies the
> primary source, science itself, dynamic by its very nature and con-
> tinually producing not only new conceptual schemes but also the
> possibility of new applications of those schemes in the form of tech-
> nological inventions.[52]

The rapid increase in scientific knowledge during the present age
(often called the age of science) is evident. It has been calculated that
recent measures of scientific activity show a doubling time of somewhere between ten and fifteen years, whereas other human activities
double approximately every forty years.[53] If science itself has a high
rate of increase, one may indeed expect a high, and probably increasing, rate of socio-cultural change in the years ahead. Science thus has
a special and key importance for the subject of socio-cultural change—
in those areas, it must always be added, where it is firmly established
and positively valued.

Evolution, Change, and Progress

The term *evolution* has already been contrasted with that of revolution. Social evolution has been a long-term interest of sociologists,
dating back to the nineteenth century when the Darwinian and other
studies in biological evolution stimulated interest in their social coun-
terpart. But the study of social evolution ran into difficulties about
the 1920s. Strong objection developed to the notion that human so-

---

52 Bernard Barber, *Science and the Social Order* (Glencoe, Ill.: The Free Press,
Inc., 1952), pp. 210–212.

53 Rosenblith, *op. cit.*, p. 509. Measurement is made on the basis of the increase in
the number of scientific societies and journals, memberships in scientific societies,
and similar indicators. See also, Derek J. Price, "The Exponential Curve of Science,"
Chap. 30 in Bernard Barber and Walter Hirsch (eds.), *The Sociology of Science* (New
York: The Free Press of Glencoe, Division of The Macmillan Company, 1962). Price
warns of an approaching "period of saturation when there cannot be enough scientists
to meet all demands, and when those scientists will tend to be stifled by their own
flood of literature and intense overspecialization." P. 524.

cieties evolve in a unilinear way, with each society going through various stages, and many felt that sociologists were too slavish in copying the biological explanations. The phrase social change was increasingly used at this time. However, the problem of how societies evolve has remained, and during the 1960s—probably due to the growing interest in historical and comparative studies—a revival of interest in the evolutionary view has taken place. This does not imply a return to the nineteenth-century perspectives; rather it is assumed, as Eisenstadt declares,[54] that the earlier theory will be revised and reappraised in the light of current theory and research. This approach to the study of socio-cultural change will be discussed further in Chapter 3.

Here a basic point needs to be made, however, concerning social evolution and social change. In describing the unfolding of a given system or of a total society or the modification of systems, a *neutral* viewpoint is maintained by the observer. No evaluation of the development (or stages of development) is made. The phrase social change has particularly been used to connote objective, scientific description, but in both cases there is an utter absence of moral or other evaluation.

The concept of *progress* is different. Here evaluation is made, and the new development is defined as desirable change, improvement (in some respect), something good. Progress is, however, a subjective term. Defining something as good or desirable clearly relates to one's values. We may *believe* in progress, but, as MacIver and Page state,[55] we cannot demonstrate it to others unless they first accept our valuations. A given population may observe the same changes: racial integration, the coming of automation, greater freedom in discussion of sex subjects, establishment and functioning of the United Nations. To some people these changes spell progress, to others retrogression. Evolution and change, then, can be shown with certainty; they are objective matters. Belief in progress depends on the standard of value chosen for measuring it and on the time perspective in which it is measured. If we look back a hundred years, it seems clear that mankind has had progress in the mastery of physical forces. If we look back two thousand years, it is not at all sure that man has had progress in intelligence and in the art of living.[56] At least this is arguable.

The subject of fluctuations in the belief in progress at various times and in various places is itself interesting. During the nineteenth century a generalized belief in progress was held in the United States; life

54 S. N. Eisenstadt, "Social Change, Differentiation and Evolution," *American Sociological Review*, Vol. 29, No. 3 (June, 1964), 375.

55 Robert M. MacIver and Charles H. Page, *Society, An Introductory Analysis* (New York: Rinehart and Co., 1949), p. 610.

56 Carl Becker, "Progress," an article in the *Encyclopaedia of the Social Sciences*, Vols. XI–XII (New York: The Macmillan Company, 1933).

was thought to be getting better and better. This viewpoint has hardly prevailed to the same extent—and for good reason—in the present century. Some have linked the growing sense of disillusionment with the German experience under Hitler wherein a civilized nation went barbarian. That the mass extermination of some 18 million people (about six million were Jews) could occur in a supposedly civilized nation was indeed jolting. Others became skeptical regarding progress with the advent of ominous war weapons, especially the H-bomb. Other factors played a part too.[57] Increasing violence during the 1960s in connection with crime, riots, and the assassinations of public figures such as President John F. Kennedy, Dr. Martin Luther King, Jr. and Senator Robert F. Kennedy were also disillusioning.

Notions about progress, at any rate, need to relate to the yardstick used to measure it. Some have sought to introduce a scientific consideration of progress—to "objectivize" the subjective concept. Thus, if one defines increasing education on the part of the average American citizen as progress, *this* can be demonstrated. If one defines a rising standard of living or a decreasing death rate as progress, *these* matters can be shown as occurring in the United States. On such points as these evaluations are not likely to differ much. On other matters—the mechanized way of life, the over-all commercial emphasis in the United States, present-day movie and television presentations, jazz as a type of music, modern art, to name a few—differences of opinion are likely to be vigorously expressed. In general, evaluatory agreements are often made with regard to organic matters and items that are a means to an end; consensus concerning the ultimate ends of life are often more difficult to obtain.[58] Inevitably, however, one returns to the thesis that progress is necessarily subjective in nature; it is not a scientific concept. Its determination depends on values of time and place (as well as of the individual person). It may relate to vested interests. If one agrees that X (decrease in crime, smaller number of divorces, increased monetary saving from income, increasing use of seat belts in cars) constitutes progress, then progress can be measured on that basis. But one's views may be colored by the fact that one is a banker or a seat-belt manufacturer. Some factor as the divorce rate may in turn relate to divorce laws and other considerations; even then differences of opinion can

---

57 Pitirim A. Sorokin, we may remind ourselves, characterized the first part of the twentieth century (up to the time of his writing) as "the bloodiest and the most turbulent period—and therefore one of the cruelest and least humanitarian—in the history of Western Civilization and perhaps in the chronicles of mankind in general." Sorokin, *Social and Cultural Dynamics*, 1 Vol. (Boston: Porter Sargent, 1957), pp. 594–595.

58 MacIver and Page, *op. cit.*, pp. 614–615. In general, their Chap. 28, entitled, "Social Evolution and Social Progress," is recommended.

occur. Progress can be defined, moreover, not in terms of evaluations of people, but regarding whether some behavior is functional or dysfunctional for the social system. Thus, having the average American citizen achieve a greater amount of education than formerly would be defined as functional (thus progress) for the social system. It should enhance the operations of the political, economic, and other systems. Similarly, to have a lower rate of mental disease would be functional for the system. But the same sort of difficulty remains: Is there general agreement that modern movies, current television programs, or "X" type educational curriculum are functional or dysfunctional? Even rough agreement is not always possible.

Planned and Unplanned Change

As one reflects on the many and diverse socio-cultural alterations that have occurred in nations, states, communities, and subsystems (corporations, colleges, churches, and others), it seems evident that many of the changes are spontaneous, unwitting, accidental, products of quick decisions, the result of a person's individual interest (for instance, an inventor's), consequences of system interaction, consequences of a cultural process (as diffusion). In brief, they are socially unplanned. Again, systems and subsystems change immanently, often with no particular planning involved. Fads and fashions seem to spread without rhyme or reason. Sometimes inventions and discoveries are even made by accident. But if not, can one say that the inventor of the automobile *planned* that his vehicle would affect vacation patterns or courtship behavior? Did the inventor of the airplane *plan* that his ship would increase international contacts and foster the spirit of "one world"? Did Columbus *plan* to discover a new world during the 1490s? Hardly; he was seeking a trade route to India.

On the other hand, other changes have been carefully planned. One thinks of the many programs of state or nation, of community or neighborhood, of corporation or university. There are some people who regard the Tennessee River project performed by the Tennessee Valley Authority (TVA), beginning in 1933, as a shining example of planning; this is especially so if one factually compares the welfare of the region's people *before* and *after* the TVA. Some will oppose the TVA accomplishments, however, from the special standpoint of the private power interests or in the light of undiluted free-enterprise ideology. Other planning projects—metropolitan regional planning, urban renewal programs, interstate highway programs, planning that deals with problems due to automation (associated with the Area Redevelopment Act of 1961), antipoverty planning (stimulated by the Economic Develop-

ment Act of 1965), planning for special areas (for instance, resulting
from passage of the Appalachian Regional Development Act of 1965)—
all testify to the current lively interest in setting goals and then trying
to devise the most efficient and workable means of reaching them.[59] On
the international scene it is clear that planning in underdeveloped
areas is a vast subject in itself. It may also be noted that, although
we have said leaders often make spur-of-the-moment decisions and
inventors may invent on the basis of sudden inspiration, nevertheless
they may also act and invent in relation to systematic plans. Indeed
we shall advance the thesis in a later chapter that the increased planning of inventions (both mechanical and social) is socially beneficial.
So, also, in modern times would be decision making on the basis of
carefully considered plans.[60]

A proposition can be stated that as *social conditions become more
complicated and fast-moving, planning is increasingly needed.* Even at
the present time, as Gross declares, changes due to conscious, goal-
oriented activities are "probably far less than intellectuals would like
to think." [61] In contrast to the slow, simple, rural times of one century
ago in the United States, however, it seems difficult to deny today that
the application of intelligence and foresight to human endeavors is
more and more necessary if man aspires to reach goals. The wish for a
better life may be a noble sentiment. In order to attain it man often
needs to study and plan, work and persevere, be able to cope with
human resistances and natural obstacles, and show wisdom in choosing
between alternative courses of action. This is as true in building interstate highways within the United States as in securing economic development in Latin America, Asia, or Africa. In any case the subject
of planned change and development is an important interest of many
peoples and governments today.[62]

[59] We do not say, of course, that "politics" will not enter into the execution of
the plans, nor that immense projects of these kinds will not encounter a variety of
problems.

[60] It seems to us, furthermore, that there is a middle area in which leaders, administrators, inventors, legislators, and others, do *some planning.* Their actions and
endeavors are not entirely based on planning, but neither are they entirely hit-or-
miss. Lawmakers (working in committee) may do a great deal of studying concerning
a subject before the law is written; it may be the same with inventors. Neither are
social movements as spontaneous and as unstructured as many may believe. The
planning espoused in various activities may be a matter of degree.

[61] Bertram M. Gross, "The State of the Nation: Social Systems Accounting," Chap.
3 in Raymond A. Bauer (ed.), *Social Indicators* (Cambridge, Mass.: The MIT Press,
1966), p. 176.

[62] Wilbert E. Moore observes that "deliberate change is increasingly characteristic
of the contemporary world." "The Utility of Utopias," *American Sociological Review,* Vol. 31, No. 6 (December, 1966), 765–772.

Summary

This chapter has briefly examined such fundamentals in the study of socio-cultural change as conceptualizations and definitions; the need of setting space and time limits; assessing change in relation to the social structure; observing differential rates of change; distinguishing between *evolution* and *revolution* and between *change* and *progress;* and noting that changes may be planned or unplanned, with the former more characteristic of the present era.

A review of the conceptualizations of the basic terms *social change* and *cultural change* suggests that most sociologists (and other social scientists) are in substantial agreement as to the meaning of these terms. Change in human affairs is seen as including both the social and cultural elements. Nevertheless, emphasis has sometimes been placed on one or the other, and semantic confusions have existed in the past. In this book, at all events, we shall consider the unit of investigation in the sociological study of dynamics to be the society and its culture (or some division thereof). The social and cultural elements in change are assumed to be approximately equal in importance, to warrant about equal attention, and (probably) to provoke about an equal amount of interest in the minds of most observers.

ANNOTATED BIBLIOGRAPHY

Barber, Bernard, *Science and the Social Order* (Glencoe, Ill.: The Free Press, Inc., 1952).
>   Rapid change is virtually guaranteed if science is highly valued and is established in the social order. Interrelationships between science and society are considered. The book is well written.
Becker, Carl, "Progress," an article in the *Encyclopaedia of the Social Sciences,* Vols. XI–XII (New York: The Macmillan Company, 1933).
>   Worthwhile reading.
Durant, Will and Ariel, *The Lessons of History* (New York: Simon and Schuster, 1968), Chap. XIII, "Is Progress Real?"
>   The distilled ideas on world progress of these two renowned philosophers and historians (authors of an entire series on The Story of Civilization) are of special interest. The Durants' basic conclusion is that: "If progress is real . . . it is not because we are born any healthier, better, or wiser . . . , but because we are born to a richer heritage, ... The heritage rises, and man rises in proportion as he receives it."
Hostetler, John A., *Amish Society* (Baltimore, Md.: The Johns Hopkins Press, 1963).
>   An American subsystem (the rural, patriarchal, religiously oriented

Amish) tries with difficulty to resist change. A fascinating account. The author, a sociologist, is a former Amishman.

Kroeber, A. L. and Parsons, Talcott, "The Concepts of Culture and Social System," *American Sociological Review*, Vol. 23, No. 5 (October, 1958), 582–583.

An admirable and much-needed clarification of these fundamental concepts.

MacIver, Robert M. and Page, Charles H., *Society* (New York: Rinehart and Co., 1949), Chapter 28, "Social Evolution and Social Progress."

This is a high-quality discussion of change and progress; penetrating, wise, and unusually well written.

Moore, Wilbert E., "Social Change," an article in the *International Encyclopaedia of the Social Sciences*, Vol. 14 (New York: The Macmillan Company and The Free Press, 1968).

The conceptualization of *social change* of a leading contemporary sociologist. The cultural influence is subsumed under this term.

Parsons, Talcott, "Introduction" to Part IV, "Culture and the Social System," in Parsons, *et al.* (eds.), *Theories of Society*, Vol. II (New York: The Free Press of Glencoe, Inc., The Macmillan Company, 1961).

This is a rewarding discussion of the interrelations of culture and social system written by an eminent social theorist.

Ryan, Bryce, *Social and Cultural Change* (New York: The Ronald Press, 1969).

Ryan's general (socio-cultural) perspective is similar to that found in the present book. He emphasizes invention, diffusion, social movements, and integrative patterns.

Washburne, Norman F., *Interpreting Social Change in America* (Garden City, N. Y.: Doubleday & Co., 1954).

This booklet helpfully discusses the fundamentals of change.

von Wiese, Leopold, "The Sociological Study of Social Change," *Transactions of the Third World Congress of Sociology*, Amsterdam, 1956 (Amsterdam: International Sociological Association, 1956).

Professor von Wiese laments past conceptual and semantic confusions in the analysis of change. Well-considered observations.

Yang, C. K., *The Chinese Family in the Communist Revolution* (Cambridge, Mass.: The MIT Press, 1959; paper edition, under the title *Chinese Communist Society: The Family and the Village*, 1965).

An illuminating example of drastic change in a social subsystem. Role behavior in the traditional Chinese family is recast, and such mores as filial piety and veneration of age are swept aside amid a political-economic-social revolution. An engrossing, well-done study.

3

Approaches to the Study
of Socio-cultural Change

Having realized the immensity of change in the United States and in other areas and having reviewed and clarified certain issues related to conceptualization and other fundamentals of change, we now come to the vast subject of *causes*. Why have socio-cultural alterations occurred? As new, sometimes unexpected, events take place on the human scene and new forces are generated—resulting in exhilarating or sometimes tragic consequences—social scientists, community or national leaders, self-styled "sages," and ordinary citizens understandably have much interest in the "Why?" Perhaps the reader—contemplating events of history or current items of major significance—has also wondered what lay back of this or that change. Possibly "it" was the coming of the Hitler regime in Germany or the advent of Castro in Cuba or the Communist takeover in China. Or it may have been the great build-up of cities and metropolitan centers or the rising status of Blacks in the United States during the present generation. Or one may be much interested in the vast population increase in this or that part of the world or the strong wish of underdeveloped nations—dormant for so many years—to modernize. Or, returning to the American scene, one may be curious regarding the modern accent on education whereby millions of youth want to attend college; fifty years ago it seems that only a small number had this wish. To be more inclusive, what causes predominated in the all-around evolution of the United States from its condition of one century ago (as briefly portrayed in Chapter 1) to its present state of development? Similarly, what caused the development of Australia and Austria, Belgium and British Guiana, Canada and China, India and Israel, Poland and Peru—indeed the entire world if we incline to the macroscopic—to its present state? We know from the account of history that many developments have occurred. But why?

To attempt to explain all these things would be, of course, a large undertaking. Is it foolish·to try to give explanations at all? Is the unfolding of historical occurrences to be left—with a shrug of the shoulders—as a series of haphazard, unique, unexplicable details? We think not. Sociological explanations are possible and available.[1] Hundreds, perhaps even thousands, of ideas have been advanced in the attempt to illuminate the fascinating, sometimes puzzling, course of human happenings. These explanatory ideas—sometimes simple, sometimes elaborate and sophisticated—have been debated, criticized, sometimes related to other known occurrences, and occasionally tested by research. Sociological explanations of change are close to what is called the philosophy of history. Indeed, only a fine line separates the two.[2] We shall discuss the more substantial and enduring explanations of change as they have appeared during the years and shall consider some of the still-controversial items.

Some selectivity is necessary in considering explanations of change, otherwise the sheer bulk of the subject would overwhelm us. First, explanations based on magic will be completely ignored. If increasing human fertility is believed to be caused by a tribal incantation, or if the coming of economic prosperity is held to reflect the benign favor of the Gods, that will have to be recognized. But such assumptions are beyond rational analysis, and we shall have nothing to do with this type of explanation here. We shall insist on scientific accountings, ones that—however convincing or unconvincing—at least attempt to link cause and effect on the basis of factual evidence. We acknowledge that the degree of scientific rigor in these accountings will vary considerably, but the obligation to follow scientific method is central to the enterprise. Secondly, we shall strive to emphasize higher-quality explanations with some regard for timeliness. Thus we shall allot more space to explanations thought to have significance for the present and immediate future. If an issue is of the past and is essentially decided, we shall cut drastically on space allotment. If an issue is truly dead, we may merely mention it—with no real discussion at all. Thirdly, we shall give attention to explanations of change in the light of their believed importance.

---

1 A prominent sociological thinker, Pitirim A. Sorokin, has revealed that his extensive work in studying socio-cultural dynamics began with attempts to see reason behind the events of the First World War and the Russian Revolution. He declares: "What were the reasons, the causes, and the meaning of these [events]? The leading principles of the social science that I had learned did not help much in my attempt to understand. Quietly, sincerely, only for myself, I began to meditate, to study, and to look for the answer. This personal quest has continued for a number of years. . . . After many trials and errors the central idea . . . emerged. . . . After preliminary tests of its truth, I undertook its systematic elaboration." *Social and Cultural Dynamics*, Vol. I (New York: American Book Co., 1937), Preface.

2 To turn again to Professor Sorokin, he states: ". . . almost all great sociological systems are a brand of philosophy of history, and . . . most of the great philosophies of history are a sort of sociology of cultural change." *Ibid.*, p. x. This writer suggests that a major aspect is whether one studies the data of history from the perspectives of and uses the methods of sociology or philosophy.

The plan of operation is to discuss broad approaches to socio-cultural change in the present and following chapter. Different perspectives toward the subject will be outlined even if, thus far, no person is known to have presented any systematic theory or set of ideas using the approach. If none has done so, maybe this should be remedied. At all events, our discussion is designed to present different viewpoints. These two chapters will be followed by four others that will deal with specific theories. Thus the six chapters together are regarded as a unit describing explanations of change. Insofar as is possible, the first two chapters will be cross-checked with the following four.[3] Attention may also be called to the fact that the theories deal with socio-cultural *change* only, not with society in other respects. In many cases the ideas relating to change compose only a fraction of the total output of their authors.

This may be a proper time to emphasize the extensiveness of the study of socio-cultural change. It is an omnibus kind of subject. The many and varied approaches, as well as the contrasting theories, indicate this. We shall have illustrations of some approaches being related to social phenomena and others being associated with the cultural. Some approaches, furthermore, are primarily linked with the internal factors of a system, and some are primarily connected with external influences. In a specific situation involving empirical change only a few of these approaches may be involved. However, it appears wise to inspect the wide gamut of approaches to change—approaches that may occur *anywhere*—before examining detailed cases.[4] The varied alternative approaches may thus be perceived, before a theoretical framework is considered that may be a serviceable connection with a given set of concrete data.

Finally, the question may be raised as to what we expect to find in ranging over the different approaches to change. Do we anticipate

[3] That is to say, when discussing some approach mention will be made of significant theories that are based on that approach. Later, in discussing the theories, it will be pointed out that X theory is an illustration of the Y approach—if any doubt or ambiguity seems to exist concerning the matter. In the present discussion of approaches little attention will ordinarily be paid to individual theories.

[4] Bertram M. Gross is also impressed with the idea of "exploring the entire field" before analyzing specific situations. With regard to his "state-of-the-system" type of analysis he declares: "An infinite number of permutations may be created by combining various elements and subelements of structure and performance. In this way the system states of nations, as well as their major subsystems may be described for any period of time, past, present, or future. . . . The value of a general system approach to all possible variables is that it provides a background for selecting those variables most appropriate to specific situations and for changing one's focus as the occasion warrants." "The State of the Nation: Social Systems Accounting," Chapter 3 in Raymond A. Bauer (ed.), *Social Indicators* (Cambridge, Mass.: The MIT Press, 1966), p. 185.

discovering any *one* approach that will be the key to explaining many different types, or even all types of change? Is any viewpoint *the* correct one or do we expect to encounter a collection of valid approaches? Do they function in concert? We have previously suggested that some approaches receive greater emphasis in societies having certain kinds of value orientations; thus the scientific-technological factor is a major source of change in the industrial-type society. We have also maintained that some approaches are evidently important in all societies— for instance, the leadership factor in change. We grant that differences or nuances of emphasis in such a factor may occur in the light of varying cultural values. A fundamental proposition is, at any rate, that no one explanation has been found adequate for the panoramic range of socio-cultural change. Different explanations are required. Moreover, we must bear in mind MacIver's point [5] that most social changes are enmeshed in a tangled web of different orders or levels of reality— physical, biological, psychological, and social. Hence, different levels of explanation may be given.[6] Contending that one factor is the dominant cause of something usually evades the full explanation; a glimpse at the different kinds of explanations at least shows that none is suffi-

---

[5] Robert M. MacIver, *Social Causation* (New York: Ginn & Co., 1942), pp. 74–76 and 113–114.

[6] The late Professor Samuel A. Stouffer illustrates this humorously with a "parable of the dead duck." Quoting from Stouffer:

> *Sometimes it seems as if there are almost as many theories of social change as there are sociologists writing about it. Some of these writers, wedded to a particular theory, are quite dogmatic. The monolithic cause of change through the ages is found convincingly to reside in ideology, or in geography, or in psychology, or in technology, or in some other single "ography" or "ology."*
>
> *. . . To take an eclectic position is to invite doubts and confusion, and whatever clarity is achieved is likely to be equated with superficiality. . . . [Let us illustrate with] the parable of the dead duck. The story is simple. A duck was shot dead by a hunter at daybreak in a Michigan marsh. Now the problem. What was the cause of the duck's demise?*
>
> *Well, there is a physiological explanation. The duck died because of a hemorrhage, which left the heart no blood to pump. And there is a psychological explanation. The duck died because the hunter was the kind of person he was—if he had had different frustrations in his youth, he might not have become a bird-killer. We might take quite a psychoanalytic dive on this one, but let's skip it. And there is an ideological explanation. . . . And there is a geographical explanation. Note that our duck died in a marsh. No hunter probably would have been waiting for him on top of a hill. Finally, consider a technological explanation, ...*
>
> *Now the point of this parable is, first, that every one of these explanations of the cause of the duck's death is correct. And, of course, many additional explanations could be dreamed up. Second, the explanations are at different levels.*

Social Research to Test Ideas (New York: The Free Press of Glencoe, Division of The Macmillan Company, 1962), pp. 238–239.

cient in itself. One-factor explanations tend to oversimplify (if they do not do gross violence to the empirical data of situations). It is often claimed that simplification delights many people, but, unfortunately, the simpler explanations have not stood the test of time well.[7] Remembering, moreover, that many different types of change occur in different situations and cultures, we raise an additional question: "Can we tell how important is X cause or factor in a given type of change as compared with Y and Z factors?" The questions raised here are difficult ones to answer in the present state of sociological knowledge, but they should be raised in any case. Sooner or later sociology should be able to provide better answers.

From the standpoint of research an explanation of change is known as an *independent variable*. If factor X changes, society and/or its culture (or a segment thereof) will register a change (as a dependent variable). The former change is the cause of the latter. There are many possible independent variables in changing situations, even if no single factor is thought to be sufficient to explain all changes.

With this orientation we begin discussion of the various explanations of change. First, two "old-timers"—the geographical and race factors— are examined.

The Geographical Explanation

The geographical factor (which includes climate) has been alleged to bring many changes in society and/or its subsystems by a collection of writers: H. T. Buckle, Ellsworth Huntington, R. H. Whitbeck, Ellen Semple, W. S. Jevons, H. L. Moore, and Sir Arthur Shuster. Others, however, could be listed.[8] Changes in weather conditions have been alleged to affect the business cycle and thence the total economy. Variations in climatic energy have been held to affect industrial output and also academic achievement. Huntington postulated that ranges of climate affected the level of civilization in the different continents of the world. For one reason or another, these varied attempts to relate geography and climate to change have failed to make a case in the eyes of most people who have examined the evidence. Some of the propositions, as the effects of weather on the business cycle, were not estab-

[7] Solutions that reduce the varied and complicated causes of social phenomena to some single idea as an all-determining source have thus far met with criticisms and, in the end, discredit. For discussion see Sorokin, *op. cit.*, Vol. I, p. 45; Wilbert E. Moore, "A Reconsideration of Theories of Social Change," *American Sociological Review*, Vol. 25, No. 6 (December, 1960), especially pp. 811–812; and Ely Chinoy, *Society* (New York: Random House, 1961), pp. 70–71.

[8] For a full list, as well as the specific beliefs and titles of their works, see Pitirim A. Sorokin, *Contemporary Sociological Theories* (New York: Harper, 1928), Chap. III.

lished factually. Huntington showed high correlations between range of climate and level of civilization, but he was not convincing, because he failed to note that the latter was related to many other variables too.[9] Some of the variables were far more meaningful than range of climate, as others saw the situation. After all, correlation does not establish causation; it may reflect mere chance.

Geographical factors in specific instances bring changes without question. Coal, iron, water, or other resources may become depleted, thus necessitating some kind of change. Wind or water erosion may destroy a formerly productive land, leading to a dust-bowl situation and population out-migration. It is simply that the amount of change produced by the geographical-climatic influence is regarded as small in comparison with the over-all immense change that has taken place in Western civilization. Moreover, the real influence of geography and climate is not so much direct as it is in setting limits on socio-cultural growth. This or that activity may be permitted or prohibited in an area in the light of its geography. Other factors (often cultural) will then cause some phenomenon to develop or fail to do so.

One may, on the other hand, take an opposite stand, maintaining a view that might be called geographical impotency. Thus, instead of declaring that geography has an all-determining influence on social behavior and change, it may be declared that it has no influence at all. This, in our opinion, is not acceptable either. For example, one sociologist has stated that geography and climate are incapable of producing socio-cultural change.[10] But essentially the issue of the geographical explanation of change is a past one, and we believe that this comparatively brief discussion is all that is required at this time.

The Racial Explanation

The discussion of racial composition and related biological phenomena as a cause of socio-cultural change will be even briefer than the preceding section. So far as we are concerned, this is a completely dead issue (and has been for several decades); the only reason for mentioning it is to make clear that it is a *possible* approach. We do not

---

[9] MacIver, *op. cit.*, p. 117.

[10] ". . . geographic factors are necessary but not sufficient to explain social structure and social change. . . . For no period of human history do we have information of a geographical character which will adequately account for the social changes that occurred." Robert Bierstedt, *The Social Order* (New York: McGraw-Hill Book Co., Inc., 1957), p. 504. But, for one case, did not the wind erosion in the American Southwest (Oklahoma area) destroy the wheat-producing land, causing population out-migration (social change) during the 1930s? Somehow we believe that Bierstedt's choice of words makes his stance seem more extreme than it really is.

mean by the racial approach attempts (such as demonstrations and picketing) to bring greater justice for racial groups or to improve their living conditions in other respects; they are cultural in nature and will be discussed under the heading of collective behavior. We refer entirely to the biological phenomena themselves: That members of X race will have this or that greater achievement or other change because of their higher endowment with respect to biological characteristics. Thus, if a certain area (as Northwestern Europe) has a higher standard of living than another area (as sub-Sahara Africa or China) what is the explanation? It is not predominantly geographical or cultural (according to this view) but racial. The racists will stoutly declare that the people living in Northwestern Europe are of a superior racial stock, and that their "higher civilization" merely reflects this "fact."

During the nineteenth century ideas of this sort were widely held. Count Arthur de Gobineau (1816–1882) of France is well known for his belief that the inequality of races is sufficient to explain the destinies of people. Superior races (such as the Nordics, who were Gobineau's favorites) were held to be capable of great progress, whereas others would be forever limited. Gobineau, however, never precisely defined the term *race;* and he confused the proper meaning (a biological division of man) with an ethnic group living according to a certain culture.

We believe that Timasheff's assessment of this approach (he refers to Gobineau specifically) is generally correct:

> *Gobineau's theory is in error anthropologically: there are no superior and inferior races. In other words, man's innate capacities are not determined by race. And the theory is wrong sociologically: racial mixture as well as interpenetration of cultures often result in a blossoming of culture.*[11]

Others have held views approximating those of Gobineau, Hitler being the most famous—or infamous—exponent during recent times. No doubt other persons will hold similar views in the future, but one hopes that the number who choose this false trail will be small.

SOCIO-CULTURAL APPROACHES

In recent decades sociologists have come to an important conclusion in the quest for valid explanations of socio-cultural change, namely: That whatever the precise cause or combination of causes involved in change, they are increasingly thought to involve socio-cultural variables. These are likely to constitute the major explanations of change.

---

[11] Nicholas S. Timasheff, *Sociological Theory,* 3rd. ed. (New York: Random House, 1967), p. 53. For a more extensive treatment see Sorokin, *op. cit.,* Chap. V.

In other words, if one considers at random various *results* that one would like to have explained: the rising standard of living in the United States, the rising status of Blacks in this nation, the trend toward early marriage or increasing employment of wives, the extension of governmental regulations, the increasing crime rate, the impetus for higher living standards in underdeveloped nations, and the like, the *cause* (or causes) of these phenomena is thought to lie with socio-cultural variables.

At this point we begin discussion of various socio-cultural explanations. Our first approach is one that has several subheadings. It has early antecedents, dating back to the nineteenth century, but it is receiving much attention today.

Evolution, Differentiation, and Immanency

This approach, which is similar and essentially allied, stems from the evolutionary doctrine of the late nineteenth and early twentieth centuries. The early evolutionary view, as represented by Morgan,[12] Tyler,[13] Spencer,[14] and Durkeim,[15] postulated that social forms (such as institutions) and entire societies have the tendency to develop in sequence and to pass through various stages. The family, for instance, was held to have evolved from a state of early promiscuity to a stage of matriarchal rule to one of patriarchal emphasis to (finally) the small conjugal family of today. The economy—to take another example— was thought to have evolved through the successive stages of food collecting, hunting, animal breeding, agriculture, and then to industrial emphasis. Technology, similarly, was stated to have evolved through the various ages of wood, stone, bronze, iron, and so on. Entire societies went through a similar process, and Spencer declared (although he partly retracted it later) that, in doing so, it evolved much as individual persons do. This is called the organic analogy. Thus, just as the infant evolves to become the youth, man, and finally the senior citizen, so the small community grows to become the large town, then the bustling city, and then the metropolis. The entire society is like an organism, moreover, in increasing in size as well as in complexity of structure. Then, increased differentiation of structure is declared to be accomplished by greater differentiation of functions. The evolutionary thesis emphasizes this transition from simple to com-

[12] Lewis Henry Morgan, *Ancient Society* (New York: Holt, 1877).

[13] Edward B. Tyler, *Primitive Culture*, 3rd. American ed. (New York: Holt, 1889).

[14] Herbert Spencer, *First Principles* (New York: Appleton, 1890) and *Principles of Sociology*, 3 Vols. (New York: Appleton, 1898–1899).

[15] Émile Durkheim, *The Elementary Forms of the Religious Life* (New York: The Macmillan Company, 1915).

plex society and from simple to elaborate differentiation of structure and function.

Difficulties began to arise, however, for this viewpoint. Stubborn facts, unearthed from various kinds of scientific investigation, opposed the scheme. From ethnographic data Westermarck demonstrated convincingly, for example, that the early stage of human family life was *not* one of sexual promiscuity.[16] Elaborate controls were evident in the most primitive groupings. The sequences of economic growth were also firmly disputed. Then, of special importance, growing knowledge of diffusion and of imitation showed that people did not necessarily have to pass through various stages of development. The early evolutionary models further broke down at another point: namely, they failed to specify characteristics of the system that were related to the process of evolving. What was the detailed process whereby the institution or society changed from one stage to the next? Similarly—relative to the organic analogy—if communities were postulated to grow to cities and then to metropolitan centers, why was it that some communities did this and others did not? One would say the same for societies: If some grew in size and structure, why was it that others did not? Even though, during the second decade of the twentieth century, Albert G. Keller sought to make the evolutionary view more scientific [17] and Leonard T. Hobhouse endeavored to formulate objective criteria related to the evolutionary advance of societies,[18] this viewpoint suffered some decline at the time.[19]

Social Differentiation. Differentiation, similar as it is to the evolutionary view, has a different focus. It contrasts the simple, undifferentiated, homogeneous, peasant or primitive society (where social solidarity is based on the similarities of people) with the large, differentiated, specialized, interdependent, complex modern society (where

[16] This occurred as early as the turn of the century. Edward A. Westermarck's *The History of Human Marriage* was published in London in 1901.

[17] In his *Societal Evolution* (New York: The Macmillan Company, 1915), Keller was particularly concerned with the relationship between the developing mores and organic evolution. Keller was an associate of Sumner at Yale.

[18] Hobhouse explored the use of such criteria as size, efficiency, and freedom. See Hobhouse, *Social Development* (New York: Holt, 1924), and Leonard T. Hobhouse, M. Ginsberg, and G. Wheeler, *The Material Culture and Social Institutions of the Simpler Peoples* (London: Chapman and Hall, Ltd., 1915). See also H. E. Barnes, "Leonard T. Hobhouse: Evolutionary Philosophy in the Service of Democracy and Social Reform," Chapter 32 in Harry Elmer Barnes (ed.), *An Introduction to the History of Sociology* (Chicago: University of Chicago Press, 1948).

[19] But the evolutionary view as an approach did not die out: indeed renewed interest in it cropped up in the 1960s as we shall see. Because the *early expression of it* has been considerably discredited, however, the statement of one of the early theories (such as Spencer's) is not thought to be necessary in our discussion of theories.

social solidarity is based on the division of labor and need for the services of others). As primitive societies break up, the process of differentiation begins. Subsystems are formed. The latter may further break up into branches or substructures—more specialized organizations.

Differentiation tends to emphasize not stages of increasing complexity or specialization, but the ways through which major functions or institutional spheres of society have become disassociated from one another and have become attached to special collectivities and roles. Differentiation is often seen as the continuous development away from the ascriptive basis; here the division of labor is based on kinship and family units. What causes the differentiating? In a general way, it may be said to lie with dissatisfactions with the old structure. The earlier equilibrium is disturbed by some influence within or external to the system. An informal dealing with tensions first takes place in order that group objectives may be met. New ideas are considered, and eventually a new way of doing things becomes routinized. However, not all changes lead to differentiation, nor (in the modern view [20]) do all societies at the same level of differentiation necessarily have the same institutional contours. Differing types of results may occur. The process may not always be successful; in some cases it may regress. The presence or absence of innovating elites in one or several institutional spheres may be of major importance.[21] Not all the answers concerning the process are currently known.

Early contributions toward the differentiation view were made by Durkheim and Tönnies—the former with his brilliant study concerning the division of labor and the latter with his famous contrasting of the close solidarity of the *community (gemeinschaft)* with the looser, contractual system of the *society (gesellschaft)*.[22] During recent times Robert M. MacIver has emphasized social differentiation as a major view of change. Talcott Parsons has used this view in conjunction with the structural-functional perspective, and some of Parsons' followers— such as Neil Smelser and Winston White—have done the same. In

---

[20] See, for example, S. N. Eisenstadt, "Social Change, Differentiation, and Evolution," *American Sociological Review*, Vol. 29, No. 3 (June, 1964), 375–385.

[21] *Ibid.*, p. 384.

[22] In contrasting the "relationships which have grown naturally out of sympathetic sentiments" with those "which have been set up consciously and for a definite purpose," Tönnies saw them as ideal types. They will be found in varying proportions in the empirical world. See Ferdinand Tönnies, *Gemeinschaft and Gesellschaft* (Leipzig, 1887) 8th ed., 1935; English translation, *Fundamental Concepts of Sociology: Gemeinschaft and Gesellschaft*, Charles P. Loomis (New York: Harper & Row, 1963), Harper Torchbook ed. See also Rudolf Heberle, "The Sociological System of Ferdinand Tönnies: 'Community' and 'Society,'" Chapter 10 in Barnes (ed.), *op. cit.*

Chapter 6 we shall discuss the theories of Durkheim, MacIver, Parsons, and (more briefly) the applications and modifications of Smelser and White. MacIver made additions to differentiation theory, and Parsons and his followers refined it to a marked degree.

Immanent Change. Immanency, whose outlook is broadly similar to the evolution and differentiation views, has, however, some distinctive features of its own. The late Pitirim A. Sorokin was the major exponent of this view, being widely known for his theory of immanent change; Moore is a contemporary supporter.[23] This theory makes no mention of *stages of growth* (in institutions or in the total society, which is called the "super-system" by Sorokin), nor is there emphasis per se on *disassociation from other units* (or freedom from ascriptive ties). *Immanent change* states that the forces bringing change come from within; they are internal for the system. Let us see Sorokin's own phrasing of the concept:

> *Any socio-cultural system changes by virtue of its own forces and properties.* It can't help changing, even if all its external conditions are constant. *The change is thus immanent in any socio-cultural system, inherent in it, and inalienable from it. It bears in itself the seeds of the change.*[24]

Any socio-cultural system evolves, then, on the basis of its own forces and properties. If one takes the example of changes in the family during the past hundred years (Sorokin cites this example),[25] the immanent theory declares that changes are derived largely from within the family. External factors may accelerate or retard some process, they may reinforce or weaken a realization of the immanent potentialities, or they may even at times crush the system; but the system bears in itself the seeds of its future destiny. Moreover, a monogamous family cannot unfold itself into a Christian Church or develop the properties of the Royal Scientific Society. So develop other systems—economic, political, religious, educational, and so on—according to this process of inner unfolding.

The preceding brief descriptions, then, are of the immanent approach. This is not the place for a lengthy evaluation of it (evaluation will be attempted in Chapter 5 as we consider Sorokin's various contributions to socio-cultural change). Here we merely point out that immanency is a proper and major viewpoint in the study of change,

---

23 Wilbert E. Moore, "Theories of Social Change," *American Sociological Review,* Vol. 25, No. 6 (December, 1960), 811.

24 Pitirim A. Sorokin, *Social and Cultural Dynamics,* Vol. IV (New York: American Book Co., 1941), p. 590. The underlining is Sorokin's.

25 *Ibid.,* Vol. IV, p. 588.

and Sorokin has performed a service to the field of sociology in emphasizing it during recent times.[26] Before Sorokin expressed the immanent view in Volume IV of the *Dynamics,* most sociologists had stressed external factors in change.

It is time for some stocktaking concerning the trio of viewpoints: evolution, differentiation, and immanency. First, it may be observed that all three viewpoints emphasize the changing *social system.*[27] Then, one may point out that the first two show *what* has happened—what change has occurred—rather than lay stress on *why* it has occurred. Thus, the society or institution X has evolved to a different stage; functions or institutional spheres have become disassociated; behavior has moved away from the ascriptive basis. As over-all approaches they have not explained why, and a note has been made that the evolutionary view has been taken to task for this omission. In the instance of differentiation, individual theories state the reasoning as to why (as will be noted in Chapter 6). The immanent approach does indicate the general nature of the why: Forces within the system have brought the change. This might well be tested in detailed situations, however, in case doubt exists as to why result A occurred rather than result B.

Critics may raise the question as to whether all three of these views (although especially the evolutionary and immanent ones) have come to a sufficient assessment of the relationship between internal and external sources of change. Sometimes the historical factor is minimized. Kenneth E. Bock [28] believes, for instance, that this factor is currently underplayed, and that it shows itself in the failure to explain why changes occur *when* they do. The *time* element is left out.

With some dissatisfaction apparent with regard to current answers, American sociology during recent years has, interestingly enough, revived its attention to evolutionism. This has apparently occurred because of a growing interest in historical and comparative studies; the historical neglect may thus be in the process of being remedied. A renewal of evolutionary thinking does not imply, however, a return to the assumptions of nineteenth-century ideas.[29] The evolutionary

---

[26] Sorokin points out that he did not actually *originate* the idea of immanency. It can be traced back to Plato and Aristotle. But he was the sociologist who brought it to the attention of his contemporaries.

[27] We refer here to conceptualizing with respect to social change and cultural change in Chapter 2 of this book. Sorokin, however, emphasized the cultural, and probably would have been inclined to refer to the socio-cultural system.

[28] Bock declares, for example, that "the argument of this essay is that theory-building for attacking the problem of change has been hampered in both evolutionist and functionalist analyses by an orientation that encourages the derivation of sources of change from the nature of the thing changing." "Evolution, Function, and Change," *American Sociological Review,* Vol. 28, No. 2 (April, 1963), 229–237.

[29] Eisenstadt, *op. cit.,* p. 375.

ideas will be reappraised and revised in the light of recent advances in theory and research. This is especially likely to mean a merging of ideas of the evolution and structural-functional approaches (the latter to be discussed here subsequently). Characteristics of each evolving society will be systematically observed, and the mechanisms and processes of change will be fully specified. The latter will clearly relate to characteristics of institutional structures and values.

Talcott Parsons is a leader in expressing the new evolutionary perspective, and he describes his outlook well in an article entitled "Evolutionary Universals in Society." [30] He further extends his views and applies them to societies at the primitive and intermediate levels of development in his *Societies: Evolutionary and Comparative Perspectives.*[31] In the first seminal article he thinks of "complexes of structures and associated processes the development of which so increases the long-run adaptive capacity of living systems in a given class that only systems that develop the complex can attain certain higher levels of general adaptive capacity." [32] Religion, communication through language, social organization developing through kinship, and technology are cited as evolutionary universals at even the earliest human level. Two other universals are related to the process of breaking out of the primitive stage of evolution: a system of stratification and a system of legitimatizing differentiated functions (especially the political one) apart from kinship. A second pair of evolutionary universals develops in societies as they move well beyond the primitive stage. These are (1) administrative bureaucracy and (2) the money and market complex. Finally, for modern societies a generalized legal system and a democratic association with elective leadership (that will support the legal order) is necessary.[33] These complexes are thus prerequisites for socio-cultural development.

These Parsonian formulations have recently found empirical support. Buck and Jacobson,[34] applying a Guttman scaling technique to fifty contemporary societies, scored each nation regarding its performance relative to Parsons' ten universals. The testers were thereupon

[30] Talcott Parsons, "Evolutionary Universals in Society," *American Sociological Review,* Vol. 29, No. 3 (June, 1964), 339–357.

[31] Talcott Parsons, *Societies: Evolutionary and Comparative Perspectives* (Englewood Cliffs, N. J.: Prentice-Hall, Inc., 1966).

[32] Parsons, *op. cit.,* "Evolutionary Universals in Society," 340–341.

[33] Parsons suggests that a highly generalized legal order is a necessary prerequisite for the democratic association. In citing the latter he realizes that he is taking the position that "communist totalitarian organization will probably not fully match 'democracy' in political and integrative capacity in the long run." *Ibid.,* p. 356.

[34] Gary L. Buck and Alvin L. Jacobson, "Social Evolution and Structural-Functional Analysis: An Empirical Test," *American Sociological Review,* Vol. 33, No. 3 (June, 1968), 343–355.

able to identify groups of nations with similar patterns of relative development. Five levels were postulated. The fifth level, showing the most advanced development, included the industrialized societies of the world (the Western European and North American countries). The first (most primitive) level included such nations as India, Indonesia, Pakistan, Haiti, Ghana, Uganda, Nigeria, and the Congo. Then they were able to show the effects of each universal in furthering social change. They did this by computing the scale error at each level of development, and by observing for each universal whether the error was greater or less than the random error pattern (which is 5 per cent). On this basis they determined whether that universal facilitated or impeded social change at each level and to what extent.[35] This empirical analysis tends to confirm generally the existence of universals as set forth by Parsons, as well as to support the order of their influence (which universals have the greatest influence at which level) in the evolutionary sequence.

The Structural-Functional Approach

Having just discussed Parsonian ideas regarding the evolutionary view, and having previously alluded to his works (as well as to those of several of his followers) concerning differentiation, we now examine his theoretical ideas relative to the structural-functional approach itself. That part of the Buck-Jacobson study has functional relevance, it may be noted. Moreover, we shall also explore the contributions of certain other structural functionalists besides Parsons.[36]

The study of change has been a sensitive area for structural functionalists. Some critics have maintained that this approach is more appropriate for a society in equilibrium than for one undergoing size-

---

35 *Ibid.*, 350–352 (note Table 2).

36 The general remarks that follow are based on such sources, in addition to Talcott Parsons' works, as: R. K. Merton, *Social Theory and Social Structure*, rev. ed. (Glencoe, Ill.: The Free Press, Inc., 1957); Neil Smelser, *Social Change in the Industrial Revolution* (Chicago: University of Chicago Press, 1959); Wilbert E. Moore, *Social Change* (Englewood Cliffs, N. J.: Prentice-Hall, Inc., 1963) and "Theories of Social Change," *American Sociological Review*, Vol. 25, No. 6 (December, 1960), 810–817; Francesca Cancian, "Functional Analysis of Change," *American Sociological Review*, Vol. 25, No. 6 (December, 1960), 818–827; S. N. Eisenstadt, "Institutionalization and Change," *American Sociological Review*, Vol. 29, No. 2 (April, 1964), 235–247; Kingsley Davis, "The Myth of Functional Analysis As a Special Method in Sociology and Anthropology," *American Sociological Review*, Vol. 24, No. 6 (December, 1959), 757–772; Charles P. Loomis, *Social Systems* (Princeton, N. J.: D. Van Nostrand Co., 1960); and Alvin Boskoff, "Functional Analysis As a Source of a Theoretical Repertory and Research Tasks in the Study of Social Change," Chapter 8 in George K. Zollschan and Walter Hirsch (eds.), *Explorations in Social Change* (Boston: Houghton Mifflin Co., 1964).

able change.[37] Nearly all functionalists have maintained, however, that understanding the existing structure is a necessary prelude to the analysis of change. Parsons has also emphasized that "if theory is *good* theory, . . . it will apply equally to statics and to change." [38] Theory should also indicate why change has *not* occurred in this or that situation; values or the opposition of vested or other interests may prevent it from taking place.

Sources of change in social systems, according to the structural-functional view, include the following: inherent tendencies to deviate; imperfections in the integration of value orientations; and strains inherent in the system, including conflict between normative alternatives and unattained ideals (significant gaps between actual and ideal functioning of groups and institutions).[39] Lastly, an important source of change is the establishment of cultural configurations that promote change. Science, with its technological applications, is a notable example of this. In general, values favoring achievement and universalistic (broad and impersonal) orientation promote change.

The structural-functional type of investigation systematically notes the value orientations and structures related to the change in question, as well as relevant functions (manifest and latent). Change is seen as the alteration of structures and functions from a former equilibrium to a new one. For a social system to remain in equilibrium, four functional exigencies have to be met. These are (1) latent pattern maintenance and tension management; (2) goal attainment; (3) adaptation; and (4) integration. Motivation for a change is likely to be associated with dissatisfaction or frustration with respect to one or more of these exigencies. If goals of the system, for example, are not being attained, frustration in this boundary of the system tends to manifest itself. The disturbance of an old equilibrium may be either endogenous or exogenous. The full change process cannot be described here, but roles and collectivities are likely to be modified in reaching the new equilibrium. Finally, sanctions (legal norms, and so forth) will be established to fit the new structure. Cancian [40] has described some of the more detailed

---

[37] The use of an equilibrium model would seem to so focus attention on structural relationships that change would be deemphasized. However, as Cancian states (*Ibid.*, p. 825) "using this model of a functional system does not imply that the system *is* in equilibrium." Moore comments that this model "would predict only such other complementary changes as would restore the equilibrium." (*Ibid., Social Change,* p. 10.) In general, he favors the view of society as a tension manager rather than as a self-equilibrating system.

[38] Talcott Parsons, *The Social System* (Glencoe, Ill.: The Free Press, Inc., 1951), p. 535. The underlining is Parsons'.

[39] On the latter point see Moore, *Social Change, op. cit.,* p. 18.

[40] Cancian, *loc. cit.* She follows the formal statement on functional analysis made by the philosopher Ernest Nagel (which is the type used by Parsons).

processes involved in functional analysis. For instance, one must specify the system under study including the G(s)—namely, the property of the system that is maintained or that is stable—and the state coordinates (which are variables determining the presence or absence of G). Then, types of change can be predicted on the basis of the functional analysis: The disappearance of G is predicted if there is a failure to meet the conditions of the equilibrium and so on. There are four types of change altogether.[41]

Recent examples of this approach include the Parsons-Smelser examination [42] of the differentiation of ownership from control in the American economy—a finding of the 1933 Adolf A. Berle—Gardner Means classic [43]—and Smelser's analysis of the effects of the growth of the British cotton industry on the family structure of the working classes.[44] Both of these excellent studies apply structural-functional analysis to previously well-explored subjects. The analysis is systematic and thorough. It remains to be seen what further studies will uncover, what theoretical breakthroughs will be achieved in the years ahead, and how this approach will be allied with other approaches.[45] It is axiomatic that with structural-functionalism attention is centered on the social system. Bock [46] considers that functionalism is no more successful than evolutionism in accounting for the *time* factor in change; moreover, he declares that its explanation of change relies too much on the nature of the thing changing. Also, in this case should external factors be given greater recognition, granting that the adaptive function of the system is related to such influences? At any rate, the functional view has many active adherents at the present time, and these problems may be worked out.

It must not be forgotten, moreover, that variations of the structural-functional theory of change have been formulated. In Chapter 6 we shall discuss the variations of Wilbert E. Moore and Charles P. Loomis.

The Cybernetic Analysis of Change

Cybernetics as an approach began during the 1940s with new developments in communications engineering. It was also affected by

41 *Ibid.,* p. 823.

42 Talcott Parsons and Neil J. Smelser, *Economy and Society* (Glencoe, Ill.: The Free Press, Inc., 1956), Chap. V.

43 *The Modern Corporation and Private Property* (New York: The Macmillan Company, 1933).

44 Smelser, *op. cit.*

45 Kingsley Davis contends that structural-functional studies of change are not basically different from nonfunctional studies. He cites Marion Levy's analyses of institutional factors in Chinese and Japanese economic development, Merton's studies of the rise of science, and Robert Bellah's study of religion and change in Japan. Davis, *op. cit.*, 766–767.

46 Bock, *op. cit.*, pp. 235–237.

certain convergences in mathematics and statistics, neurophysiology, and psychology. Cybernetics, as the leading mathematician Norbert Wiener called it, is the science of communication and control in all kinds of organizations.[47] All organizations are thought to be alike in that they are held together by communication. Because the subjects of communication and control have been regarded as vital in science for many years, cybernetics can be said to comprise a new science concerned with old subjects. As Wiener observes,[48] however, human and social communication is extremely complicated as compared with patterns of machine communication. Whether or not the information measured and communicated will include all relevant phenomena in a complicated social system may be a real issue. It would seem that for proper cybernetic analysis of social data many contributions will be needed during the coming years.

The essentials of cybernetics can be stated in summary fashion as follows: (1) This new science focuses attention on "steering" organizations; thus, interest is maintained in systems of decision making, regulation, and control. Cybernetics is useful, then, for ongoing systems (the concept is incompatible with systems in static equilibrium). (2) It emphasizes self-controlling machines that react to their environment as well as to the results of their own behavior. (3) Cybernetics stresses the storage and treatment of information in machines; the general concept is that of a self-modifying communications network or "learning net." Such a learning net would be any system that has a relevant degree of organization, communication, and control. Every open system (more about this presently) must have mechanisms for the selective storage and recall of information. Furthermore, the network must acquire information that makes learning and innovating behavior possible.[49] The information may be electrically transmitted. Patterns

---

[47] *Cybernetics,* 2nd ed. (Cambridge, Mass.: The MIT Press, 1961, paper edition, 1965). See also Wiener, *The Human Use of Human Beings: Cybernetics and Society* (Boston: Houghton Mifflin, 1950, paper edition, Doubleday Anchor Books, 1954); W. Ross Ashby, *An Introduction to Cybernetics* (New York: John Wiley & Sons, Inc., 1956); Stafford Beer, *Cybernetics and Management* (New York: John Wiley & Sons, Inc., 1959, paper edition, 1964). Regarding social science aspects, this writer has leaned somewhat heavily on Karl W. Deutsch, *The Nerves of Government* (New York: The Free Press of Glencoe, Division of The Macmillan Company, 1963, paper edition, 1966). See also, Mervyn L. Cadwallader, "The Cybernetic Analysis of Change in Complex Social Organizations," *American Journal of Sociology,* Vol. LXV, No. 2 (September, 1959), 154–157; this has been reprinted in A. and E. Etzioni (eds.), *Social Change* (New York: Basic Books, Inc., 1964), Chap. 19; and Richard L. Meier, "Communications and Social Change," *Behavioral Science,* Vol. I (January, 1956), 43–50.

[48] Wiener, as quoted in Deutsch, *op. cit.,* p. 77.

[49] From the general ideas of cybernetics various propositions are suggested such as the following: that the rate of innovation is a function of the quantity and variety of information, and the rate of change for the system will increase with an increase in the rate of change of the environment.

of information "can be measured in quantitative terms described in mathematical language, analyzed by science, and transmitted or processed on a practical industrial scale." [50] (4) The self-modifying process is based on *feedback*. The communications network produces action in response to the input of information; this includes the results of its own action, which then modifies its subsequent behavior. This notion of feedback is regarded as a more sophisticated concept than the simple mechanics of equilibrium. Useful for all kinds of organizations, feedback promises to become a powerful tool of the social sciences.[51] And (5) the capacity of a social system to persist over time through a change of structure and behavior is called ultrastability. Thus, corporations and other systems survive in a changing environment through a process of self-transformation or adaptation. The system changes in a changing environment, in short, or it perishes. Often, change in a fluctuating environment is made through learning and innovation as already mentioned. Hence, organizations are treated as open problem-solving systems. "Any such system capable of purposeful problem-solving behavior and of learning from the past and innovating for the future is an ultrastable system." [52] Thus, a theme of cybernetics is *maintaining stability through adaptation (change) using feedback.*

An extended discussion of cybernetics is not possible at this time. The frontier is being steadily advanced. Although the new science is not highly developed in the social field as yet, various social scientists have shown much interest in it. Deutsch has set forth the promise of cybernetics in his *The Nerves of Government* (see footnote 47), and he has analyzed nationalism in political communities on the basis of it.[53] Boulding [54] has pioneered with this approach in economics. Quastler and others [55] have applied cybernetics in experimental psychology. Etzioni,[56] in his theory of the active society, points to cybernetics as one of the three foundations of modern macroaction. The technologies of communication, knowledge, and energy were drastically transformed following the Second World War; the development of the computer and its use in automation were important elements. Cybernetic factors,

---

[50] Deutsch, *op. cit.*, p. 83.

[51] *Ibid.*, p. 89.

[52] Cadwallader, *op. cit.*, p. 155.

[53] Karl W. Deutsch, *Nationalism and Social Communication* (New York: John Wiley & Sons, Inc., 1953).

[54] Kenneth E. Boulding, *The Organizational Revolution* (New York: Harper & Bros., 1953).

[55] Henry Quastler (ed.), *Information Theory in Psychology* (Glencoe, Ill.: The Free Press, Inc., 1955).

[56] A. Etzioni, *The Active Society: A Theory of Societal and Political Processes* (New York: The Free Press, Collier-Macmillan Limited, Division of The Macmillan Company, 1968).

relating to the use of knowledge and to decision making, are discussed in Part Two of his book. We shall further discuss Etzioni's ideas in later chapters.

Bertrand Gross, in his treatise on social systems accounting in the *Social Indicators* volume,[57] is receptive to the cybernetic model. He maintains that this model of the controlled feedback or self-governing system has become the new classical image in systems theory. He suggests that further computer models of man and of social systems will require a greater recognition of social-system complexity. We shall explore in a later chapter Gross' elaborate proposal of social systems accounting, setting forth seven elements each of social-system *structure* and of social-system *performance*. Moreover, Robert A. Rosenthal and Robert S. Weiss, in *Social Indicators*,[58] focus attention on the feedback process. The very survival of an organization, they assert, indicates a feedback process of at least minimal effectiveness. They discuss feedback from both external and internal sources, effects of feedback on policy, and research in maintaining feedback.

Certain allied developments—namely, systems theory, information theory, decision theory, game theory, and simulation—will be briefly discussed at this point. Because systems theory has already been mentioned in connection with Gross' ideas, we shall begin with it. *Systems theory* is a broader concept than cybernetics. As von Bertalanffy [59] declares, cybernetics is but a part of the general theory of systems; other types of regulation may be followed by other than cybernetic systems. *General* system theory is interested in formulating principles that are valid for systems in general. This theory, then, tends to unite and integrate the various scientific disciplines, seeking to develop principles that run vertically through the various individual sciences. It focuses on organized wholes (systems) of interrelated entities. Systems can be closed or open. In conventional physics the systems are closed; that is, the interacting elements are isolated from their environment.[60] Thus, in physical chemistry the reactions and chemical equilibria are established in a closed vessel where a number of reactants are brought together. *Social* systems are by nature open. The family, corporation, or university is affected by outer social or cultural influences. Von Bertalanffy makes the important point that social systems differ from their physical and biological counterparts in that human

[57] Bertram M. Gross, "The State of the Nation: Social Systems Accounting," Chapter 3 in Bauer (ed.), *op. cit.*

[58] "Problems of Organizational Feedback Processes," Chapter 5 in Bauer (ed.), *op. cit.*

[59] Ludwig von Bertalanffy, *General System Theory* (New York: George Braziller, 1968), p. 17.

[60] *Ibid.*, p. 39.

beings are significantly influenced by *culture* and its various elements (such as values, norms, symbols, and artifacts).[61]

Buckley,[62] who directs his attention largely to sociology and *social* systems, agrees with von Bertalanffy that the cultural factor constitutes a prime reason for contrasting social from physical or biological systems. Buckley asserts that, because of this, social systems should be denoted as socio-cultural ones. Accordingly he uses the term socio-cultural throughout his book.[63] Buckley's main thesis, however, is that the modern systems perspective is more appropriate for analyzing socio-cultural systems than are the equilibrium and organismic models that dominate much of current social science thinking. He suggests that the systems perspective is especially advantageous for treating large, complex organizations because it visualizes the socio-cultural system in terms of information and communication nets ("the heart of sociology"), it emphasizes interrelationships (not entities), and it focuses attention on purposive, goal-seeking behavior. The emphasis all along is on socio-cultural *dynamics,* whereas the earlier models, in his contention, defend the system too much (and, hence, are unduly static in conceptualization). Buckley [64] also notes certain differences between closed and open systems that are relevant to sociology. The open (social) system not only engages in interchanges with its environment, but this interchange is *an essential factor* (Buckley's italics) underlying the system's viability. Moreover, the open system tends to decrease in entropy (it elaborates its structure) with change, whereas the closed one increases in entropy and tends to run down. Furthermore, open systems are vastly more complicated with regard to the energy factor than closed systems. With such closed systems as mechanical ones, energy per se (raw energy) is the main source of action, points out Buckley; with complex, adaptive systems (biological and social, open ones) more complex forms of force are found—for instance, reactions may take the form of collective behavior, enthusiasms, aggressions, deviations, creativity, productivity, competition, and the like. Buckley's major interest relates to "those processes which tend to elaborate or change a system's given form, structure, or state" [65]—which are collectively termed *morphogenesis*. These processes, he feels, have been underemphasized at the expense of those that preserve or maintain a system's form or state.

[61] *Ibid.,* pp. 196–197.

[62] Walter Buckley, *Sociology and Modern Systems Theory* (Englewood Cliffs, N. J.: Prentice-Hall, Inc., 1967).

[63] This of course is the type of reasoning followed in the present volume, as the reader may recall from the preceding chapter.

[64] *Op. cit.,* p. 50.

[65] *Ibid.,* pp. 58–59 and 62–66, and Chaps. 4 and 5.

Robert Boguslaw [66] similarly relates cybernetics to systems theory. The new system engineers, computer programmers, and the like are indeed the "new utopians," according to his view. Boguslaw distinguishes four approaches to system design, which he illustrates from the social science literature. These are (1) the formalist approach, in which models, implicit or explicit, are used; (2) the heuristic approach, in which principles are set forth and used as guides for action; (3) the operating unit approach, wherein the people involved have particular characteristics and the system will reflect these special characteristics; and (4) the *ad hoc* approach, in which the present state of affairs constitutes the starting point and the design concerns itself with moving to some desired system state.

Our comment with respect to information theory, decision theory, game theory, and simulation, which are all related to systems analysis, will be briefer. *Information theory,* based on the work of Claude E. Shannon and Warren Weaver, has enabled man to make progress in understanding the relationship between information and organization and information feedback as a control mechanism. This development has gained importance in communication engineering although its application to science has seemingly been less successful so far.[67] *Decision theory* is a mathematical theory concerned with choices among alternatives. This assumes that the understanding of decisions involves knowledge of the roles and personal traits of decision makers as well as of the environment in which they operate. The major issue is "Just how do the various personal and environmental characteristics interact with each other to affect the decision?" [68] *Game theory,* which is closely associated with simulation, involves the participation of human actors in a simulated system. Often the games are of a competitive nature. As exemplified by the early work of von Neumann and Morgenstern,[69] game theory is concerned with the behavior of supposedly "rational" players to obtain maximum gains by appropriate strategies. In a "game," declares Raser,[70] the rules for translating "real life" variables into simulation variables are less demanding as compared with simulation itself; thus, a game is more tentative and more informal. However,

[66] *The New Utopians: A Study of System Design and Social Change* (Englewood Cliffs, N. J.: Prentice-Hall, Inc., 1965).

[67] von Bertalanffy, *op. cit.*, p. 22.

[68] See, for example, Herbert A. Simon, D. W. Smithburg, and V. A. Thompson, *Public Administration* (New York: Alfred A. Knopf, 1950); and Richard C. Snyder, H. W. Buck, and B. Sapin (eds.), *Foreign Policy Decision-Making: An Approach to the Study of International Politics* (Glencoe, Ill.: The Free Press of Glencoe, 1962).

[69] John von Neumann and Oskar Morgenstern, *Theory of Games and Economic Behavior,* 3rd ed. (Princeton, N. J.: Princeton University Press, 1944, 1953).

[70] John R. Raser, *Simulation and Society* (Boston: Allyn and Bacon, Inc., 1969), p. x.

game theory has provided a valid method for considering actions of conscious opponents when there is a conflict of interests.[71] Finally, *simulation* is close to gaming as we have said, but in this case salient variables are more formally programmed and the model is a complete and accurate analogue to some referent system. The simulation model is dynamic; changes over time in the model correspond to changes over time in the system being modeled. Therefore, notes Raser,[72] simulators must try not only to build a model of system structure, but also one that will incorporate system processes. The potential value of simulations is great. One may have the answer to the "what-would-happen-if" questions involving decision alternatives, in which the answers are usually supplied by the computer. Then, too, simulations permit the researcher to reproduce many times a situation that might occur only once in real life. Thus he can examine certain variables and relationships concerning the effects in real life situations.[73]

Each of these developments has considerable potential for the years ahead. Game theory and simulation, in particular, have much momentum at the present time.[74] Because these various forms of systems analysis are for the most part computer based, one may inquire regarding the future developments of the computer itself. Just as cybernetics, information theory, and game theory (for instance) are essentially post-Second World War developments,[75] so the related computer industry emerged during this period. These various "stars" have risen together. A bright future for the computer, too, is indicated.[76] Currently in use are the third generation of computers; the fourth and later generations loom over the horizon and will undoubtedly bring many improvements. This is a time to anticipate further major accomplishments. If, then, we view such developments as cybernetics, gaming, and simulation with considerable if cautious optimism, this assumes that social scientists will steadily improve their techniques. As always, problems

---

[71] *Ibid.*, p. 139. See the Robbers' Cave experiment conducted by Muzafer Sherif and the Simulation of Society (SIMSOC), developed by William Gamson. Sherif, *et al., Intergroup Conflict and Cooperation: The Robbers' Cave Experiment* (Norman, Okla.: University of Oklahoma, 1961); W. Gamson, *SIMSOC: A Manual for Participants* (Ann Arbor, Mich.: Campus Publishers, 1966).

[72] Raser, *op. cit.*, p. 10.

[73] *Ibid.*, p. 17.

[74] For a reasonably full bibliography, see *ibid.*, pp. 160–173.

[75] von Bertalanffy, *op. cit.*, p. 15. Each had antecedents, of course.

[76] The computer itself has had a fabulous development. As John Diebold states, the speed of the computer has been enormously increased since the first electronic computer was built in 1945. Between 1945 and 1951, he declares, the speed increased one hundred times and, from then until 1969, it increased one thousand times again. He summarizes that "the computer industry, while still in its childhood, has become a central factor in the operations of our economy." *Man and the Computer* (New York: Frederick A. Praeger, 1969), pp. 8–9.

connected with these areas have to be met. We can only hope that many of the seemingly enormous potentialities that lie within these subjects will eventually be realized.

ANNOTATED BIBLIOGRAPHY

Older Evolutionary Doctrines

Morgan, Lewis Henry, *Ancient Society* (New York: Holt, 1877); Tyler, Edward B., *Primitive Culture,* 3rd American ed. (New York: Holt, 1899); Spencer, Herbert, *First Principles* (New York: Appleton, 1898–1899); and Durkheim, Émile, *The Elementary Forms of the Religious Life* (New York: The Macmillan Company, 1915).

Modern Evolutionary View (which in part compares it with other approaches)

Parsons, Talcott, "Evolutionary Universals in Society," *American Sociological Review,* Vol. 29, No. 3 (June, 1964), 339–357; Parsons, Talcott, *Societies, Evolutionary and Comparative Perspectives* (Englewood Cliffs, N. J.: Prentice-Hall, Inc., 1966); Eisenstadt, S. N., "Social Change, Differentiation, and Evolution," *American Sociological Review,* Vol. 29, No. 3 (June, 1964), 375–385; and Bock, Kenneth E., "Evolution, Function, and Change," *American Sociological Review,* Vol. 28, No. 2 (April, 1963), 229–237. For an imaginative, ably performed, empirical test of the Parsonian "Evolutionary Universals," see Gary L. Buck and Alvin L. Jacobson, "Social Evolution and Structural-Functional Analysis: An Empirical Test," *American Sociological Review,* Vol. 33, No. 3 (June, 1968), 343–355.

General Discussion Relative to the Causes of Change

Ginsberg, Morris, "Social Change," *British Journal of Sociology,* Vol. 9 (September, 1958), 205–229.
> Ginsberg takes a position similar to MacIver's maintaining that social causation differs importantly from natural causation (because of the psychological factor). He discusses forces that cause strains, the "Great Man" theory, other causes. It is ably written.

MacIver, Robert M., *Social Causation* (New York: Ginn & Co., 1942; Harper Torchbook edition, 1964).
> Valuable discussion of causes of change in relation to scientific fundamentals. Emphasizes the psychological element. Helpful bibliography has been added in the 1964 paperback edition.

Moore, Wilbert E., "Theories of Social Change," *American Sociological Review,* Vol. 25, No. 6 (December, 1960), 810–817; also see *Social Change* (Englewood Cliffs, N. J.: Prentice-Hall, Inc., 1963).
> Worthwhile and helpful discussion. Moore notes the abandonment of single-factor explanations of change. He holds a modified structural-functional position, as is indicated in the *Social Change*.

Nisbet, Robert A., *Social Change and History* (New York: Oxford University Press, 1969).

> A controversial but interesting work, one to be considered. Nisbet champions the historical view, and even defends the early evolutionists. He is critical of the functional and immanent perspectives. Well written.

Concerning the Cybernetic Approach

Ashby, W. Ross, *An Introduction to Cybernetics* (New York: John Wiley & Sons, Inc., 1956).

> General statement of the principles of cybernetics, including the concept of ultrastability.

Boguslaw, Robert, *The New Utopians: A Study of System Design and Social Change* (Englewood Cliffs, N. J.: Prentice-Hall, Inc., 1965).

> Sets forth four approaches to system design: The formalist, heuristic, operating unit, and *ad hoc,* which are of interest to the "new utopians" (system engineers and computer programmers) as well as to social theorists. Recommended.

Cadwallader, Mervyn L., "The Cybernetic Analysis of Change in Complex Social Organizations," *American Journal of Sociology,* Vol. LXV, No. 2 (September, 1959), 154–157; reprinted in Etzioni, A. and E., *Social Change* (New York: Basic Books, Inc., 1964), pp. 159–164.

> Illustrates sociological thinking with regard to cybernetics.

Deutsch, Karl W., *The Nerves of Government* (New York: The Free Press of Glencoe, Division of The Macmillan Company, 1963).

> Probably the best explanation of the essentials of cybernetics that this writer has seen for social scientists. Deutsch, a political scientist, feels that cybernetics bears much promise for social science.

Wiener, Norbert, *Cybernetics,* 2nd ed. (Cambridge, Mass.: The MIT Press, 1961; paper edition, 1965).

> Valuable discussion by the "Father of Cybernetics." Highly mathematical. Chapter VIII is likely to be of special interest to social scientists.

Concerning Systems Theory

Bertalanffy, Ludwig von, *General System Theory* (New York: George Braziller, 1968).

> A very rewarding exposition by a leader of the *systems* perspective. The author makes the case for systems theory as a general science of "wholeness" that integrates the various scientific disciplines. Chapter 8, "The System Concept in the Sciences of Man," is valuable for social scientists.

Buckley, Walter, *Sociology and Modern Systems Theory* (Englewood Cliffs, N. J.: Prentice-Hall, Inc., 1967).

> The modern systems perspective is recommended as a theoretical framework for the socio-cultural system, which is seen in terms of information and communication nets. Buckley is especially interested in the morphogenetic process that tends to elaborate or change a system's structure. A worthwhile, pioneering book.

Concerning Scientific Gaming and Simulation

Gamson, William A., *SIMSOC: A Manual for Participants* (Ann Arbor, Mich.: Campus Publishers, 1966).
   An interesting and rather elaborate "game." Based mostly on Parsonian concepts, it involves the simulation of society.
Raser, John R., *Simulation and Society* (Boston: Allyn and Bacon, 1969).
   A most helpful, all-around introduction to simulation and gaming.

4 *Approaches to the Study of Socio-cultural Change* (Continued)

In this chapter we shall discuss the economic, technological, demographic, leadership, collective behavior, legal, ideological, religious, educational, and conflict approaches to the study of socio-cultural change. Most of these approaches have been pursued for many years, although this in no way lessens their importance; some (as the technological, collective behavior, educational, and conflict) have taken on new meaning and significance during recent years. Many of these approaches constitute primarily *external causes* in relation to ongoing social systems.[1] Not all, however, are of this type. We shall conclude with one that is assuming critical importance at the present time, namely: the self-determinative or active approach as we shall call it. This approach manifests an attitude toward *change* itself. Adherents of this view maintain that man should actively chart an intelligent course of conduct, be increasingly responsive to human needs, deal with problems and other impedimenta encountered in following that course, and attain the goals that have been set—thus attempting to direct change and in significant measure even to master the society's future. This would apply to underdeveloped as well as economically advanced societies. Such a perspective implies that at this period of the twentieth century man's knowledge base and his ability to plan and to reach goals are sufficient for these purposes. Because this approach gathers others—such as the political, leadership, educational, and technological—under its folds, some may prefer to think of it as an *over-all point of view* or a *master approach*.

The basic self-determinative view is not new. Many social thinkers have had ideas along this line, beginning with Lester F. Ward; but the number has increased in recent years, and the ideas have been

---

[1] Thus, if one were to study the changing *university* or *hospital* as a social system, he might observe the effects of economic influences, various technological inventions, population changes in the relevant area, the passage of (Federal, state, or local) laws affecting the university or hospital, and the like. Such external influences are in contrast from internal ones such as modifications of the system due to failure to meet functional needs or changes precipitated by "strains" in the system (some of the latter were discussed in Chapter 3). The external and the internal may be related, of course.

extended. Greater competence in moving toward these objectives is indicated because of accumulating social science and other knowledge, significant technological advances, developments in communication, increased education, and other factors. The prospects of man's shaping his future in the light of predetermined goals seem better than ever. On the other hand, major frustrations of contemporary society have impelled many people to seek a social transformation in the quest of better conditions. Actually the active society would presume to engage in a perpetual self-transformation. Many claim that majority convictions as to desirable behavior and change should have overriding influence in the shaping process; thus they should take precedence over the dictates of the established institutional order. Many self-determinists would indubitably affirm that, in instances where these two forces are in conflict, the convictions of the people should prevail in determining policy. This would be the case whether the entire social order or a specific subsystem were concerned. Potentially, then, this approach is a source of revolutionary change. Whatever our attitude toward it, it is clear that the deterioration of the traditional order and its authorities is at stake. That problems, dilemmas, and controversies are involved in this approach will be evident in our later discussion. That it is highly relevant to the current American scene should similarly be realized.[2]

The Economic Approach

Sociologists have long been interested in the interrelations between economic and social phenomena, and the significance of the economic [3] as a factor in socio-cultural change. As an independent variable the economic factor is shown to have considerable importance. The number of marriages and divorces has been demonstrated to be markedly correlated with the business cycle. Political preferences have been shown to be significantly affected by economic status; many years ago Charles A. Beard pointed to the role of economic factors in shaping the

---

[2] This self-determinative or active approach should not be equated with cybernetics per se. It has wider compass than cybernetics. The latter, as the science of communication and control, may be *used* in reaching the goals of the society as Etzioni and others have set forth (as was noted in Chapter 3). On the other hand, one could obviously attempt to seek out and attain goals without the use of cybernetics. We shall partly follow Amitai Etzioni's broad theme in *The Active Society* (New York: The Free Press, Division of The Macmillan Company, 1968) in describing the self-determinative approach. This point of view, at any rate, came to the fore during the 1960s. Because of its recency as well as its all-encompassing nature, it may appropriately conclude our discussion of approaches to socio-cultural change.

[3] The technological factor is excluded from this.

Constitution of the United States.[4] Studies such as *The Material Culture and Social Institutions of the Simpler Peoples* by Hobhouse and associates [5]—previously mentioned—have indicated that the level of material culture and other aspects of culture are significantly associated in primitive societies. A change in the organization of productivity (such as automation) clearly has many effects throughout the society. Details are hardly necessary. Later in this book the subject of under-developed areas will be discussed. Again, the effect of economic change brings many repercussions throughout the society; it is also true that prerequisites must be present before the economic change itself can occur. In Chapter 7 the theory of Karl Marx will be examined, one part of which maintains that the means of economic production determine the nature of development of the superstructure (the other institutions) of the society. Marx at least believed in the major influence of the economic system in this way.

However, some restraint in considering the economic approach is in order—and this is not intended solely in reference to the excesses of Marxian thinking. At this point the views of structural functionalism have considerable value. One may say that economic influences may obtain (leading to social repercussions) *if* the end goals continue and *if* the social values favor the change.[6] But if the goals or values should themselves change—for instance, if a nation changes its condition from peace to war (or cold war), or its value emphasis should be altered from laissez-faire orientation to one favoring governmental intervention—the same economic forces might produce entirely different social effects. Thus the characteristics of the society and the nature of its value system are of crucial importance. This is the opposite side of the coin: The external influence of the economic system is considerable, but the social-system factor cannot be neglected either.

The Influence of Technology

Many social scientists have commented on the importance of the technological influence on society and on socio-cultural change. Ralph

---

4 C. A. Beard, *An Economic Interpretation of the Constitution of the United States* (New York: The Macmillan Company, 1913). His main thesis is that the Constitution was essentially an economic document: Those who favored it generally had an economic interest in it, and those who opposed often had an opposite economic interest.

5 Leonard T. Hobhouse, G. C. Wheeler, and M. Ginsberg, *The Material Culture and Social Institutions of the Simpler Peoples* (London: Chapman and Hall, Ltd., 1915).

6 Talcott Parsons and Neil J. Smelser, *Economy and Society* (New York: The Free Press, Division of The Macmillan Company, 1956; Free Press paperback edition, 1965); and Wilbert E. Moore, *Economy and Society* (Garden City, N. Y.: Doubleday & Co., 1955), Chap. 5.

Linton declares that "in the last analysis it is technology which sets the ultimate limits within which culture can develop." [7] Walter Goldschmidt maintains that ". . . the fundamental feature in evolution is technological development, which . . . is progressive. The important thing is that with the various technical developments—starting with fire, string, and the use of clubs or missiles—man has increased his capacity to produce the necessary wherewithal to sustain life." [8] Two sociologists who are *not* particularly known for their technological orientation—Robert M. MacIver and Charles H. Page—nevertheless declare that "it is scarcely too much to say that every major problem of modern society is either initiated by or at least strongly affected by technological change." [9]

Although technology is as old as the stone-age axe, the great era of technological development has been the past century when, based largely on science, nearly all of what we call modern technology has been established.

The rate of technological development has been accelerating. Increasing the productivity of the land, increasing the total goods available to the population, fostering a division of labor and the separation of social and economic functions, and enabling man to have more leisure, technology has brought a sweeping tide of change in societies where it is well developed. Individual inventions such as the automobile, airplane, radio, television, nuclear reactor, computer, and space satellite have had (or are having) such a tremendous impact on man's way of life that the age has often been named after them.

Hundreds of social effects, direct and derivative, have ensued from these great inventions.[10] Now that man is well along in the air age, has made solid accomplishments in the nuclear age, and is moving ahead steadily in the computer and space ages, the main question is, "What comes next?" Accustomed as mankind has become relative to the wonders of science and invention, individuals—and sociologists too—must be certain that they do not become so blasé as to fail to recognize one of the great social influences of all time. In particular, the sociology of change must clearly give adequate recognition to the science-technology factor as a ranking one in transforming the socio-cultural

[7] Ralph Linton (ed.), *The Science of Man in the World Crisis* (New York: Columbia University Press, 1945), p. 212.

[8] *Man's Way* (New York: World Publishing Co., 1959), p. 112.

[9] *Society: An Introductory Analysis* (New York: Rinehart and Co., Inc., 1949), p. 557.

[10] For treatment of some of the effects, see F. R. Allen, Hornell Hart, Delbert C. Miller, William F. Ogburn, and Meyer F. Nimkoff, *Technology and Social Change* (New York: Appleton-Century-Crofts, 1957), Part II. For a more negative, sometimes extreme, view of the effects of science and technology and their values (which the author lumps together under the term *technique*), see Jacques Ellul, *The Technological Society* (New York: Alfred A. Knopf, 1964).

environment in both constructive and destructive ways. If one considers the changing city, for instance, one can hardly be coy regarding this influence. The Industrial Revolution itself set in motion forces that gave impetus to urbanization; the motor vehicle, telephone, and other inventions (mechanical and social) had much to do with the advent and flourishing of suburbs; more recent technological and industrial developments, in relation to other forces, have brought such problems as air pollution; and even the potential destruction of the large city is an ever-present reality thanks to the making and stockpiling of nuclear bombs (Hiroshima and Nagasaki constitute exhibits A and B in this, except that the job can be accomplished more efficiently today). Concerning these many technological inventions, the sociology of change has the task of ascertaining how major each is in terms of ongoing social systems and their functional requirements. This is a considerable task that, by the way, has barely been begun. Automation is a case in point. This development is unquestionably important. Will the age of the computer, when fully developed, be a new order? In the previous chapter we discussed cybernetics because we believe that this new science of communication and control merits discussion apart from the over-all influence of technology; but it is related to automation. What will be, in fact, the extent of social impact from both? Will dislocations be devastating as some experts have predicted? What social subsystems will be especially affected? Or could it be that dysfunctional effects have somehow been overstated or perhaps overimagined? What effects seem highly probable (or in the "proven" category) and which are uncertain and arguable?

During the past decade or two the technological influence has not been especially accented by sociologists espousing the structural-functional view. Some have taken the tack that technology rests overwhelmingly upon scientific achievement in modern times, and that it is *science* rather than technology that is embedded in Western society and "really" causes the vast amount of change. This view has been effectively stated, for instance, by Bernard Barber.[11] Others may coun-

11 Barber maintains that

> . . . *perhaps the analysis of the nature of science and its inevitable social consequences which we have been developing here will permit us to see the "technological theory" of social change in a new light. This theory, which has had a great vogue among some social scientists, holds that it is change in technology which always produces change in the rest of the society.* . . . *The technological theory of change, we can now see, does not search far enough.* . . . *behind the technological and social innovations lies the primary source, science itself, dynamic by its very nature and continually producing not only new conceptual schemes but also the possibility of new applications of those schemes in the form of technological inventions.*

Science and the Social Order (Glencoe, Ill.: The Free Press, Inc., 1952), p. 212.

ter, on the other hand, that anthropologists often point to the importance of technology in primitive society—a human setting in which, it must be noted, the influence of science is nil. One can further observe, if he wishes to be fine-pointed about it, that in many instances of change brought about by the science-technology cluster in modern civilization, the change is actually caused by the technological invention—not by the scientific finding per se.[12] Thus the many social effects of aviation have been caused by the use of the airplane, not by earlier scientific discoveries concerning the physics of flight. Similarly, many effects are currently being produced by the use of the computer (a technological product). They were *not* brought about by prior developments in the science of electronics, magnetic tapes, transistors, tunnel diodes, and microminiaturized circuits that were used in making the computer. If technology, then, is often the influence that actually produces the changes,[13] we suggest that it is safer—and arguments on this matter are rather futile anyway—to merely declare that science and technology together bring many socio-cultural changes. The impact of these influences on social systems, including the functional needs of systems, remains an important area of study.

Sociologists and others have often stressed the effects of *values* in connection with the technological influence.[14] Thus the many effects of technology are conceded, but it is the influence of values that has been decisive. This pays tribute to the intertwining influences of culture and social system. It is indeed true that in areas where the science-technology influence is sizeable, values tend to favor the pursuits of science and technology as they also favor the resultants (products) of these activities. Thus, to conduct research in physics or chemistry is by and large looked on as a good thing; moreover, the marketing of a new technological product in such an area having beneficent values generally finds an air of positive expectation with regard to the product unless specific and often individualistic factors have intervened. Recent research has focused on the reverse aspect of the subject, namely: the

[12] For discerning this point this writer is indebted to his friend and one-time student, Professor John Alston.

[13] In rare cases the threat of producing a technological product might bring changes without the production actually taking place.

[14] Talcott Parsons, *Structure and Process in Modern Societies* (Glencoe, Ill.: The Free Press, Inc., 1960), especially Chapters 1 and 4; Robin M. Williams, Jr., *American Society*, 3rd ed. (New York: Alfred A. Knopf, 1969). The connection between technology and values has been a notable interest of several members of the Harvard University program on Technology and Society staff, especially of Dr. Emmanuel Mesthene (director of the program), Dr. Irene Taviss, Dr. Harvey Cox, and Dr. Edward Shils. Shils and Taviss are sociologists; Mesthene's original academic field was philosophy; Cox is a professor of divinity at Harvard. Studies are in process. The ten-year program, which was established in 1964, is being financed by IBM.

impact of technology on values. Mesthene has explored the mechanisms by which values are shaped by technological change and also the effects of contemporary technology on religious and aesthetic values. Taviss has examined the effects of technology on change within value systems. Cox analyzes religious change as a mediating mechanism through which technology affects values. Shils is exploring the effects of science and technology on individuality and on individualistic values.[15]

Because technology has caused a steady, persistent transformation of the social environment in areas where values favor its influence; because it has been shown to be an exceedingly important variable as related to the changing character of war, the practice of medicine, and other institutions; [16] because, even in primitive societies, recent research [17] has indicated that level of technology is the single, most important component of cultural dimensions in 71 societies; [18] and because technology is moreover an underlying factor in relation to certain other variables—such as the division of labor and population changes—the technological impact has to be acknowledged as one of the first-order variables bringing socio-cultural change. Its relationship with other elements of the social system is admitted and indeed proclaimed. If, however, one compares present-day American society with that of one century ago, some of the most decisive differences would be found to relate to the many direct and derivative influences of advancing technology. In Chapter 7, consideration is given to more specific ideas regarding the technological influence—as embodied in the theories of Thorstein Veblen and William F. Ogburn.

The Demographic Influence

Population is another fundamental influence on socio-cultural change. According to circumstances it can be, like technology, at times an independent variable and at other times a dependent one. Population growth or decline is influenced by various values (of the total social system, of family, of religion); it is also affected by the level of technology, although a reasonably high level is not a requirement for

[15] For brief summaries of the Mesthene, Taviss, Cox, and Shils studies, see Harvard University Program on Technology and Society, *Fourth Annual Report,* 1967–1968, pp. 22–24 and 53–64.

[16] Allen, *et al., op. cit.,* Part III.

[17] Alvin W. Gouldner and Richard A. Peterson, *Technology and the Moral Order* (Indianapolis, Ind.: Bobbs-Merrill Co., 1962).

[18] *Importance* was operationally defined by Gouldner and Peterson in terms of explaining the greatest amount of variance of the total variance in the correlation matrix. Although this study is of a pioneering nature, its findings are not to be dismissed casually. Gouldner and Peterson used data from the Human Relations Files of Yale University. *Ibid.,* p. 55.

having a large population, as witness the "Malthusian nations" of India and China.

On the other hand, population operates as the independent variable in many situations: An expanding population (such as that occurring in the Western world in the "Demographic Revolution" or "population explosion") brings expanding markets: more people to buy homes, automobiles, refrigerators, scooters, baseball bats, and baby rattles. It causes an expansion of institutional facilities: A "baby boom," such as the one of 1946–1963 [19] in the United States, inevitably brings an acute need for expanded junior high and high schools (buildings, teachers, principals, and allied personnel and equipment) and other community facilities some 13–14 years later. Just as inexorably (since the death rate at this age is low) college and other facilities and appropriate personnel will be much in demand some 18 years after the period of the baby boom; this assumes favoring values. Life-cycle interests and needs, then, rest on the population factor, which is thus a driving force of change. Derivative effects of this may come later. The fact that many more 18–22-year-olds have experienced a college education is itself likely to have some repercussions on the total society-culture. Growing communities will need new churches, larger police forces, expanded fire protection, water reservoirs with larger capacity, more restaurants, and so on. In areas where population is expanding very rapidly—as in California, Arizona, Texas, and Florida, in this country—keeping the dependent variables in reasonable relationship with the population variable may indeed be difficult.

Changes in the composition of the population bring socio-cultural changes of a different kind. Whether it be a nation or a community, the population may evolve an unusual or unaccustomed percentage of young people or of oldsters, of male or female, of this or that racial group. The character of a nation, region, or community is likely to be affected not only by population characteristics but by modifications in them. Not only are institutions affected but so are problems. A large percentage of teen-agers may bring (although not necessarily) a step-up in juvenile delinquency. The South, with its large Negro population, has had acute racial problems for many years, whereas the Northwest, by way of contrast, has had an insignificant Negro problem. The early West—in its frontier days—was male-dominated, and its problems were predominantly male-linked: lawlessness, fighting, gambling, and the like. California, with an ample Chinese population, has had problems related to this group, although it is granted that factors other than

[19] Donald J. Bogue, "Population Growth in the United States," Chapter 5 in Philip M. Hauser (ed.), *The Population Dilemma,* The American Assembly (Englewood Cliffs, N. J.: Prentice-Hall, Inc., 1963), pp. 73–81.

population are also involved. With heavy Negro in-migration, Los Angeles has experienced racial difficulties, especially in its Watts area. The main principle, in any case, is clear: Population composition and change are the source of socio-cultural change.

Later in this book we shall discuss the underdeveloped areas of the world; here the population factor is frequently a major one. Dilemmas often accompany population developments on both the domestic and world scene. Alternate choices of action frequently need to be made and appropriate policies formulated in order to deal with changes.[20]

Leadership and Socio-cultural Change [21]

One durable and time-honored explanation of change is that the latter is brought by gifted and dynamic leaders. Washington, Lincoln, and Franklin D. Roosevelt; Gladstone, Disraeli, and Churchill; Lenin and Khrushchev; Gandhi and Nehru, and others too numerous to mention are said to have changed their eras. The "Great Man" is held to have led the way—to have made the times. This "romantic" view, emphasizing the great abilities and accomplishments of a president, prime minister, or other leader, requires some modification. The leader may indeed accomplish notable things and he or she may be endowed with fine abilities; a comparison of different presidents, secretaries of state, and prime ministers shows that some have been particularly able. What is often left unsaid is that other influences play a real part in the accomplishments too. Especially in a democracy, the leader alone cannot bring forth the major changes. His programs must be acceptable to public opinion or, great as the person may be, the programs are

20 Philip M. Hauser tells us that the importance of these dilemmas prompted him to give the volume cited in the preceding footnote its title. See Hauser (ed.), *op. cit.,* p. 6. On the subject of population see also Charles B. Nam, *Population and Society* (Boston: Houghton Mifflin Co., 1968); William Petersen, *Population,* 2nd ed. (New York: The Macmillan Company, Collier-Macmillan Ltd., 1969); and Ralph Thomlinson, *Population Dynamics* (New York: Random House, 1965). Incidentally, Chapters 5–8 of this book do not contain any theory of population as a cause of (or factor in) socio-cultural change. So far as this writer is aware, none exist. The nearest, perhaps, is the thesis of David Riesman and associates, *The Lonely Crowd* (New Haven: Yale University Press, 1950) that population, along with other factors, has produced a change in the American character from a tradition-directed to an inner-directed to the other-directed type. Many theories relate to population growth itself—from Malthus to Pearl, Gini, Carr-Saunders, and others—but this is another matter.

21 The reader should appreciate that classification of these influences as internal or external to the social system needs to be regarded with due flexibility. One may assume that leadership will usually constitute an internal type of influence.

not likely to be established. Leaders thus are only one type of role player and must be supported by the rank and file; an equilibrium exists between the former and the latter.[22] Leadership must function in the light of its acceptability to others having varying statuses in the social system. The actions of the leader often must be adjudged proper (legal) by the courts. Those actions must be at least reasonably consistent with the society's mores. Ordinarily the leader who defies the mores of the group is himself defeated.

But not all leaders are of the political type. The commanding figure may be a man or woman of science, of invention, of religion, of education, or of the military: Darwin, Pasteur, Edison, Einstein, Horace Mann, John Dewey, and James Bryant Conant, to name a few from varied fields. These creative minds may explain the nature of man and his universe in new terms, may inaugurate magnificent ethical concepts, conquer communicable diseases, visualize the possibilities of splitting the atom, or enable man to fly or to orbit in space. Tremendous as these achievements are, and remarkable as the people may be who have made the contribution, these benefactors of the human species have always depended on others. Others have set the stage for their final accomplishment. Again, if their ideas too grossly flaunt society's mores and values, they may not be accepted as leaders at all. They have to function along with others in the social system.[23]

When one considers the tens of thousands of leaders in many fields—direct and indirect leaders—corporation presidents, editors, university presidents, senators, cabinet members, members of regulatory boards, officers of institutions—one wonders if somehow the significance of leadership has not been underplayed? Aren't these people the great decision makers of society? It is granted that the various publics will pass judgment on those decisions, but don't these decision makers and problem solvers have much to do with society's course of change? We pose this question: Is the downgrading of the influence of leaders being overdone as easily as the earlier romantic view was overstated? Superior leadership in a state, corporation, or university may spell a vital difference. Often the spirit of a forceful, imaginative, high-quality leader permeates an entire organization, or even a nation, just as the presence of an inept, sluggish person at the top may bog down the group's activities and its morale. In instances of marked change occurring in primitive societies, moreover, one can often point to the vital role of a

[22] Harry C. Bredemeier and Richard M. Stephenson, *The Analysis of Social Systems* (New York: Holt, Rinehart, and Winston, Inc., 1962), pp. 381–388.

[23] The structural-functional view is useful in pointing out likely sources of resistance to a leader's actions or other accomplishments.

leader.[24] It is proper to acknowledge the influence of public opinion and other social forces, yet leadership needs to be given its due.[25]

The Approach of Collective Behavior

Socio-cultural change often has its source in collective behavior—that special area of behavior exhibiting itself in crowd and mass behavior, publics, and social movements. This type of behavior arises spontaneously; it is not based on preestablished understandings or on tradition; it is relatively uncertain and unpredictable; it attempts to meet needs in undefined or unstructured situations.[26] It is often related to some deprivation, dissatisfaction, or frustration. Frequently society has not attacked the sources of its own strains; in this sense, collective behavior may be thought of as "action of the impatient." [27] Even though the most stable society has some collective behavior, heightened manifestations depend essentially on two things: the arousal of discontent and a sense of unfulfilled opportunity. The latter presents new possibilities for coping with the discontent.[28]

Social movements, in particular, have their essential meaning in the context of change. The very definition—for example, that "a social movement is a collectivity acting with some continuity to promote a change or resist a change in the society or group of which it is a part" [29]—bears this out. Social movements tend to have a cycle of development, and the final stage of the cycle (assuming that the move-

[24] Margaret Mead cites the importance of the native leader Paliau in her account of drastic change in Manus society. See *New Lives For Old: Cultural Transformation —Manus,* 1928–1953 (New York: Mentor Books, 1961), pp. 27–28 and Chap. 8, "Paliau: The Man Who Met the Hour." Similarly, Robert Redfield emphasized the leadership of Don Eus Ceme in his study of major change in Chan Kom village in Mexico, *A Village That Chose Progress: Chan Kom Revisited* (Chicago: University of Chicago Press, 1950), pp. x and 168–169.

[25] In assessing the over-all significance of the factor of leadership, the reader will have his or her own opinion. This sociologist-writer suggests that, as may be recalled from Chapter 1, leadership *is* a vital element in socio-cultural change—that the role of leaders has often been underrated.

[26] Ralph H. Turner and Lewis M. Killian, *Collective Behavior* (Englewood Cliffs, N. J.: Prentice-Hall, Inc., 1957), Chap. I; and Neil J. Smelser, *Theory of Collective Behavior* (New York: The Free Press of Glencoe, Inc., 1963), Chap. I.

[27] N. Smelser, *op. cit.,* pp. 72–73.

[28] R. H. Turner and L. M. Killian, *op. cit.,* pp. 523 and 526.

[29] This definition is that of Turner and Killian (*ibid.,* p. 308). However, Smelser, Lang and Lang, Heberle, and others have definitions that similarly connect social movements with social change. See Smelser, *op. cit.,* Chap. 4; Kurt and Gladys Lang, *Collective Dynamics* (New York: Crowell, 1961); and Rudolph Heberle, *Social Movements* (New York: Appleton-Century-Crofts, 1951), p. 6. L. M. Killian makes the apt statement elsewhere that "unless a social movement results in significant social change, it becomes merely an interesting sidelight to history, a curiosity." "Social Movements," Chapter 12 in R. E. L. Faris (ed.), *Handbook of Modern Sociology* (Chicago: Rand McNally and Co., 1965).

ment is successful) is the establishment of the new idea or grouping in the social organization. The change is then completed; a new equilibrium is established. Many social movements illustrate this—the labor movement, women's rights, child labor, public health, civil defense, the current civil rights movement, and many others in the United States; the cooperative movement in the Scandinavian countries; the Nazi movement in Germany; and so on. The final stage is the passage of a significant law or series of laws; establishment of public health departments or a civil defense administration; establishment of a cooperative organization; voting in a new party such as the Nazi party in Germany; or sometimes the mere public acceptance of the new order. A series of steps are observed in moving toward the change. The social movement begins with a basic discontent or deprivation. It may be low status or status inconsistency; or the feeling that a certain category of people, such as women or Negroes, are not receiving just rights or their economic due; or worry (and occasionally panic) relative to raging epidemics of cholera, yellow fever, smallpox, and other diseases such as occurred during the 1870s and 1880s in the United States; or the dissatisfaction and frustration of a people due to having lost a war. Eventually, if the movement is successful, a new concept or organization, which it is felt can cope with the need, is established. The historical record indicates that many changes are made from struggles of people to remedy some source of dissatisfaction. Collective behavior, and especially social movements,[30] may thus be considered as positive responses seeking to remedy strain or disequilibrium.[31]

The Legal Approach to Change

The impact of laws (or court decisions having the effect of law) is a different kind of influence from the sometimes tumultous, "nature-in-the-raw" activities of collective behavior. The law emphasizes formal, abstract reasoning. Conflicts will certainly occur, but they will be intellectual battles. Reliance on the law is often considered a significant index of civilization, although perhaps one could also hold that the amount and nature of collective behavior is also an important index of society. The racial desegregation Court decisions of 1954 and subse-

[30] We are not so much concerned here with other forms of collective behavior as fads, crazes, or even crowd behavior per se.

[31] See H. Fallding's discussion in "Functional Analysis in Sociology," *American Sociological Review*, Vol. 28, No. 1 (February, 1963), 11. Also see Smelser, *op. cit.*, p. 387. As Fallding observes, people could have other reactions in these situations that are less positive; for instance, they could exhibit the *anomie* reaction or some might even commit suicide. Collective behavior at least attempts to redress the situation.

quent ones are notable reminders of the force of law in promoting socio-cultural change. For many problem situations the cry arises, "There ought to be a law!" in order to bring needed control. The law, presumably, brings a desired change. As such, in the formula of change, the law acts as an independent variable. On the other hand, we have just seen that collective behavior (especially social movements) has led to the passage of many laws—for civil rights, child labor, public health, and scores of other causes. Advancing public opinion, moreover, has brought the enactment or revision of many laws. Frequently laws on the books have become "dead letters" because public opinion has advanced beyond them.

The law, then, is another factor in socio-cultural change that operates, according to circumstances, sometimes as an independent variable and sometimes as a dependent one. In the latter situation it is apt to lag, although the lag may not always be pronounced. When socio-economic forces indicate that the law needs to be modified from time to time in the quest for justice,[32] the process of legal revision—or it might be original legal enactment—takes time. Careful study has to be made in order to decide precisely what the law should provide. If corporations seem to require regulation, exactly what (and by whom) should be the regulation? If various grounds for divorce are to be permitted in a state, precisely what grounds should be stipulated? When a new problem or concept arises and requires legal control, what should be the content of the law? [33] Then, the formation and passage of the law by the appropriate legislative body sometimes encounters obstruction and other difficulty. The implementation and enforcement may lag. All in all, the law commonly has much inertia. Comparing the rate of legal change with that of scientific and technological change in the Western world, says one jurist,[34] is like putting the tortoise next to the hare.

[32] Relative to *justice,* which is the *raison d'être* of the legal system, Georges Gurvitch writes: "Law represents an attempt to realize in a given social environment the idea of justice (that is a preliminary and essentially variable reconciliation of conflicting . . . values embodied in a social structure), through multilateral imperative-attributive regulations based on a determined link between claims and duties; . . . ." *Sociology of Law* (New York: Philosophical Library, 1942), p. 59.

[33] Current dilemmas concerning outer space are a case in point. For instance, a nation's sovereignty extends three miles from its shores with regard to shipping, but how far up does this sovereignty extend in space? The astronauts have made many orbits into space, and remarks Lincoln P. Bloomfield: ". . . a brand new situation is already in existence, with law and order, as usual, lagging well behind." "The Prospects for Law and Order," Chapter 7 in Bloomfield (ed.), *Outer Space* (Englewood Cliffs, N. J.: Prentice-Hall, Inc., 1962), p. 151.

[34] Earl Warren, "The Law and the Future," *Fortune* (November, 1955), 106. This article by ex-Chief Justice Warren has been reprinted in John E. Nordskog, *Social Change* (New York: McGraw-Hill Book Co., Inc., 1960), pp. 335–342.

The influence of the law in socio-cultural change is intertwined, as we have seen, with such other influences as collective behavior, public opinion, leadership, and the mores.[35] If forward-looking leaders secure passage of a law that expresses "advanced sentiments," public opinion generally will have to catch up with the views expressed. Thorough-going enforcement may have to wait until the latter has at least partly occurred. Reasonable synchronization needs to be obtained between the law, the mores, and public opinion. If the latter is a reality, the unique importance of the law is that it *is* the controlling force. To some extent the law may be seen as social engineering; it must answer to the community.[36]

The Influence of Ideologies

Guiding the march of social movements, the passage of laws, and the actions of leaders, is often another factor—ideology. A basic idea or kernel of a doctrine often provides the spark, as well as the nucleus, for an action program. An ideology may be defined as "the aggregate of the ideas, beliefs, and modes of thinking characteristic of a group, such as a nation, class, caste, profession or occupation, religious sect, political party, and so on." [37] We shall think of ideas and ideologies together.[38] Their motivating influence in change is considerable, and many sociologists have emphasized change in ideas as extremely important in initiating impulses in social dynamics generally. Conflicting ideologies are all about us: democratic ideology, capitalist ideology, conservative ideology, liberal ideology, business ideology, ideology of the medical profession, ideology of the middle class, revolutionary ideology, and others.

Sometimes ideologies and idealistic conceptions may seem to be visionary and impractical; they may occasionally appear to be the

---

[35] Concerning the law amid such intertwining of forces, see N. S. Timasheff, *An Introduction to the Sociology of Law* (Cambridge, Mass.: Harvard Committee on the Social Sciences, 1939), Chap. 15.

[36] Relative to the philosophy and nature of the law, see Morris R. Cohen, *Law and the Social Order* (New York: Harcourt, Brace, 1933); Warren, *op. cit.;* and Karl N. Llewellyn, "Law and the Social Sciences—Especially Sociology," *American Sociological Review*, Vol. 14 (August, 1949), 451–462.

[37] "Ideology," Henry Pratt Fairchild (ed.), *Dictionary of Sociology* (Ames, Iowa: Littlefield, Adams and Co., 1955). F. X. Sutton and associates have defined *ideology* as "any system of beliefs publicly expressed with the manifest purpose of influencing the sentiments and actions of others." Sutton, Seymour E. Harris, Carl Kaysen, and James Tobin, *The American Business Creed* (Cambridge, Mass.: Harvard University Press, 1956; Schocken paperback edition, 1962), p. 2. Also see Harry M. Johnson, *Sociology* (New York: Harcourt, Brace and Co., 1960), pp. 587–588.

[38] Robert Bierstedt, *The Social Order* (New York: McGraw-Hill Book Co., Inc., 1957), pp. 523–524.

product of escapist thinking. Sometimes they *are* visionary and escapist, of course. On the other hand, the force of ideas in history is considerable. People seem to require ideas and ideals. Ideologies are, therefore, not to be underestimated. They may lead to beneficent or dire consequences when they form the basis of social movements. Many Germans during the 1930s were converted to the Nazi ideology. The Nazi experience should be a telling lesson to any and all who are inclined to take ideologies lightly. Certainly the ideological blueprint was efficiently carried out by the Nazis in power.[39] But ideologies can be influential without being officially adopted as a basis for an action program. Sometimes ideological beliefs are taken over by other groups in power; the Socialist party of the United States has had an influence in this way. Also, utopian thinking may be partially absorbed. Or people may almost silently aspire to an ideal over generations. The masses in underdeveloped nations may currently have the vision of improved economic conditions even though their actual realization may take some time. The basic ideal of freedom—a part of the democratic ideology—is still seen by the American people as a beacon of inspiration and a continuing rallying point for effort.

Sometimes an idealistic conception is negative in nature and is put forth as a "shocker"—hoping that some development will *not* come to pass. Orwell's *1984* [40] is an illustration of that. As modern society has become more complicated and more and more regulation has occurred, the vision of the land of "Big Brother," where the extension of controls reaches the ultimate, is jolting. Various utopian conceptions, moreover, are essentially exercises in social criticism. The picture of the perfect society, as contrasted with the realities of the present, is often intended by utopian writers to underscore current shortcomings. The nature of the ideal and the actual, as presented, shows the particular point of criticism that the author is striving to make.

Ideas and ideologies may themselves, then, constitute underlying bases for socio-cultural change, and indeed constitute a major force in history. Their influence is both internal and external. Because the various systems in a society are interinfluencing as functioning parts of a total social network, the greater impact would seem to come from external sources—at least as seen from the standpoint of any one system. We shall discuss in Chapter 8 two theories—one a classic and one contemporary. These are the theories of Max Weber and Don Martindale.

---

[39] William L. Shirer, *The Rise and Fall of the Third Reich* (New York: Simon and Schuster, 1960). For the ideological blueprint see Chapter 4; for the real, if horrible, results see Chapter 27.

[40] George Orwell, *1984* (New York: Harcourt, Brace and Co., 1949); Signet Books (paperback, 11th printing, 1954).

Religion and Socio-cultural Change

Religion is a specific instance of the influence of ideas and ideologies. As with other influences religion operates both as an independent and a dependent variable in change. Moreover, at various times and in different places it functions as an initiator and also as a brake on change. More often, however, religion serves as a conserving force—a brake—but the initiating influence should not be overlooked.

Is religion a prime mover in history, or perhaps, as some contend *the* prime mover, the clue to history? If this is true, how does one explain changes in religion itself? Oppositely, is religious change a mere reflection of other changes, a symbol, but not a part of the causal interaction? Or is religion one of several levels of causation, a force that once set in motion is part of a complex of causes that mutually condition each other? If this is the most adequate position, as we shall contend, it is likely that the influence of religion will vary from situation to situation.[41]

It is clear that many religious changes that have occurred in the United States [42] have been due to the adjustment of religious ideas or of the churches as organizations to other influences. The secularization of religion is, of course, a most significant point. A notable religious recrudescence or revival has occurred in this nation in recent years, but this comeback (as it has been called [43]) has been one of a strongly secularized religion—with emphasis upon "belonging," obtaining "peace of mind," and other needs of man. In a word, modern religion is man-centered rather than god-centered.[44] It illustrates the over-all view that religions are imbedded in the society in which they are a part. Religion serves its members, and the latter are subject to many influences—and have many beliefs—apart from their church.

Yet religion is in many ways a conserving force.[45] Reliance on its symbols, traditions, and sacred writings turns one more to the past than to the future. This is illustrated by the many policy statements of the Catholic Church toward divorce, birth control, and other subjects. The fact that many individual Catholics practice birth control rather than follow Church doctrine is itself an indication of the influence of

[41] J. Milton Yinger, *Religion, Society and the Individual* (New York: The Macmillan Company, 1957), pp. 265–266.

[42] See *ibid.*, Chaps. 10–11, especially pp. 272–294; and Herbert W. Schneider, *Religion in Twentieth Century America* (Cambridge, Mass.: Harvard University Press, 1952); and many other books.

[43] Schneider, *ibid.*, p. 16.

[44] Will Herberg, "Religious Revival in the United States" Chapter 26 in Amitai Etzioni and Eva Etzioni (eds.), *Social Change* (New York: Basic Books, Inc., 1964), especially pp. 233–234.

[45] Yinger states: "All but the most ardent defenders of religion agree that it is more likely to be a conserver of old values than a creator of new." *Op. cit.*, pp. 300–301.

external, secular views on them. Many religions, at any rate, have attempted to prevent change. Parsons [46] notes that religion operates mostly as a conserving force in most primitive societies and in traditionalized higher cultures. He also restates Max Weber's sage observation that classical Greece was a land of great cultural creativity because a traditional priestly class did not have great social power; furthermore, the converse fact that Indian caste society is perhaps the most resistive large society the world has ever seen is linked with the social ascendency of the Brahmin priestly caste.

But if religion often serves as a brake on the occurrence of sociocultural change, we must recognize that it often acts importantly as an initiator too. Religious ideas spring from the basics of human life itself. These ideas shape perceptions of the world. Once started, these ideas may have marked later development and community influence. One illustration of this in the United States is that of the Mormon Church: "A Mormon community is different, not only in the days of the charismatic leadership of Joseph Smith, but today." [47] Even more, from simple beginnings, the Mormons now have much power, including economic power, if some secular thinking about a religion may be added.[48] However, on the world scene over the centuries of history the creative innovations of religion have been especially notable. Parsons [49] (following Max Weber) calls attention to the fact that the great religious movements of the seventh to fifth centuries B.C.—Confucianism in China, philosophical Brahmanism and the beginnings of Buddhism in India, and Prophetic Judaism in Israel—laid the foundation for great civilizations for the following two thousand years. The values of these religions provided the main frameworks of the great civiliza-

---

[46] Talcott Parsons, "Religion As a Source of Creative Innovation," adapted from his essay entitled, "Religious Perspectives of College Teaching in Sociology and Social Psychology" (New Haven, Conn.: Edward W. Hazen Foundation, 1951), pp. 29–34. It has been reprinted in Nordskog, *op. cit.*, pp. 295–299 (see especially p. 295).

[47] Yinger, *op. cit.*, pp. 306–307.

[48] This, of course, is another illustration of "from small acorns great oaks grow." Nevertheless one records that beginning in 1830, with a meeting of six men (led by Prophet Joseph Smith), on a farm near Palmira, New York, this religious grouping (now called The Church of Jesus Christ of Latter-day Saints) had, in 1962, about two million members. The membership is now centered in Utah; indeed about three fourths of the residents of Utah are members of the Mormon Church. It is now elaborately organized; is stated to be probably the wealthiest per capita of any religious denomination in the United States; has considerable political power. *The New York Times*, August 1, 1962. For another assessment of the Mormon Church, its beliefs, power, ideas, educational and welfare policies, and even its attitude toward current race problems, see Seymour Freedgood, "Mormonism: Rich, Vital, and Unique," *Fortune* (April, 1964), 136–139 and 166–172.

[49] Parsons, in Nordskog, *op. cit.*, pp. 295–298.

tions of the Orient, except that Islam came later. These must be regarded as considerable influences.[50]

The Educational Approach

Theorists on socio-cultural change have not usually stressed the influence of education—which this writer considers to be a mistake. Education, as here defined, includes both formal schooling and informal influences, especially via the mass media. Education is clearly involved in the other approaches that have been discussed, such as public opinion, leadership, inventions, and the research process. Moreover, education functions sometimes as an independent variable, sometimes as a dependent variable, and sometimes in an intervening manner. Education is an influence, furthermore, that has much to do with a person's entire world view. The college graduate is often markedly different from those who have had only a grammar school education.[51] Education, moreover, has important effects on society, aside from its significant effects on the individual.

Education is a prerequisite for many other social developments. If democracy as a political process is to be successfully achieved, education of the citizenry to a reasonable extent is necessary. If occupations are to become more involved and highly skilled, education is again necessary for this.[52] If science is to become a fundamental activity in the social system, then education is surely needed.[53] If the problem of leisure time is to be well met, once again education (including adult

[50] So considerable, in fact, that the thoughts of some have turned toward the viewpoint of religious determinism. Parsons, however, is at pains to point out that the religious movements he mentions had roots in various other social and psychological forces. The religious is fused with others, including the economic. He affirms the common consensus of sociologists that there is no single dominant factor in social change. *Ibid.*, p. 298.

[51] The complete range here would be between the extreme of being almost completely uninformed (the person might be illiterate) and, on the other hand, of being extremely well informed on a wide variety of subjects. Education, moreover, bears significant relation to the traits mentioned by Robert K. Merton of locally oriented or of cosmopolitan orientation. *Social Theory and Social Structure*, rev. ed. (Glencoe, Ill.: The Free Press, Inc., 1957), pp. 393–394. Even a person's sense of tolerance, as S. A. Stouffer pointed out, is related to the extent of his education. *Social Research to Test Ideas* (New York: The Free Press of Glencoe, Division of The Macmillan Company, 1962), pp. 121–124.

[52] See John K. Folger and Charles B. Nam, "Trends in Education in Relation to the Occupational Structure," *Sociology of Education*, Vol. 38, No. 1 (Fall, 1964), 19–33; and Otis Dudley Duncan and Robert W. Hodge, "Education and Occupational Mobility: A Regression Analysis," *American Journal of Sociology*, Vol. 68 (May, 1963), 629–644.

[53] For a broad view of this subject, including an elaborate appraisal of the production of knowledge, see Fritz Machlup, *The Production and Distribution of Knowledge in the United States* (Princeton, N. J.: Princeton University Press, 1962).

education) is related. If culture is to grow, the creative people in different activities must first be informed as to the current stock of knowledge. Thus, advances in physics or medicine are hardly made by individuals who have never been near a physics lab or medical lecture hall. However, education is not to be equated with being informed only on the basis of formal instruction. Sometimes a person will impressively make up in informal learning what he lacks from the formal, although this is not very likely in such areas as physics and medicine.[54] Education, furthermore, usually aids the solution of social problems: to understand the nature of a problem and its ramifications is often the first step. Lastly, given our present "knowledge explosion," education is more and more needed merely to understand what we already have.

Results in the field of education, especially as allied with science, sometimes give rise to further changes. Thus, Darwin's theory of evolution in biology had dozens of social repercussions. Also, Thorstein Veblen's socio-economic doctrines led to much social regulation of business in the United States.[55] Another example would be Gunnar Myrdal's distinguished volume, *An American Dilemma,* which disturbed America's conscience relative to the Negro problem and was one of the basic influences leading to the Supreme Court desegregation decisions of 1954 and thereafter.[56] All three of these examples—taken only as illustrations—were notable in arousing public opinion, which then led to legal or other changes.

At the present time a worldwide educational revolution is occurring. We are thinking here of the drastic increase in the number of people being educated. The uneducated person is becoming an economic and social liability even more than during past years. The median school years completed in the United States in 1969 (both sexes, all races) was 12.1 for all persons 25 and older; [57] that is to say, the average American at this time had slightly more than a high school education. The average is steadily rising, and Drucker [58] points out that it is

54 The case for informal learning is often made with reference to such individuals as Thomas Edison. Edison, one of the world's great inventors, had only a grammar school education. Nevertheless, one may reflect that the probabilities of making such total achievement as Edison's *today* among, let us say, 1,000 young boys possessing only a grammar school education would be exceedingly small.

55 See a discussion of Veblen's theories in Chapter 7 of this book.

56 Relative to the effects of the Myrdal book, see Oscar Handlin, "A Book That Changed American Life, Review of the Twentieth Anniversary Edition of Gunnar Myrdal, *An American Dilemma,*" in *The New York Times Book Review* (April 21, 1963), p. 1.

57 U. S. Bureau of the Census, *Statistical Abstract of the United States: 1970,* 91st Annual edition (Washington, D. C., 1970), Table No. 157, p. 109.

58 Peter F. Drucker, "The Educational Revolution," Chapter 27 in Etzioni and Etzioni (eds.), *op. cit.,* p. 238.

increasing in other nations too—especially in the Soviet Union. Several causes may be responsible for this change, but one of the main ones is undoubtedly that modern work is increasingly mental and conceptual. "The man who works exclusively or primarily with his hands is the one who is increasingly unproductive." [59] The automation trend is directly related to this. The manual-labor (unskilled) job is the one that often is taken over by machines.

If education is on the rapid march today, what of the future? Daniel Bell [60] maintains that education is likely to be *vastly* important in the years ahead. In the coming (postindustrial) society Bell believes that business will no longer be the predominant element. The intellectual will be predominant. Such institutions as universities, research institutes, and research corporations will be even more important than they are today. This prediction is allied to developments in science and technology, and especially important in Bell's eyes are such factors as (1) the exponential growth of science; (2) the growth of intellectual technology, such as the computer; and (3) the growth of research and development activities. In the light of such trends as these—which Bell extends from the present state—education rises to a new plateau of importance.[61]

The Conflict Approach

The conflict approach to the study of socio-cultural change shows a sharply increased relevance at the present time. If *conflict* is defined as "a process-situation in which two or more human beings or groups seek actively to thwart each other's purposes . . . even to the extent of injuring or destroying the other" [62] and it is kept in mind that this "often involves a struggle over values and claims to scarce status, power, and resources," [63] it seems clear that conflicts are not only common but they are virtually intrinsic to the social process; and they are, needless to say, the source of much social change. They will relate to

[59] *Ibid.*, p. 239.

[60] "The Post-Industrial Society," Chapter 2 in Eli Ginzberg (ed.), *Technology and Social Change* (New York: Columbia University Press, 1964), p. 44 ff.

[61] It is in the light of such thinking that this sociologist underscored the influence of education in Chapter 1 as of special importance. The time-honored functions of education (with respect to public opinion, leadership, innovation, and the rest) are important enough. From this point the role of education in relation to change will assume a higher level of importance still.

[62] "Conflict," an article in Fairchild and others, *op. cit.*, pp. 58–59.

[63] Lewis A. Coser, *The Functions of Social Conflict* (Glencoe, Ill.: The Free Press, Inc., 1956), p. 8. See also "Conflict," by Lewis A. Coser, in Julius Gould and William L. Kolb (eds.), *A Dictionary of the Social Sciences* (New York: The Free Press of Glencoe, Division of The Macmillan Company, 1964), pp. 123–124.

changes *within* and changes *of* social systems. Conflicts may involve individuals, small groups, organizations, community residents, social classes, racial groups, and nations (in short, they may be intranational or international). Conflicts may be physical, intellectual, or spiritual.[64] J. Novicow and others have stressed that "eternal struggle is a universal and everlasting law." [65]

Conflict theory has had a lengthy development in social science. Its foundations lie in the ideas of Machiavelli, Jean Bodin, Thomas Hobbes, David Hume, Adam Ferguson, Turgot, Adam Smith, and Thomas R. Malthus. All-important contributions were made by Karl Marx and Georg Simmel, but a host of lesser contributors could be listed.[66] In the United States Robert E. Park and Ernest W. Burgess were considerably influenced by Simmel (and by Small who introduced Simmel to Americans). The Park-Burgess, *Introduction to the Science of Sociology*,[67] emphasized the social processes such as competition, conflict, accommodation, and assimilation. Finally, on the contemporary scene, followers of Marx and Simmel (in particular), such as Ralf Dahrendorf and Lewis A. Coser, have been active as we shall see.

During the 1930s and 1940s (and much of the 1950s) the *conflict* emphasis in sociology appeared to be in eclipse.[68] In the 1960s it rose dramatically. During the earlier period Parsonian structural-functionalism had gained attention, and it was mainly concerned with maintaining the social structure. Parsons tended to view conflict as primarily disruptive, and hence dysfunctional for the system.[69] He, like many sociologists, mostly ignored positive functions of conflict. He saw conflict as partly inevitable and partly avoidable but, in any case, undesirable. Coser, writing in the mid-1950s, summarized that the generation of sociologists of that time had generally less interest in social conflict than the preceding generation. For the most part the mass of sociologists seemed to agree with Parsons' negative dysfunctional view of conflict.

Coser's essential view is that conflict has positive features along with

---

64 Fairchild and others, *loc. cit.*

65 Pitirim A. Sorokin, *Contemporary Sociological Theories* (New York: Harper, 1928), p. 314 ff.

66 In Martindale's quite inclusive review he summarizes the contributions of the Social Darwinians such as Herbert Spencer and William Graham Sumner; of such racial adherents as Arthur de Gobineau, Houston Chamberlain, de Lapouge, Lothrop Stoddard, and of course Hitler; and of others such as Walter Bagehot, Ludwig Gumplowicz, Gustav Ratzenhofer, E. A. Ross, and Albion W. Small. Don Martindale, *The Nature and Types of Sociological Theory* (Boston: Houghton Mifflin Co., 1960), Chaps. 6–8.

67 (Chicago: University of Chicago Press, 1921.)

68 Jessie Bernard, "Where Is the Modern Sociology of Conflict?" *American Journal of Sociology*, Vol. LVI (1950), 11–16.

69 Coser, *The Functions of Social Conflict, op. cit.*, pp. 21–23.

the negative. He holds, first, that conflict is a form of socialization. No group can be entirely harmonious. Moreover, conflicts are not entirely disruptive. Group life is built up through cooperation *and* conflict. The latter has important functions as well as dysfunctions.[70] Following the ideas of Simmel, Coser states a series of propositions relative to conflict. Some of these are that (1) Conflict has various group-binding functions. A certain amount of discord and controversy is organically tied up with the elements that ultimately hold the group together.[71] (2) Conflict has group-preserving functions. The power to rebel against tyranny is something of a safety valve. Social systems provide institutions that serve to drain off hostile sentiments. (3) The closer the social relationship, the more intense the conflict.[72] Coser states 16 propositions in all. Then, concerning social conflict in relation to social change, he observes that the former may lead to inner adjustments of social systems (hence gradual changes take place); but changes *of* social systems may also occur.[73] He concedes that the details of conflicts relate to each social system with its given type of structure, patterns of social mobility, and ways of allocating scarce power and wealth. At any rate, aggressive groups may become sufficiently powerful that vested interests of the system will be overcome; hence, a breakdown of the system and a new distribution of the social values will result. A new social order is thereby established.

Recent interest in conflict has stemmed from an additional source. The German sociologist Ralf Dahrendorf [74] similarly developed his ideas in response to Parsonian integrationism. After thoroughly examining the Marxian theory of social class, Dahrendorf proceeds to launch his own thesis; this follows from his view that the ubiquitous elements of conflict and social change have thus far been given insufficient emphasis. Dahrendorf holds that (1) distributions of authority may generate conflicts and disruptions; (2) that social classes are essentially conflict groups (he follows Marx in this); (3) that conflicts are basic features of social structure and process ("wherever there is life, there is conflict"); (4) that conflict, although not necessarily "functional" for the society, is nevertheless "desirable"; (5) that conflicts bring structural changes (a major point); (6) that the factors of "in-

70 *Ibid.*, pp. 27–31.
71 *Ibid.*, pp. 33–38.
72 *Ibid.*, pp. 67–72.
73 *Continuities in the Study of Social Conflict* (New York: The Free Press, Collier-Macmillan Ltd., 1967), Chap. I, pp. 24–33.
74 Ralf Dahrendorf, *Class and Class Conflict in Industrial Society* (Stanford, Calif.: Stanford University Press, 1959). Chapters V and VI are especially relevant. Then, in Chapters VII and VIII, he applies his ideas to industrial conflict and political conflict.

tensity of the conflict" (that is, degree of energy expenditure and involvement of the parties) and violence are very consequential; (7) that intensity and violence are in turn significantly affected by contexts and types of conflict, rewards enjoyed by authority figures, possibilities of vertical mobility in the society, and regulation of conflicts; and (8)— the over-all culmination of the preceding—that the structural changes brought by conflicts tend to be of three types: (1) A total or near-total exchange of personnel in positions of domination occurs; this is, in short, the case of revolutionary change; (2) a partial exchange of personnel occurs, which may be called evolutionary change; or (3) personnel are not exchanged at all, but ideas are incorporated by the majority party and structural changes are made.[75] Dahrendorf interrelates these three elements such that they constitute an embryo theory (they do not comprise a formal theory, he declares).

In any case, it was during the 1960s that sociological (and public) interest in conflict rose to a higher pitch. It may be recalled that in the brief summary of socio-cultural conditions in present-day American society in Chapter 1, discussion was made of racial protests, confrontations, sit-ins, takeovers, protests directed against the Vietnam war, and varied demonstrations and rebellions. As was stated at that time, protesting groups have been a mixed army of idealists, racial dissidents, revolutionaries (such as the Students for a Democratic Society), general nihilists, and others. Whatever attitude one may espouse toward these groups and activities, it seems unarguable that *conflict* was the chosen method of social change. Conflict theory is indeed relevant for current race relations.[76] In these various matters some may attempt to justify the recourse to conflict and violence. Others may condemn it.[77] One can trace the rise of conflict and confrontation, beginning with the sit-ins, wade-ins, and freedom rides of the early 1960s—which were relatively peaceful compared with later developments. The civil rights movement gradually became more militant, and the urban riots of 1964–1967 followed.[78] The New Left became more active with its concerns for both the black ghetto and the white poor. Amid this, college students became increasingly disapproving of the Vietnam war and of

[75] *Ibid.*, pp. 232–233.

[76] See Lewis M. Killian and Charles M. Grigg, *Racial Crisis in America* (Englewood Cliffs, N. J.: Prentice-Hall, Inc., 1964), especially pp. 18–20 and Chap. VII; also see Joseph S. Himes, "The Functions of Racial Conflict," *Social Forces*, Vol. 45, No. 1 (September, 1966), 1–10.

[77] For example, see the statement of Dean Franklin L. Ford of Harvard's Faculty of Arts and Sciences following the seizure of University Hall by militants during April, 1969. *The New York Times* (April 12, 1969).

[78] For a suggestive explanation and interpretation of changing race relations in the United States, 1963–1968, as they affected the urban riots, see Howard Hubbard, "Five Long Hot Summers," *The Public Interest* (Summer, 1968), 3–24.

relationships between universities and the military-industrial complex; many had previously been concerned with racial injustices. Clashes and confrontations with university administrators became common. Indeed college campuses more and more became the "new battle-ground." To seek objectives by conflict activity (taking over buildings and the like) was the new strategy.

It is useful to note that the various conflict areas of activity (racial, antiwar, New Left-inspired, and so on) are in part interrelated, just as specific campus demonstrations (Berkeley, Columbia, San Francisco State, Harvard, Cornell) and even the individual urban riots of 1964–1967 bear reference to preceding events. The mass media have been, of course, an indispensable factor in linking each specific occurrence with the preceding. It is also of value—and with this we conclude the discussion on this subject—to observe that, even though American society has had other major eras of protest, certain characteristics appear to characterize the present one. Here we tend to follow, indeed we quote, Boskin and Rosenstone.[79]

1. *The current protest has occurred in a period of prolonged prosperity.*
2. *It has reflected the increasingly pluralistic nature of society, including not only ethnic groups, but also emerging subcultures centering around school, youth, and dropouts from society.*
3. *It has been essentially activist rather than ideological in orientation.*
4. *It has seen the emergence of nationwide black organizations which have excluded white membership.*
5. *It has been led by the younger generation, which has set the tone and direction of the movements.*

The Self-determinative or Active Approach

At the beginning of this chapter it was stated that the self-determinative or active approach to socio-cultural change refers to the motivation of people to actively guide their own concerns and behavior; to demand greater responsiveness on the part of their government to human needs; and, all in all, to seek to determine and procure (insofar as is possible) the type of life pattern that they desire in their society. If we follow Professor Etzioni's [80] description of a society that is based on these interests, which he calls the active society, the latter tends to be master of itself. It continually responds to the needs of its members; it is a society under perpetual self-transformation. Components

[79] Joseph Boskin and Robert A. Rosenstone, Introduction to "Protest in the Sixties," *The Annals of the American Academy of Political and Social Science,* Vol. 382 (March, 1969), ix.

[80] Amitai Etzioni, *The Active Society* (New York: The Free Press, Division of The Macmillan Company, 1968).

of the active orientation, declares Etzioni,[81] are (1) self-conscious and knowing actors, (2) one or more goals that the actors are committed to realize, and (3) access to levers or power that will allow the actors to reset the social code. Self-determinative or active societies make a greater effort to realize values and to explore barriers that deter societies from realizing these values. If the institutional structure, wholly or in part, were itself to represent some departure from value concepts —and its behavior were to show inconsistencies with such values as justice, rightness, and the like—an effort would be made to transform the structure to a condition more consistent with the values. In transforming the society such that social groups would better realize their collective wants and goals, the self-determinative or active society would improve the public opinion process by striving for more adequately informed publics and more active participation. Knowledge would be increasingly used as a transforming force; research and development work would be used as much as possible; improvements would be made in the decision-making process. An effort would be made to develop channels for transmitting data relative to a developing consensus upward to the leaders and other elites, so that a more responsive policy would result. The society would especially endeavor to avoid conditions that alienate persons and groups. An important cause of this phenomenon in contemporary American society, maintains Etzioni,[82] is a condition known as inauthenticity. This means that people are given the illusion of participating in social affairs with little actual effect; that is, there is the appearance of responsiveness while the underlying condition is alienating. In transforming society in order to reduce alienation and inauthenticity, Etzioni would use various principles of societal guidance, cybernetic mechanisms, mobilization of power, and mechanisms of consensus.[83]

But, with modern American society still in mind, the reader may inquire if this society does not *already* take many measures seeking to realize its values—use social knowledge (indeed initiate countless studies and surveys), liberally support research and development, respond to the needs of the people, pass many laws and inaugurate programs dealing with problems, and so on? Yes, it does—all these things—but not to the degree that the self-determinists say is needed.

The extent to which contemporary American society already does these things and the degree of success that it realizes in relation to the

[81] *Ibid.*, p. 4.

[82] *Ibid.*, Epilogue, p. 619.

[83] There is too much material here for detailed discussion. This material constitutes the bulk (Parts I–V) of his *The Active Society*.

need are complicated issues. Each person will have his own answers. People differ in their expectations as to the role of government in these matters, in any case. We shall have more to say on this subject later. The self-determinists or activists would maintain, at least, that they would devote *more active* efforts in behalf of the commonweal and would be *more responsive* to social needs than is done at present.

The Individual Component. In his portrayal of the active society Etzioni is less clear as to the role of the individual person. His main interest centers on the transformation of the society.[84] If we are to supplement his ideas as thus far presented, we would suggest that the individual similarly shows the active outlook to greater extent than at present in his personal behavior, affirmations, dissents, protests, and the like. He should base his actions to a greater degree than formerly, moreover, on his personal convictions. The individualistic emphasis in American society has always been strong; yet, if a person disagreed with national policies regarding, let us say, the prosecution of a war or the treatment of a minority group, he would be more likely than ever to protest and take some symbolic action of renouncing the existing legal authority, such as by burning a draft card. His convictions would count heavily in these actions. The expectation of adjusting to others or especially to the social order itself, which was generally assumed in earlier years, may often be scorned. Indeed because he has an interest in a transformation to new social conditions, he may be quite indifferent to the future of the present order.

Such behavior is often highly idealistic, although pure unadulterated idealism will in many cases not be the sole motivation. Marxist sentiment, the influence of Students for a Democratic Society, nihilistic views, or other miscellaneous revolutionary strivings may also be in evidence. Diverse motives and political affiliations, in short, may be included under this banner. Typically, the self-determinist or active person is young, although not all young people are self-determinist. The person has usually come to believe that the social order is hypocritical, corrupt, or incompetent; hence, it needs replacement or major transformation. Sometimes it is not the entire social order (the establishment) that needs to be transformed but only one part of it: the

---

[84] In general, Etzioni would say that many individuals will join with others to form collectivities that will expend their efforts with respect to social transformation. Of course, the individual has the option of "accepting passivity." However, he may gradually participate. "A major step in many personal chains of activation," says Etzioni, "is the decision not to accept the system any longer, and that it must be changed basically." *Ibid.*, p. 648 (including footnote).

"educational establishment," [85] corporate structures, or (frequently at this time) the military establishment. Protests may be expressed in active confrontations or sometimes more indirectly (antimilitary news sheets are printed and issued near military bases). If such active efforts are sufficiently effective so as to persuade more and more people to their views, it is clear that extensive social change may be in the offing.

Are the Hippies to be counted with the self-determinist or active group? We would reply in the negative. They do determine, it is true, their own social system to a large extent, protesting as they do against the dominant American cultural pattern with its emphasis on "success," money, and maintaining a certain standard of living. The Hippies renounce all that. In some respects they live the traditional American life in reverse: Instead of using time wisely, the Hippie usually has no regard for time; instead of striving for upward mobility, the Hippie is content to live in voluntary poverty; instead of working hard at education in quest for a later job and other rewards, the Hippie often drops out of school; instead of following the expected standards of personal cleanliness and hygiene, the Hippie is indifferent to these matters. But in all this, including the flaunting of traditional morality, the Hippies are passive. They are not self-determinists as the self-determinist group is envisaged here. They have established an alternative to the traditional American socio-cultural system, but their implicit theory of change can be summed up in the phrase "transformation by example." [86] They only want freedom to "do their thing," hoping that their life will appeal to others and that others will then emulate them. The *active* emphasis, then, is lacking. The self-determinists that we are describing in this section are motivated to transform society according to their convictions and in light of the cultural values; the *active* perspective is necessary and important.

Origin of the Self-determinative or Active View.   It was noted earlier that the emergence of the self-determinative or active approach to social change occurred quite recently. It was a development of the 1960s. Its origin, we suggest, was rooted in the protest movement of that decade, which concentrated on racial and minority group injus-

85 As one example among many, the considerable student opposition at Harvard University during April, 1969, to the Harvard Corporation, the major administrative board made up of the president of the university, the treasurer, and five elected Fellows, may be cited. In an editorial entitled, "The Corporation Must Go," *The Harvard Crimson* (student newspaper) declared that "The Corporation as it is now constituted cannot legitimately act as the principal governing body of the university." *The New York Times* (April 12, 1969).

86 John R. Howard, "The Flowering of the Hippie Movement," *The Annals of the American Academy of Political and Social Science*, Vol. 382 (March, 1969), "Protest in the Sixties," especially p. 45.

tices, poverty conditions (especially in the cities), and the Vietnam war. Gradually a new attitude toward change itself developed; it seems that the years 1964–1967 were transition years in this regard.[87] What was before this time a viewpoint *against* the preceding conditions (and several other lesser issues) became in addition a *positive* and *active* attitude to secure conditions and a social structure that one *did* want. The need for a general social transformation was sensed. Gradually the broadening of this viewpoint took hold. It should be emphasized that this was indeed a broadening (not a negative-to-positive switch), because the race-poverty-war protests were still ardently made. However, the same type of person who engaged in the protests of the 1960s now *also* constituted the bulwark of those espousing the self-determinative view of social change.

What are the roots of self-determinism? We have alluded to conditions and problems of American society in relation to the self-determinative approach to social change, but it must be emphasized that this active outlook and performance can occur in any society. Moreover, the more active approach does not mean that *ipso facto* the resulting programs in the society must be radical or militant. Programs of social transformation might be moderate in nature; in whatever nation they might constitute little more than a "New Deal." Of course, if alienation or inauthenticity in the society are indicated to be of sizeable proportions, it would probably follow that the transformation sought would be substantial. Such a change might take place along Marxist or other radical (or militant) lines. It would seem difficult if not impossible at the outset of such a period of intended, self-propelled change to tell how thorough-going the transformation will finally be; both resistances and new ideas on the part of the elites are likely to make their appearance as the programs proceed. One can hardly deny that the *potential* for revolutionary change would be present.

Lengthy consideration of the self-determinative approach is not possible at this point; the attempt in this chapter is merely to describe different approaches to social change. Because this subject is one of major current interest, however, we shall extend the treatment in Chapter 13. At that time attention will be centered on American society, which is viewed as an example.

[87] It is probable that a number of influences converged to make this period a key one. Of course, the Civil Rights Act itself was passed in 1964. But civil rights workers were learning that a more active struggle would be necessary before the goals of that movement would be attained; the killing of three workers in the Mississippi Summer Project of 1964 was a case in point. However, the totality of protests during the 1960s was gradually leading toward a new attitude concerning change. For an illuminating discussion of the Mississippi experience and its impact, see Robert Coles, "The Words and Music of Social Change," *Daedalus* (Summer, 1969), 684–698. For a well-done summary description of the diverse protests of the 1960s, see the entire issue of *The Annals* as cited in the previous footnote.

Concluding Comment

There are, then, many approaches to the study of socio-cultural change.[88] The approaches discussed in this and the preceding chapter have hopefully included most of the important ones. All have merit in the sense that they illuminate some aspect of the subject. One may be a governing factor in one situation, another in a different situation. Usually a number of the factors will combine, thus operating as a cluster, in causing some change. Factors, moreover, may often be enmeshed at different levels of reality—as the biological, psychological, and socio-cultural—in producing the new result. Marked complexity in the combining of causative agents is especially to be anticipated in modern times. The importance of different factors in causing change varies according to time, circumstance, and especially the value emphases of the society in question; perhaps chance historical events may have effects. The conflict and self-determinative approaches are regarded as of especial importance on the current American scene. The notion of monocausality, on the other hand, has to be regarded as completely false. One-factor theories, which had some vogue in earlier years, are indeed discredited today.

The student is encouraged to investigate and analyze *change situations* of his or her own choosing. Perhaps five changes each in relation to one's college campus, community, state, nation, and the world society might be selected. Selections should be such that the student in each case is able to set forth the general social structure and other relevant conditions *before* the change takes place. For each instance of change, indeed, the student should describe (1) just *what* was altered over a given period of time, (2) what were the relevant socio-cultural and other conditions *before* the change occurred, and (3) what were the influences that produced the change? If the importance of the various causative factors can be approximated, so much the better. It is likely that such exercises will bring a sharpened realization of the complexities of the change process.

With appreciation of the many approaches to socio-cultural change we proceed to a second step in considering causes. At this time we turn to specific theories that have been advanced by leading social thinkers

[88] Professor Daniel Bell, Chairman of the Commission on the Year 2000 of the American Academy of Arts and Sciences, divides models of social change into three types. These are (1) *crescive changes,* which are long-run, ground-swell changes, largely unplanned; the most important of these, he declares, are population changes and technological innovations; (2) *social demands,* which are conscious demands by specific social groups for redress in society; the civil rights revolution, he says, is an obvious example of this in our time; the extension of welfare services is another example; and (3) *planned social change,* whether it be on a national or on a local scale. Daniel Bell, in "Toward the Year 2000: Work in Progress," *Daedalus* (Summer, 1967), pp. 975–976.

in explaining change. Each theory may be assumed to embody the author's precise ideas, following some approach, of how changes are produced. Every theory, too, is a product of time and place.

ANNOTATED BIBLIOGRAPHY

Concerning the Technological Approach

Allen, F. R., Hart, H., Miller, D. C., Ogburn, W. F., and Nimkoff, M. F., *Technology and Social Change* (New York: Appleton-Century-Crofts, 1957).
> Describes the technological influence on modern Western society, regarding it as *a* major (not *the* major) influence.

Ellul, Jacques, *The Technological Society,* Translated from the French by John Wilkinson (New York: Alfred A. Knopf, 1964).
> Recommended, not because Ellul's views are believed to be correct but because they are likely to stimulate the reader's thinking. Ellul's "technique" (which includes science as well as technology and the associated values of rationality and efficiency) influences all human activity. It takes over; it is irresistible and irreversable. Man adapts, tends to conform, and often becomes a means to an end. Many criticisms are carried to the extreme, and many have been made before. Favorable influences of technique are underplayed.

Gouldner, Alvin W. and Peterson, Richard A., *Technology and the Moral Order* (Indianapolis, Ind.: Bobbs-Merrill, 1962).
> A pioneering study using factor analysis, which finds level-of-technology to be the single, most important component in explaining variance in 71 primitive societies. Data from the Yale Human Relations Files are used.

Ogburn, William F., *Social Change* (New York: B. W. Huebsch, Inc., 1922; The Viking Press, 1950; Dell paper edition, 1966). See also Ogburn, "The Influences of Invention and Discovery," Chapter 3 in President's Research Committee on Social Trends, *Recent Social Trends in the United States* (New York: McGraw-Hill Book Co., Inc., 1933); Otis Dudley Duncan (ed.), *William F. Ogburn on Culture and Social Change* (Chicago: University of Chicago Press, 1964).
> From 1922 until his death in 1959, Professor Ogburn was a sociological leader in emphasizing the impact of technological change on society.

Concerning the Demographic Approach

Hauser, Philip M., "The Chaotic Society: Product of the Social Morphological Revolution," *American Sociological Review,* Vol. 34, No. 1 (February, 1969), 1–19.
> Hauser sees modern American society ("The Chaotic Society") as crucially influenced by the population variable. The significance of changes in size, density, and heterogeneity of population are depicted. In this presidential address before the American Sociological Association he stimulatingly discusses consequences of population change,

lags in adjusting to changes, and the role of the social sciences in dealing with problems. Contains many valuable insights.

Concerning Collective Behavior

Smelser, Neil J., *Theory of Collective Behavior* (New York: The Free Press of Glencoe, Inc., 1963).
> The "value-added" concept is adapted from economics. This theory is also based on the components of social action. Application is made to panics, crazes, and other behaviors. Ably written.

Turner, Ralph H. and Killian, Lewis M., *Collective Behavior* (Englewood Cliffs, N. Y.: Prentice-Hall, Inc., 1957). See also R. E. L. Faris (ed.), *Handbook of Modern Sociology* (Chicago: Rand McNally, 1964), Chap. 11, "Collective Behavior," by Turner and Chapter 12, "Social Movements," by Killian.
> Recommended. Social movements are particularly consequential for socio-cultural change.

Concerning the Religious Approach

Herberg, Will, *Protestant-Catholic-Jew,* rev. ed. (Garden City, N. Y.: Doubleday & Co., 1960).
> Stimulating and valuable analysis of religion in modern America.

Lenski, Gerhard, *The Religious Factor* (Garden City, N. Y.: Doubleday & Co., 1961).
> Well-done analysis of religious behavior and related socio-cultural elements.

Yinger, J. Milton, *The Scientific Study of Religion* (New York: The Macmillan Company, 1970). Also see Yinger, *Religion, Society and the Individual* (New York: The Macmillan Company, 1957).
> The final chapters especially relate to change. Religion is seen as a force that is apt to retard change but sometimes initiates it. Very able study; much recommended.

Concerning the Educational Approach

Bell, Daniel, "The Post-Industrial Society," Chapter 2 in Eli Ginsberg (ed.), *Technology and Social Change* (New York: Columbia University Press, 1964).
> Predicts an accelerated influence of education and research in the coming society. Stimulatingly written.

Machlup, Fritz, *The Production and Distribution of Knowledge in the United States* (Princeton, N. J.: Princeton University Press, 1962).
> Comprehensive inventory of the "knowledge industry."

Concerning the Conflict Approach

Coser, Lewis A., *The Functions of Social Conflict* (Glencoe, Ill.: The Free Press, Inc., 1956). See also Coser, *Continuities in the Study of Social Conflict* (New York: The Free Press, Collier-Macmillan Ltd., 1967).

Coser makes the case for conflicts being in part a positive factor in change. Conflicts disrupt, but they also integrate. Conflict theory is proposed not to *replace* consensus (or equilibrium) theory but to *supplement* it. Worthy contributions to conflict theory in the tradition of Simmel.

Dahrendorf, Ralf, *Class and Class Conflict in Industrial Society* (Stanford, Calif.: Stanford University Press, 1959).

After thoroughly examining the Marxian thesis concerning social class, Dahrendorf launches his own ideas. Chapters V and VI are especially relevant for approaches to change. Conflict is a basic phenomenon of life and is essentially "good." Dahrendorf comes close to stating a theory of conflict as he relates (1) power and authority and (2) intensity of conflict and violence to (3) radicalness and suddenness of change. Original and penetrating discussion. The author, youthful when he wrote this, qualifies as an intellectual "heavy-weight."

Concerning the Self-determinist or Active Approach

Etzioni, Amitai, *The Active Society* (New York: The Free Press, Inc., Division of The Macmillan Company, 1968).

The active society, one that is master of itself, is viewed as an option of the present era. Leaders and active publics will be responsive to the needs of actors, and the society will engage in continual transformation.

Informed, plausible, and written with a sense of purpose. American society *is* becoming more active-minded. Still, social scientists and others will soberly reckon the likely results of taking this charted course; alternative versions might be proposed. However this is decided and whatever the percentage of Americans that think their society is inauthentic, Etzioni's provocative work deserves a careful reading.

Theories of Change:
Accent on Immanent Factors

The main interest of this chapter relates to Professor Pitirim A. Sorokin's theory of immanent change and allied theories. Because, however, the chapter leads off a series of four that deal with different perspectives toward socio-cultural change, we shall make certain initial and introductory remarks with respect to theories in general. First, the theories that are described in this and the next three chapters incorporate the approaches summarized in Chapters 3 and 4. Not all approaches, however, will be represented by one or more theories. In some cases an adequate theory using an approach has not as yet been formulated. We shall endeavor to emphasize theories that have stood the test of time. We shall give special attention to some that we consider underrated. We shall discuss several that we view as unsubstantiated, holding that the subject is sufficiently important that even an imperfect formulation is better than none. Discussion might stimulate a restatement or alternative statement of the essential idea. The spatial allotment for each theory will no doubt reflect biases and special concerns on our part, for which we make no particular apology. In at least one instance we would have devoted more space to a theory did we not believe that it had been exceedingly well covered in the literature. All in all, the amount of space given to a theory will in a general way reflect our judgment as to its importance, whether or not we agree in all respects with its content.

In the discussion that follows we shall bear in mind Merton's distinction between *sociological theory in the strict sense* and *general orientations to a subject*. He declares that theory in the strict sense consists of "sets of interdependent and verifiable statements of relations between specified variables," whereas general orientations to a subject are statements that "only suggest the types of variables that are somehow to be taken into account" in understanding the subject. The two should not be confused. This does not mean, however (as Merton adds), that "general orientations" are accordingly downgraded in importance.[1] At any rate, much of the theory that we are about to discuss

---

[1] Robert K. Merton, *Social Theory and Social Structure*, rev. ed. (Glencoe, Ill.: The Free Press, Inc., 1957), p. 9 and Chap. II; also see Merton, Introduction to

must be classed as *general orientations to the subject of socio-cultural change.* We suggest that strict theory will increasingly be constructed often using such key ideas as a base.

Hans L. Zetterberg has stressed the pursuit of sociological theory, viewing the latter as "systematically organized, law-like propositions about society and social life." [2] This would seem to be close to Merton's conception of "theory in the strict sense." Zetterberg and many others hope that sociologists will increasingly concern themselves with the discovery of general propositions. This is meant to be applied to the entire field of sociology, of course. As one ruminates over the special situation of socio-cultural change he is conscious of the need to "walk before attempting to run." One has only to recall the substance of Chapter 2 of this text, which deals with semantic and conceptual difficulties involved in studying social dynamics. Nevertheless, whether unduly optimistic or not, we do hope that students of socio-cultural change will master the semantic and conceptual problems and will gradually proceed with the development of systematically organized propositions.

We further subscribe to Merton's view that sociology is not yet ready for high-level abstraction in theory, and that it is currently wiser for sociologists to concentrate on theories of the middle range, substantiating them with empirical data.[3] The viewpoint of this volume is that a dozen or more *change* theories of the middle range have validity; no *one* theory of socio-cultural change dominates the field. But they must be recognized as *general orientations to socio-cultural change,* not strict theory.

The discussion of sociological theory in this volume, it should be emphasized, concerns itself solely with the subject of *change.* This means the study of change in relation to both social systems and culture, including ways in which they may affect each other, and effects in either case that are due to inner or external factors. The society-

---

Allen H. Barton, *Social Organization Under Stress: A Sociological Review of Disaster Studies,* Disaster Research Group, Study No. 17, National Academy of Sciences, Publication 1032 (Washington, D. C., 1963), p. xxiv.

[2] He contrasts this type of theoretical interest with (1) that which "designates all of the better sociological writing of older vintage," which is better termed "sociological classics"; (2) "critical commentary on sociological writing, usually made from an historical perspective," which is better called "sociological criticism"; and (3) development of an "orderly schema of anything to which sociologists (and other social scientists) should pay attention," which may be called "sociological taxonomy." See Hans L. Zetterberg, *On Theory and Verification in Sociology,* rev. ed. (Totowa, N. J.: The Bedminster Press, 1963), Chap. I, especially pp. 4–5. Also see discussion of theory in George C. Homans, "Bringing Men Back In," *American Sociological Review,* Vol. 29, No. 6 (December, 1964), especially pp. 811–812.

[3] Merton, *Social Theory and Social Structure, op. cit.,* p. 9.

culture is the unit of study.[4] Some theories will have greater emphasis on the social system than on changing culture, others the reverse. The ideas of a thinker, moreover, reflect time, place, interests, life experiences (in part), and perhaps other factors.

Finally, we shall note, while considering the various theories, whether the study of change constitutes (or constituted) for the theorist (1) an exceedingly strong interest, perhaps his strongest one; a select few will be in this category; (2) a relatively strong interest; or (3) a relatively minor interest even though the person has somehow made a notable contribution. The latter cases are of course unusual, but sometimes a theorist concentrates on a different subfield of sociology (or anthropology) and achieves major results that have a *crucial bearing* for socio-cultural change. Nevertheless, the most important consideration of all is undoubtedly the *validity* and *over-all worth* (amount of explanatory power) provided by the theory. We would encourage readers to decide for themselves: (1) How *valid* is each theory; that is, to what extent is it substantiated by empirical data? and (2) How *important* is each theory, and why?

In commencing discussion of our chief interest in this chapter—Professor Pitirim A. Sorokin's theory of immanent change (several others have followed the immanent perspective but are less known in connection with it)—we note that the late Professor Sorokin had an exceedingly strong interest in the subject of socio-cultural change. His greatest single effort related to this area, and he also wrote extensively concerning a particular type of change, namely: revolutions. At the same time, as a versatile and very productive sociologist, he also authored books on rural-urban sociology, on the totality of social theory, on social mobility, on altruism, and on other subjects. Because of the magnitude of his efforts in the field of socio-cultural change, we shall devote more-than-average attention to the Sorokin views.

PITIRIM A. SOROKIN (1889–1968)

Before discussing Sorokin's theories of change, let us endeavor to place him as a person. Briefly, he was born among the Komi people of north Russia; he received his doctorate in sociology at the University of St. Petersburg; he served as personal secretary to Alexander Kerensky, head of the Russian provisional government in 1917; was imprisoned six times by the (Communist) Russian government; was condemned to death but freed by order of Lenin; was banished from

---

4 As was observed in Chapter 2, this term is cumbersome; hence we do not necessarily recommend its use. However, the "society and its culture" is always the implied unit.

Russia and came to the United States in 1923; served as a professor of sociology at the University of Minnesota, 1924–1930; was appointed first chairman and professor of sociology at Harvard University in 1930 —and served as chairman for thirteen years and as a professor until his retirement in 1955; and was elected president of the American Socio-logical Association in 1964–1965.[5] Professor Sorokin was the author of many important volumes,[6] most of which were widely translated (which means that he was internationally renowned in the study of society). His death occurred on February 10, 1968.

Because we are concerned here with his contributions toward the subject of socio-cultural change, we shall focus attention on his four-volume work, *Social and Cultural Dynamics*. This is widely considered to be his magnum opus, and it has been translated into seventeen languages. It is comparable in scope and effort to Spencer's *Sociology,* Marx's *Capital,* Toynbee's *A Study of History,* and Spengler's *Decline of the West.* Sorokin brought out a one-volume, abridged edition of the work.[7] Various popularizations have also been written, one by Sorokin himself entitled *The Crisis of Our Age.* What was the content of this major work?

Sorokin's goal in the *Social and Cultural Dynamics* volumes (which will hereafter be referred to as the *Dynamics*) was nothing less than to study socio-cultural fluctuations (change) in Graeco-Roman and West-ern cultures, concentrating on the period 600 B.C. to approximately

[5] Sorokin tells his remarkable story in "Sociology of My Mental Life," in Philip J. Allen (ed.), *Pitirim A. Sorokin in Review* (Durham, N. C.: Duke University Press, 1963). Probably few sociologists can equal this for a colorful and exciting life story. Philip Allen's volume is itself of interest. Authors of the various chapters are Joseph B. Ford, Arnold J. Toynbee, O. F. Anderle, Gosta Carlsson, David R. Mace, T. Lynn Smith, Alex Inkeles, N. S. Timasheff, Robert Merton, Bernard Barber, and others. Each chapter deals with some aspect of Sorokin's work. In the concluding chapter, Sorokin answers his critics. Arnold J. Toynbee wrote the chapter dealing with Sorokin's ideas concerning socio-cultural change. Sorokin's full-length auto-biography, *A Long Journey* (New Haven, Conn.: College and University Press, 1963) is also recommended.

[6] Sorokin's book publications include *A System of Sociology,* 2 Vols. (St. Peters-burg: 1920); *Leaves from a Russian Diary* (New York: 1924, and Boston: Beacon Press, 1950); *Sociology of Revolution* (N. Y.: H. Fertig Company, 1967) (Philadelphia: 1925); *Social Mobility* (New York: Harper, 1927, and Glencoe, Ill.: The Free Press, Division of The Macmillan Company, 1959); *Contemporary Sociological Theories* (New York: Harper & Bros., 1928); *Principles of Rural-Urban Sociology,* with C. C. Zimmerman (New York: Henry Holt & Company, 1929); *Social and Cultural Dy-namics,* 4 Vols. (New York: American Book Company, 1937–1941); *Crisis of Our Age* (New York: E. P. Dutton & Co., Inc., 1941); *Society, Culture, and Personality* (New York: Harper & Bros., 1947 and 1962); *Altruistic Love* (Boston: Beacon Press, 1950); *The Ways and Power of Love* (Boston: Beacon Press, 1954); *Fads and Foibles in Modern Sociology and Related Sciences* (Chicago: Henry Regnery Company, 1956); and *Sociological Theories of Today* (New York: Harper & Row, 1965). A full listing, including articles, is found in Allen (ed.), *op. cit.,* pp. 497–506.

[7] *Social and Cultural Dynamics* (Boston: Porter Sargent, 1957).

A.D. 1935. He also made shorter excursions in Hindu, Chinese, and Arabian cultures. During the preceding time period, he declares,[8] records applying to the areas studied were fuller and more accurate than they were in earlier times. Sorokin thought of his project as covering roughly 2,500 years in all. "Long-time fluctuations cannot be studied properly in a shorter space of time, especially the profounder 'waves' of history." After outlining his major points of interest—a kind of preview of what is to come—he examines fluctuations in the ideational, idealistic, and sensate forms of different departments of culture: the broad field of art (painting, sculpture, architecture, music, and literature) and the three systems of truth and knowledge: ethical and juridical culture mentality, the systems of social relationships, and war and internal disturbances. Finally, he states various conclusions that take form in the principle of immanent change, the principle of limits, his discussion of linearity and of circular forms of change, and the prediction of the decline of modern sensate culture and the emergence of a new ideational or idealistic socio-cultural order.[9]

Sorokin's Findings and Conclusions [10]

The initial finding of the *Dynamics* volumes relates to Sorokin's description of the panorama of Graeco-Roman and Western cultural change over the approximate 2,500 years. He classifies the range of developments on the basis of the three cultural types: [11] (1) the *ideational* type, which places emphasis upon nonmaterial, spiritual, and religious qualities; (2) the *sensate* type, which views reality in terms of the senses and whose interests emphasize the physical and the epicurean; and (3) a mixed type—the *idealistic*—which represents a balanced combination of the first two, usually with, however, a predominance of the ideational elements. What has been the nature of the cultural fluctuations during this lengthy time period? The over-all trends for art, truth and knowledge, ethics and criminal law, war

---

8 *Ibid.,* Vol. I, p. 189.

9 In this vast undertaking Sorokin had some help: ". . . The main body of materials were collected not by me, but by various scholars, each working independently without knowledge either of the objective for which the data were needed, or of my theories." *Ibid.,* I, p. xii. Accordingly this was a cooperative project on the order of Quincy Wright's *A Study of War* (Chicago: University of Chicago Press, 1942) or Gunnar Myrdal's *An American Dilemma* (New York: Harper & Row, 1944).

10 This section attempts to present the "straight Sorokin"—his ideas kept scrupulously free of commentary, interjection, or evaluations; evaluatory comment will follow.

11 The first two are profoundly contrasting types, even though neither necessarily exists in pure form. The third is a balanced mixture of the first two. *Op. cit.,* Vol. I, pp. 66–75.

and internal disturbances, show—not a steady, linear course of change —alternating fluctuations, a waxing and waning of the ideational, idealistic, and sensate cultural emphases. For the most part, the various elements of culture (the arts, systems of truth, and the rest) fluctuated together; that is, if the arts in a certain century changed from the ideational to idealistic emphasis, the other elements made the same change at roughly the same time (occasionally one would lag). In general, the ideational culture mentality dominated the early part of the 2,500–year period; and the sensate mentality and culture rose and dominated from the fifteenth to the twentieth century. Now the sensate culture is at an advanced stage, and Sorokin predicted that it will decline and be superseded.[12] Its spirit is exhausted. Sorokin vividly paints a dark picture of the coming end of the sensate:

1. *Sensate values will become still more relative and atomistic until they are ground into dust devoid of any universal recognition and binding power. The boundary line between the true and false, the right and wrong, the beautiful and ugly, positive and negative values, will be obliterated increasingly until mental, moral, aesthetic and social anarchy reigns supreme.*

2. *These progressively atomized Sensate values, including man himself, will be made still more debased, sensual and material, stripped of anything divine, sacred, and absolute. . . . They will be progressively destructive rather than constructive, representing in their totality a museum of socio-cultural pathology rather than the imperishable values of the Kingdom of God. . . .*

3. *With all values atomized, any genuine, authoritative and binding "public opinion" and "world's conscience" will disappear. . . .*

4. *Contracts and covenants will lose the remnants of their binding power. The magnificent contractual socio-cultural house built by Western man during the preceding centuries will collapse. . . .*

5. *Rude force and cynical fraud will become the only arbiters of all values and of all interindividual and intergroup relationships. Might will become right. As a consequence, wars, revolutions, revolts, disturbances, brutality will be rampant. . . .*

. . .

8. *The family as a sacred union of husband and wife, of parents and children will continue to disintegrate. . . .*

. . .

10. *Its creativeness will continue to wane and wither. The place of Galileos and Newtons, Leibnitzes and Darwins, Kants and Hegels, Bachs and Beethovens, Shakespeares and Dantes, Raphaels and Rembrandts will be increasingly taken by a multitude of mediocre pseudo thinkers, science-makers, picture-makers, music-makers, fiction-makers, show-makers, one group more vulgar than the other.*

. . .

11. *In the increasing moral, mental, and social anarchy and decreasing*

12 *Ibid.*, Vol. IV, Chap. 17, "The Twilight of Our Sensate Culture and Beyond."

> *creativeness of Sensate mentality, the production of the material*
> *values will decline, depressions will grow worse, and the material*
> *standard of living will go down.*[13]

After the complete sensate decline has occurred, the beginnings of
the new ideational (or possibly idealistic) order will appear. New
leadership will emphasize the new values; knowledge will affix itself to
the new cultural mentality. The final determination of a new socio-
cultural order prevailing over the outworn and decaying sensate will
depend largely on whether mankind can avoid a new world war.[14]

In Sorokin's long review of the developments during 2,500 years of
Graeco-Roman, Western, and other cultures, how was he able to classify
the various fluctuations in art, music, truth systems, ethics, law, and
other subjects? What methods did he use? On what basis did he conclude that—now in Greece or Rome, now in Europe—the ideational
emphasis in this or that department was changing to the idealistic or
sensate? Sorokin's methodology was to make first a qualitative and
then a quantitative assessment for each department of culture. For
example, he first described developments in art and in other fields
based on samplings and on prominent works, aided by an expert or
qualified person. This was followed by a "mass," quantitative study.
To make an objective (scientific) study of such subjects as trends and
emphases in arts and systems of truth or of ethics may sound difficult.
Sorokin points out that many subjects of this kind are surprisingly
objective in nature: simple landscape scenes (in paintings); portraits of
the Madonna, priests, landowners, peasants, laborers; or similar por-
trayals. But Sorokin concedes that a subjectivity problem does exist
in various cases. For instance, does a work of art represent the ideational or sensate mentality? In this sort of situation he asked experts
to judge the question and he accepted the majority opinion.[15] Nevertheless using these methods Sorokin was able to make a classification of
fluctuations of the various departments of culture.[16]

The Principle of Immanent Change.   A major conclusion of
the *Dynamics* study is that socio-cultural change is largely caused by

[13] *Ibid.*, Vol. IV, pp. 775–777.

[14] This last sentence was added in the 1958, one-volume edition, *op. cit.*, p. 704.

[15] One of the more difficult matters concerns interpretations as to whether nudity
in art, for example, is ideational or sensate in nature during a certain time period.
Sorokin and his experts concluded that in England during the fifteenth and sixteenth
centuries nudity tended to be more ascetic (ideational) in nature, whereas erotic
(sensate) nudity grew during the seventeenth century and was more prevalent during
the eighteenth and nineteenth centuries. (See *op. cit.*, Vol. I, Table 17 on p. 425.)

[16] For another difficult item see Sorokin's classification of fluctuations of ethical
systems. (*Ibid.*, Vol. II, Tables 29 and 30 on pp. 487–489.)

immanent factors. Changes of the system are generated from within. This view, the reader may recall, was briefly discussed in Chapter 3.

Sorokin declares that there are three possible explanations of socio-cultural change: (1) The latter is caused by external factors to the phenomenon studied; thus, changes in the family can be explained by economic, technological, biological, legal, and climatic factors—anything external to the family system. (2) Changes in any socio-cultural system are caused by internal or *immanent* factors; the system changes by virtue of its own forces and properties. It is bound to change, maintains Sorokin, even if all its external conditions are constant. Any system such as the family thus bears the seeds of the change. (3) Changes are attributable to the combined external and internal forces. This would assume that they are approximately equal in importance in bringing change.

Sorokin's answer is that immanent factors provide the major thrust of change, admitting, however, that external factors have some influence. The latter may retard or accelerate the unfolding of the immanent destiny; in some cases they might even crush the entire system. Nevertheless he believes that the major cause of change is internal. The character of the system determines the nature of its development: Just as an acorn must develop into an oak, so the business corporation must develop in ways consistent with its nature; it cannot develop the functions and life career of a monastery or of a branch of the military service or of a university. He thinks that the principle of immanent change is supported by empirical observation.

Because any socio-cultural system is composed of human beings as one of its components, and because any organism, so long as it exists, cannot help changing, the socio-cultural system is a going concern and cannot help changing so long as it exists, according to Sorokin; this is true regardless of its external conditions, even if they could be absolutely constant. The very performance of any activity, any reaction or response, to a given environment A, changes the system and makes it react differently a second time, and then a third time, and subsequent times. Gradually or abruptly, rapidly or slowly, the system has to change, just because it exists as a going concern. Change thus is immanent in it and rooted in its very nature.[17]

In summary, the socio-cultural system and its subsystems—art, philosophy, science, law, religion, and forms of social, political, and economic organization—change because each of these is a going concern and bears in itself the impelling reason for its change.[18]

[17] *Ibid.*, Vol. IV, p. 594.
[18] *Ibid.*, Vol. IV, p. 600.

The Principle of Limits.   Another basic conclusion of the *Dynamics* study concerns the principle of limits. The latter is, in a sense, a corollary of immanent change. If changes result largely from immanent (inner) factors of a socio-cultural system, the questions may be raised: How great may such changes be? Are there any limits to change? To what extent do changes reoccur in cyclical form (hence history repeats itself)?

Sorokin sets forth some contrasting situations. If a socio-cultural system has only one possible way of changing immanently, it will of course change along this one linear trend. If, on the other hand, the system has many (or unlimited) possibilities of change, the result is bound to be one of no reoccurrence and no rhythm, with everything unique and unrepeated. Systems are likely to have a situation somewhere in between these two extremes. However, some socio-cultural processes seem to be quite linear in their development.[19] Indeed, if the time period is short, many processes show an approximate linear change. Sorokin believes, however, that beyond a certain limit the growth is more likely to be a long-time parabola or other nonlinear trend.[20] But apart from this, people are creative: New processes are very likely to occur—inventions, discoveries, and other novel elements. The possibilities of developing new forms and changes are, therefore, great. Even incessant change is indicated. At the same time systems and processes have their distinctive properties, and the range of possibilities of change is definitely restricted for each system.[21]

Sorokin then shows the limited number of available forms in various departments of culture—economic and political organization, marriage and the family, systems of truth, systems of ethics and of law, principles of science, and socio-cultural systems and processes.[22] From this evidence it seems clear that a large number of systems and processes cannot help repeating the forms already used, either in the same order or in different order; repetition and recurrence of the forms become inescapable.

But the diverse and new processes of culture—invention and discovery—occur in relation to the limited change of systems. There is no possibility, then, of *identical* developments occurring in the same system (recurring in time) or in differing systems (reoccurring in space).

[19] Sorokin cites population growth, growth of knowledge and inventions, and growth of social differentiation (including division of labor). But will population, for example, grow forever, he asks? *Dynamics, op. cit.,* one-volume edition (1957), pp. 667–668.

[20] *Ibid.,* p. 669.

[21] *Dynamics, op. cit.,* Vol. IV, p. 702.

[22] *Ibid.,* IV, pp. 704–707.

The inherent (immanent) changes of the system prevent this.[23] Thus, cyclical processes do not take place.

Sorokin's over-all conclusion on this matter is that "the most general pattern of socio-cultural change is that of incessantly varying recurrent processes." [24] Socio-cultural processes and systems are limited in their possibilities of change; yet changes are guaranteed (precise static conditions do not obtain). Therefore, history repeats itself in part—although never entirely.

Evaluation and Commentary

An initial observation is to remind one that in studying socio-cultural change Sorokin emphasizes the *cultural* phase of the subject, not the social.[25] Sorokin is primarily interested in change from the ideational to the sensate (cultural) epoch and further onward. This, to be sure, affects the organization of people (the social system). His theory of immanent change is socio-cultural in nature; Sorokin thought of systems as comprising the two elements in close interaction and liked to refer to them as socio-cultural.

The Sorokin Statistics. Comment is needed concerning his full qualitative and quantitative review of the 2,500 years of Graeco-Roman and Western cultures, particularly the quantitative results. A notable display of numerical data and percentage changes is unveiled —a "scientific show." Yet, are we to be greatly impressed by the fact that in Europe during the fourteenth and fifteenth centuries works of art were 95.2 per cent spiritual and 4.8 per cent sensual, whereas during the seventeenth century they were 46.4 per cent spiritual and 53.6 per cent sensual? As precise figures (concerning this kind of data) they seem dubious. Many sociologists and sociology students who might be willing to accept Sorokin's major point—the culture change from ideational to sensate—might regard such individual figures unconvincing. Concerning other departments of culture, this problem might not exist.

---

[23] Sorokin says:

> *Time is different; details in the components are different: in the system of meanings, in vehicles, in agents; society and environment are different; and so on. Every one of us, from day to day, has dinner or sleep, but each dinner or sleep is not identical with the former ones: we ourselves are changed; time has elapsed irretrievably; and a number of traits of the dinner or sleep are varying.* Dynamics, op. cit., *one-volume edition (1957), p. 673.*

[24] *Ibid.*, pp. 674–675.

[25] Sorokin himself comments on this. See his "Sociology of my Mental Life," in Allen (ed.), *op. cit.*, p. 24.

Critics have argued over these statistics. Stark [26] observed that in some instances Sorokin attempted to quantify data that are qualitative in nature. Merton and Barber [27] countered by asking what is "inherently" and "exclusively" qualitative? They assert that only selected aspects of the socio-cultural material were subject to quantitative assessment, which was proper. Matilda White Riley and Mary E. Moore [28] comment that the usual statistical checks to ensure reliability of data could have been used.

Sorokin, replying to these critics,[29] seems to have an ambivalent attitude toward statistics generally. He concedes difficulties with the statistics from the beginning, both factual and methodological difficulties. The main problem, he says, is that of trying to make a perfect translation of qualitative-quantitative material into purely quantitative language. He admits that he did not use modern statistical techniques such as sampling, data processing, content analysis and the like; he "preferred to use the entire universe of facts, instead of mere samples of it." In any case, he has added, he was more interested in substantive studies than in techniques.[30] Without prolonging this discussion unduly, one may suggest that some question does exist as to whether quantitative treatment was advisable for *some* of the subjects with which Sorokin dealt—at least at the time the work was written.[31] As social scientists know well, many concepts are effectively quantified

[26] Werner Stark, *The Sociology of Knowledge* (Glencoe, Ill.: The Free Press, Inc., 1958), p. 280.

[27] Robert K. Merton and Bernard Barber, "Sorokin's Formulations in the Sociology of Science," in Allen (ed.), *op. cit.*, p. 352.

[28] Matilda White Riley and Mary E. Moore, a chapter (they are unnumbered) in Allen (ed.), *op. cit.*, p. 206 ff.

[29] "Reply to My Critics," in Allen (ed.), *op. cit.*, especially pp. 441–447.

[30] Sorokin has some distrust, it is clear, of quantitative methods, although he declares that they are "necessary and most fruitful if and when they have been shown to be applicable and competently and expertly used." He believes that some seemingly quantitative procedures, however, are "pseudo-mathematical, quasi-statistical, and 'quantophrenic.'" *Ibid.*, p. 492 ff.

[31] Arnold J. Toynbee has commented regarding the Sorokin use of statistics:

> The four volumes of his Social and Cultural Dynamics . . . are sown generously—one might say almost recklessly—thick with statistical tables and figures, and a majority of these are concerned with subjects that most of the conventional statisticians have fought shy of. . . . Laboriously, they (his critics) will pick perhaps as much as 90 per cent of Sorokin's findings to pieces. But Sorokin will come out strategically victorious from any number of tactical defeats. . . . Sorokin's use of the "numerically quantitative" method of presentation is one of the most distinctive, as well as controversial, features of his work. I admire, as I have said, his boldness in his use of it. At the same time, I do think that, on occasions, it plays him false.

"Sorokin's Philosophy of History," in Allen (ed.), *op. cit.*, pp. 69–71.

today that were in the "qualitative" category only a few years ago (perhaps when Sorokin wrote the *Dynamics*).

As an equally important issue: Are Sorokin's final conclusions and explanatory theory surely based on his tabular material? Or, after making the massive display of tables and graphs, did he conclude much as he wished? We have in mind especially the principle of immanent change itself. We see no evidence that the facts so laboriously gathered back up *this* principle; they do comprise the empirical grounding for the ideational-to-sensate formulation. Immanent change is initially mentioned in Volume I of the *Dynamics*,[32] which was published in 1937, it may be recalled. Indeed the first three volumes, published at this time, contain the descriptions of types of culture, the lengthy review of fluctuations in art, truth and legal systems, and other departments of culture during the 2,500 years. Volume IV, issued in 1941, contains the final explanations. When we suggest that the principle of immanent change appears to be unrelated to the many factual tables, this does not, it is clear, constitute criticism of the content of the principle. It still could be a brilliant and valid explanation of change even if it is a thing apart from the data. However, one is obligated to point out that his array of data does not necessarily *prove* or sustain the principle of immanent change.[33]

On the other hand, Sorokin did establish (at least in our judgment) important points properly on the basis of his data, namely: That culture and its parts fluctuated periodically during the 2,500 years; that culture did not evolve in a linear progression, as Spencer had declared; that it did not move in cycles, as Spengler had set forth; that it did not move toward some final utopia, as Marx had asserted; and that it changed in recurrent but incessantly varying processes. At least we feel that Sorokin generally established the latter point through logical discourse. Eventually, quantitative techniques may be brought to bear on this problem. Simulation techniques, for example, may prove to be useful sooner or later relative to this kind of problem.

The Twilight of the Sensate.   We have earlier described Sorokin's view of the approaching decline of the sensate period: the deterioration of values, the further debasing of the sacred and absolute, the disappearance of a genuine public opinion, loss of the binding power of contracts, the dominance of force and fraud, and other

---

[32] *Op. cit.*, p. 51.

[33] If the theory is not empirically based, perhaps it could be tested in the future —especially in view of widespread interest in internal versus external causes of change.

occurrences. Sorokin declares that he does not consider this a pessimistic utterance because he feels that the sensate will be followed by a bright new age—a far better one.

We do not dispute that the modern scene contains some of the conditions that Sorokin depicts, even though others might be challenged (for example, is a genuine public opinion disappearing?). The declining phase of the sensate indeed presents a black picture.[34] Somehow this writer is not convinced that Sorokin's predictions will necessarily occur. We do not know, of course, whether this era will grind to a miserable, power-minded, materialistic, debauched end. Who can do more than guess? If it does, we doubt that the decline will occur in the manner of Sorokin's "trends."[35] It is not that we object to pessimism per se; in fact, one does not have to be either optimistic or pessimistic regarding the future of the sensate. We do not say that modern Western civilization will not end. It *could be* that the devastating impact of nuclear-germ-chemical war will be such that civilization will go under. Or pollution, ecological crises, and other problems might possibly overwhelm the present order.

But we do not particularly expect that such a debacle will occur, admitting that some civilizations of the past have declined. Leaders are continually grappling with problems—from nuclear testing and automation to racial injustice and pollution. Modern problems are sometimes critical, yet resources for solving them are also greater than during past times. We simply question whether Sorokin's predictions are likely to be fulfilled as he states them. For one thing, it is not to be assumed that humanity will passively sit back and wait for the sensate to glide to its lowly end. On the contrary, the active spirit is decisively rising. Leaders, government officials, scientists, all kinds of workers and thinkers will be devising solutions and taking measures— sometimes heroic—to control problems. Sensate culture may still decline. Or, it may persist for many decades and generations, with many

---

34 It reminds one, even if the details differ, of Lewis Mumford's picture of the paleotechnic period of the machine age. The authors in both cases seem to let themselves go in painting the black picture. For Mumford's description, see *Technics and Civilization* (New York: Harcourt, Brace & Co., 1934), pp. 172–195.

35 For example, we cannot agree with some trends that were quoted earlier, certainly if the United States is used as Exhibit A: That material values are declining; that depressions are getting worse (rather greater success has been realized in controlling economic depressions); and that the standard of living is going down (quite the contrary, it has doubled in the United States during the first half of the twentieth century and is still rising). The public opinion issue (just mentioned) will be discussed in Chapter 13. In all these matters it is true that one can maintain that, even if they do not seem to be occurring, these predictions *will* come; man has not reached the time of arrival *yet*. We simply choose not to take this dismal view.

problems gradually being solved, others being partially remedied, and others still eventually fading away. Science may bring constructive influences; many social scientists today are intent on applying their knowledge for the betterment of society. Will such efforts have *no* effects? Mechanical and social inventions will continue to be made. To link science and technology entirely with the destructive is to render the incomplete, one-sided picture. Constructive answers from many sources, then, are to be expected unless society takes Sorokin literally and merely waits for the sensate to finish (like a clock that must eventually unwind). Such a notion, however, is not convincing.

The Theory of Immanent Change.　Sorokin has rendered an important service in explaining the principle of immanent change to the past and present generations of sociologists and their students.[36] He may, however, have overemphasized the principle. This writer respectfully suggests that he did. One may say that the internal, self-determining properties of a social system are important in accounting for many changes in the system and in preventing other changes from occurring. It is quite another to declare that these immanent factors are *the* major sources of change, admitting only of some external influence. Socio-cultural systems are *open* ones, as leaders in systems theory such as von Bertalanffy and Buckley have explained (see Chapter 3). Indeed, many environmental factors will influence an ongoing socio-cultural system. A given system (as the family or school) will be affected by other systems and by the total society, by population factors, inventions, passage of new laws, interpretation of laws, and even by international influences.[37] Then, too, we would hold that Sorokin has considerably underestimated the influence of diffusion. Some diffusion may take place within the system as we shall see; but the diffusion of ideas and material objects from culture to culture as anthropologists have studied it over the years can be exceedingly important.

Linton declares:

[36] It is true, however (as Sorokin declares and Toynbee agrees), that the Chinese and other earlier writers called attention to the phenomenon of immanent change. Arnold J. Toynbee in Allen (ed.), *op. cit.*, pp. 85–86.

[37] American society, for example, was considerably affected by the external challenge of Sputnik I's launching during October, 1957. The impact of this Russian space satellite brought an invigoration to the American space program; caused the creation of the office of Science Advisor to the President of the United States; had varied effects on American education—it caused a tightening in education (harder work, removing frills, and the like) and increased the prestige of the fields of mathematics, physical science, and engineering; caused the passage of an important law (the National Defense Education Act of 1958) designed to strengthen education; and so on. The Sputnik *challenge*—for it was interpreted by the American people as precisely that—was keenly felt because of the existence at the time of a cold war.

> *The comparatively rapid growth of human culture as a whole has been due to the ability of all societies to borrow elements from other cultures and to incorporate them into their own. This transfer of culture elements from one society to another is known as* diffusion. *It is a process by which mankind has been able to pool its inventive ability.*[38]

Kroeber points out that culture is transmitted both geographically (by area—which is diffusion) and over time (which is tradition). He then states that "the total part played by diffusion in human culture is almost incredibly great." [39]

Hoebel, among others, makes the following point:

> *It is clear that cultures grow more through cross-fertilization and diffusion than in isolation through independent invention. . . . Isolated cultures invariably stagnate. . . . The peripheral cultures of the Australians, Tasmanians, Fuegians, and African Bushmen are all testimonials to the sterilizing effects of isolation.*[40]

In short, without outside culture contact most societies tend to stagnate. How is it, then, that so much change is alleged to come from the immanent, self-generating process?

Nor must we forget Linton's famous dictum to the effect that the vast majority (about 90 per cent) of changes in a society are due to diffusion, whereas only about 10 per cent of the new elements, *at most,* are derived from the members of a given society.[41] As an illustration of the power of diffusion he cites the now well-known description of the "average day of an average American." Most of the articles that the average American consumes or deals with were spread from outside the area.

Diffusion is affected, to be sure, by the receiving social system—being affected by the latters' values, emphases, and actions (especially actions of elite officials). Some ideas or articles, indeed, may not spread at all to some areas; the values or other cultural factors of some societies may be grossly incompatible. Yet, even after making an allowance for these influences, it appears that Sorokin has underestimated the importance of diffusion. Considering *all* the external influences on socio-cultural systems, we think that the immanent principle may have had undue emphasis and that some reassessment is in order.

As we see it, then, immanency may be overstated; it is not invalid. Socio-cultural systems do in part generate their own changes, and we

---

[38] Ralph Linton, *The Study of Man* (New York: D. Appleton-Century, 1936), p. 324.

[39] A. L. Kroeber, *Anthropology*, rev. ed. (New York: Harcourt, Brace, 1948), p. 412.

[40] E. A. Hoebel, *Man in the Primitive World* (New York: McGraw-Hill Book Co., Inc., 1958), p. 607.

[41] Linton, *op. cit.*, p. 325.

are indebted to Sorokin for pointing to this important factor. As he states it, a university will not develop into a corporation or a hospital because of its inherent nature. But systems are affected by many outer influences too, and this is what Sorokin has underestimated. Indeed, after logically setting forth the three alternative hypotheses of causes of change—external, immanent, and combined external-internal—we suggest that he may have erred in postulating the second one. Would he have done better to have selected the third? [42] We merely affirm that such influences as have been described tend to favor the third (combined external-internal) alternative. We, therefore, suggest that this matter should be reconsidered.

However the reader reacts to the preceding argument that external influences on socio-cultural systems (which are open systems) are more important than Sorokin posited in immanent theory, Sorokin has unquestionably opened up a significant and interesting issue: the relative importance of internal and external influences in causing institutional or total-system change. Empirical studies in this context of several dozen systems and subsystems would be expected to shed light on the issue. This writer does not know of many studies performed in this context. One ably executed modern study of this nature that illuminates external influences on a system is the study of the American public school performed by Robert E. Herriott and Benjamin J. Hodgkins for the U. S. Office of Education.[43] Herriott and Hodgkins (viewing the school as an open socio-cultural system) devote considerable attention to aspects of the school's environment such as regional, metropolitan, and social-class influences.[44] They relate the characteristics of

---

[42] Professor Robert M. MacIver criticized the theory of immanent change as follows:

> It is not enough . . . to regard a social organization as having its source of change within itself. The system A. we are told, is "destined to have a life career B.," and cannot have another for which it lacks potentiality. A criminal gang does not become a "society of real saints," nor does a state become a night club. But who can reckon the potentialities of a state—or even of a criminal gang? They are not inherent in the organization, the character of which can undergo almost any transformation according to the changing demands of its members, the external compulsions put upon them, and the environmental conditions to which they are subject. The future of a social organization is not inherent in the social organization as such, in the sense in which the future of an organism is inherent in the organism as such.

A review of *Social and Cultural Dynamics*, Vol. IV, in the *American Sociological Review*, Vol. 6 (1941), pp. 904–906.

[43] *Sociocultural Context and the American School: An Open-Systems Analysis of Educational Opportunity*, U. S. Department of Health, Education, and Welfare, Office of Education, Bureau of Research (Washington, D. C., January, 1969).

[44] *Ibid.*, Chaps. 5–7.

the school to the extent of modernity *of the environment.* Their over-all working hypothesis (stating that the more modern the socio-cultural context of the American public school, the more modern will be the organizational structure and functioning) is *generally* supported.[45] Certainly the external impact on the school is amply demonstrated. Similar studies of other subsystems or of total systems would of course be of value.

It is clear that developing nations are much affected by external influences. The industrialization program itself is imported, and many social subsystems are then likely to be much affected by the general social transformation that follows. Changes in the *family* subsystem (the institution that Sorokin gave as an example of immanent causation of change) are shown to be notable.[46] In fact, ongoing institutions in a society (whether traditional or advanced) affect each other considerably; they operate as a network. From the standpoint of an individual institution, therefore, the external influence tends to be sizeable.

In concluding this discussion of immanency we mention several points that need further exploration; so far as we are aware, little is known concerning them. First, it would seem that the more activist an influence in a society, the stronger will be the immanent influence; activism implies social self-direction. Efforts of leaders and others to guide and direct change will bring effects of this nature. Secondly, we reflect that Sorokin brilliantly called attention to the immanent principle in change, but he did little to supply details as to *how* the changes from within would occur. Moore [47] seems to have filled some gaps here, noting the role of tensions and strains in generating change. Empirical studies might supply further details of the inner dynamics of this process.[48] Finally, what kind of relationships exist, if any, between the external *and* the internal influences? Again, so far as we are aware, this represents unexplored territory.

The Principle of Limits. This principle is well stated, and our brief comment here consists of an extension of the remarks that we have made concerning immanent change; they must be carried over to the matter of limits. If change results from external factors to a greater

45 *Ibid.,* p. 20.

46 William J. Goode, "Industrialization and Family Change," Chapter 12 in Bert F. Hoselitz and Wilbert E. Moore (eds.), *Industrialization and Society* (Unesco, The Hague: Mouton, 1963).

47 Wilbert E. Moore, *Social Change* (Englewood Cliffs, N. J.: Prentice-Hall, Inc., 1963), pp. 10–11.

48 On this and allied matters this writer is indebted to Mr. Curt Craeger, graduate student, for helpful discussion.

extent than Sorokin believed, then these same external factors will bring even more variation than he predicted. We agree with Sorokin that incessantly varying recurrent processes are responsible for the phenomena of change; but the variation is likely to be even greater than he has postulated, if he has underplayed the external influences. Many factors external to the social system in question will have an impact on the system's development. History will in part repeat itself, but more and more we predict that it will *not* do so; it will not do so because more and more *other factors* influence the system.

Having criticized the *Social and Cultural Dynamics* at various points, we nevertheless pay tribute to it as a great work. It is indeed one of the most impressive macroscopic studies of socio-cultural change ever made. The lengthy consideration that we have given to this magnum opus is itself a measure of our high estimate of its importance. Sorokin asks the right questions.[49] Whether his principal explanatory answer— the theory of immanent change—is entirely valid or whether it under-estimates the external influences, the reader must judge.[50] Sorokin's presentation of the long view of change is at any rate something akin to the vista from a mountaintop.

ANNOTATED BIBLIOGRAPHY

Sorokin, Pitirim A., *Social and Cultural Dynamics,* 4 Vols. (New York: Ameri-can Book Co., 1937, 1941); *Social and Cultural Dynamics,* 1 Vol. abridg-ment (Boston: Porter Sargent, 1957).

> Whether one reads the full four volumes or the one-volume abridg-ment, it is a rewarding experience. It will be rewarding whether or not one accepts the author's conclusions. The theory of immanent change was underplayed for many years; it is an important idea even though Sorokin may have exaggerated it.

Sorokin, Pitirim A., "Sociology of Yesterday, Today, and Tomorrow," *Ameri-can Sociological Review,* Vol. 30, No. 6 (December, 1965), 833–843.

> Ideas concerning the state of sociology and things to come, which have a bearing on socio-cultural change. Sorokin believes that a synthesizing phase lies ahead. This is his presidential address before the American Sociological Association.

---

[49] Robert Bierstedt, in reviewing *Pitirim A. Sorokin in Review,* edited by P. J. Allen, has a similar reaction to Sorokin's writing. "Whatever one may think of his answers, no one can possibly doubt that he asks the right questions. He knows what sociology is. . . . We learn from Sorokin." A review of *Pitirim A. Sorokin in Review,* Allen (ed.), in *Social Forces,* Vol. 42, No. 2 (December, 1963), pp. 247–249.

[50] Sorokin, of course, may have the correct view here, and we may have erred. On the other hand, if it is *we* who have come to the more correct conclusion, we must acknowledge that we would undoubtedly not have done so if Sorokin had not written his work first. It is a clear-cut case of standing on the shoulders of a giant.

Allen, Philip J. (ed.), *Pitirim A. Sorokin in Review* (Durham, N. C.: Duke University Press, 1963).

> An enlightening volume. The chapters by Arnold Toynbee, Robert Merton and Bernard Barber, and Matilda White Riley and Mary Moore concern Sorokin's ideas on *change*. Toynbee's criticisms of the Sorokin *Dynamics* are the most judicious and convincing that this writer has seen. The Merton-Barber and Riley-Moore comments —concerning Sorokin's methodology and measurement—are eminently worthwhile. Sorokin weighs the criticisms in the final chapter.

Schneider, Louis, "Toward Assessment of Sorokin's View of Change," Chapter 15 in George K. Zollschan and Walter Hirsch (eds.), *Explorations in Social Change* (Boston: Houghton Mifflin Co., 1964).

> Further criticisms, in a somewhat philosophical vein. Again, Sorokin replies in a following chapter.

6

Theories of Change: Differentiation, Functionalism, and Functional Variants

In this chapter we shall discuss various theories of socio-cultural change espousing the approaches of social differentiation and structural functionalism. This will include the theories of Émile Durkheim, Robert M. MacIver, Talcott Parsons, several of Parsons' followers—notably Neil Smelser and Winston White—and, finally, several structural-functional variant theorists—namely, Wilbert E. Moore and Charles P. Loomis. The theories of change of these sociologists vary in some consequential respects, but they do nevertheless have a certain common core of interpretation.

ÉMILE DURKHEIM (1858–1917)

Émile Durkheim's ideas concerning socio-cultural change are largely contained in his *De La Division du Travail Social (On the Division of Labor in Society)*, which was first published in 1893 and went through a total of five editions. It was his first sociological publication. Durkheim's interest in social change at this time was to trace the development of social solidarity within human society. It was written in the pattern of the early evolutionists. As Nisbet declares, *On the Division of Labor in Society* can be placed "within the same realm occupied by, say, Comte on human knowledge, Marx on economic society, Morgan on kinship, and Tylor on religion." [1] After this publication it seems that Durkheim's concerns moved away from the larger patterns of evolution, and he was generally interested in relating social change to social order. His volume on the *Rules of the Sociological Method* (1895), his large monograph on *Suicide* (1897), and his *Elementary Forms of Religious Life* (1912) were major contributions. Even his works on education and other subjects have commanded considerable attention. Durkheim is also well known for his emphasis on the so-ciologistic (collective) view. In any case Durkheim's insights concerning social differentiation were clear-cut and succinct, and they opened up a basic and major approach toward the understanding of change in

[1] Robert A. Nisbet, *Social Change and History* (New York: Oxford University Press, 1969), p. 229.

society. It happens that these ideas can be discussed more briefly than in the case of Sorokin.

In *On the Division of Labor in Society,* Durkheim's main thesis is that there are two kinds of solidarity: *mechanical* and *organic.* The mechanical type is based on "states of conscience which are common to all the members of the same society." [2] In short, it is rooted in likenesses and collective sentiments.[3] The organic type, on the other hand, is brought about by the division of labor; it is based on differences and on the need of people for the goods and services of others.[4] Primitive societies tend to have a solidarity of the former type, advanced societies of the latter. With advanced societies, moreover, the division of labor is not just permitted; it is necessary. It always occurs. Societies having the organic type of solidarity show a significant disassociation between religion and law, and contractual law tends to become highly developed. As a society develops and as the division of labor steadily occurs, various results ensue: (1) Behavior results less from common beliefs and traditions and more and more on the basis of individual beliefs and tastes. (2) Social control is based less and less on the common views and "collective conscience"; it becomes less rigid and repressive and more individualistic with increased emphasis on contractual law. (3) Solidarity and social ties have less reference to the homogeneity of individuals and a unanimity of public opinion and a much greater reference to the division of labor and the need for one another and one another's services. (4) And political affairs are run less and less by the whole body of the group and more and more by specialized bureaus and officials—and with greater emphasis on contractual relationships.

Durkheim has postulated the division of labor, then, as an independent variable in the evolution of societies. As the society develops, the ties based on resemblances and common beliefs become loosened. If no other force were to take the place of the homogeneous ties, the system would fall apart. The division of labor, however, fills the vacuum, and becomes the principal social bond in more advanced societies. Durkheim expresses it this way:

[2] *On the Division of Labor in Society,* translation by George Simpson (New York: The Macmillan Company, 1933), p. 109.

[3] Durkheim declares: "Solidarity which comes from likenesses is at its maximum when the collective conscience completely envelops our whole conscience and coincides in all points with it. . . . The term *(mechanical solidarity)* does not signify that it is produced by mechanical or artificial means." *Ibid.,* p. 130.

[4] This type of solidarity, he observes, "resembles that which we observe among the higher animals. Each organ, in effect, has its special physiognomy, its autonomy. And, moreover, the unity of the organism is as great as the individuation of the parts is more marked. Because of this analogy, we propose to call the solidarity which is due to the division of labor, organic." *Ibid.,* p. 131.

> *In sum, since mechanical solidarity progressively becomes enfeebled, life properly social must decrease or another solidarity must slowly come in to take the place of that which has gone. . . . It will become still more evident that social solidarity tends to become exclusively organic. It is the division of labor which, more and more, fills the role that was formerly filled by the common conscience. It is the principal bond of social aggregates of higher types.[5]*

Then Durkheim addresses himself to the question of the cause of the appearance of the division of labor. At this point he considers the latter as a dependent variable. Disagreeing with the prevailing belief of his time that the quest for happiness [6] is the cause, he contends, on the contrary, that the latter must be sought in other variations of the social scene. He formulates the following proposition:

> *The division of labor varies in direct ratio with the volume and density of societies, and, if it progresses in a continuous manner in the course of social development, it is because societies become regularly denser and generally more voluminous.[7]*

Increasing population, therefore, is the general cause. This leads to an intensification of the struggle for life. If the population is large, many people have to be served, and to be a "jack of all trades" becomes more and more difficult. One almost has to specialize. The fields of business, the professions, and the trades become more involved. In order to compete satisfactorily one has to narrow one's sphere of operations. The increase in the density of population thus leads inevitably to an increase in the division of labor. The latter, moreover, has a moral character, and is set forth in the law. "If the division of labor produces solidarity," declares Durkheim, "it is not only because it makes each individual an 'exchangist' . . . ; it is because it creates among men an entire system of rights and duties which link them together in a durable way. . . . The division of labor gives rise to rules which assure pacific and regular concourse of divided functions." [8]

This treatise on social solidarity thus constitutes a significant theory of socio-cultural change. As societies grow in population, the nature of the solidarity changes from the *mechanical* type (dominated by a collective conscience) to the *organic* type (characterized by specialization, division of labor, and interdependence). Effects are then registered in behavior, customs, the law, public opinion, and government as noted. Durkheim states that in advanced societies it is the duty of

[5] *Ibid.,* p. 173.
[6] That is to say, mankind would be happier with greater production and a higher level of living. But Durkheim shows that material progress and civilization do not make people any happier.
[7] *Ibid.,* p. 262.
[8] *Ibid.,* p. 406.

people to concentrate and specialize. It is an illusion to believe that personality is "more complete" when the division of labor is less. Moreover, public sentiment, he declares,[9] opposes the dilettante who concerns himself only with general culture.

Comment Relative to the Durkheim Theory.

The principle that an important aspect of the change from primitive to civilized modes of social living is found in the increase in the amount of division of labor—in a word, specialization—is both basic and important. Are there any objections to it at all? Sorokin questions various assumptions and related statements associated with the division-of-labor theory:[10] For example, that if a society has little division of labor and greater emphasis on the moral conscience of the group, the law will be more repressive and punishments more cruel; that a greater division of labor results in more freedom, independence, and solidarity for the society; and that with an increase in division of labor the inheritance of social position and the caste principle invariably decrease. These all appear to be factually arguable. Certainly exceptions to the generalizations appear to exist. Our principal comment relates to the point that division of labor is itself explained on the basis of increasing population. Because this is a biosocial explanation, it is evident that nonsocial factors are involved, then, with a developing division of labor. Is it, moreover, as simple a matter as declaring that increasing population leads to greater density, to a greater struggle in living, and thence to increasing division of labor? It appears at the present time that population increase itself is a complicated matter—with class and other differences, with factors involved in migration, and with effects of other variables. Furthermore, one may ask if the division of labor is considerable in such highly populated societies as India and China. Again, we suggest that Durkheim oversimplified. Other variables would seem to have an influence. The theory has much merit, but it needed some refining, as indeed it was later refined.

Various research projects using the division-of-labor concept may be noted. Gibbs and Martin [11] have confirmed such certain anticipated correlates of the division of labor as urbanization and an efficient level of technology. Gibbs and Browning [12] have explored the relationship

[9] *Ibid.*, pp. 401–404.

[10] Pitirim A. Sorokin, *Contemporary Sociological Theories* (New York: Harper, 1928), p. 479. Sorokin discusses them at length in footnote 73.

[11] Jack P. Gibbs and Walter T. Martin, "Urbanization, Technology, and the Division of Labor: Further Evidence," *Pacific Sociological Review*, Vol. 7 (Spring, 1964), pp. 3–9.

[12] Jack P. Gibbs and Harley L. Browning, "The Division of Labor, Technology, and the Organization of Production in Twelve Countries," *American Sociological Review*, Vol. 31, No. 1 (February, 1966), pp. 81–92.

between division of labor, technology, and organization of production in 12 nations in North, Central, and South America (including the United States, but unfortunately excluding Brazil, Argentina, and Mexico because of unavailable data). They found that, consistent with expectations, the estimated size of productive associations did vary directly with the degree of division of labor in these nations. However, the division-of-labor variables were even more closely related to indicators of technological efficiency than to the estimated size of productive associations. They regarded their project as exploratory, however, because some of the measures employed were crude.[13]

A research area that bears promise relative to social differentiation and the division of labor has been suggested by the systems theorist, Ludwig von Bertalanffy.[14] General systems theory, he points out, is interested in the relative growth of components within a system over time. The Gibbs-Browning research project examined the size of productive associations in relation to the division of labor and technology in the Western Hemisphere. The idea suggested by von Bertalanffy was to compare such growth with that of other associations in various areas; and this would be performed over a period of time as the statistics of nations would permit. Some components might manifest only slight growth. The relative growth of components in American society could be assessed over the years in the general context of the sketches that were presented in Chapter 1 of this textbook. Measurement might be made, in short, of 1870, 1910, 1940, and the present; or, if preferred, other years could be selected. The measurement would need, however, to be more elaborately and more rigorously performed.

ROBERT M. MACIVER (1882–1970)

Because the late Professor MacIver was a productive writer (like Sorokin and Durkheim) it is necessary to concentrate on his contributions relative to socio-cultural change and momentarily ignore his various other volumes on sociology and political science except as they are relevant to the *change* subject.[15] Born in Stornoway, Scotland, and educated at Edinburgh University and at Oxford, MacIver taught at

13 *Ibid.*, p. 92.

14 *General System Theory* (New York: George Braziller, 1968), p. 103.

15 Again we are considering the ideas of an eminent figure who wrote a total of about twenty books. Among the more notable of these are *Social Causation* (1942); *The Web of Government* (1947; paper edition, 1965); *The More Perfect Union* (1949); *The Pursuit of Happiness* (1955); and *Power Transformed* (1964). See MacIver's comments regarding his own books in *As a Tale That Is Told: The Autobiography of R. M. MacIver* (Chicago: The University of Chicago Press, 1968), pp. 171–173.

Edinburgh University (1907–1914), the University of Toronto (1915–1927), and Columbia University (1928–1950); at the latter he was Lieber Professor of Political Philosophy and Sociology.[16] He was president of the American Sociological Association in 1939. MacIver's theory concerning socio-cultural change is found in *Society: Its Structure and Changes* (1931), Part Four; in *Society: An Introductory Analysis,* with Charles H. Page (1949), Book III, which was a rewriting and amplification of the earlier text; and in *Social Causation* (1942). It is of note that the subject of socio-cultural change occupies a prominent place in MacIver's over-all sociological system, as was the case with Sorokin.

In discussing social change, Professor MacIver emphasized the process of *social differentiation.* However, his manner of following Durkheim is affected in part by his general sociological orientation; moreover, MacIver had some other (not necessarily Durkheimian) ideas relative to social change. Social evolution is held to bring increasing specialization of organs and units within the society. A greater division of labor occurs as a result, and the number and type of institutions and associations multiply. Communal customs pass into differentiated communal institutions, which become embodied in differentiated associations.[17] As an illustration of the process, he describes the evolution of the church as a social form. Beginning cults lead to specific related institutions. Finally, religious associations—churches—are formed. However, this kind of evolution does not cover all of the society. The MacIver view is that only the part denoted as *civilization* (the utilitarian order of material instruments, techniques, and means to the ends, including organizations) evolves in this way. The remaining portion, *culture,* which is the realm of final valuations and the ends or goals of striving, does not advance unless the human spirit somehow is able to extend its scope or perfect its cultural achievements. MacIver and Page explain it as follows: "Our means of transportation grow constantly more swift and more efficient. They are vastly superior to those which the ancient Greeks employed. But can we say the same of our dramas and our sculptures, our conversation and our recreation? . . . Our plays are not necessarily better today because of the achievements of Shakespeare. There is no 'march' of culture." [18]

Following Durkheim, MacIver states that the phenomenon of social differentiation is best illustrated by the contrast between primitive and civilized society. Life in the former is undifferentiated and in the latter

[16] Following his retirement from the Sociology and Political Science Departments at Columbia, he became president (1963–1964) and then chancellor (1965–1966) at the New School for Social Research, New York City. He died on June 15, 1970.

[17] Robert M. MacIver and Charles H. Page, *Society: An Introductory Analysis* (New York: Rinehart and Co., 1949), p. 598.

[18] *Ibid.,* p. 500.

vastly ramified and proliferated. In the "great associations"—political, economic, and cultural—much differentiation within each structure has occurred. One consequence of this is the effect on social solidarity. In the primitive world solidarity is "natural," it is not deliberately willed; it is based on the social character of man and the unity of the closely knit group. In the conditions of modern civilization such solidarity is no longer attainable.[19] Social cohesion is looser, less profound, and more contractual, as Tönnies and Durkheim stated. Indeed, the individual has to choose his loyalties and decide his own attachments to a far greater degree.

Other Ideas and Relevant Perspectives. Several other basic ideas of MacIver have relevance to the study of change. These mainly concern his over-all ideas relative to sociological study—in particular, to differences between studying social and physical data. First, efforts to find causes of *social* phenomena involve different procedures from such efforts in the physical and biological realm; in the case of the former the socio-psychological nexus is involved. Indeed any social change that we seek to explain is meshed in a tangled web involving conditions within different orders of reality—the physical, biological, psychological, and social. Because of this complicated situation, some individuals are likely to jump to simple, one-factor explanations. Others may overemphasize their own order in suggesting explanations; MacIver cites Durkheim as one who tries to explain social phenomena exclusively in social terms, not leaving a "proper place" for biological and individual psychological factors.[20] Finally, the relation of phenomena to different orders of reality means that tracking down causes is a difficult matter. At the end of the effort to establish the cause of social phenomena one will still have just an approximation.[21] To find the whole truth—the quest for the specific why—is difficult.

In seeking social explanations, moreover, the researcher needs to use more than statistical analysis. Counting and measuring are only first steps. Correlations, trends, and periodicities give the external facts of behavior. They show how phenomena are related to other phenomena. But the researcher must look beyond these objective data, discover the

[19] "In the more advanced social system, with its specializations, its cultural diversities, its numerous groups and associations, its mingling of many elements into a complex whole, we cannot expect to find the all-embracing solidarity of a simpler society." *Ibid.*, p. 634.

[20] Sorokin's criticisms of Durkheim are similar. See Pitirim A. Sorokin, *Contemporary Sociological Theories* (New York: Harper, 1928), pp. 466–467 and 476.

[21] ". . . causal discovery in the social sciences is often insecure, generally incomplete, and at best approximate." MacIver, *Social Causation* (New York: Ginn & Co., 1942), p. 378.

meaning of the correlations, and understand the processes involved. It is here that the social scientist will probably have only approximate results. It must also be kept in mind that even high correlations do not mean that causation has been established.

The organizing principle for *social* causation, he holds, is the *dynamic assessment* of the situation. Here all the factors determining conscious behavior are brought to a focus. This is the moment of decision and the confronting of alternatives. This applies not only to individual people but to groups; it is "interindividual," to use MacIver's term.[22] This dynamic assessment takes note of objective conditions, and it also considers the inner, subjective ideas of people. To omit the latter, says MacIver, is to miss a most significant part of the content of human relationships.

Comment on the MacIver Views. The *social differentiation* emphasis calls for little comment. MacIver has refined the ideas of Tönnies and Durkheim in describing how customs change into differentiated communal institutions and thence into differentiated associations. He has made clear that the instrumental, means-to-ends, and organizational elements are altered in this fashion; the final valuations and goals do not so change. MacIver gives some apt illustrations of communal customs differentiating into institutions and associations. In general, he has followed an eminently acceptable view of change. The discussion of the "Quest of the Specific Why" is convincing. His role of the *precipitant* in change, motives in relation to causation, and the principle of responsibility are reasonable. His statement of the role of inner psychological factors (as well as external ones) in social causation was controversial during earlier years, but this has been generally resolved in MacIver's favor. Many, although not all, sociologists have agreed with his insistence that social causation differs significantly from physico-biological causation in the fact that the former involves the psychological nature of man. The problem was to reconcile the use of inner, subjective factors with the principles of scientific method. At any rate, the issue was resolved logically: The hopes, ambitions, and feelings of people must be dealt with factually (objectively), and such data must be amenable to scientific treatment. Sociology has made steady progress in the objective analysis of attitudes and other subjective elements.[23] It has accomplished much since MacIver stated his ideas in the first textbook on *Society* (1931). Treating subjective data objectively in the causation process will sometimes be difficult. Prob-

[22] *Ibid.*, p. 374.
[23] This subject will be discussed in further detail in Chapter 9, "The Measurement of Change."

ably few sociologists today, however, are so "objectified" in their thinking that they would wish to dispense with this element altogether.[24]

As to other points, we express agreement with MacIver relative to the following: (1) Establishing social causation, hence denoting explanations of change, is often difficult inasmuch as it relates to different orders of reality. (2) In view of the foregoing, the final explanation of causation will be approximate. (3) Social science does need to go beyond correlations and other statistical data in the quest for causation; correlations need to be made meaningful, and underlying processes have to be understood. (4) The primary organizing principle in understanding social causation lies with the *dynamic assessment* of the situation. The preceding may be seen in many examples. These principles seem to comprise meaningful and important keys to the understanding of changing situations.

MacIver's ideas seem to wear well. They show balance and maturity of judgment. The *Social Causation* is undoubtedly more highly esteemed today by sociologists than at the time it was published. The publishing of the paper edition in 1964 is mainly responsible for this, but for some reason sociologists lagged in showing appreciation of this work. His contrasts of the inner and outer orders of human reality and his emphasis upon the vast web of relationships convey the feeling of the complicated social order as well as any. Then, in conclusion, we would mention Professor MacIver's clear, unusually attractive, and smoothly flowing style of writing.[25] The ideas themselves are necessarily the vital consideration and the mode of expression secondary. Nevertheless, when ideas are unusually well expressed, one is duly grateful and full of admiration.

TALCOTT PARSONS (1902–   )

With respect to socio-cultural change, Talcott Parsons resembles MacIver in that he generally follows the viewpoint of social differentiation, while maintaining other views toward *change* that reflect his over-all position in sociology. These other views are, however, different from those of MacIver. But Parsons differs from MacIver with regard to the importance of the *change* subject: The former's interest in this subject has been less dominant than was the case with MacIver—and

---

[24] It seems likely that this represents a considerable change in perspective on the part of the average sociologist as compared with a generation ago.

[25] Professor Harry Alpert has written "He [MacIver] has positively demonstrated that sociological writing can be beautiful, clear, artistic, and literate." "Robert M. MacIver's Contributions to Sociological Theory," Chapter 13 in M. Berger, T. Abel, and Charles H. Page (eds.), *Freedom and Control in Modern Society* (New York: D. Van Nostrand, 1954), pp. 286–287.

Sorokin. Indeed Parsons has been criticized for his slight attention to change. His emphasis on the social structure and on the maintenance of equilibrium has brought forth the comment that his theory over-emphasizes statics, although, as we will see, he rejects this charge. Whatever one may say about the Parsonian emphasis or lack of emphasis on change,[26] one notes his statement that any sociological system must account for change as well as for the existing social structure. Because Parsons is a sociologist of high productivity and one whose views have grown over the years, he may yet come to place greater emphasis on changing society. However, his advancing age now might prevent this.

Born in Colorado Springs, Colorado, Talcott Parsons attended Amherst College (A.B., 1924), the London School of Economics (1924–1925), and earned his Ph.D. at Heidelberg (1927). He taught economics at Amherst (1926–1927) and Harvard (1927–1931), and then turned to the field of sociology. Remaining at Harvard, he went through the ranks, becoming a full professor in 1944. He is the author of *The Structure of Social Action* (1937), *The Social System* (1951), *Economy and Society,* with Neil J. Smelser (1956), *Societies: Evolutionary and Comparative Perspectives* (1966), and many other books. He is another sociologist who has written about twenty books. He was president of the American Sociological Society in 1949. During the past generation Parsons has evoked the attention and interest of large numbers of sociologists in the subject of sociological theory.[27] Indeed this past generation might be characterized as the "Parsons generation" in American sociology, which pays a considerable tribute to him.

Structural Differentiation

Parsons has indicated repeatedly that his views concerning socio-cultural change are centered on the theory of structural differentiation.

---

[26] This writer agrees with Nisbet that Parsons (like Durkheim) is essentially interested in order *and* change. It just happens that Parsons' own efforts have largely related to the existing order (structure). Nisbet, *op. cit.,* p. 228. One can say of course, as Parsons has, that knowledge of structure is a necessary prelude to the analysis of change. *The Social System* (Glencoe, Ill.: The Free Press, Inc., 1951), pp. 483 and 486.

[27] Parsonian theory has been dominant in American sociology during this period, but it has also received major criticisms. See D. Martindale, *The Nature and Types of Sociological Theory* (Boston: Houghton Mifflin Co., 1966), and N. S. Timasheff, *Sociological Theory,* 3rd ed. (New York: Random House, 1967). For recent vigorous criticism, including the charge that functionalism has failed to explain why social changes occur, see George C. Homans, "Bringing Men Back In," *American Sociological Review,* Vol. 29, No. 6 (December, 1964), pp. 809–818. See also, Walter Buckley, *Sociology and Modern Systems Theory* (Englewood Cliffs, N. J.: Prentice-Hall, Inc., 1967), Chap. 2.

In his first major publication, *The Structure of Social Action*,[28] he discusses Durkheim's ideas at length—along with those of Max Weber, Pareto, and Alfred Marshall—although he was not concerned with the division of labor here. Parsons has used the approach of structural differentiation in analyzing such diverse subjects as economic institutions and their relationship to the total social system,[29] modern industrial (bureaucratic) organization,[30] and the separation of functions in the American farm family.[31] Concerning the first, Parsons and Smelser view the economy as a subsystem differentiated from other subsystems of a society. It is a special case of the general theory of the social system. Total societies differentiate into subsystems that specialize in various functional exigencies: adaptive functions (economy), goal attainment (government or polity), the integrative functions, pattern maintenance (the family), and so on. The economy becomes further differentiated into subsystems: production finance and capitalization, entrepreneurship, and economic commitments.[32] Each is examined in detail and illustrated with charts. Structural changes in the American economy, such as the separation of ownership and control, are noted. A model of institutional change is stated, showing (1) dissatisfactions with the existing situation, (2) experimentation with ways of making changes, (3) the establishment of the organizational innovation that seems to deal satisfactorily with the situation, and (4) establishing patterns of sanctions that back up the new practice.[33]

Other examples of the Parsonian treatment of change are similar, hence they can be discussed briefly. In seeking to account for the emergence of modern industrial structure, Parsons is interested in the family business firm and its emancipation (in the sense of structural differentiation) from the political system.[34] Anything approaching full bureaucratic organization independent of the political structure and the church, says Parsons, did not exist before the nineteenth century.[35] The social structure was heavily oriented to ascription of status, hence kinship factors were consequential. With the emergence of larger-scale units, such as factories, the lower levels of employment become more

28 (New York: McGraw-Hill Book Co., Inc., 1937).

29 Talcott Parsons and Neil J. Smelser, *Economy and Society* (Glencoe, Ill.: The Free Press, Inc., 1956).

30 Talcott Parsons, *Structure and Process in Modern Societies* (New York: The Free Press of Glencoe, Inc., A Division of The Macmillan Company, 1960), Chap. 3.

31 Talcott Parsons, "Some Considerations on the Theory of Social Change," *Rural Sociology*, Vol. 26, No. 3 (September, 1961), pp. 219–239.

32 Parsons and Smelser, *op. cit., Economy and Society,* p. 196.

33 *Ibid.,* pp. 267–271.

34 Parsons, *op. cit., Structure and Process in Modern Societies,* p. 108 ff.

35 *Ibid.,* p. 110.

achievement-oriented; the ascribed kinship component, then, was at the top, bringing an unstable arrangement. As the corporation developed further and became disassociated from the private property interests of the owning kinship lineage, the important change was made of a fiduciary board of directors to replace the legitimate owning lineage. Although elected by stockholders, the directors have the *real control* of managing other people's money. Moreover, business management has become more professional.[36]

Then, finally, the separation of functions in the American farm family shows a similar process, hence we can comment quite briefly. Before discussing this illustration, however, Parsons systematically reviews the process of structural differentiation as one type of change in social systems.[37] He then shows the differentiation of collectivities in which the farm family shifts to the urban occupational pattern. The occupational role is separated from the kinship group in which the individual's personal security and consuming interests are anchored. The process is now familiar. The new role subserves a higher-order function than the old. Differentiation is a process of emancipation from the former ascriptive ties. Again, successful differentiation has taken the following steps: (1) A need factor (that is, some dissatisfactions) is present; (2) experimentation is tried in the effort to find an answer to the situation; (3) facilities that previously were ascribed to less differentiated units are now freed and made available for use in the new higher-order units; (4) new collectivity structures are established; and (5) legal and other norms are developed to back up the new arrangement.[38] The values of the new system are different from those of the original unit.

Elsewhere Parsons has affirmed that the division of labor tends to bring freedom from ascriptive ties. Moreover, he notes Durkheim's view that technological innovations nearly always lead to an increasingly more elaborate division of labor and a concomitant more-elaborate social organization.[39] He hails Durkheim's insight that "a whole complex of institutionalized norms must be established as a condition of the stability of a functionally differentiated system." [40] On the other hand, Parsons observed that Durkheim did not distinguish between

36 *Ibid.*, p. 114.

37 Parsons, *op. cit.*, "Some Considerations on the Theory of Social Change," pp. 219–226.

38 *Ibid.*, 235–236.

39 Talcott Parsons, *The Social System* (Glencoe, Ill.: The Free Press, Inc., 1951), p. 507.

40 Talcott Parsons, "Durkheim's Contribution to the Theory of Integration of Social Systems," in Kurt H. Wolff (ed.), *Émile Durkheim, 1858–1917: A Collection of Essays* (Columbus: Ohio State University Press, 1960), p. 138.

the levels of generality achieved by the cultural patterns—values, norms, collectivities, and roles.[41] Societal values have the highest level of generality, declares Parsons. Then come (in order) the norms, collectivities, and roles.

Before turning to certain of Parsons' general ideas concerning sociocultural change, comment should be made of contributions using the approach of structural differentiation on the part of certain of Parsons' followers, Neil J. Smelser and Winston White. Professor Smelser's *Social Change in the Industrial Revolution* [42] uses the model of structural differentiation to examine changes occurring in the British Industrial Revolution between 1770 and 1840. He focuses attention particularly on the growth of the cotton industry and the transformation of the family structure of the working class. Smelser summarizes the model of structural differentiation as follows:

> *The model of structural differentiation is an abstract theory of change. When one social role or organization becomes archaic under changing historical circumstances, it differentiates by a definite and specific sequence of events into two or more roles or organizations which function more effectively in the new historical circumstances. The new social units are structurally distinct from each other, ... The differentiation of an economy's distribution system into "retail" and "wholesale" is an example. . . . Any sequence of differentiation is set in motion by specific disequilibrating conditions. Initially this disequilibrium gives rise to symptoms of social disturbance which must be brought into line later by mechanisms of social control. Only then do specific ideas, suggestions, and attempts emerge to produce the more differentiated social units.*[43]

Observing that the model can be used for many types of social structures—the economy, family, class system, and others—Smelser examines the cotton industry in England and the family economy because of the rapid and dramatic changes in these phenomena and because he wishes to apply the structural-differentiation theory to the familiar happenings of the Industrial Revolution. He outlines seven steps by which the structural-differentiation process occurs: [44] (1) There is dissatisfaction with the goal achievements of the social system in question and there is the feeling of an opportunity for change with the available facilities; (2) symptoms of disturbance are shown in the "unjustified" negative emotional reactions and "unrealistic" aspirations of the people in the system; (3) a covert handling of these tensions

---

[41] *Ibid.*, p. 42.

[42] Neil J. Smelser, *Social Change in the Industrial Revolution* (Chicago: University of Chicago Press, 1959). This is based on his doctoral dissertation at Harvard.

[43] *Ibid.*, p. 2.

[44] *Ibid.*, pp. 15–16.

and an attempt to realize the implications of the existing value system occurs; (4) there is an encouragement of new ideas; (5) positive attempts are made to attain new ideas and institutional patterns that will become objects of commitments; (6) the responsible implementation of innovations is carried out by persons or collectivities that are either rewarded or punished in terms of the existing value system; and (7) if the implementations of step (6) are received favorably, they are gradually routinized into usual patterns of performance and sanction.

We are not so much concerned with Smelser's detailed results except to say that major changes in the roles of labor and of family structure did occur, and to note that new social units (trade unions, cooperative stores, savings banks) were created in the proliferation process that is the essence of the structural-differentiation theory.[45]

Winston White is concerned with a vastly different subject—conformity.[46] Intellectuals have maintained that American values have changed during the past generation from an emphasis on freedom to one on security; from the Protestant ethic (hard work, self-reliance, thrift) to a social ethic; from the goals of inner-direction to the approval seeking of other-direction. White rejects the interpretation of this presumed change as stated by the intellectuals: namely, that pressures for conformity have stifled individualities, and that the newer, inferior conformity values operate as a social Gresham's law in driving out the good.[47]

Briefly, White feels that the preceding value change has occurred, but he explains it on the basis of the theory of structural differentiation. The intellectual ideologies are reacting to the strain in modern times of greater demands on personality development. In the differentiated society each individual plays an increasing number of roles, and he can no longer be guided by the same patterns of behavior characteristic of the ascribed society. Even though conformity may be of the approval-seeking type—it may also be of the type bringing uniformity of behavior, he says—this is likely to decrease as behavior is increasingly emancipated from the former ascriptive ties. Moreover, as the society continues its development [48] and as human resources and

45 George C. Homans commends the Smelser treatment, but argues that the latter used functional theory only as window dressing; the "real" explanation of change (as revealed in the seven steps) lies in psychological factors, he asserts. Homans, *op. cit.*, pp. 815–817. Others might retort, on the other hand, that the Homans views are "*overly* psychological."

46 *Beyond Conformity* (New York: The Free Press of Glencoe, Inc., A Division of The Macmillan Company, 1961).

47 *Ibid.*, Chaps. 1–2 and pp. 70–72.

48 *Ibid.*, p. 160. The development, says White, will be along the lines indicated in W. W. Rostow's *The Stages of Economic Growth* (Cambridge, England: Cambridge University Press, 1960).

education are further emphasized, the other-directed type of conformity will become less evident.

Other Parsonian Ideas Concerning Change

Parsons has expounded certain general ideas concerning change, most of which ensue, however, from his sociological system. The following can be mentioned briefly: (1) He declares that there are two broad ways of considering social change: change *of* systems as systems and accounting for changes *within* some system. He believes that explaining the former is not possible given the present state of sociological knowledge. The latter may be assayed, however, and one must show why, given relevant conditions, the constant pattern of some system is altered over a specified period of time. Thus there is always an initial and a terminal pattern as points of reference, and one must account for alterations that have occurred during the time period.[49] (2) The occurrence of change involves the overcoming of resistances. Vested interests are especially important; they tend to be derived from the processes of equilibrium in a boundary-maintaining type of system.[50] (3) Once a change is made, a significant matter concerns the tracing of repercussions of the change throughout the social system. Finally (4) Parsons recognizes that certain factors of the social system tend to produce changes. These are mainly (a) inherent tendencies to deviation, (b) imperfections of the integration of value orientations, and (c) positively institutionalized sources of change, such as a commitment to a cultural configuration.[51] If the latter emphasizes achievement and universalistic orientation, the impetus toward change is likely to be considerable. The obvious example of this, declares Parsons, is science with its technological applications.[52]

Comment and Criticisms

Parsons has been mainly concerned with constructing and refining general sociological theory at the higher level of generality—a considerable task. Our principal comment relative to his ideas concerning social

---

[49] Parsons, *The Social System, op. cit.,* pp. 482–483.

[50] *Ibid.,* p. 491.

[51] Talcott Parsons and Edward A. Shils (eds.), *Toward A General Theory of Action* (Cambridge, Mass.: Harvard University Press, 1951), pp. 231–232.

[52] We remind the reader that we discussed Parsons' neoevolutionary ideas, as stated in the "Evolutionary Universals in Society," *American Sociological Review,* Vol. XXIX, No. 3 (June, 1964), pp. 339–357, and in his *Societies: Evolutionary and Comparative Perspectives* (1966), in Chapter 3. Further comment is not deemed necessary.

change has been partly expressed before: namely, he has not been a major contributor to *this* subject. We have cited his studies of the structural differentiation of economic institutions, of modern industrial (bureaucratic) organization, and of the American farm family. These bring improvements, in our judgment, to the social-differentiation theory of Durkheim. Yet it is clear that such studies do not constitute a significant new lead or a major contribution otherwise to social dynamics. It appears that Parsons has interest in both order *and* change, but also that he is mainly attracted to the "statics" of the social structure so far as his own writing is concerned.

Let it be recorded that the elaborate Parsonian discussions of types of social structure, the pattern variables, and the functional needs of social systems, as well as other matters, are highly relevant for social change to be sure. Cultural values affect such major processes as industrialization, invention, and diffusion in basic ways. Nonetheless, while explaining these elements of the social structure, often in a sterling manner, Parsons has not seen fit to extend and apply them in a major way to the *changing* social system. He has outlined such application;[53] but he has not applied them to the subject of social change in any major work. One could say, then, that Parsons has made major contributions to sociological theory in general but not to social change. Some might phrase it that if Parsons has a magnum opus (*The Social System* or another volume), it again would *not* be classified in the field of social change. Some critics [54] would want to go further. They would maintain that his emphases relative to the social structure actually impede the analysis of social change. Many sociologists believe that Parsonian theory *in toto* underplays social dynamics.

His use of the equilibrium model has been widely discussed. Does this model bring a bias favoring "social statics"? Parsons declares that the concept of equilibrium is a corollary of that of the social system itself. A continuing stability, whether it be static or a "moving stability in change," is found. Thus, equilibrium essentially means "regularity under specified conditions," although some variation within a range of tolerance may be present. Parsons gives the illustration (from physiology) of the relatively constant body temperature and to Cannon's concept of homeostasis. He maintains, at any rate, that no static bias is necessarily postulated; at the same time he holds that socio-cultural systems tend to maintain a continuing stability (or relative equilib-

---

53 For example, in *The Social System, op. cit.,* Chap. XI.
54 See W. Buckley, *Sociology and Modern Systems Theory* (Englewood Cliffs, N. J.: Prentice-Hall, Inc., 1967), Chap. 2. We shall not repeat the various Buckley arguments here. Nor shall we restate the Coser and Dahrendorf contentions concerning the neglect of conflict processes (which were discussed in Chapter 4).

rium) unless affected by some outside force. However, it seems that social forms and systems develop immanently to some extent even if external influences are constant (which they are not likely to be); also, the population is gradually aging, birth and death rates may change, resources may be gradually depleted, and so forth. Life and society are evidently always in flux, and this view (emphasizing inevitable change) seems preferable to one that posits an initial equilibrium to remain constant unless disturbed by specific forces. Sympathetic as we are to many of the Parsonian views, we suggest in this case that the equilibrium model does bear a certain bias toward staticism.[55]

Structural-Functional Variants: Moore and Loomis

Because Parsons has not devoted major attention to socio-cultural change thus far, and because some of his followers have much interest in it, these other structural functionalists have inevitably spoken out concerning the subject. In particular, we would single out for attention the ideas of Wilbert E. Moore and Charles P. Loomis.

Wilbert E. Moore. Professor Moore, a former student of both Sorokin and Parsons at Harvard, mixes an interest in social change with comparative institutions and industrial sociology. Moore is a leading figure in the study of social change on the current scene; he is a recent president of the American Sociological Association. We have already noted Moore's views favoring the doctrine of immanent change; his calling attention to inherent strains in societies as likely areas of change; his emphasis on society as a tension-management system rather than as a self-equilibrating one; and his espousal of the significance of unattained ideals (where a lack of correspondence exists between the *ideal* and the *actual* state of affairs) as a source of change. Because this was discussed previously we shall be brief here.

At this particular juncture we are especially interested in Moore as a modifier of the Parsonian equilibrium theory. Moore believes that this is best replaced with the tension-management view, with which this writer concurs. Indeed Moore's *Social Change*,[56] although a volume of only 118 pages, is probably the best single statement of the structural-

[55] See the discussion of this model by Robin Williams, Jr., Black, and Parsons in Max Black (ed.), *The Social Theories of Talcott Parsons* (Englewood Cliffs, N. J.: Prentice-Hall, Inc., 1961). Williams (pp. 89–90) and Black (pp. 274–276) believe that the equilibrium notion emphasizes staticism, but Parsons disputes the criticism. In the final chapter ("The Point of View of the Author") Parsons states that, "On this point I have thus remained completely unimpressed by the barrage of persistent criticism." (pp. 337–338).

[56] (Englewood Cliffs, N. J.: Prentice-Hall, Inc., 1963).

functional perspective on change.[57] Moore has also written various high-quality articles on social change.[58] Furthermore, he has been active in the measurement and monitoring of social change, and we shall be interested in his contributions on that subject in Chapter 9. Finally, Moore has been a leader in the study of developing nations; [59] in Chapter 14 we shall assess his ideas on that subject. Moore's total contribution to the study of social change, then, is very diversified. His general productivity during the years, including his contributions to industrial sociology, has been impressive.

Charles P. Loomis.   Professor Loomis is also a former student of Sorokin and Parsons. Loomis has been a professor of sociology at Michigan State University for many years (and for much of this time was chairman of the sociology department). He has written many books, of which the most relevant for socio-cultural change are *Social Systems* [60] and, with Zona Loomis, *Modern Social Theories.*[61] Starting with the social-action and social-system emphases, Loomis nevertheless strikes out anew in setting forth a new scheme for understanding both social structure and social change. This formulation is called the Processually Articulated Structural Model (PASM). It consists of nine elements [62] that, whether one is considering a total society (called a master system) or a subsystem, comprise the system. Then nine processes [63] articulate the elements; of the nine, six are designated as comprehensive or master processes [64] that involve several or even all elements. Using this model Loomis examines various social systems:

57 This is also the opinion of Nisbet. See Nisbet, *op. cit.*, p. 236.

58 "Theories of Social Change," *American Sociological Review,* Vol. 25, No. 6 (December, 1960), 810–817; "Predicting Discontinuities in Social Change," *American Sociological Review,* Vol. 29, No. 3 (June, 1964), 331–338 (this was the written statement of the MacIver Award Lecture for 1964); and "The Utility of Utopias," *American Sociological Review,* Vol. 31, No. 6 (December, 1966), 765–772 (this was the presidential address delivered before the American Sociological Association in August, 1966).

59 Moore's Chapter Five in the *Social Change* is the best brief statement on modernization that this writer has seen. He and Bert F. Hoselitz have also edited the *Industrialization and Society* (The Hague: Unesco, Mouton, 1963).

60 (Princeton, N. J.: D. Van Nostrand Co., 1960).

61 (Princeton, N. J.: D. Van Nostrand Co., 1961) See especially the final chapter.

62 These elements are belief, sentiment, end or goal, norm, status role, rank, power, sanction, and facility.

63 The processes are cognitive mapping and validation, tension management, goal attainment, evaluation, status-role performance, evaluation of actors, decision making, application of sanctions, and utilization of facilities. Thus they relate to the elements.

64 The master processes consist of communication, boundary maintenance, systemic linkage, socialization, social control, and institutionalization.

systems under stress (disasters), religious systems, the Amish, educational systems, and health systems.

Loomis' model, pointing to significant elements and processes that need to be considered in understanding social systems, seems well considered. Somehow one is not clear as to the results that might be obtained by its use in studying change. Many would see the importance of a theory in relation to its ability to illuminate arrays of facts in a given area. This writer prefers to withhold judgment on PASM until further research and perhaps theoretical refinements have been made; in particular this writer would like to see research uses of PASM demonstrated in studying socio-cultural change.

Loomis has recognized that both immanent and external factors are important in the changes of social systems.[65] He generally ignores broad cultural change (as did Parsons and Moore). The question may be raised as to whether Loomis, given his interest, still includes all significant processes. Alvin L. Bertrand has suggested that a tenth element should be added to PASM, namely, stress-strain. Then a tenth process would also be added—Bertrand calls this disorganization-distintegration—and he recommends that a seventh "master process" be added (social change itself).[66] This amendment is desirable as this writer sees it; it fits in well, incidentally, with Moore's view of strains in the system as a source of change. If both culture and social system are to be emphasized, then certain cultural processes—such as innovation and diffusion—would unquestionably need to be added to his model.

Summary

In this chapter theories emphasizing *social differentiation* have been examined. Whatever the relative contributions made by different sociologists (Durkheim's is unquestionably the greatest), this is a basic and notable perspective concerning social change. Most of the theories have maintained the social-system view. These theories have varied in numerous ways, but, by and large, the branching out (proliferation) of the social system has been emphasized. Specifically, we have reviewed and criticized the theories of Émile Durkheim, Robert M. MacIver, Talcott Parsons, and, more briefly, those of Neil J. Smelser, Winston

---

[65] *Social Systems, op. cit.*, pp. 40–44; see also, Loomis, "Social Change and Social Systems," found in Edward A. Tiryakian (ed.), *Sociological Theory, Values, and Sociocultural Change* (New York: The Free Press of Glencoe, Division of The Macmillan Company, 1963), especially p. 185.

[66] "The Stress-Strain Element of Social Systems: A Micro Theory of Conflict and Change," *Social Forces*, Vol. 42, No. 1 (October, 1963), 1–9.

White, Wilbert E. Moore, and Charles P. Loomis. Beginning with Parsons, the *differentiation* perspective is merged with the views of structural functionalism. Although we believe that Professor Moore has thus far made the ablest exposition of *change* from this perspective, it must be said that a full-scale, definitive statement of the functional view toward change remains to be made.

In the next chapter we turn to theories emphasizing economic and technological causation.

ANNOTATED BIBLIOGRAPHY

Durkheim, Émile, *On The Division of Labor in Society,* translated by George Simpson (New York: The Macmillan Company, 1933).
> A classic. This volume pioneered a fundamental and valued perspective on change.

MacIver, Robert M., *Social Causation* (New York: Ginn & Co., 1942; Harper Torchbook edition, 1964).
> Excellent on the causes of change. This book, which received little attention when first published, may be on its way to becoming a classic. It represents nonmechanistic thinking. The role of the precipitant idea may be further developed.

For the Parsonian ideas on change, *see*

Parsons, Talcott, *The Social System* (New York: The Free Press of Glencoe, Inc., 1951), Chap. XI; Talcott Parsons and Neil J. Smelser, *Economy and Society* (New York: The Free Press, Division of The Macmillan Company, 1956; Free Press paperback edition, 1965), especially Chap. V. Also see Neil J. Smelser, *Social Change in the Industrial Revolution* (Chicago: University of Chicago Press, 1959).
> Modern refinements on the theory of structural differentiation. Well considered; but Parsons' major contribution relates to the analysis of social structure rather than to accounting for change.

For Criticisms of the Parsonian ideas, see

Black, Max (ed.), *The Social Theories of Talcott Parsons* (Englewood Cliffs, N. J.: Prentice-Hall, Inc., 1961).
> These criticisms by a group of Cornell professors are generally relevant to socio-cultural change. Worthwhile reading. Parsons answers back in the final chapter.

Buckley, Walter, *Sociology and Modern Systems Theory* (Englewood Cliffs, N. J.: Prentice-Hall, Inc., 1967), especially Chap. 2.
> An indictment of Parsons' equilibrium-function model. Even though some of the points have been made previously (for example, that Parsons has overemphasized adjustment to the existing system and underplayed the factors of deviance and strains), Buckley's arguments

form a base for contending that the Parsonian model has grave difficulty in dealing with social change.

Homans, George C., "Bringing Men Back In." *American Sociological Review,* Vol. 29, No. 6 (December, 1964), 809–818.

Vigorous criticisms of structural functionalism. Homans charges that functionalism has failed to explain why changes occur. He would accent psychological factors. Some might hold that he (Homans) has accented the latter *too much.*

Concerning Functional Variations

Moore, Wilbert E., *Social Change* (Englewood Cliffs, N. J.: Prentice-Hall, Inc., 1963).

Moore prefers the view of society as a tension-management rather than as a self-equilibrating system. An able, although rather brief, statement.

Loomis, Charles P., *Social Systems* (Princeton, N. J.: D. Van Nostrand Co., 1960).

Loomis presents the Processually Articulated Structural Model (PASM) as a means of understanding social structure and change. Although systematic and indeed elaborate, time will have to tell regarding its usefulness in guiding research.

7

Theories of Change: Economic and Technological

In this chapter we shall concentrate on theories having an economic or technological orientation. Some limitation is, once again, necessary for reasons of space. Of the many theories that might be reviewed and evaluated we have selected those of Karl Marx, Thorstein Veblen, and William F. Ogburn.

KARL MARX (1818–1883)

The intellectual accomplishments of Karl Marx may be divided into (1) contributions to economic theory, (2) contributions to sociological theory, and (3) endeavors connected with scientific socialism as an action program. In this volume we are not concerned with (1) and (3); and, even with regard to his sociological theory, we shall restrict our interest to socio-cultural change.[1] Having this limitation of interest we can obviously be briefer in discussing the ideas of Marx than would otherwise be the case. Even so, Marx ought not receive too scanty a treatment. Frederick C. Mills' observation that Marx cannot be ignored by the student of social change any more than he can be by the student of economics, is well expressed.[2] Moreover, few question that Marx possessed one of the great minds among those who have examined and sought explanations of socio-economic questions—whatever else one may say about him. Harris comments that "probably no one since Christ has affected the course of history and influenced the world of ideas more than this brilliant, original, erratic, and vituperative bourgeois."[3] Parsons[4] observes that Pareto, Durkheim, and Max Weber

[1] Most academicians have tended to place Marx as an economist primarily, although Seymour E. Harris (himself an economist) has described him as "economist, philosopher, historian, political theorist, and, above all, sociologist." A review of Clinton Rossiter's *Marxism* in *The New York Times, Book Review* (October 9, 1960). Joseph A. Schumpeter is among those who have effectively distinguished between Marx the economist, Marx the sociologist, Marx the prophet, and so on. See *Capitalism, Socialism, and Democracy*, 3rd ed. (New York: Harper, 1950).

[2] Introductory Comments at Round Table Commemorating the Centenary of the Communist Manifesto, *American Economic Review*, Vol. 39 (1949), 13. Dr. Mills was chairman of the Round Table.

[3] Harris, *loc. cit.*

[4] Talcott Parsons, "Social Classes and Class Conflict in the Light of Recent Sociological Theory," *American Economic Review*, Vol. 39 (1949), 16–17.

were profoundly concerned with the problems raised by Marx and took the Marxian view most seriously—even if none of them ended up as a Marxist. Indeed, over the decades thousands of economists, sociologists, and other social scientists and social thinkers have grappled with Marx's views—with reactions ranging from high enthusiasm to utter disbelief.[5] Many have proceeded to express their reactions volubly. Marx has been, in short, a tremendous stimulator of thought. The tenor of one's reactions, however, will be different depending on whether one is thinking of Marx the scholar or Marx the revolutionary advocate. Concerned with the former as we are here, we shall endeavor to weigh his views in the scientific spirit. A lamentable thing about Marx, as Mills declares[6] (and with which this writer agrees), is that during the past century Marx the revolutionary advocate has triumphed over Marx the scholar. The figure of the revolutionist is the one that bulks large in the contemporary world. But the Marxian theories relating to socio-cultural change are important, and they need to be carefully assessed.[7]

Karl Marx was born in Trier, Germany, the son of a lawyer. He was educated at the Universities of Bonn and Berlin and was granted the Ph.D. degree in 1842.[8] Marx had first hoped for a university career, but his radical views made this difficult. He began work on a radical newspaper in Germany, and soon became one of its editors. However, within a year the newspaper was suppressed, and Marx left for Paris— then a center of socialist thought. He met Friedrich Engels there. In 1848 they issued the *Communist Manifesto* pamphlet. At about this time Marx was banned from Germany; he was, moreover, told by French authorities that in that country he could live only in a small provincial community; hence he decided to move on to London where he remained for the rest of his life. He wrote *The Critique of Political Economy* in 1859, and Volume I of *Das Kapital*[9] in 1867. He died in

---

[5] Some in the "especially enthusiastic" category have regarded Marx (and his associate Engels) as the Darwins or Galileos of the social sciences. Pitirim A. Sorokin, *Contemporary Sociological Theories* (New York: Harper, 1928), p. 545. Sorokin himself does not agree with such a characterization.

[6] Mills, *op. cit.*, 14–15.

[7] Indeed it is of the greatest importance to come to grips with the *ideas* of Marx. See Robert L. Heilbroner, *The Worldly Philosophers* (New York: Simon and Schuster, 1953), p. 131.

[8] This summary of Marx's vita is taken from the articles on "(Heinrich) Karl Marx" in the *Encyclopaedia Britannica*, Vol. 14 (Chicago: Encyclopaedia Britannica, Inc., 1964) and in the *Columbia Encyclopaedia*, 2nd ed. (New York: Columbia University Press, 1950). The latter article declares that Marx took his Ph.D degree at the University of Jena. This is corroborated in a helpful "Chronology of Marxism" found in the Appendix of Clinton Rossiter, *Marxism: The View from America* (New York: Harcourt, Brace, 1960).

[9] *Das Kapital,* as the article in the *Columbia Encyclopaedia* notes, has had an incalculable influence, an influence comparable to that of the Gospels, the Koran, and Newton's *Principia*.

1883 without completing the remainder of *Das Kapital*. However, Engels (using Marx's partially completed manuscripts and notes) later issued Volumes II and III.

The Economic Interpretation of History

The first basic idea of Karl Marx concerning socio-cultural change is embodied in his theory of the economic interpretation of history.[10] This states that the means of economic production tend to determine the social organization of production and, furthermore, the entire superstructure of society—the political organization, law, religion, philosophy, art, and other elements. In Marx's words:

> In the social production of their material life, men enter into definite relations that are indispensable and independent of their wills; these relations of production correspond to a definite state of the development of their material forces of production.
>
> The sum total of these relations of production makes up the economic structure of society—the real foundation on which arises a legal and political superstructure and to which correspond definite forms of social consciousness.
>
> The mode of production of material life determines the social, political, and intellectual life process in general. It is not the consciousness of men that determines their existence, but rather it is their social existence that determines their consciousness.[11]

The mode of economic production—on which man depends to sustain himself—is, then, the fundamental condition of life. It is a key cause of change—a prime condition, an independent variable on which other influences and factors depend. One may observe that Marx was not entirely clear in his expression of this and other ideas. He acknowledges that other secondary factors operate, such as political and cultural influences. He holds, nevertheless, that the economic or material factor is fundamental. In view of some of Marx's obscurities and inconsistencies, Bober declares that an argument can be raised as to whether the economic interpretation of history is intended to emphasize technological advances or something more comprehensive. But after carefully examining the evidence Bober concludes that Marx and Engels repeatedly stressed the mode of production as the prime mover of history, and that the broad interpretation of production is the one intended.[12] Indeed, he believes that when Marx and Engels speak of

---

[10] This theory goes under various names, being also known as historical materialism, the materialist conception of history, and economic determinism. It runs through all the writings of Marx and Engels. See M. M. Bober, *Karl Marx's Interpretation of History*, 2nd ed. (Cambridge, Mass.: Harvard University Press, 1948), p. 3.

[11] Karl Marx, *A Contribution to the Critique of Political Economy* (New York: International Library Publication Co., 1904), pp. 11–13.

[12] Bober, *op. cit.*, p. 6 ff.

production they have in mind the following components: (1) the organization of labor in a scheme of division and cooperation; (2) the geographical environment and knowledge of the use of resources and materials; and (3) technical means and processes and the state of science generally.[13]

However one may choose to construe this meaning, the theory did serve as an antidote to views emphasizing the all-determining influence of great men, the effects of political and diplomatic maneuverings, history seen as the clash of races, and the course of events as affected by great migrations. This more materialistic view of Marx was "at the bread-and-butter level." It looked below the surface of things and emphasized influences ordinarily not in the limelight. The common view of history has tended to underscore the actions of emperors, kings, presidents, generals, admirals, prime ministers, and the like and Marx felt that the basic economic (materialistic) influences had been grossly neglected. Some [14] have claimed that Marx and Engels revised their theory later in their lives and declared that history cannot be explained in economic terms alone. Economic phenomena wield a *preponderant* influence, the revised view is alleged to state, not an exclusive one. Gouldner [15] has recently declared that, at least applying to Engels if not to Marx himself, even a social-system influence may have been favored more than is realized. However, most doubt that any real backtracking on the economic emphasis was made by Marx. At least he continued to place a strong emphasis on the economic factor.

The Dialectic, the Class Struggle, and Inevitable Revolution

Whereas the first theory, then, proclaimed that the cause of change is rooted in the economic factor, several other Marxian theories together indicated the processes involved as well as certain *specifics* of societal change. Marx followed the Hegelian dialectic of thesis, antith-

[13] *Ibid.*, p. 24.

[14] See E. R. A. Seligman, *The Economic Interpretation of History*, rev. ed. (New York: Columbia University Press, 1924), pp. 67 and 144.

[15] Gouldner refers to the following quotation from Engels:

> *Marx and I are ourselves partly to blame for the fact that younger writers sometimes lay more stress on the economic side than is due it. We had to emphasize this main principle in opposition to our adversaries, who denied it, and we had not always the time, the place, or the opportunity to allow other elements involved in the interaction to come into their rights.*

Karl Marx and Friedrich Engels, *Selected Correspondence, 1846–1895* (New York: International Publishers, 1942), pp. 477, 475 and 114. The preceding quote is from Alvin W. Gouldner, "Reciprocity and Autonomy in Functional Theory," Chapter 8 in Llewellyn Gross (ed.), *Symposium on Sociological Theory* (Evanston, Ill.: Row, Peterson and Co., 1959), p. 269, footnote 46.

esis, and synthesis in explaining the steps involved in change. Affirmation of an idea is made; opposition to it will then inevitably be expressed; and finally, a synthesis of the idea and its antithesis will culminate the process. Although he followed the philosophy of Hegel (who had a commanding influence in Germany when Marx was a young man), Marx changed the basis of Hegel's thought from the idealistic to the materialistic. At any rate, the Hegelian dialectic is applied to the case of the capitalistic economic system. This system of production is established (affirmed) and controlled by the business (bourgeois) class. The system becomes entrenched, and it opposes new inventions. The laboring class opposes the system because workers do not receive their due and their life becomes more and more miserable. But the capitalist class prevents a synthesis from being made; hence a revolution is made necessary for the opposition to overcome the entrenched order and create a new one.[16] If the revolution is successful, the proletariat (laboring class) takes over the means of production. The system is collectively owned in a socialistic regime; but this is transitional. Eventually a communistic State will be established.

The doctrine of the class struggle is an important part of this process. In the capitalistic economy those who own the means of production and those who toil in the laboring class inevitably oppose each other. As Marx and Engels phrase it in the *Communist Manifesto:*

> *The history of all hitherto existing society is the history of class struggles. Freeman and slave, patrician and plebian, lord and serf, guildmaster and journeyman, in a word, oppressor and oppressed, stood in constant opposition to one another, carried on an uninterrupted, now hidden, now open fight, a fight that each time ended, either in a revolutionary reconstitution of sociey at large, or in the common ruin of the contending classes . . . . The modern bourgeois society that has sprouted from the ruins of feudal society has not done away with class antagonisms. It has but established new classes, new conditions of oppression, new forms of struggle in place of the old ones . . . . Society as a whole is more and more splitting up into two great hostile camps, into two great classes directly facing each other—bourgeoisie and proletariat.[17]*

In capitalist society, says Marx, people have no choice but to exploit or be exploited. If the workers are not more and more ground under

[16] Rossiter's interpretation of the dialectic as applied to capitalism is similar (but not precisely the same) to this. See *Op. cit.,* p. 106. Also, some have suggested that Marx did not necessarily mean that proletariat conditions would progressively worsen prior to the revolution; rather he may have had the idea of relative deprivation—that wages might rise but less rapidly than profits. See James C. Davies, "Toward a Theory of Revolution," *American Sociological Review,* Vol. 27, No. 1 (February, 1962), 5–18, especially p. 5.

[17] Edited, with introduction, by Samuel H. Beer (New York: Appleton-Century-Crofts, Inc., 1955).

foot, they at least suffer relatively. The class struggle is the driving force of history that leads, then, to revolution as the form of change.

Marx's theory of socio-cultural change may, therefore, be summarized as follows: (1) The key factor and determinant of change in society is economic, the mode of production being the specific cause. (2) The process of change is patterned after the dialectic of Hegel—the sequence of thesis, antithesis, and synthesis. (3) A struggle between the business and laboring classes occurs because of the nature of the capitalistic economic system.[18] (4) This inevitably leads to revolution, which arises as the proletariat class overthrows the capitalistic order and itself takes over the means of production. These ideas are tied in with other Marxian theories that are, however, exclusively economic and, hence, are not discussed here. These are the labor theory of value, the theory of surplus value (with its three laws), and the theory of the falling rate of profit.

Comment and Evaluation

Marx's ideas, forcefully expressed, have received much criticism. The following seem to be justified and significant criticisms: (1) Marx has *stated* his idea concerning the economic interpretation of history, but he has not proven it. In no sense did he establish any correlation between the economic base of a society and its superstructure. Some have maintained, in fact, that such cannot be proven. Timasheff has pointed out that, contrary to Marxian doctrine, the same capitalistic economic system can coexist with various political institutions, including absolute monarchy and democracy. Moreover, a considerable variety of philosophies, arts, and other cultural phenomena have flourished throughout the capitalistic era. Then, too, change from one type of social organization of production to another is not necessarily due to the consequences of a victory of the exploited class. In European history, Timasheff adds, the destruction of feudalism was due more to the activities of a small yet powerful bourgeoisie than to the serfs.[19] (2) Marx's emphasis on the mode of economic production as the key or primary cause of socio-cultural change has met with widespread objection. His original statement of this, as we have quoted it from his

18 Thus Marx holds this to be an inevitable development—an unfolding of the system. Veblen comments on this Marxian view that the capitalistic system is almost entirely "self-conditioned and self-acting." See Max Lerner (ed.), *The Portable Veblen* (New York: The Viking Press, 1958), p. 280. See also Heilbroner, *op. cit.,* pp. 131 and 160. As Heilbroner declares, the Marxian contention is that capitalism must inevitably and necessarily collapse; the essence of the system is self-destruction.

19 N. S. Timasheff, *Sociological Theory,* 3rd ed. (New York: Random House, 1967), p. 50.

Contribution to the Critique of Political Economy, is quite unacceptable because it is factually incorrect.[20] All monistic theories are unacceptable, to be sure, because they tend to oversimplify and often distort the process of socio-cultural change; they overlook the important influence of other factors, which often have a major effect on the economic one. Sorokin [21] has noted, for instance, that a series of investigators (Durkheim, Malinowski, Mauss, and others) have shown that, even in primitive stages, the technique of production and the whole of economic life are absolutely inseparable from religion, magic, science, and other phenomena. At any rate, the social process is exceedingly complex. Many influences tend to affect social phenomena.

Some may take the view that Marx and Engels moderated their views later in their lives, and that they finally reached a more proper and acceptable view.[22] Economic factors are now declared to be the predominating (not sole) cause of change; political and other factors are admitted beside the economic one. But this pluralistic theory practically means an abandonment of their original contention. It is indeed more satisfactory than the original, but we are inclined to agree with Sorokin [23] that this modified view had been expressed before and it signified merely that they corrected the early untenable position (if in fact they surely did so).

(3) Concerning Marx's specific ideas regarding the change process (dialectic, class struggle, revolution), the power of his thinking is indicated. The social process, it is true, did not take place as stated by Marx. The middle class did not wane in capitalistic nations as he predicted. Nor did a revolution occur in industrial nations. However, a theory is not to be faulted because specific events do not follow a prediction.[24] What Marx thought must inevitably fall was the exploitation of the worker by the capitalist. In this situation collective bargaining, unionization, various forms of social welfare programs, and the like were developed to take care of these problems of the economic order in "tension-management" fashion as Wilbert E. Moore would phrase it (see Chapter 6).

More and more intervention in and regulation of economic processes were found necessary, as Berle [25] and others have shown. Increasingly

20 See Bober, *op. cit.,* Chap. 16; Sorokin, *op. cit.,* pp. 527–533; Robert M. MacIver, *Social Causation* (New York: Ginn & Co., 1942), pp. 115–119; and Clinton Rossiter, *Marxism: The View from America* (New York: Harcourt, Brace, 1960), Chap. 2, especially pp. 50–52.

21 Sorokin, *op. cit.,* p. 530.

22 See Engels' correspondence mentioned in footnote 15.

23 Sorokin, *op. cit.,* pp. 535–536.

24 Robert A. Nisbet, *Social Change and History* (New York: Oxford University Press, 1969), pp. 251–253.

25 Adolf A. Berle, *The American Economic Republic* (New York: Harcourt, Brace & World, Inc., 1963), Introduction and Chap. 5.

the laissez-faire free market ceased to be more than an abstraction. By the time of the major depression of the early 1930s, a comparatively small percentage of people stoutly defended the earlier notion that the free market operated automatically in the best interests of man. In short, the age of the regulated economy had arrived. Wages, hours of work, safety, and other factors were regulated. The worker received compensation if injured in an industrial accident. Unions, moreover, brought many benefits for the worker, and indeed were a potent force in obtaining wage increases, restricted work hours, and the like. All in all, the worker today works amid quite acceptable conditions (and sometimes is a stockholder in his company). Even if the life of the worker *had* been one of increasing misery (following Marxian theory), we are inclined to agree with Veblen that such individuals are by no means certain to revolt. The experience of history, says Veblen, teaches us that abject misery carries with it deterioration and utter subjection.[26]

Dahrendorf,[27] whose ideas were partly discussed in Chapter 4, has extended the Marxian ideas in important ways. Rejecting the Marxian model of class conflict and revolution [28] and observing Marx's errors in prediction, Dahrendorf is interested, first of all, in citing changes in the structure of industrial societies since Marx's time; such changes would presumably explain why the polarization of the capitalist and working classes in the Western nations did not become extreme, leading to revolution. Dahrendorf maintains that industrial development during the past century has brought a *new* middle class (instead of the old one "fading out" as Marx posited). Fritz Croner and others believe that this new middle class has linked itself largely with the capitalist, ruling class, whereas Theodor Geiger, C. Wright Mills, and others consider that it is mostly oriented toward the working class.[29] Dahrendorf suggests that both may be correct. His view is that some salaried employees occupy positions in bureaucratic hierarchies and will link themselves to the capitalist class; on the other hand, employees in stores, restaurants, commercial firms, and other white-collar situations will, he thinks, relate themselves to the working class even though some of them will have higher salaries and higher prestige than industrial workers. Then Dahrendorf declares that the factor of upward mobility,

---

26 Lerner (ed.), *op. cit.*, p. 34.

27 Ralf Dahrendorf, *Class and Class Conflict in Industrial Society* (Stanford, Calif.: Stanford University Press, 1959).

28 One should point out that Marx did maintain on occasion that revolution might not be "necessary."

29 See Fritz Croner, *Die Angestellten in der modernen Gesellschaft* (Frankfurt-on-Main, and Vienna, 1954); Theodor Geiger, *Die Klassengesellschaft in Schmelztiegel* (Cologne and Hagen, 1949); C. Wright Mills, *White Collar* (New York: Oxford University Press, 1951).

which was ignored by Marx, militates against the increasing polarization of the classes. Talented people, in short, may rise to the higher-salaried, more-prestigious, positions, thus changing over to the capitalist class (instead of venting their frustrations against it). Even more, the spread of social equality during the past century (suggests Dahrendorf) has rendered class struggles and revolutionary changes "utterly impossible." [30] The idea of equality is highly dynamic; again, Marx seems to have minimized it. Although the tendency toward "leveling" can be exaggerated, nevertheless Dahrendorf explains that income taxes have brought a redistribution of incomes and that technical products (automobiles, radios, TV, and the rest) are increasingly available to everybody. Finally, the techniques of class struggle are recognized and now are "ordered" on both sides according to the rules of the game. Hence, the class struggle has "lost its worst sting"; it has been converted into a "legitimate tension between power factors which balance each other." [31]

Dahrendorf's own perspective is to see the distribution of power and authority as the determining factor in producing social conflicts of the type envisaged by Marx.[32] He follows Max Weber's definition of *power*, namely, that it is "the probability that one actor can carry out his own will despite resistance. . . ." On the other hand, *authority* is the "probability that a command within a given social context will be obeyed by a given group of persons." [33] In conflict analysis, says Dahrendorf, one is concerned with the generation of conflict groups by the authority relations of coordinated associations. Power and authority can be seen in relation to functions in behalf of the social system and *also* as productive of conflicts; Talcott Parsons and C. Wright Mills have taken the respective positions regarding this. Dahrendorf maintains indeed that authority has two faces—the Parsons and Mills aspects—and that "it is illegitimate to emphasize either of these to the exclusion of the other." [34] The important thing to see is that *one* fundamental aspect of power and authority is that they have disruptive and conflict-generating consequences. In brief, the distribution of authority in associations may generate conflicts and the formation of conflict groups.

If the Dahrendorf beliefs comprise a significant revision of Marxian theory, the former acknowledges that Marx's denoting classes as conflict

---

[30] Dahrendorf, *op. cit.*, p. 61.

[31] *Ibid.*, p. 65. Dahrendorf holds that "Marx displayed a certain sociological naiveté when he expressed the belief that capitalistic society would be entirely unable to cope with the class conflict generated by its structure."

[32] *Ibid.*, p. 165.

[33] *Ibid.*, p. 166.

[34] *Ibid.*, pp. 169–170.

groups is generally correct. Classes, declares Dahrendorf in a final summary, "signify conflict groups that are generated by the differential distribution of authority in imperatively coordinated associations." [35] Dahrendorf also comments approvingly on Marx's interest in social change itself. Focusing on the economic sphere, the latter saw conflict groups and their clashes, then, as forces producing change.

Talcott Parsons, finally, criticizes Marx on some different points. Parsons holds, first, that Marx was incorrect in treating the socio-economic structure of capitalism as a single indivisible entity rather than breaking it down into a set of distinct variables.[36] Secondly, Parsons develops the theme of tendencies of the American social system to develop class conflicts—which states in so many words that various other factors were involved in such conflicts in addition to those emphasized by Marx. Parsons speaks of these tendencies: [37] (1) Class conflicts are likely to develop because of the inherently competitive nature of the occupational system; occupations differ on a prestige scale, and fair competition may not always prevail; (2) discipline and authority are generally needed, yet they may engender some resentments; (3) the powerful may exploit the weaker, not only by capitalistic exploitation, which Marx mentioned, but in other ways that he did not describe; (4) people at different points in the social structure develop different cultures; Marx did not go far enough in analyzing this; (5) different occupational systems lead to a differentiation of family types; and (6) absolute equality of opportunity in the occupational system is impossible in reality.

Parsons doubts, moreover, that a sharp and fundamental sociological distinction can be made between capitalistic society and all noncapitalist industrial societies. He believes [38] that class conflict is endemic in modern industrial society, although he does not think that the case has been made for believing that it is the dominant feature of every such society.[39] His over-all view is that the Marxian position on class conflicts requires considerable modification.[40] For one thing, systems

---

[35] *Ibid.*, p. 204.

[36] Talcott Parsons, "Social Classes and Class Conflict in the Light of Recent Sociological Theory," *American Economic Review*, Vol. 39 (1949), pp. 16–17.

[37] *Ibid.*, pp. 22–24.

[38] *Ibid.*, p. 25.

[39] Noting that knowledge of comparative social structures has increased immensely in recent years, Parsons feels that

> *capitalistic and socialist industrialisms tend to be seen as variants of a single fundamental type, not as drastically distinct stages in a single process of dialectic evolution. . . . Marxian thought appears as a strait jacket rather than a genuine source of illumination of variant facts of institutional life.* Loc. cit.

[40] *Ibid.*, p. 26.

of stratification have certain positive functions in the stabilization of social systems. Davis and Moore [41] have discussed this in more detail, although many (following Dahrendorf) would hold that the conflict-producing consequences should also be stressed. Parsons feels, incidentally, that the Marxian ideal of a classless society is probably utopian, and that the differences between capitalist and socialist societies—with reference to stratification—are not as great as Marx and Engels thought.

THORSTEIN VEBLEN (1857–1929)

Thorstein Veblen is another economics–oriented thinker—he accents the technological—but his ideas differ considerably from those of Marx. He is in some agreement with Marx, it is true, in their belief in the economic interpretation of history,[42] indictment of capitalistic operations (although for different reasons), and linking war with property—yet he disagrees as strongly as, or more strongly than, he agrees. Veblen stressed institutional conflict (we shall see details presently), not class conflict. He dismissed Marx's labor theory of value as an unproven assumption. Similarly, he cast aside the Marxian theory of surplus value and the accumulation of capital out of unpaid labor value as unproven. We noted earlier that Veblen disagreed with Marx's conclusions in the doctrine of the increasing misery of the working class; he did not think that this condition would lead to a proletarian revolution. Veblen had fewer illusions concerning the common man, certainly he did not picture him as a great hero who would overturn the existing order. He found fault with the Marxian theory of the class struggle, which assumed that the laboring class would follow its logical and rational interest. Veblen's psychology proclaimed that men act on the basis of instinct and propensity, and that they tend to adhere to habits and thoughtways that have become institutionalized. Veblen's conception of social process was not Hegelian; it stressed the Darwinian processes of ceaseless adjustment and cumulative change. In fact, summarizes Lerner,[43] Veblen was critical of Marxism at almost every step. Furthermore, Veblen was no revolutionary figure—no firebrand [44]—although he was very much out of the ordinary.

---

[41] Kingsley Davis and Wilbert E. Moore, "Some Principles of Stratification," *American Sociological Review*, Vol. 10 (April, 1945), pp. 242–249. See also, Wilbert E. Moore, "But Some Are More Equal Than Others," *American Sociological Review*, Vol. 28, No. 1 (February, 1963), pp. 13–18.

[42] It is significant, says Max Lerner, that in every one of Veblen's teaching positions his main course had the title "Economic Factors in Civilization." Lerner (ed.), *op. cit.*, Editor's Introduction, p. 25.

[43] *Ibid.*, p. 33.

[44] That is to say, Veblen was no firebrand in the sense that Marx was. Veblen

Thorstein Veblen [45] was born of Norwegian immigrants in a Wisconsin farm community, one of twelve children. His father was a master carpenter who, however, had strong intellectual interests. As a boy Thorstein could speak German and Latin as well as Norwegian (he learned English later). At the age of 17 he was sent to Carleton College (Minnesota) for preparatory training and college. Following graduation he spent one year (1881) at Johns Hopkins. He then transferred to Yale, staying there for three years and earning his Ph.D. degree. He has been characterized as a penniless, hard-working, and rather eccentric student.[46] Unfortunately, he contracted malaria while at Yale, and his health failed. From 1884–1891, even though he possessed the Ph.D, he held no job.[47] Then he returned for a year of graduate study at Cornell and made a connection there that resulted in his being made a teaching fellow at the University of Chicago. After four years he became an instructor—which could scarcely be characterized as a meteoric rise up the academic ladder although he was located at a leading university. At this time Veblen began writing articles for economic and other journals, and in 1899 he produced his first—and probably greatest—book, *The Theory of the Leisure Class.* This led off a series of altogether remarkable volumes: *The Theory of Business Enterprise* (1904), *The Instinct of Workmanship and the State of the Industrial Arts* (1914), *The Higher Learning in America* (1918), and *The Engineers and the Price System* (1921).[48]

Veblen clearly had arrived as a socio-economic thinker. But he still did not reach the academic pinnacle or even approach it as one would expect, mainly due to personal family difficulties; the latter always seemed to plague him.[49] Indeed, he had to give up his position at the

certainly did not have the personality of a firebrand (being, on the contrary, very quiet and nonaggressive). However, in *The Engineers and the Price System* he urges engineers and technicians to take over the operation of the economic system, which is obviously a drastic course of action. But he was not personally militant.

45 Veblen's biographical data are taken from Alvin Johnson's article on Veblen in the *Encyclopaedia of the Social Sciences,* Vol. 15 (New York: The Macmillan Company, 1934); Joseph Dorfman's *Thorstein Veblen and His America* (New York: The Viking Press, 1934); and Lerner (ed.), *loc. cit.*

46 Lerner, *op. cit.,* p. 4.

47 Dorfman cites details concerning Veblen's extremely difficult time during these years in trying to secure a position. *Op. cit.,* p. 78 ff.

48 This list by no means exhausts his publications, however. His other volumes (of less interest to us here) include: *Imperial Germany and the Industrial Revolution* (1915), *An Inquiry into the Nature of Peace* (1917), *The Vested Interests and the Common Man* (1919), *The Place of Science in Modern Civilization* (1919), and others.

49 In Max Lerner's words, "Veblen's domestic economy [that is to say, his private family life] was even more original and radical than his political economy. . . . It was on this rock that his academic career seemed repeatedly to break." Lerner (ed.), *op. cit.,* p. 9; see also Dorfman, *op. cit.,* pp. 271 and 304–305.

University of Chicago. He moved to Stanford, but after a few years
again had to pack and leave. Then it was the University of Missouri
where he taught for seven years and wrote his criticisms of the conduct
of universities by businessmen. After this he made his final move (1918)
to New York where he edited a journal for a time, and then taught at
the New School for Social Research. Here he reached his greatest
influence. But his age was advanced and his health failing. He retired
from teaching in 1927; he died on August 3, 1929—several months
before the crash of the predatory (in his view) American economy.
Veblen had been a forceful and acute critic of American business
civilization.[50] Many thought him eccentric, he was mostly isolated, and
his career was checkered; yet his ideas merit serious attention.

The Veblen View of Change

At least three of Thorstein Veblen's major ideas relate to socio-
cultural change:

*Socio-cultural change results from a basic conflict between man's
productive (industrial) interests and his business (exploitive) interests.*
Veblen equated the productive interests with the institutionalized
machine system and the exploitive interests with the capitalistic business system. Thus industry is the productive process of making goods
and business the predatory or exploitive process of making profits. He
hailed the technologists and engineers devoted to efficient production.
He castigated the business interests—in which he lumped together
absentee owners, major executives, financiers, investment bankers, advertising men, stockbrokers, promoters, and others—for being parasitic
and useless. Their objectives, he claimed, are domination of others and
self-aggrandisement; their methods involve such procedures as cut-
throat competition, price wars, limiting production to increase prices
and profits, and attaining monopolies.

Veblen traced these activities from the cultural past. Man's predatory
interests are derived from a hunting, fighting tradition.[51] The roots
of "pecuniary emulation" rest in the belief that booty, trophies, and
other fruits of conquest are valid; they are indeed considered as legitimate as the rewards of productive labor. Thus work and ownership
become differentiated. To take the results of some one else's labor and
live on it, is just as honorable as to work for one's bread. Veblen says

[50] "If America has produced the most finished and tenacious brand of business
civilization," says Lerner, "it has also produced the most finished and tenacious
criticism of that civilization. That is perhaps the core meaning of Veblen's
work. . . . Veblen has worn well. Very little in him dates. . . ." *Ibid.,* pp. 1–2.
[51] *The Theory of the Leisure Class* (New York: The Modern Library, 1934),
Chap. I.

that this is not a cynical judgment on his part but simply how the "taking" class feels about it. Then one engages in conspicuous consumption in order to make a showing and so establish economic respectability.

At an even more basic level Veblen explains socio-economic behavior in terms of (1) group-regarding proclivities and (2) self-regarding proclivities. The former are illustrated by the parental bent, which is conserving and is interested in community welfare; the instinct of workmanship, representing man's tendency to produce effectively and to avoid shoddy craftsmanship; and idle curiosity, which is the drive to explain things and to pursue knowledge for its own sake. Opposed to these are the self-regarding proclivities. They include the tendencies toward conspicuous consumption, prowess, domination, prestige, and self-aggrandisement.

The social process, then, represents a conflict between the two broad forces noted here. If socio-economic conditions are to advance, says Veblen, the instinct of workmanship needs to be taken as the guiding principle. The machine-industrial system is of basic and great value; the predatory business system is dysfunctional (using Parsonian or Mertonian terminology). These considerations lead to Veblen's second over-all idea.

In the change process the values and functioning of the production system are more basic and more necessary for the society than those of the business system and will eventually defeat, undermine, or take precedence over the latter. Veblen's view, in short, is that production and business systems are incompatible, and that eventually the former will assert itself over the latter. This is the basis for placing Veblen in the camp of the technological determinists. The extent of the market must always be limited by the state of the industrial arts (technology). The industrial technology, then, is the "real substance" of the modern economy, to quote Ayres.[52] It is the independent variable, the business price system a dependent variable. Most economists had previously stated it the other way around. Let us examine the argument in Veblen's own words:

> The "social problem" presents this singular situation: The growth of business enterprise rests on the machine technology as its material foundation. The machine industry is indispensable to it; it cannot get along without the machine process. But the discipline of the machine process cuts away the spiritual, institutional foundations of business enterprise; the machine industry is incompatible with its continued growth; it cannot, in the long run, get along with the

52 C. E. Ayres, "The Legacy of Thorstein Veblen," in *Institutional Economics: Veblen, Commons, and Mitchell Reconsidered* (Berkeley: University of California Press, 1963), Chap. 2, pp. 52–53.

> *machine process. In their struggle against the cultural effects of the machine process, therefore, business principles cannot win in the long run; since an effective mutilation or inhibition of the machine system would gradually push business enterprise to the wall; whereas with a free growth of the machine system business principles would presently fall into abeyance.*[53]

The technological base of every society is thus the key factor. He illustrated this from primitive societies—indeed he placed much emphasis on anthropological evidence. In the instance of modern civilization the role of the machine is crucial, and society has to adjust to its machine technology.[54] This belief in the primacy of the machine production system leads to a further, the third, proposition.

For the advancement of the society, the production experts (the engineers and technicians) should operate the economy, not the predatory business interests. This is Veblen's final answer to the problem, his answer to "What can be done?" Here he is at his most revolutionary. This urging the engineers to take over control—which in his later years was translated into the technocracy movement, to be described later—no doubt had the financial interests worried, at least for a while. Dorfman comments that Veblen and some of his radical colleagues were disappointed that no revolution of this sort occurred when the depressed conditions of 1921 arrived.[55] Veblen felt that more and more the engineers recognized the wastes of economic life brought by the business interests—the sabotaging of production in favor of greater profits, the unearned increments, the many abuses and malpractices. He realized, however, that many engineers were in the employ of great corporations and, hence, themselves operated under the aegis of the business interests. It is to be noted that Veblen denied that the Marxian solution of proletarian revolt and assumption of control was satisfac-

---

[53] *The Theory of Business Enterprise* (New York: Mentor Books, 1958); paperback edition, p. 177.

[54] Heilbroner observes that Veblen's proposition was

> *more than an acid treatment of the business system. It was, as well, a theory of social change. For Veblen believed that the days of the business leaders were numbered, that despite their power, there was ranged against them a formidable adversary. It was not the proletariat . . . , but a still more implacable foe: the machine.*
>
> *For the machine, thought Veblen, "throws out anthropomorphic habits of thought." It forced men to think in terms that are matter-of-fact, precise, measurable, and devoid of superstition and animism. Hence those who came in contact with the machine process found it increasingly difficult to swallow the presumptions of "natural law" and social differentiation which surround the leisure class.*

Heilbroner, *op. cit.*, p. 227.

[55] Dorfman, *op. cit.*, p. 462.

tory. He does not necessarily link industriousness and productivity with the proletariat class. Moreover, Veblen thought that labor does not understand the necessities of modern industry any better than does the business class. His faith, therefore, rested with the production-minded people who—as technicians—were capable of bringing peace and abundance. Such, in brief summary, is the last element in the Veblen credo.

One may observe that Veblen developed these ideas gradually. They constitute a logical, continuing thesis begun in *The Theory of the Leisure Class,* extended in *The Instinct of Workmanship* and in *The Theory of Business Enterprise,* and concluded in *The Engineers and the Price System.* The range of his knowledge was most impressive, the phrasing picturesque and novel. Some of the core ideas go back to his youth, and Veblen himself is said to have remarked that ideas in *The Theory of the Leisure Class* were derived to a considerable extent from those of his father.[56] Veblen, at any rate, was very influential—not as a popular writer or as a teacher, but as a professor's professor.[57]

Criticisms and Evaluation

Two preliminary comments are in order before we suggest certain criticisms of Veblen's ideas. One concerns his use of concepts and terms. In some cases the latter are out-of-date. This, however, is unavoidable, remembering that he wrote essentially during the 1900–1920 period; obviously he has to base his ideas on the accepted usages of *his* day. We must note nevertheless that some of these usages are unacceptable *today.* One of these is the concept of *instinct.* For example, one pauses to consider his volume, *The Instinct of Workmanship and the State of the Industrial Arts.* Is there an *instinct* of

[56] *Ibid.,* p. 174.

[57] According to reports Veblen was a poor teacher. He generally spoke in a low, monotonous voice. He had no interest in undergraduate students (and showed it). His classes were almost always small. *Ibid.,* pp. 273–274 and 307. His public popularity was greatest during his New York years (around 1919–1920). Dorfman declares that he was the center of intellectual attention at this time, succeeding William James and John Dewey in this respect. "Everyone of intellectual pretensions read Veblen." *Ibid.,* p. 423. Soule states that

> *Veblen's influence is of the kind which spreads, not through a wide popular audience, but through its impact on minds of men who in turn influence others. He had no celebrated disciples who preached and elaborated his doctrine as a whole; it never got into the accepted text-books. But American economics—even American apologetics for big business—has never been quite the same since he wrote. Defenders of capitalism today emphasize technical achievements and great productivity rather than supposed automatic equilibrium of the system.* Op. cit., *p. 140.*

workmanship? Are there any instincts applying to human behavior? As Sorokin declares,[58] the very starting point of this investigation is incorrect in its conceptualization. Allowance clearly has to be made for the disparity between the stock of knowledge of his day and the present time, with special reference to economics, psychology, sociology, and occasionally philosophy.

Another comment similarly relates to the *time* factor. As a product of his time and place, Veblen's attention was sharpened to the conflict between predatory, exploiting people and industrious people. This was most meaningful to him, seeing the world as he did from the vantage point of post-Civil War America. As a product of the Wisconsin-Minnesota area he noted at close range the problems of the wheat farmers in relation to "big business." Veblen's formative years were roughly those of 1875–1890: a period of the emerging trusts, of maneuverings by shrewd and often ruthless "captains of industry" (the "robber barons"), and of America's greatest emphasis on laissez faire.[59] This was the era in which a prominent industrialist could say "The Public be damned. I owe the public nothing." [60] What could be more natural than for this intellectual from the agrarian Northwest to develop a profound skepticism if not hatred for big business and its financial center, Wall Street? When misfortunes came to the hard-working wheat farmers—traceable to the usual problems of weather, wheat prices, plant diseases, storage problems, shortages of railway cars, and the like—radicalism was common. Some of the problems (especially, of course, falling prices) were often laid at the door of the financial East. The picture was of the hard-working farmer versus the predatory financial manipulator. Ignoring Veblen's use of terms (admittedly sometimes now out-of-date), his unique coining of phrases, and countless nonessential details, his over-all message is that the capitalistic system needs redressing. Nothing however is to be overthrown, the institution of business enterprise is simply dysfunctional. This is the part of the system that needs correcting. The machine-industrial system is the valued part—the real producer. Its leaders (the

[58] *Op. cit.*, p. 615, footnote 34. See also David Riesman and Staughton Lynd, "The Relevance of Thorstein Veblen," *American Scholar*, Vol. 29 (1959–60), 544–545.

[59] Adolph A. Berle describes this situation, not in terms of villainy, but more neutrally:

> [*The unregulated free market*] . . . *acted quite normally. The strong and powerful eliminated or absorbed the weak and undefended, and monopolies proliferated. . . . They* [*men in a free market*] *used competition not for the purpose of keeping prices down but for the purpose of putting their competitors out of business, and becoming monopolists. . . . Where they could not drive out competitors, they consolidated with them.* Op. cit., p. 234, Notes.

[60] Quoted from Riesman and Lynd, *op. cit.*, p. 546.

engineers) should be entrusted with the operation of the entire system, said Veblen.[61]

If this is regarded as the essence of Veblen's message, how shall we comment? *First, Veblen's perspectives toward business enterprise bring forth criticisms on his part that are too broad. He improperly lumps together different economic activities, roles, and individual behavior that are then a collective target for his criticism.* It seems clear, for example, that not all businessmen are predatory. Are they all villains because they aspire to make a profit? Many, on the contrary, exemplify group-regarding proclivities; they are constructive community leaders. It is perhaps true that between approximately 1865 and 1900 business ethics in the United States were at their lowest ebb; [62] at this time "might makes right" was in considerable vogue. But, even if this is granted, in all periods the ranks of businessmen (as with all occupations?) contain the honorable, the fairly honorable, and some dishonest manipulators and merciless exploiters. Moreover, Veblen was also indiscriminate, and hence again incorrect, in grouping together absentee owners, major executives, financiers, salesmen, advertising men, stockbrokers, promoters, and others not directly concerned with production and essential distribution to receive his pronouncement of being parasites and worse than useless. Intent on getting something for nothing they are alleged to kill off competitors, sabotage industry, and endeavor to keep the supply of goods scarce and prices high. Yet it can hardly be denied that executives *are* necessary in order to operate a business; salesmen similarly are necessary; stockbrokers *do* have a legitimate function; and advertising men *are* needed in mass society in order to market the vast amount of goods produced by machine production.[63] Not only do these activities perform a valid function, but thousands of persons engaged in these pursuits are honest, upright, and hardworking individuals. However, it is with the practices, not individual people, that Veblen was concerned. Some undesirable practices un-

61 Riesman and Lynd describe the legacy of Veblen in their statement that the social environment of capitalism is hostile to a peaceful, cooperative life. In phrasing it this way they follow Veblen's anthropological usages in contrasting two stages of life: savagery and barbarism. Savagery, for Veblen, was peaceful, cooperative, and good; barbarism, on the other hand, was competitive, warlike, and spiritually oriented to personal rather than communal achievement. Thus modern society, to Veblen, was latter-day barbarism. *Ibid.*, p. 550.

62 Some may contest this generalization, but most historians and social scientists agree that unrestricted laissez-faire individualism was at its height at this time. See the works of Harold U. Faulkner, Louis M. Hacker, B. B. Kendrick, Charles and Mary Beard, and other historians.

63 See, for example, Don Martindale, *American Society* (Princeton, N. J.: D. Van Nostrand, 1960), p. 12. Also, David Potter points out the great need for advertising in an economy of abundance. See *People of Plenty* (Chicago: University of Chicago Press, 1954), Chap. 8.

doubtedly needed regulation by law. In castigating such total groups and their work Veblen overshot the mark. Probably all occupational groups have some unscrupulous and dishonest practitioners. Chase [64] comments that Veblen's general emphasis could later be seen in such volumes as *The Modern Corporation and Private Property* [65] and in the Ferdinand Pecora investigations of high finance during the 1930s. The spirit of Veblen can be seen in the (United States) Security and Exchange Commission's 17-month investigation of the security markets in 1962–1963.[66] Some manipulation and fraud were detected; and additional controls and improvements were recommended. The prosecution of certain brokerage houses is made from time to time, and campaigns for more truth in advertising are instituted. These activities represent Veblen's thinking. Thus many corrections in business practices have now been made, although continued vigilance as to practices is needed.

Secondly, Veblen did not prove his case, in our judgment, that the industrial order is the basic and primary factor (the independent variable) in socio-economic affairs, and the business system is secondary (a dependent variable). He *stated* this, to be sure. He applied some logic to the contention. But he did not prove it. Veblen followed the tack that the machine (industrial) system and the business-enterprise system are the two prime movers in modern culture; but they are in basic conflict. The machine system, being more essential (the key influence), will eventually cause the business system to yield. The thought patterns of the industrial system—matter-of-factness, precision, rationality, and scientific orientation—cut into the foundations of profit-minded business enterprise.

Can the preceding be established? Is it not, rather, that the production system and business enterprise *affect each other* in various respects? Even in severe depressions the business system has not collapsed. It has been defensive-minded—yes. However, its values and leadership were able to ride out difficult times. But, in broader scope, the industrial system has hardly been all-determining in its influence. What has happened is that it and other parts of the economy have been affected by laws, governmental decisions, and other elements of the social system. *All* the social institutions affect each other. Abuses and malpractices, then, have often been corrected; neither the industrial system nor business enterprise has driven the other to the wall. Thus, in the absence of scientific proof, we have turned to predictability (as we did

---

[64] Stuart Chase, Foreword in Thorstein Veblen, *The Theory of the Leisure Class* (New York: The Modern Library, 1934), p. xiii.

[65] Adolph A. Berle and Gardner C. Means, *The Modern Corporation and Private Property* (New York: The Macmillan Company, 1933).

[66] For a lengthy summary see *The New York Times* (April 4, 1963).

with Marx). It has not worked out as Veblen predicted. Even in the severest of depressions (as in 1929–1934) the business-enterprise system did not go down. Such has been the record, at any rate, since Veblen expressed this idea—in 1904—in *The Theory of Business Enterprise*. On the other hand, the forces of government have taken strong measures—setting up public works projects, attacking the unemployment problem, and encouraging industrial production in varied ways—when the market economy has encountered critical times.

Finally, if abuses and malpractices have occurred in business affairs, is the best solution to the problem that of turning over operation of the economic system to the production-minded engineers? We think not. In saying this we intend no animosity toward engineers. Rather, we do not believe that any one professional group should be the masters of society. Different occupational groups have diverse outlooks and types of ability; many of them are useful in controlling a society. It seems that the real solution to the issue is to correct the abuses and evils that are found. This indeed is the general course of action that American society, in its gradual and no doubt imperfect way, has taken. Veblen, perhaps, in this respect, made the same mistake as Marx: He relied too much on one factor—treating it in an immanent manner and failing to see that it would be modified by other factors in the social system. The evils in the business-enterprise system during the post-Civil War period constituted an important influence in the overthrow of laissez faire. The philosophy of government intervention has grown steadily. As Heilbroner expresses it, Veblen underestimated the capacity of the democratic system to correct its excesses.[67] Moreover, the *climate* of business could change, as indeed it did, in adjusting to a changing world.

At only one time to this writer's knowledge did American society seem to develop an interest in the possibilities of control by the engineers. This was during the early 1930s when the technocracy movement began to make headway. The major business depression had set in, and technocrats such as Howard Scott were receiving more and more attention.[68] Here was action beginning along the lines of Veblen's *The Engineers and the Price System*. It began to be asked whether Scott's group was preparing seriously for their "Revolution of the Engineers" and whether it dared to follow Veblen's lead.[69] What is technocracy? In broad terms Chase answers the question as follows:

[67] Heilbroner, *op. cit.*, p. 233.

[68] For a concise statement on technocracy, see Stuart Chase, *Technocracy, An Interpretation* (New York: John Day Co., 1933), pamphlet. For a fuller discussion, see Howard Scott and others, *Introduction to Technocracy* (New York: John Day Co., 1933).

[69] Dorfman, *op. cit.*, p. 513.

> *It [technocracy] is Veblen pushed a few steps forward, modified by recent industrial history and Mr. Howard Scott. It is an attempt to measure by means of figures and charts the impact of energy (the machine, if you like the term better) on civilization. It is an expedient into the higher mathematics. It is a prophecy and a challenge. It has hinted at a blueprint of a possible new society where economic activity is controlled by the technician, with a sixteen hour work week, but the blueprint has not yet been divulged. It is the name of a group said to consist of some 350 engineers and technical men.*[70]

Does this sound potentially important? Does such a movement seem to bear promise? Perhaps. Many would declare that the implications of advancing technology are crucially important. The technocrats, led by Mr. Scott, did organize in 1933, and they published a magazine, *Technocracy*. But the early strong interest in the movement soon declined. It is true, to be sure, that many meetings were held in various American cities for about fifteen years; but by 1948 the group had split into factions. The remnants of the movement gradually faded into obscurity and isolation.[71] In this manner the specific technocracy movement came to an end in the United States, although the term *technocracy* is sometimes used in Europe (especially in France) to convey the generalized use of political power on the part of technologists.

It is conjecture whether many engineers would like to be masters of society in the Veblen or Howard Scott sense. However this is answered, it is undeniable that modern society is vastly complicated; many issues cannot be settled on the basis of lines on engineering charts. We suspect, furthermore, that other occupational groups would similarly shrink from the notion of being elite managers of an economy and society. At present, lawyers are prominent in the various branches of government, but at least the governing processes are not officially turned over to the legal profession. Veblen saw well the flaws and malpractices of the business operations of his time, but it may be that the control of society is best distributed among many occupational and other groups with free interplay between them.

WILLIAM F. OGBURN (1886–1959)

Like Veblen, the late Professor William F. Ogburn taught a course entitled "The Economic Factor in Culture" for many years. Again like

---

[70] Chase, *op. cit.*, p. 11.

[71] For a more detailed description of this rather colorful movement (including the enigmatic personality of Howard Scott), see Henry Elsner, Jr., *The Technocrats: Prophets of Automation* (Syracuse, N. Y.: Syracuse University Press, 1967). For an example of the current generalized treatment of technocracy in Europe (especially France), see Jean Meynaud, *Technocracy,* translated by Paul Barnes (New York: The Free Press, Division of The Macmillan Company, 1969).

Veblen, he emphasized the influence of technology—although in a different way. Ogburn was impressed with the over-all social impact of technology, not with its conflict with the business enterprise system. Finally, Ogburn—like Sorokin and MacIver—was dominantly concerned with the subject of social change. He had other interests (as did the others), but this—centering on the impact of technology on society [72]—was his greatest sociological concern.

Ogburn began his professional career around 1910, and at this time many leaders of the social sciences emphasized reform and social philosophy. To produce verifiable knowledge, therefore, was for him a matter of first importance (just as Giddings, under whom he studied, had advocated it). "How do you know It?" was a favorite question of Ogburn's. Research became for him a strong interest, with emphasis on the use of statistical methods.

William Fielding Ogburn was born in Butler, Georgia, on June 29, 1886. He was granted a B.S. degree from Mercer University in 1905, and received A.M. and Ph.D. degrees from Columbia University in 1909 and 1912, respectively. He taught at Princeton University (1910–1912) and Reed College (1912–1917). During 1917–1918 he was an examiner and head of the cost-of-living department of the National War Labor Board, and in 1919 he became special agent of the U. S. Bureau of Labor Statistics. At the end of this year he left government service to become a professor of sociology at Columbia where he remained until 1927. At this time he was made professor of sociology at the University of Chicago. He became Sewell L. Avery Distinguished Service Professor in 1933, and remained at Chicago until his retirement in 1951.[73]

Professor Ogburn's bibliography runs to twenty books and approximately 200 articles, in addition to many chapters written for books edited by others. His more noteworthy volumes include *Social Change* (1922), *American Marriage and Family Relationships* (with E. R. Groves, 1928), *Social Characteristics of Cities* (1937), *The Social Effects of Aviation* (1946), and *Technology and the Changing Family* (with M. F. Nimkoff, 1955). His ideas were made known to hundreds of

[72] Ogburn's co-worker, the late Professor M. F. Nimkoff, expressed it this way: "for the most part the titles of his (Ogburn's) many volumes and articles cluster around a single general theme, social change; more specifically, the impact of technological change on society." Nimkoff, "William Fielding Ogburn, 1886–1959," *American Sociological Review*, Vol. 24, No. 4 (August, 1959), pp. 563–565.

[73] After his retirement from Chicago he served as visiting professor of sociology at Florida State University until the time of his death. This stay, however, was interspersed with other visiting professorships: at the University of Calcutta (1952), at Nuffield College, Oxford (1952–1953), and at the Indian School of International Studies, University of Delhi (1956–1957). Professor Ogburn was the first American sociologist to receive an appointment at Oxford.

thousands of college students in the United States and elsewhere through the various editions of the *Sociology* (general textbook) that he wrote with Professor Nimkoff.[74] Concerning governmental service, several of his positions have already been mentioned; more importantly, he was director of research and a member of President Hoover's Research Committee on Social Trends. Here he supervised a team of America's leading social scientists in writing the volumes, *Recent Social Trends in the United States*.[75] He held the office of president of the American Sociological Society (1929), president of the American Statistical Association (1931), chairman of the Social Science Research Council (1937–1939), vice-president of the American Association for the Advancement of Science (1932), and first president of the Society for the History of Technology. He was holding the latter office at the time of his death on April 27, 1959.

Professor Ogburn also made signal contributions as a teacher, academic statesman, and public servant.[76] It appears that his personal qualities, as well as his important academic positions, offices, and publications, fitted him admirably for the role of academic statesman.[77] Jaffee calls him a "scholar who could best present the case of the social scientist to the world of nonscientists." [78] Another [79] has described Ogburn as "a great man who looked the part."

Principal Ideas

But our immediate interest lies, not in the man, but in his ideas. Ogburn's basic ideas surely are mostly outlined in his first book, *Social Change* [80]—probably his most important single volume. Like Sorokin, his main interest related to the effects of cultural change on social change. But, writing in the early 1920s, he had to approach his thesis by first demonstrating the importance of cultural explanations of social phenomena; this meant showing that biological explanations (then

[74] An official of the Houghton Mifflin Company, publishers, informed this writer as of mid-1965 that sales of the four editions of this volume amounted to more than a half-million copies—and the 4th (1964) edition was still at that time "much in the market." This has to be regarded as a remarkable record of continued acceptance by the field of sociology. Letter to F. R. Allen dated August 27, 1965.

[75] (New York: McGraw-Hill Book Co., 1933.)

[76] Philip M. Hauser, "William Fielding Ogburn, 1886–1959," *American Journal of Sociology*, Vol. LXV, No. 1 (July, 1959), p. 74.

[77] A. J. Jaffe, "William Fielding Ogburn, Social Scientist," *Science*, Vol. 130 (August 7, 1959), pp. 319–320.

[78] *Ibid.*

[79] Helen MacGill Hughes, "William Fielding Ogburn, 1886–1959," *Social Forces*, Vol. 38, No. 1 (October, 1959), pp. 1–2.

[80] (New York: B. W. Huebsch, 1922; ten printings); (New York: The Viking Press, 1950; Delta (paperback) edition, 1966).

much in vogue) are not nearly as important in relation to social data as are the cultural.[81] Such a thesis is completely assumed today, but, it must be realized, it is thanks to the work of social scientists like Ogburn. He showed how culture accumulates by the addition of new elements and the discarding of old elements. Cultural additions result from inventions and discoveries. Inventions, defined as any new element in the culture, may be either mechanical or social. Even in making inventions Ogburn held that the cultural factor was exceedingly important, more so than the biological. Inherited mental capacity is needed in order to invent things, but the existing culture must provide requisite elements if an invention is to be possible. Thus, it is essentially correct to say that the existing culture, not necessity or inherited capacity, is the mother of inventions. Indeed, if the culture base is ready for some invention to be made (that is, if the needed elements are available), the invention will often be made independently by several people. Ogburn (with Dorothy Thomas) cited many illustrations of this.[82] Diffusion is another process that promotes rapid culture growth; some diffusion is inevitable when cultures are in contact. The rate of growth of material culture, resulting from inventions and from diffusion, bears an approximate relationship to the compound interest law, said Ogburn; however, culture growth is not constant or even, because some inventions are far more important than others and bring many more social changes. Ogburn points out that, even though culture has been rapidly advancing in recent years, biological evolution has been slow.[83] Mutations occur infrequently. The point is to be made, then, that cultural evolution is not accounted for by biological evolution.

In the *Social Change* volume Ogburn also discusses (Part III) why cultures do not change faster than they do. The reason is that certain resistances are apt to be made to inventions or to diffused ideas or objects. These resistances are based on vested interests, traditions, habits, social pressures, conservatism as an outlook, and glorification of the past as a psychological tendency. Ogburn then considers social maladjustments (Part IV) that often result from the change process. At this point he states the well-known hypothesis of cultural lag: Lag occurs because two or more cultural elements are related, yet they change at different rates of speed. We shall return presently for further discussion of this hypothesis. At any rate, Ogburn became exceedingly well known for the *lag* hypothesis, which was popular for many years.

[81] *Social Change* (1950 edition), pp. 40 and 50.
[82] *Ibid.*, pp. 90–102.
[83] Ogburn declares that biological change during the last 2,000 years "must be exceedingly slight, if it has occurred at all." *Ibid.*, p. 141.

Interestingly enough, as Duncan has put it,[84] "as the vehemence of critics has increased, the concept, or at least the terminology, has won widespread use, and 'cultural lag' may now be found in the dictionary, written with initial lower-case letters and without Ogburn's name attached." Ogburn discusses the adjustment between human nature and culture in Part V of the *Social Change*. This rests on the earlier conclusions that man has changed little biologically (he is essentially primitive in nature) while his culture has been fast-changing and is now complicated. Hence, the picture is of a cave man dwelling in the modern city. Many problems arise (such as war, crime, sexual difficulties, and disease) because of man's inability or slowness in adapting to modern artificial conditions. Evidences of lack of adjustment are also seen in nervousness and insanity.

In the 1950 edition of *Social Change*, Ogburn added a fresh and notable statement: Part VI, entitled, "Social Evolution, Reconsidered" that concisely summarizes his views on cultural evolution. Cultural evolution, he declares, is explained by four factors, namely: invention, accumulation, diffusion, and adjustment.[85] Invention is the central factor. Thus, cultural evolution is caused by these factors much as Darwin explained biological evolution in terms of variation, natural selection, and heredity.

The essential elements of the Ogburn theory of socio-cultural change have been stated here, but he continually added to his ideas. Restatements and an occasional expansion of ideas are found in the various editions of the Ogburn-Nimkoff general textbook as well as in such volumes as *The Social Effects of Aviation* (1946), *Technology and International Relations* (1949), which he edited and to which he contributed three chapters, and the *Technology and the Changing Family* (1955).

In *The Social Effects of Aviation*, he introduced a novel type of sociological inquiry: predicting the future effects of a major invention. Knowing the process by which inventions produce social changes,[86] he maintained that the coming social effects of a new invention could be set forth with scientific validity; that is, coming effects can be fore-

---

84 Otis Dudley Duncan, Introduction, in Duncan (ed.), *William F. Ogburn on Culture and Social Change* (Chicago: University of Chicago Press, 1964), p. xv.

85 Ogburn, *op. cit.*, p. 377.

86 Ogburn described this process on several occasions. See, for example, W. F. Ogburn (ed.), *Technology and International Relations* (Chicago: University of Chicago Press, 1949), Chap. 2; Ogburn and M. F. Nimkoff, *Sociology* (Boston: Houghton Mifflin Co., 1940, 1950, 1958, and 1964 edition), Part 7; and Ogburn, "How Technology Causes Social Change," Chapter 2 in F. R. Allen, *et al.*, *Technology and Social Change* (New York: Appleton-Century-Crofts, 1957).

seen and anticipated with varying degrees of probability. He illustrated this in the case of the airplane. At the time he was writing this volume (roughly 1945), he suggested that man was standing at the threshold of the air age just as he had entered the automobile age at about the turn of the century. His objective, therefore, was to discuss the coming effects of the airplane on customs, institutions, groups, and communities as seen from the time-position of approximately 1945.[87] He suggested that, with more and more practice, sociologists could perfect their ability to predict future effects of inventions.

Professor Ogburn then outlined procedures for making predictions and discussed related phenomena: extrapolating trends, observing factors that influence projections, differentiating between major trend lines and fluctuations around a major trend, making predictions by means of correlation, dealing with unmeasured data over a period of time, controlling biases and wishful thinking, dealing with fashions, and dealing with the problem of being too conservative (because many social scientists are shown to have erred on the side of underprediction).[88] He then summarized his views on predicting coming inventions, uses of inventions, resistances to these uses, and coming social effects.[89]

This over-all approach is summed up in a paragraph entitled, "A Forecast of Forecasting." Conceding that this is a pioneering type of investigation for sociology, Ogburn writes

> Not many social scientists have seriously tried to find out in advance what an important invention will do to society. Indeed, most social scientists prefer to be historians and are less willing to venture an estimate of the future than the businessman or the ordinary citizen. The ability to look ahead with some success is particularly important in a changing society. The best way to learn to do anything is to go ahead and try it. . . . What is needed is many social scientists working at the problem of forecasting the future as well as social scientists writing histories of past events. With many social scientists working on the future, we should gradually accumulate a set of useful procedures.[90]

After some years, this advice to assay predictions or anticipations of the future was indeed taken by the American Academy of Arts and Sciences, which established its notable Commission on the Year 2000; Professor Daniel Bell serves as the Commission's chairman. Moreover, the World Future Society, with its journal *The Futurist*, has also

---

[87] William F. Ogburn, *The Social Effects of Aviation* (Boston: Houghton Mifflin Co., 1946), p. 10.
[88] *Ibid.*, Chap. 3.
[89] *Ibid.*, Chap. 4.
[90] *Ibid.*, p. 80.

sponsored and encouraged scientific studies of the future, as have The Hudson Institute (headed by Dr. Herman Kahn) and other organizations.

The remainder of Professor Ogburn's *Aviation* volume, in fact the larger part of it, is given over to the uses and effects of aviation involving population, family life, business, cities, health, education, international relations, and many other institutions and activities. We are not concerned here with the specific predicted social effects.

The *Technology and International Relations* volume can be mentioned briefly. In Ogburn's part of this project (he served as editor and wrote three chapters), the perspectives of the research are reversed from the preceding: Instead of investigating the many social effects resulting from one invention, many different technological inventions are studied with regard to their effects on one subject: international relations. Ogburn describes, in an introductory chapter, various effects of inventions in causing the growth of states, the changing power of states, and the increasing destructiveness of war. He then outlines the process of adjustment to inventions generally, and, finally, explores further the effects of aviation on international relations. Other authors discuss the influence of communications inventions, atomic energy, and other inventions on international relations.

In *Technology and the Changing Family* the Ogburn-Nimkoff team again maintains the reverse perspective from the *Aviation* study. This time they are interested in the effects of many technological inventions and scientific discoveries on one social institution: *the family*. Hence the methodology of the study again differs significantly from that used in the *Aviation* volume. Eighteen (18) family experts in the United States [91] were asked to list significant changes in the American family occurring during the past century. Professors Ogburn and Nimkoff compressed the resulting list into the following eight important changes: (1) the increasing emphasis on romantic love as a basis for marital choice, (2) the increasing occurrence of early marriage, (3) the trend toward a smaller family, (4) the trend toward fewer functions being performed by the family, (5) the increasing number of working wives (outside employment), (6) a lessening of patriarchal authority (the trend toward equality in maintaining control), (7) the placing of greater emphasis on the child, and, finally, (8) the trend toward more family disruption (the increasing divorce rate). They anticipated changes in family life that would result in the future from the influence of technological invention and scientific discovery. Many changes

---

[91] William F. Ogburn and M. F. Nimkoff, *Technology and the Changing Family* (Boston: Houghton Mifflin Co., 1955), p. 4. A list of the eighteen experts is given in a footnote.

are here predicted ranging from the effects of new types of home construction to the effects of biological discoveries concerning the reproductive processes, sex hormones, and the process of aging.

In emphasizing inventions, then, as a factor in socio-cultural change (calling invention the central factor), Ogburn pointed out that both mechanical and social inventions may bring change. Moreover, the influence of scientific discoveries, as already noted with the Ogburn-Nimkoff study, is to be included.[92]

> *Science and technology are the most dynamic elements of our material culture. Through technology men transform the physical environment, so that men, natural resources, and inventions and discoveries are the primary factors which determine the wealth, standard-of-living, and well-being of a people.*
>
> . . .
>
> *Social changes of today are connected with inventions of the past and inventions of today will no doubt foreshadow the social changes of the future.*[93]

Professor Ogburn defined the word *technology* comprehensively:

> *[It] includes all the objects of a material culture. Technology would thus encompass the making of a great variety of objects, such as bows and arrows, pottery, harness, plows, dynamos, engines, jewelry, and nylon. . . . Is technology different from applied science: It may be said that the making of mechanical objects rests upon the application of science, though in cases the science may be very crude and simple, as in the making of a trap or a spear by primitive hunters. Technology may therefore include the applied science that aids in making material objects.*
>
> . . .
>
> *In popular language we often find word symbols that are roughly equivalent to the term* technology. *The word* machine *is an abbreviated symbol that stands in a rough way for technology. So also is* factory *or the* factory *system as a referent for the technology that has developed since the invention and use of the steam engine.*[94] *(italics are Ogburn's)*

Ogburn illustrated the *importance* of inventions in bringing social change in such volumes as those concerning aviation, international relations, and the family (as already discussed). Concerning the *number* of effects that might be produced from a significant invention, he drew up a list of 150 social effects resulting from the use of the radio.[95]

---

92 See also Ogburn's earlier study, with the assistance of S. C. Gilfillan, "The Influence of Invention and Discovery," Chapter III in the President's Research Committee on Social Trends, *Recent Social Trends in the United States* (New York: McGraw-Hill Book Co., 1933), pp. 124 and 149–151.

93 *Ibid.*, p. 122.

94 "The Meaning of Technology," Chapter 1 in Allen, *et al., op. cit.,* pp. 8–9.

95 *Recent Social Trends in the United States, op. cit.,* pp. 153–156.

He maintained that many major inventions would produce at least this number of social effects.

Mention should be made of Ogburn's many, often significant, journal articles. Of Ogburn's total of approximately two hundred, Duncan [96] has selected twenty-five (25) relating to the subjects of (1) social evolution, (2) social trends, (3) short-run changes, and (4) methods. Many of the articles play on dominant Ogburn themes: inventions, population, and history; technology as environment; technology and governmental change; technology and the standard of living; trends in social science; the great man versus social forces; and cultural lag as theory. A different kind of article, which might be extremely helpful to graduate students in performing their own research, is entitled, "Some Observations of Sociological Research." [97] Here Ogburn expresses his ideas on scientific research in sociology—not in the manner of a formal treatment of research methods, but as informal commentary with respect to choice of subjects for research, working habits, perfectionism, functions of criticisms, and the final writing up of the project. This article reflects his many years of experience in directing dissertations at Columbia and at the University of Chicago. The ideas may be classed as opinion (as Ogburn himself declares) or advice, but for the most part the commentary is *not* dated.

This concludes our statement of the Ogburn views on socio-cultural change and on certain other matters. Some additional observations relative to the cultural-lag hypothesis will be made presently. His other volumes have less relevance to the subject of change.

Reactions, Criticisms, and an Over-all Assessment

It seems evident from the discussion up to this point that the main contribution of Professor Ogburn regarding socio-cultural change relates to the development of the cultural perspective concerning the subject, including the exploration of associated processes; this new perspective in Ogburn's time replaced the earlier biological emphasis. Ogburn was by no means the only sociologist during the 1920s who emphasized the influence of culture on human affairs, but he was a leading one—and perhaps even *the* leading one—in stressing its importance in the study of social change. We may also observe that Ogburn's general standing as a sociologist was very high—having in mind such considerations as his positions at Columbia and the University of Chicago, his elected offices, and other honors. It seems apparent, all in all, that we are dealing with an eminent sociologist here who, even in preliminary reaction, must be regarded as *one of the*

96 Duncan (ed.), *loc. cit.*
97 *Ibid.*, pp. 328–347.

leading thinkers on the subject of socio-cultural change. We chiefly address ourselves, then, to the question of just *how eminent* was Professor Ogburn's contribution to this subject.

It is interesting that even though Ogburn did not write an autobiography as Sorokin and MacIver did, he nevertheless made an assessment of his own sociological contribution. This was done in response to a request from Howard W. Odum. Ogburn replied as follows:

> *I shall be bold. I claim that the problem of social evolution is solved and that I have played a considerable part in solving it. By solving I mean solving in the sense that Darwin solved the problem of biological evolution. Darwin did it by pointing out three factors, variation, natural selection, and heredity. Darwin added the factor of natural selection. The problem of social evolution is solved by four factors, invention, exponential accumulation, diffusion, and adjustment. My contribution has been largely in the factor of exponential accumulation and also in the development in the factor of invention. I also think that my role has been significant in the adjustment of one part of culture to another [cultural lag].*[98]

This assessment is forthright (telling what he really thought), and we suggest that for the most part it is sustained by the record. The main point of disagreement, as many sociologists would probably see it, relates to his reference to the adjustment of one part of culture to another (the culture lag hypothesis). Here criticisms have mounted. This does indeed warrant further comment. However, his important contributions regarding inventions and exponential accumulation seem indisputable. His emphasis on diffusion is also commendable, although it rests on the accomplishments of anthropologists. In brief, Ogburn made first-order contributions in the realm of the impact of cultural processes on social change, which, as was declared in Chapter 1 here, was the main development in the study of change during the 1920–1940 period. Moreover, he was a conspicuous leader in this, granting that Hornell Hart, F. Stuart Chapin, and others also made contributions. Sorokin emphasized cultural change, as was observed in Chapter 5, but his major explanation took a different turn (the notion of immanent change); a comparison of Ogburn's and Sorokin's contributions is difficult to make. At all events, the high tide of the cultural influence on social change occurred during Ogburn's producing years, and it appears correct to say that his own efforts comprised an important part of this entire development. The cultural influence still constitutes a major perspective regarding social change, and, needless to say, it continues to be widely followed. Indeed, with such inventions as the computer,

[98] This is published in Howard W. Odum, *American Sociology* (New York: Longmans, Green and Co., 1951), p. 151. Duncan has also included it in Duncan (ed.), *op. cit.*, pp. xiv–xv.

space vehicle, intercontinental missile, and laser producing many effects, and with the increasing interest in social inventions and the continuing interest in diffusion, no major slackening of interest in this sector seems evident at all.

If we turn to the criticisms of Professor Ogburn's views, we can begin at this precise point: Because he was so largely concerned with cultural factors in change, some consider that he neglected social-system factors. Of course, it must be realized that if the onset of sociology's interest in and emphasis on the social system is dated about 1940, this criticism is *ex post facto;* certainly Ogburn's early work, including the important *Social Change* volume, came well before this time. Structural functionalists may contend, furthermore, that Ogburn's analysis of the effects of inventions on social institutions is too simple. Because they have called attention to the importance of the functional exigencies of systems and also to the significance of manifest and latent functions, they hold that the impact of inventions and discoveries on these elements should be elaborated. But, again, this is clearly a hindsight criticism so far as Ogburn is concerned. As was maintained in discussing equivalent criticisms of Marxian and Veblenian theory, all social scientists have to express ideas in terms of the stock of ideas of *their* time. Besides, it might be agreed (as was stated in the preceding chapter) that structural functionalists have themselves yet to issue a definitive, full-scale statement on the *changing* social system. These matters testify as much as anything to the fact that the field of sociology continues to move ahead now emphasizing cultural factors, now the social system, then newer concerns still. *Ex post facto* criticisms of many thinkers can doubtless be made. Technically the criticisms may be correct.

Another criticism was mentioned previously, and we allude to it briefly. It has been held that the "technological theory of change does not search far enough." [99] The implication is that technology is based on science, especially during modern times, and that hence science is the real cause of change. This criticism may properly apply to some thinkers, but we simply declare that in our judgment Ogburn is not vulnerable on this point. Time and again he used the phrase "science *and* technology"; it is apparent that he linked them. Indeed, in this section we have quoted him to that effect.

The Hypothesis of Cultural Lag. The *lag* hypothesis requires more extensive discussion. Curiously enough, the concept that probably brought Professor Ogburn more fame than anything else in his

[99] Bernard Barber, *Science and the Social Order* (Glencoe, Ill.: The Free Press, Inc., 1952), p. 212.

productive career has become highly controversial, markedly distorted by many, and much overemphasized. As Ogburn himself took pains to point out, "the concept of cultural lag is not a fundamental part of the theory of social evolution." [100] It is only one of the four factors involved in that theory (and the last one at that). Nevertheless, various sociologists persist in referring to the *lag* statement as Ogburn's theory of social change. Lags do not constitute a basic part of the theory for the additional reason that during the long sweep of history "lags are not visible because they have been caught up." [101] Then, the content of the theory is commonly distorted. All lags are *not* initiated by mechanical inventions to which social institutions must adapt. As Duncan states it, ". . . this proposition is suggested as an empirical generalization for a specific historical period and is not assumed to be without exception, even for that period. In other settings, the sequence of change may run in the other direction." [102] Ogburn was clear enough about this in his original phrasing; he was especially clear in his 1957 restatement.

We do not propose to discuss in detail the various criticisms made regarding the *lag* hypothesis during the years, as we doubt that such discussion would be fruitful at this time. Ogburn himself felt that many criticisms were based on distortions and misunderstandings.[103] We might briefly state two modifications of the hypothesis that we believe are desirable and would meet various criticisms, namely: (1) that the title of the hypothesis be changed from "cultural lag" to "socio-cultural lag," because lags can involve both social and cultural elements (a terminological objection is removed if this modification is made); [104] and (2) that the words *material* and *nonmaterial* (which were used by Professor Ogburn) be avoided in describing what lags behind what. Material and nonmaterial elements of a subject tend to form a basic unity that is best preserved. Lags can as easily be described in relation to specific scientific or technological developments, cultural complexes, institutions, and even elements, as the late Professor Hart maintained.[105] Certain conceptual difficulties are avoided if this modification is followed. At present, however, a main point is that interest in the hypothesis has declined partly because of the controversies but also

[100] *Social Change,* 1950 edition, *op. cit.,* p. 374, footnote.

[101] Ogburn, "Cultural Lag as Theory" (1957), Chap. 7 in O. D. Duncan (ed.), *op. cit.,* p. 95.

[102] Duncan, Introduction, in *ibid.,* p. xvi.

[103] *Social Change, loc. cit.*

[104] The late Professor Nimkoff adopted this suggested modification in preparing the 4th edition (1964) of the *Sociology;* Professor Ogburn had of course died in 1959. See p. 730 of the 4th edition.

[105] Hornell Hart, "The Hypothesis of Cultural Lag: A Present-Day View," Chapter 17 in Allen, *et al., op. cit.,* especially pp. 419–422.

because a fast-developing sociology has moved on to newer concerns. Yet, at the same time, one must point out that, in times of rapid change, the relationships between social forms that are changing at different rates of speed remain a durable problem. In any case the *lag* hypothesis of Professor Ogburn has to be regarded as the most controversial element in his theory of change—indeed it is the only real point of controversy—whether one chooses to think that (1) this element of the theory was properly challenged—that is, that many or most of the criticisms were valid; (2) the difficulty was due to confusions and misunderstandings; or (3) some combination of the two brought the difficulty.[106]

The role of inventions (mechanical and social) clearly occupies an important place in Ogburn's thinking, but one should observe that he avoided the pitfalls of the extreme statement. Ogburn was no technological determinist.[107] Believing that science and technology comprise a dominant force in causing change in Western society (with its given values), he nevertheless was fully aware of the considerable influence of population change, collective behavior, ideologies, resources, and the like. This is no instance of monistic thinking.

If the achievements recorded here indicate that Ogburn is an eminent leader in the study of socio-cultural change, some comparisons are in order. Weighing the relative contributions of Sorokin and Ogburn is logical, because they both laid stress on cultural factors; but unfortunately it is difficult to do. Despite his many accomplishments and enormous productivity, Sorokin's place in sociology is itself extraordinarily difficult to assess at present. If Ogburn's *lag* theory is regarded as controversial, Sorokin's *immanent* theory is in the same category. Because Sorokin was, perhaps, out of the mainstream of American sociology during the latter decades of his life, his general sociological status seems much more controversial than Ogburn's. Both men, at any rate, were highly productive. If one thinks of the total impact on the field of sociology, somehow the comparison of Ogburn and Talcott Parsons comes to mind, strange to say—strange because these two seem to be opposites in certain respects. Parsons is almost entirely a theory man, Ogburn was largely empirical-minded (his final

106 This sociologist subscribes to (3).

107 This is not to say that Ogburn was not occasionally called a technological determinist or something closely akin. See, for example, Warner E. Gettys' review of the first edition of the Ogburn and Nimkoff, *Sociology, op. cit.,* published in the *American Journal of Sociology,* Vol. 47 (1941–1942), pp. 115–119. Gettys declares that "the emphasis placed upon the social role of inventions amounts to a kind of technological determinism." (p. 118) More recently, LaPiere has alluded to Ogburn as a technological determinist. Richard T. LaPiere, *Social Change* (New York: McGraw-Hill Book Co., 1965), pp. 255 and 263.

quest was *proven knowledge,* not theory per se [108]); Parsons has been and is interested in the social system, Ogburn was interested largely in the influence of cultural factors on change; and Parsons has made his major contributions in analyzing the social structure (with comparatively little attention to change), Ogburn concentrated mainly on the subject and processes of change. Nevertheless they share some common features, even though some of them relate to their position in the field of sociology: They were each leaders of their respective viewpoints (we shall not argue over whether Merton or others equaled or surpassed the achievements of Parsons, nor to what extent Hornell Hart or others rivaled Ogburn). Each came close to leading his generation of sociologists; there was, no doubt, some overlapping of years. Each was chairman of his department at a time when that department was widely recognized as a world leader. Again, both were (Parsons still is) highly productive. Both had some difficulties relative to their theories (equilibrium theory and cultural lag, respectively), and both mainly adhered to their earlier formulations in the face of criticisms. But the theory of each was *in most ways* accepted and followed, we would say, by the field of sociology. (Some may choose to dispute this statement in either or both cases.) Both were highly regarded in the discipline, as their offices held and honors received suggest. Neither experienced the kind of personal difficulties that affect status such as Veblen had, nor the life pattern of a radical such as was the lot of Marx. Both had a dominant influence on sociology, somewhat more so, it seems, than MacIver (even despite his excellent writing). In a general way, however, Sorokin, MacIver, and Ogburn, academically located for many years at Harvard, Columbia, and Chicago, respectively, were all notable figures in the field of socio-cultural change. But we must now proceed with other theorists and theories. In the next chapter we shall consider some that have emphasized historical and ideological factors.

ANNOTATED BIBLIOGRAPHY

On the Marxian Ideas of Change

Marx, Karl, *Capital, The Communist Manifesto, and Other Writings,* Max Eastman (ed.) by (New York: The Modern Library, 1932).

    Capital (Das Kapital) is one of the most influential works of social

---

[108] Professor Ogburn was not opposed to theory; yet, theory was for him a step in attaining knowledge. Theory is not the end goal of science, in his view; it is knowledge. Nevertheless, theory stresses the organization of knowledge, which is important. See also the comments of Professor Duncan in his Introduction, Duncan (ed.), *op. cit.,* p. xv. As Duncan says, "For Ogburn the important thing was not the conceptual scheme, but the discoveries to which its application might lead."

science. It expounds the economic interpretation of history, the theory of the class struggle, and of subsequent revolt. Valuable—not for the correctness of its theories but for its practical world influence.

For Commentary and Criticisms of Marx

Bober, M. M., *Karl Marx's Interpretation of History*, 2nd ed. (Cambridge, Mass.: Harvard University Press, 1948).
    Superior, scholarly interpretation.
Rossiter, Clinton, *Marxism: The View from America* (New York: Harcourt, Brace & Co., 1960).
    Ably written, modern American interpretation.

For the Veblen Credo

Veblen, Thorstein, *Theory of the Leisure Class* (New York: The Modern Library, 1934); Veblen, *The Theory of Business Enterprise* (New York: Charles Scribner's Sons, 1904; Mentor paper edition, 1958); Veblen, *The Engineers and the Price System* (New York: The Viking Press, 1921).
    These volumes provide the essence of Veblen. Eminently worthwhile.

For Criticisms and Discussion of the Credo

Lerner, Max (ed.), *The Portable Veblen* (New York: The Viking Press, 1958).
    A lively and helpful introduction to Veblen.
Riesman, David, *Thorstein Veblen* (New York: Charles Scribner's Sons, 1953; paperback edition, 1960).
    Reflective and worthwhile; Riesman points up inconsistencies in Veblen's ideas.

For the Ogburn Ideas

Ogburn, William F., *Social Change* (New York: B. W. Huebsch, Inc., 1922; new edition, The Viking Press, 1950; Delta paperback edition, 1966). See also Ogburn, *The Social Effects of Aviation* (Boston: Houghton Mifflin, 1946); Ogburn, "Technology As Environment," *Sociology and Social Research,* Vol. XLI (September–October, 1956), 3–9.
    The *Social Change* is probably Ogburn's most important single volume; it is widely regarded as a classic. The additional Part VI in the 1950 edition should be noted. "Aviation" illustrates the Ogburn treatment of a modern invention and its social effects; it leads off with a worthy section on methodology. The "Technology As Environment" article, a product of his later years, is rewarding.

For Commentary on the Ogburn Ideas

Duncan, Otis Dudley (ed.), *William F. Ogburn on Culture and Social Change* (Chicago: University of Chicago Press, 1964).
    Duncan's Introduction is brief (15 pages) but excellent. Significant articles by Ogburn over the years and a full bibliography are also presented. A very helpful contribution.

8

Theories of Change:
Historical and Ideological

In this chapter we shall discuss theories of socio-cultural change that emphasize the influence of historical and ideological factors, namely: the theories of (1) Oswald Spengler, (2) Arnold J. Toynbee, (3) A. L. Kroeber, (4) Max Weber, and (5) Don Martindale.[1] Spengler's work led off a series of major volumes in the general category of historical sociology that appeared during the (approximately) second quarter of the twentieth century. A veritable efflorescence, as one of the authors (Kroeber) would call it, manifested itself at this time relative to the subject of socio-cultural growth. The time was apparently ripe for this productiveness. Ample opportunity is provided to consider different kinds of ideas presented in markedly different ways. Let us begin with the lead-off man: Spengler himself.

OSWALD SPENGLER (1880–1936)

Oswald Spengler was a German philosopher who was also adept in mathematics, science, history, and art. After receiving his doctorate from the University of Halle in 1904, he served as a schoolmaster for seven years.[2] After this he moved to Munich, choosing to work on a major historico-philosophical project that was finally published in 1918 (it was delayed by the war). Its title was *Untergang des Abendlandes,* which was translated as *The Decline of the West.*[3] It contained gloomy predictions, but these suited the popular mood in Germany following the end of the First World War. At any rate, the work received wide public acclaim. It is true that its reception in the universities was cool;

---

[1] At the end of this chapter we shall make a brief, over-all comment relative to the various theories discussed in Chapters 5–8, as well as to the omissions.

[2] Biographical material has been obtained from the Oswald Spengler article in the *Encyclopaedia Britannica,* Vol. 21, 1964 edition (Chicago: Encyclopaedia Britannica, Inc., 1964), p. 204, and the Oswald Spengler, article in the *Columbia Encyclopaedia,* 3rd ed. (New York: Columbia University Press, 1963), p. 2018. See also H. Stuart Hughes, *Oswald Spengler: A Critical Estimate* (New York: Charles Scribner's Sons, 1952), p. 167.

[3] *Der Untergang des Abendlandes:* Umrisse einer Morphologie der Weltgeschichte; I: Gestalt und Wirklichkeit (Munich: 1923). This was translated by Charles Francis Atkinson as *The Decline of the West,* Vol. I: *Form and Actuality* (New York: Alfred A. Knopf, 1926).

professional historians, social scientists, and philosophers on both sides of the Atlantic were sharply critical of both its methods and conclusions. The divided reception—public enthusiasm and scholarly disdain —continued for some years. Spengler proceeded to engage in other enterprises after this. But a second book, *Man and Technics,* was not as successful. A third one angered the Nazis, who by this time had captured political power in Germany.[4] Hence, with definite assists from the Nazis, Spengler's popularity in Germany gradually receded. It is clear that the *Decline of the West* was his chief claim to fame.

Spengler's Major Ideas

Two key ideas pervade Spengler's ponderous and gloomy book. The first is an emphasis on the preeminent importance of the culture— seen as a mystical and creative inner force, not as the way of life of people in a society as modern social scientists see it. World history, asserts Spengler, has to be seen as the endless formations and transformations, the waxing and waning, of organic cultural forms.[5] The meaningful element is the inner possibilities—the soul—of the culture. The idea of *destiny*—an important word for Spengler—is, again, a mystical, inner phenomenon; it contains the fate of the spiritual and artistic development of the soul's potentialities. History is the "actualizing of a soul." [6] This, it is clear, is a special brand of history. It is intuitive—the sensing of the reality of historical events—and hardly modern systematic and factual history. The second key idea is that cultures grow as an organism: youth, manhood, old age, and death. Each stage has a definite duration, and this is always the same.[7]

Spengler, then, sees history as the multiple dramas of a number of cultures each stamping its events in its own image, each having its

4 Spengler's *Man and Technics* (New York: Alfred A. Knopf, 1932) was not a work of high quality. It predicted the doom of man because of technological influences. Technology had outrun its usefulness; it was becoming man's master instead of his servant. Moreover, the black and yellow races would learn to use it and so defeat the Western (Caucasian) nations. Spengler followed this with *The Hour of Decision* (New York: Alfred A. Knopf, 1934), and this one brought forth the wrath of the Nazis. Hughes comments that the latter were angered for two reasons: Spengler repudiated the Nazis who had, up to this time, considered him one of their intellectual leaders, and he advocated policies—especially the resort to war—that Hitler intended to use but did not want publicized. See Hughes, *op. cit.,* Chap. VIII (especially pp. 131–132).

5 For comments concerning *culture, civilization,* and other terms for which Spengler gives special meanings, see Hughes, *op. cit.,* p. 72.

6 Spengler has no use for the usual divisions of history, namely: ancient, medieval, and modern. Spengler's history, one soon realizes, is not the field of history as modern historians and social scientists tend to view it.

7 *Decline of the West, op. cit.,* pp. 107–110.

ideas, feelings, life, and death.[8] If the idea of a culture is the sum total of its inner possibilities, how does a culture start? In Spengler's words:

> *A culture is born in the moment when a great soul awakens out of the proto-spirituality* (dem urseelenhaften Zustande) *of ever-childish humanity, and detaches itself, a form from the formless, a bounded and mortal thing from the boundless and enduring. . . . It dies when this soul has actualized the full sum of its possibilities in the shape of peoples, languages, dogmas, arts, states, sciences, and reverts into the proto-soul. . . . Every Culture stands in a deeply-symbolical, almost in a mystical, relation to the Extended, the space, in which and through which it strives to actualize itself. The aim once attained —the idea, the entire content of inner possibilities, fulfilled and made externally actual—the Culture suddenly hardens, it mortifies, its blood congeals, its force breaks down, and it becomes Civilization.*[9]

The nature of the destiny idea in relation to social causation is seen as follows:

> *Causality is the reasonable, the law-bound, the describable, the badge of our whole waking and reasonable existence. But destiny is the word for an inner certainty that is not describable. . . . the idea of destiny can be imparted only by the artist working through media like portraiture, tragedy, and music.*[10]

Thus destiny is not reasonable, law-bound, and describable. It is mystical in nature. This means that no factual explanation of change is attempted; Spengler's thinking is nonobjective in nature. Here we have a clue to the opposition of historians and social scientists to the Spenglerian ideas: They are not grounded in factual data; indeed there is no attempt to think objectively and factually. Spengler's approach is essentially antiscientific.[11] If doubt should exist concerning this, Spengler removes the doubt by his explicit statement that he hates mathematics.[12] He cordially dislikes conventional history. He has little confidence in scientific psychology.[13] This writer could find no references to sociology, but can well imagine the nature of his reaction.

[8] *Ibid.*, p. 21.

[9] *Ibid.*, p. 106.

[10] *Ibid.*, p. 118.

[11] Hughes comments that Spengler's use of the term *destiny*, for example, is in part a protest against one of the major tenets of positivism: the practice of assigning to historical movements and events clear and determinable causes. See Hughes, *op. cit.*, p. 70.

[12] Spengler declares: "The means whereby to identify dead forms is Mathematical Law. The means whereby to understand living forms is Analogy." He adds that Goethe hated mathematics. *Ibid.*, pp. 4 and 25.

[13] Spengler asks: "Why has psychology—meaning thereby not knowledge of men and experience of life but scientific psychology—always been the shallowest and most worthless of the disciplines of philosophy, . . . ?" Furthermore he has stated: "I maintain, then, that scientific psychology . . . has [shown an] inability to discover or even to approach the essence of the soul, ..." *Ibid.*, pp. 299 and 302.

Spengler's utterances are made in the spirit of humanistic values, not in that of science at all. His main heroes are not scientists (physical, biological, or social), rather they are humanists: in particular, Goethe, Nietzsche, and Wagner. For Spengler, in short, scientific truth is no guiding beacon.[14] Moreover, specific ideas such as the organismic succession of cultural birth, childhood, youth, manhood, old age, and death come to him as an inner revelation; they are not produced by the process of empirical investigation.

Comment and Criticisms

The fundamental difficulty with Spengler's contribution is now laid bare if we interpret that contribution from the standpoint of social *science* (as this volume does). In the first place, he provides no objective explanation of change at all—because we cannot accept his notion of inner destiny as the source of ongoing events as that. *If* we accept ideas on the basis of empirical fact and *if* we insist on objective evidence in the linking of cause and effect, Spengler's approach is totally invalid. He does not even try to make a scientific presentation. His concepts, such as the "soul of culture," its "inner possibilities," its "awakening out of proto-spirituality," and its "destiny," are all, as we have said, mystical and subjective. Could any one define them operationally? Could any one prove or disprove hypotheses involving them? They are quite wanting in scientific method.[15] Spengler's ideas, even if we gloss over their nonscientific origin and the concepts employed, have met with persistent criticisms. His organismic view of cultural growth, to take an example, presents major difficulties. His doctrine of the successive stages posits a fixed, indeed iron-clad, course of human affairs. The youth stage of culture inexorably follows the birth (after a fixed period of years). Maturity invariantly succeeds youth, and so on. Why? Because the "soul is being actualized." Its destiny is being fulfilled. Every culture is held to conform to the fixed pattern. Why? Because Spengler says so. In the meantime all the many influences and impacts known by social scientists to be consequential—wars, depressions, revolutions, migrations, racial occurrences, inventions and discoveries, industrialization, urban concentrations, and explorations—are

---

14 Indeed one recoils reading the following: "Truths are truths only in relation to a particular mankind." (*Ibid.*, p. 46.) The contrast between Spengler and Ogburn, for example, whose major interest was in *proven knowledge* (see Chapter 7), is as between night and day.

15 For comments by others concerning this matter, see Arnold J. Toynbee, *Reconsiderations* (New York: Oxford University Press, 1961), p. 43 (including footnote 4); and A. L. Kroeber, *Configurations of Culture Growth* (Berkeley: University of California Press, 1944), pp. 825–833. For somewhat different criticisms see Robert A. Nisbet, *Social Change and History* (New York: Oxford University Press, 1969), pp. 214–216.

conveniently forgotten. MacIver calls this the "closed curve theory." [16] *The main point is that the real causes of socio-cultural change are evaded.* This is an extreme example of the dogmatic neglect of a genuine explanation of change. Thus the fixed pattern linked with the mystical subjective concepts serves as a smoke screen that could discourage genuine attempts using scientific methods to find the real causes of change.[17] One may further object that if cultural maturity is at hand, death may not necessarily lie ahead. As was stated in Chapter 5 concerning Sorokin's theory, modern Western civilization (for instance) *may* succumb via nuclear-biological-chemical war or other debacle or combination of debacles. Many variables will determine what proves to be the future course of development—what actions leaders will take, what new inventions may be made, and so on. We have no way of predicting these things. But one thing we do know in an uncertain world is this: No one inevitable, inexorable course of development lies ahead that is caused by a mystical "soul" or "idea of destiny." There is no compelling reason why we should believe this. If some choose to do so, they may accept it on Spengler's terms—as a matter of faith.[18]

[16] Robert M. MacIver, *Social Causation* (New York: Ginn and Co., 1942), pp. 104–107. See also Toynbee, *op. cit.,* p. 519. MacIver also points up a related fault, namely: If one posits a fixed, predetermined course of events, one is likely to take gross liberties with the historical dating in order to justify such a scheme. This is done by Spengler in assigning a lifetime of 1400 years for each of his great cultures. Thus, says MacIver, "he makes the Egyptian 'culture' end about 1800 B. C., and the Indian and the Chinese at the opening of the Christian era." (p. 106) Indeed, how would Spengler explain the recent rise of Hindu culture following India's being granted independence in the late 1940s, or the intensified activity in Chinese culture since that nation turned Communist, also following the Second World War? These nations, in Spengler's terms, were at the advanced *civilization* stage; they were "awaiting death."

[17] It is quite possible that an intuitive idea or flash of insight may later be validated by scientific inquiry. In Spengler's case, however, further reflection on the matter has led most thinkers to doubt more than ever that one stage of cultural development must *necessarily* follow another one, especially in an inflexible manner. Moreover, they have seen many real causes of change, which Spengler overlooked.

[18] If we believe that Spengler's approach is invalid, so far as social science is concerned, and that his ideas are unsubstantiated, why have we chosen to discuss the ideas in this textbook? Actually we do not believe that such a discussion is *necessary,* as Professor A. L. Kroeber has also declared (*op. cit.,* pp. 828, 833). Spengler writes as a philosopher, not as a historian or social scientist. It may be recalled that at the beginning of Chapter 5 the statement was made that one or two theories would be discussed even though they were felt to be unsubstantiated. We specifically had Spengler in mind at this time. Nevertheless, we believe the discussion worthwhile because (1) sociologists of the present and future can learn something even from faulty statements (certainly a sociologist who is tempted to issue dogmatic, mystical, and inflexible theories might reflect on the criticisms that seem proper for this kind of treatment); and because (2) these Spenglerian ideas are often compared with those of others, especially with those of Sorokin, Toynbee, and Kroeber. Indeed, we shall later indulge in some comparisons ourselves. Hence, statement of the first ideas (even if they are regarded as invalid) is quite necessary for comparison.

ARNOLD J. TOYNBEE (1889–   )

Professor Arnold Toynbee, the English historian, has several things in common with Spengler, one being that both maintain that *civilizations* constitute the most meaningful unit for historical study. For both, the prime interest is the comparative study of civilizations. Another common point is that both had difficulties with scientific method; we shall see Toynbee's presently. However, his difficulties were not as severe as Spengler's, whose writings, as we have seen, actually had an antiscience tone.[19] In many respects Toynbee is better compared with Sorokin than with Spengler. Both Sorokin and Toynbee gave forth their interpretations of the broad chronicle of history in an outstanding set of volumes. Toynbee's *A Study of History*,[20] comprising twelve volumes, is every bit as much a magnum opus as Sorokin's *Social and Cultural Dynamics*. Toynbee's work occupied him for forty years. Each wrote the final volume of his major work after a few years had elapsed, enabling him to take note of criticisms made of the earlier volumes. This artifice is helpful in dealing with controversial ideas, and Sorokin and Toynbee were both controversialists. Toynbee was especially skillful in answering critics in the *Reconsiderations*. This volume is an outstanding example of give-and-take. Cheerful and constructive acceptance of criticism—admitting the validity of some criticisms, disputing others—may not by itself stamp an individual as a great person, but it is perhaps one element in it. More important, the sheer productivity, immense intellectual energy, and importance of their all-around contributions *do* stamp both Sorokin and Toynbee as intellectual giants in their respective disciplines.[21] Both write to a world audience, perhaps Toynbee slightly more so than Sorokin. Whatever criticisms they

[19] Toynbee's problems with regard to the scientific method were more on the order of Sorokin's: Both departed from the proper canons of science without flaying the very spirit of science as Spengler did.

[20] All volumes of Toynbee's *A Study of History* were published by the Oxford University Press, London and New York. The publication dates of the various volumes were as follows: Vol. 1–3 (1934); Vol. 4–6 (1939); Vols. 7–10 (1954); Vol. 11, written with E. D. Myers (1959); and Vol. 12, *Reconsiderations* (1961). In this textbook references will chiefly be made to the abridgement of Vols. 1–6 by D. C. Somervell (1947) and to the *Reconsiderations*.

[21] The fact that Sorokin was a sociologist and Toynbee is a historian matters little. Both are essentially giving an interpretation of history, an analysis. When a historian does not stop with presenting the historical facts but proceeds to analyze and interpret them, he approaches (perhaps steps over) the line dividing the fields of history and sociology. Toynbee was opposed to breaking up the study of human affairs into the so-called disciplines anyway. Bierstedt comments that Toynbee's *A Study of History* is a "work of pure speculative sociology." Toynbee is looking for a common pattern in the growth of civilizations, a principle of social change. Robert Bierstedt, *The Social Order* (New York: McGraw-Hill Book Co., 1957), p. 535.

may have received, each qualifies as a towering thinker of the twentieth century.

Arnold J. Toynbee was born in London, England, on April 14, 1889.[22] He was educated at Balliol College, Oxford. He served as Fellow and tutor at Oxford from 1912–1915; was connected with the British government during years of the First World War, part of that time with the Foreign Office; he was a member of the British delegation to the Peace Conference of 1919; and he was a professor of Byzantine and Greek history at the University of London, 1919–1924, where he continued as Research Professor of International History from 1925 until his retirement in 1955. Also he was Director of Studies at the Royal Institute of International Affairs in London during the latter thirty-year period. He is the author of numerous books including *Nationality and War* (1915), *The New Europe* (1915), *Greek Historical Thought* (1924), *A Study of History*, twelve volumes (1934 to 1961), *Civilization on Trial* (1948), and *War and Civilization* (1951). He has been the recipient of many honors including honorary doctorate degrees from Oxford, Cambridge, and Birmingham in England and Princeton and Columbia in the United States.

Challenge and Response

Toynbee's main key to the understanding of socio-cultural change lies in his conception of challenge and response. He initially considers the possibility that civilizations are started by superior races[23] and are a resultant of favoring geographical environments,[24] but he dismisses these explanations as inadequate. Challenges, at any rate, may come from the physical or the human environment. Civilizations get started, then, because people have had added stimulus to create a life pattern that is enduring. There are virtues in adversity. Some areas have more difficult conditions of life (he mentions Scotland and New England), but their final accomplishments may be superior to other areas that are more favored by nature. Factors in the human environment that create challenges are wars, external pressures (military, political, and others), and penalizations (handicaps that often lead to compensations, enslavement, and various types of discrimination[25]). But an important

---

[22] Toynbee's biographical data are taken from *Who's Who in America* (1968–1969).

[23] *A Study of History, op. cit.,* pp. 52–55.

[24] *Ibid.,* pp. 55–59.

[25] Among these Toynbee discusses in some detail the discriminations and persecutions undergone by the Jewish people. *Ibid.,* pp. 135–139. In all challenges, he says, the unknown quantity is "the reaction of the actors to the ordeal when it actually does come." (p. 68)

point concerning all these types of challenges, is that challenge needs to represent the Golden Mean: the challenge must be *enough and not too great*. If it is excessive, the people may be overcome. It does not follow that one can increase the severity of the challenge *ad infinitum*. Indeed, a law of diminishing returns seems to set in: If the challenge becomes quite formidable, the response is likely to be less satisfactory.[26] How does this theory apply to the *growth* of civilizations instead of their *genesis*? Toynbee points out, first, that all civilizations do not grow to adulthood; such is not inevitable. Rather, some do not survive infancy and the growth of others may become arrested. The optimum response, at any rate, is one that not only surmounts the current challenge but does so in a way that evokes new challenges it is again able to meet successfully.[27]

This may impress many readers as being reasonable and significant. One element in the theory that has constituted a point of resistance, however, is that Toynbee states it in the language of mythology.[28] Moreover, challenge and response has a religious connotation, which has bothered scientific-minded historians and social scientists. Indeed Toynbee declares that the original source of the expression was the Bible.[29] God presents a challenge to some people individually or collectively. Thus the idea expresses an anthropomorphic vision of God as a person with whom other individuals have personal encounters. In Toynbee's words:

> *Encounters taking the form of challenge-and-response are the most . . . illuminating kind of events for a student of human affairs if he believes, as I believe, that one of the distinctive characteristics of Man is that he is partially free to make choices, and that this partial freedom is not merely apparent but is genuine. Encounters are the occasions in human life on which freedom and creativity come into play and on which new things are brought into existence. God reveals himself in encounters, not in propositions; and acts of creation are one of the activities in which He thus manifests Him-*

---

[26] Toynbee gives many examples of challenges of varying severity. (*Ibid.*, pp. 146–152.)

[27] In Toynbee's words:

> *The real optimum challenge is one which not only stimulates the challenged party to achieve a single successful response but also stimulates him to acquire momentum that carries him a step farther: from achievement to a fresh struggle, from the solution of one problem to the presentation of another, from Yin to Yang again.*

Ibid., p. 187. See also *Reconsiderations, op. cit.*, p. 260.

[28] Says Toynbee: "Let us shut our eyes, for the moment, to the formulae of science in order to open our ears to the language of mythology." *A Study of History, op. cit.*, p. 60.

[29] He points out that challenge and response is the master motif of the Old Testament. *Reconsiderations, op. cit.*, p. 254.

self. . . . As I see it, the challenger is God—that is, absolute Reality approached anthropomorphically—even when the challenge comes ostensibly from Man or Nature. When a challenge has been delivered, then . . . we shall not expect the respective outcomes of these situations to conform with one another.

. . .

I believe that the outcome of a response to a challenge is not causally predetermined, is not necessarily uniform in all cases, and is therefore intrinsically unpredictable.[30]

Withdrawal and Return

A second, less basic theory of change, which is partly related to challenge and response inasmuch as it is one way for an individual to respond to a challenge, is that of Toynbee's notion of withdrawal and return. In Toynbee's words, it is "the withdrawal of an individual or a group from its social milieu, followed by a period of aloofness, during which the temporarily retiring group or individual incubates something new. . . . [then] the party in question re-enters the society from which it has returned, but re-enters it in a new role, acquired during its temporary absence." [31] He thinks that this kind of phenomenon plays an important part in the growth of civilizations, and it is illustrated by various leaders in religion and in human studies. In the religious field he mentions Paul, Saint Ignatius Loyala, the Buddha, Confucius, Jesus, Saint Benedict, and others.[32] He illustrates this in the area of human affairs by the experiences of Thucydides, Xenophon, Machiavelli, Claredon, and others. Thus, Paul withdrew after receiving the challenge of his vision on the road and returned as a Christian apostle; the Buddha withdrew after his experiences of the ills of life and returned as a preacher instead of a prince; Jesus withdrew into the wilderness after his experience at the baptism and returned as a preacher and healer instead of a carpenter; and so on. In the field of human affairs individuals may be exiled, deported, or imprisoned, after which they may return in a different role. Toynbee does not mention Hitler, who might be thought of as an example of this: Hitler spent approximately the latter half of 1924 in the Landsberg prison in Germany during which time he dictated the message of *Mein Kampf* (his autobiography). He emerged from prison with a renewed sense of mission for post-First World War Germany, but he had held most of his ideas before that time.[33] Perhaps Toynbee concluded that Hitler's sojourn in the Landsberg prison was too short to

---

30 *Ibid.*, p. 256.
31 *Ibid.*, p. 263.
32 *Ibid.*, pp. 264–265.
33 William L. Shirer, *The Rise and Fall of the Third Reich* (New York: Simon and Schuster, 1960), Chap. 4.

be of consequence. Stalin and other Communists were exiled in Siberia for varying periods of time as well. At any rate, Toynbee believes that this phenomenon of withdrawal from society and later return is a matter of significance.[34]

Models for Studying Civilizations

Also, Toynbee endeavored to set forth one or more models for the emergence and development of civilizations. He began with the Hellenic model, which was affiliated with contemporary Western civilization. He suggested that a "multiple-track chart" was needed in order to understand the totality of history, and his Hellenic model incorporated the following elements: (1) the pattern of that civilization's political history, (2) its configuration of social history, (3) its configuration of religious history, (4) the part played by the barbarians whom he called the "external proletariat," and (5) the renaissance of Hellenic culture in Byzantine and Western civilizations.[35]

However, Toynbee thought that other models were needed, and he cited the Chinese as an alternate. He constructed, furthermore, a *combined* Hellenic-Chinese model, which he believed explained the growth of civilizations quite well. He also cited a Jewish alternative model for civilizations.

Comment and Criticisms

Toynbee and Scientific Method.   The approach from which one attempts to judge the theories of Arnold Toynbee makes a considerable difference. If one appraises his theories from the standpoint of the humanistic tradition—and he was the product of a classical education himself—one would be disposed to one particular conception of his ideas. The education he received brought him an appreciation of all cultures; he had no ethnocentric emphasis on England or even on Western civilization. But Toynbee's classical emphasis did bring an underemphasis of certain contemporary values such as science and economic well-being. Moreover, as well as placing an accent on classical antiquity he frequently lapsed into metaphysics.[36] Some may accept these ideas on the metaphysical plane, but many historians, social scientists, and others will wish for a more scientific emphasis.

34 He admits that the idea has received considerable criticism. *Reconsiderations, op. cit.,* p. 264.

35 *Ibid.,* pp. 171–172.

36 Hans Kohn declares that in Toynbee's search for the ultimate meaning of all history he often "transcends history into metahistory." Kohn, "A Hopeful Vision for Humanity, a review of Toynbee's, *Reconsiderations,*" *The New York Times Book Review* (May 7, 1961).

Again, are such statements as the following acceptable from the standpoint of scientific objectivity? Toynbee declares:

> *These kaleidoscopic changes in the appearance of the past illustrate the problem of relativity which besets historians, anthropologists, sociologists, economists, and other students of human affairs—not least, perhaps, the psychologists. . . . Whatever the nature of the object that is under observation, a human observer is incapable of seeing it with the imaginary detachment of an inconceivable outsider. . . . It is impossible for one human being to think about another human being, present or absent, living or dead, without also having feelings about him and passing judgments on him.*
>
> . . .
>
> *We may say with our lips that, when we are making an historical study of our fellow human beings, we suspend our moral judgments and suppress our feelings; but, if we fancy that we can do that, we are deceiving ourselves. All interpretations of human events which profess to exclude ethics actually smuggle in uncritical ethical judgments. . . . [Judgments] are inherent in all relations between one human being and another.*[37]

In human relationships people inevitably have feelings and develop judgments with regard to others—this is granted. But for *scientists* (including scientific-minded historians) who study such behavior, subjective and ethical judgments *must* be rigidly controlled. If judgments of this kind enter into the discussion and analysis of the material—as sometimes appears to be the case with Toynbee—objections will be raised on the score of infringement of the proper scientific method. Observers will have judgments, it is conceded, even concerning remote or ancient personages.[38] Such subjectivities and biases have to be contained. This is a point of insistence for scientists, whether one is studying the most ethically laudable people in the world or the most repugnant villains.

Challenge and Response.   The flavor of the preceding comments can be carried over in part to the specific theory of challenge and response. Our emphasis is that this theory is not treated scientifically enough. It is not so much in this instance that Toynbee has mixed ethical-subjective judgments with historical data, although he may have done this occasionally. But he has not formulated hypotheses relative to challenges under various conditions in a scientific manner—various kinds of challenges bringing forth various kinds of responses.

[37] *Reconsiderations, op. cit.*, pp. 52–55.

[38] Toynbee makes the point, defending his stand, that even in the instance of the Egyptian Pharaoh Ikhnaton, who lived and died in the fourteenth century, B.C., modern Western scholars who deciphered the Egyptian scripts had strong feelings for and against him. Thus, one does not only have ethical or emotional reactions toward those on the current or recent scene—such as Nixon, Kennedy, Eisenhower, Franklin D. Roosevelt, Churchill, Nehru, Stalin, or Hitler. *Ibid.*, pp. 56–57.

Under what conditions will this or that response be made? Toynbee has not marshalled data in the effort to test such hypotheses. Consequently, the theory is so general and vague, as McClelland points out,[39] that it has little if any predictive power. K. D. Erdman has declared [40] that challenge and response, although not validated as a scientific explanation, may nevertheless have value. It can be accepted nonempirically. However, at the beginning of Chapter 5 the contrast was made (following Merton) between theory in the strict sense and general orientations to subjects. We would emphasize challenge and response as a general orientation to socio-cultural change. Thus, what is needed, from the viewpoint of social science, is a tightening and factualizing of the treatment using this orientation so that specific hypotheses can be tested, and interdependent and verifiable statements of relations between variables can thus (hopefully) be produced.[41]

The quest of a more scientific (less humanistic) theory relative to challenge and response might have considerable promise. For this writer, the basic idea has much appeal. Many changes in civilizations, societies, and smaller social systems *do* come from challenges. How these varying units react to different kinds of challenges is indeed important. One readily thinks of the challenge of Nazi Germany internally to the Jewish people or externally to the British people in 1940 (when the leadership of Winston Churchill undoubtedly assumed major importance)—or the challenge of the severe floods of the Tennessee River for more than a century until the American government "responded" by creating the Tennessee Valley Authority (TVA)—or other challenges to societies, corporations, other institutions. The idea is significant. It is just the sort of fertile and meaningful conception,

---

39 In McClelland's view,

> . . . the difficulty with Toynbee's theory is that it is so general that it cannot possibly be wrong. If a civilization has shown a creative response, it must have had just the right amount of stimulus. And since the stimulus may come from a large number of different sources—climate, the pressures of other peoples, internal conditions, etc.—the historian can always "prove" that the stimulus was "just right." Such a theory has very little explanatory power and certainly no predictive power.

David C. McClelland, *The Achieving Society* (Princeton, N. J.: D. Van Nostrand Co., 1961), p. 7.

40 *Reconsiderations, op. cit.*, p. 262.

41 As things stand, we would have to agree with Sidney Hook who states the following:

> Unless we can define what constitutes a successful response, unless we can say in advance what kind of unsuccessful response to what kind of problem spells disaster for a culture, unless we can formulate a hypothesis concerning determinate conditions under which a creative response will or will not be made, we have hardly made a beginning towards a scientific study of the rise, growth, and decline of cultures.

Ibid., pp. 259–260.

as this writer sees it, that contrasts vividly with Spengler's dogmatic and inflexible doctrine.

Withdrawal and Return. Our comment here will be brief. This Toynbee theory, as we see it, is reasonable but not very important. Many people may withdraw from society, reflect on problems, return, and provide a specific program to improve conditions; that a fairly sizeable number of leaders has done this is shown by Toynbee's list. Is it necessary for leaders to withdraw to the mountains or other secluded spots in order to provide vital programs? Don't many leaders provide a needed program without any withdrawing? We would think so—without a precise statistical accounting. Sometimes withdrawal is enforced, as when a Russian revolutionary is exiled to Siberia or any individual is sent to prison. Withdrawal (and consequent reflection) may be socially and personally beneficial. Ghandi was reputed to have set aside one day for reflection and prayer each week. Is formal withdrawal from the society necessary? We are not convinced that it is. In any case, hypotheses would need to be validated. As with challenge and response, Toynbee provides much information. He does not formulate (much less test) hypotheses.

Attractive Perspectives. Finally, we would call attention to what, for lack of better expression, we call Toynbee's attractive perspectives. His writing has enormous breadth, but here we emphasize its serenity and good temper (another contrast with Spengler). It has a happy flexibility. Toynbee writes as a Christian believer, which may have a relationship to his more optimistic conclusions (a further contrast from Spengler). Although, again, we take no stand concerning optimism or pessimism per se—it is, rather, the illuminating power of the theory that counts—it seems undeniable that Toynbee's theories make pleasanter reading than some of the others. Is this related to his public popularity? Perhaps so, at least in part. Yet, challenge and response and the other ideas, if unscientifically formulated, do have considerable appeal.[42]

ALFRED L. KROEBER (1876–1960)

Another significant macroscopic study of socio-cultural change was contributed by Professor Alfred L. Kroeber, the American anthropologist, in his work entitled, *Configurations of Culture Growth.*[43]

---

[42] For a final, over-all, reflective comment relative to Toynbee we may say, with Robert Bierstedt, that "his [Toynbee's] scope is spectacular, his learning is impressive, his concepts are imaginative—and his conclusions are unverified." Bierstedt, *op. cit.,* p. 536. And if the ideas were verified by scientific procedures, one might add, they could be of considerable significance.

[43] (Berkeley: University of California Press, 1944.)

Regardless of the precise intellectual discipline of its author, this volume is correctly placed in the realm of historical sociology.[44] The account is basically descriptive and Kroeber disavows any attempt at explaining changes in culture patterns; [45] yet, he does not stop with the historical rendition. The volume emphasizes comparative history. Then, conclusions are made based on empirical investigation, even though the conclusions do not comprise explanatory theory such as challenge and response or immanent change. From the standpoint of social *science,* at any rate, we have far more confidence in this generalization from historical data than we had in Spengler's intuitive and subjective revelations or even in Toynbee's intellectual productions with their classical and mythological orientations—even though we admittedly found Toynbee's ideas fascinating in other respects. In short, whatever else we may say about Kroeber's *Configurations of Culture Growth,* we suggest that it is a notable and impressive work of modern social science.[46]

We anticipate the discussion of Professor Kroeber's ideas with much interest for yet another reason, namely: He was a modern social scientist of exceedingly high standing. After completing his doctorate at Columbia University under Franz Boas,[47] Kroeber engaged in numerous research projects in ethnology, linguistics, and archaeology. His lengthy academic career was centered almost entirely at the University of California at Berkeley. Kroeber was the author of *Zuni Kin and Clan* (1917), *Handbook of the Indians of California* (1925), the two editions of *Anthropology* (1923 and 1948),[48] *The Nature of Culture* (1952), and *An Anthropologist Looks at History* (1963),[49] in addition

[44] Kroeber comments: "The aim of the work is obviously more or less sociological. The principal current of anthropology, and its soundest findings until now, I believe to be culture–historical. Nevertheless, if we can also generalize validly, it will be most important." *Ibid.,* Preface.

[45] *Ibid.,* p. 19.

[46] Thus, it is apparent even at the outset that the strongest criticisms we have had regarding Spengler and Toynbee—pertaining to scientific method—do not apply to this work of Kroeber's.

[47] Biographical and similar data have been taken from *Who's Who in America* (1956–1957) and from Talcott Parsons, "Alfred L. Kroeber, 1876–1960," *American Journal of Sociology,* Vol. LXVI, No. 6 (May, 1961), 616–617. Parsons refers to Kroeber as "one of the earliest, and perhaps the most distinguished" of Boas' students.

[48] Julian H. Steward called the revised (1948) edition of *Anthropology* "probably the most important single work ever written in Anthropology." See "A. L. Kroeber —Obituary," *The American Anthropologist,* Vol. 63, No. 5 (October, 1962), 1038–1087.

[49] *An Anthropologist Looks at History* is a collection of papers that Kroeber wrote during the last decade of his life. These papers, selected by Theodora Kroeber and Milton Singer, represent his thinking on the historical theme; it is clear that the growth of cultures constituted a considerable interest for Kroeber. The content of these papers, which concern such subjects as "The Delimitation of Civilizations," "Have Civilizations a Life History?" "The Time Profile of Western Civilization,"

to the *Configurations*. He was the recipient of many honors, including honorary degrees from Harvard, Yale, Columbia, California, and other institutions; the Viking Medal of the Wenner-Gren Foundation; and the Huxley Medal of the Royal Anthropological Institute. He was founder and president of the American Anthropological Association, president of the American Folk Lore Society, and president of the Linguistic Society of America. Talcott Parsons has called Kroeber "the dean not only of American anthropologists but of American social scientists generally." [50]

If Kroeber did not elect to formulate an explanatory theory of change in the *Configurations*, he was nevertheless interested in answers to some specific questions. What were the questions that piqued his intellectual curiosity? He lists them as follows: [51] As cultures grow, how far apart (or how close together) are changes in the various activities of the culture? Is there a tendency toward a norm of duration for such growths ("flowerings")? Must the florescence extend over the whole of the culture or may it be partial? Is there an order, or a tendency toward order, for the several activities to come successively to their zeniths? Can a culture pass through a cycle to full decline and then enjoy another cycle of prosperity, or are we in that case dealing with two cultures? Can the cycles or bursts be inducted from without, or must they develop from within? Do the peaks tend to come early within growths, toward the end, or is the growth curve most often symmetrical?

Kroeber's method of investigating culture growth was to assess the latter in terms of the production of superior individuals (geniuses). In the first place, he declares, a strong tendency exists to associate notable cultural periods and great men. We use a Shakespeare, a Newton, a Leonardo da Vinci, or a Michelangelo to exemplify a flowering of culture. Then one can justify the approach in reasoning that geniuses, as all persons, are products of heredity and environment. Biological heredity is, in general, a constant type of influence. Culture is the part of environment that gives rise to the uneven distribution or clustering of geniuses.[52] Thus, if many geniuses develop at a certain time and place, one can assume that a flowering has occurred in the socio-cultural environment.[53] The number of geniuses produced is considered, then, not for itself but as a measure of the growth of culture patterns. On what basis does Kroeber decide whether this or that individual is or was a genius? He tells us that he uses the conventional

---

and "The Role of Style in Comparative Civilizations," does not affect the conclusions of the *Configurations*. However, the latter was the intellectual base for this material.

[50] Parsons, *op. cit.*, p. 616.
[51] *Configurations of Culture Growth, op. cit.*, pp. 5–6.
[52] *Ibid.*, p. 12.
[53] He cites the example of Newton regarding this phenomenon. The *Principia*

ratings found in textbooks, adding that a reasonable consensus is indicated therein. He also declares that he has used data of achievement and eminence found in encyclopaedias.[54]

Kroeber's procedure is (1) to investigate the following cultural activities separately in order to appraise patterns of growth: philosophy, science, philology, sculpture, painting, drama, literature, and music; (2) to consider these activities together (as a totality) with the objective of assessing over-all changes in national cultures; political and nationalistic factors are brought into the discussion as appropriate to this; and (3) to present an over-all review and discussion of these activities.[55] The first part comprises the bulk of the volume (Chapters 1–9); the consideration of the over-all change of national cultures is found in Chapter 10; and the final review and discussion are given in Chapter 11.

Results

Kroeber's vast array of data concerning the development of philosophy, science, sculpture, painting, and the other fields, as well as his description of the total growth of many nations, are of considerable interest. However, of greatest importance are his conclusions as to the "forest" rather than the "sectors of the forest." His results may well be summarized in relation to the various questions that were stated previously. The main points are as follows: First, Kroeber finds no law or inevitable pattern in culture growth: nothing cyclical, regularly

---

could have been produced only by a genius, he declares. Yet Newton could not have produced this until a certain body of scientific knowledge was in existence, which "touched off his genius to realize itself in the *Principia*." *Ibid.*, p. 9.

54 *Ibid.*, pp. 23–24.

55 Some correspondence (and some differences) can be noted concerning this treatment and Sorokin's. Sorokin also surveyed developments in painting, sculpture, philosophy, ethics, and literature (although not in music); he also appraised fluctuations in architecture, the law, social relationships, war, and internal disturbances. Sorokin's experts provided a factual discussion of the developments as did Kroeber, but the former was interested in depicting total epochs (ideational, sensate, idealistic) and Kroeber was not. On the other hand, Kroeber had different points of interest as we have seen. Kroeber stated that he read Sorokin's *Social and Cultural Dynamics* (also Toynbee's *A Study of History*) only after completing his own study. Kroeber observed that "Sorokin's underlying data are more elaborate [than his own], Dr. Sorokin having had the benefit of a corps of research assistants." Kroeber, *op. cit.*, p. 849, bibliography. The *space* and *time* dimensions of the two studies seem to be roughly similar; this writer could find no precise statement of the *time* dimension on the part of Kroeber, but it may be inferred from his data. In general, his material seems to date back to about 500 to 1000 B.C. although he briefly discusses Egyptian and Mesopotamian sculpture and Egyptian painting to about 3300 B.C. or earlier. The discussion is carried up to about A.D. 1900 (an exception being that Kroeber discusses Nobel prize winners in science up to 1937). Sorokin concentrates on Graeco-Roman and Western civilizations as they changed from 600 B.C. until A.D. 1935.

repetitive, or necessary. "There is nothing to show either that every culture must develop patterns within which a florescence of quality is possible, or that, having once so flowered, it must wither without chance of revival." [56] The various departments of culture growth (sculpture, painting, music, and the like) are *not* necessary elements in the total culture. Some may be entirely absent. Islam had no representative art; indeed a considerable list of cultures with missing activities is made.[57] Evidently there is no activity that *must* be present in a culture, also no important relation of time and order of appearance is found with the different activities.[58] Secondly, no special *usual duration* of cultural florescences is found. The time periods vary from a single productive lifetime to approximately one thousand years.[59] Some nations, such as India, have had a slow, extremely long growth; in other instances the duration has been much shorter. Usually, declares Kroeber, "qualitatively great growths tend to be of considerable duration." [60] The question of "cultural death" is largely a matter of definition. Cultures can deteriorate and their values shrink. A population may be absorbed by other, larger societies; indeed a familiar phenomenon of the modern era has been the death of many primitive cultures in this manner. Cultures may be overcome by another culture. At any rate, cultural death (if it should occur) is not an inevitable, organismic process such as has been described by Spengler.[61] Thirdly, general nationalistic development is often related to specific activity in the cultural arts. The latter can flower without the former, says Kroeber,[62] but it is unlikely. Also, high achievements by suppressed nationalities may take place, but this is rare. Moreover, a people can do "great things in one activity while remaining mediocre or backward in all others," [63] but this again is not the usual situation. Ordinarily, national energy and higher cultural energy are related. Kroeber adds that population and wealth factors may play a part in this, conceding that he could not analyze this (as he wanted to) because data are lacking for all but this century.[64] Fourthly, the growth curves are some-

[56] *Configurations of Culture Growth, op. cit.,* p. 761. In a different context, Parsons has recently maintained that various prerequisites of the evolution of culture and society may, however, be observed. For this view see Talcott Parsons, "Evolutionary Universals in Society," *American Sociological Review,* Vol. 29, No. 3 (June, 1964), 339–357.

[57] *Configurations of Culture Growth, op. cit.,* p. 778.

[58] *Ibid.,* p. 790.

[59] *Ibid.,* p. 804.

[60] *Ibid.,* p. 805.

[61] *Ibid.,* pp. 825–826.

[62] *Ibid.,* p. 794.

[63] *Ibid.*

[64] *Ibid.,* p. 795.

times symmetrical, sometimes not. This is not always easy to measure, although he thinks that "general agreement" may often be obtained.[65] At any rate, all types of growth curves are found—symmetrical and skewed. Kroeber gives numerous examples of this.[66] Finally, Kroeber's general thesis that geniuses tend to cluster in time and space is overwhelmingly substantiated. Exceptions to this do exist, however, and Kroeber even lists some.[67] The existence of geniuses in isolation is rare.[68]

Comment and Criticisms

Our initial comment relative to this impressive work is to again underscore our view that it is confidence-inspiring because it is factually based. Whatever the conclusions, one feels that Kroeber has really looked at the evidence and made his deductions accordingly. Sorokin also presented a massive, factual review, but he may have overextended himself in this regard; he tried to be quantitative concerning subjects where it might have been wisest to confine himself to qualitative treatment (as Kroeber did).

Secondly, we believe that Kroeber's cardinal working principle— that cultural growth can be measured in terms of the production of geniuses—is essentially sound. It would appear that from the biological standpoint geniuses appear in history in an even flow except for cultural fluctuations; hence, the varying production of eminently superior individuals (who are, thus, departures from chance) can be taken as a representation of cultural florescences. We are slightly uneasy regarding the determination of genius on the basis of the consensus of textbook writers (in what proportion of cases would opinions differ?), but this is reasonably acceptable.[69]

---

65 *Ibid.*, p. 773.
66 *Ibid.*, pp. 776–777.
67 *Ibid.*, pp. 834–837.
68 We note that Kroeber never really does answer the question, although he alludes to it, of whether cultural bursts can be inducted from without or whether they must develop from within. Evidently he did not consider this proven, hence he did not want to commit himself regarding it. However, at one point he states that

> . . . no amount or type of external influence will produce a burst of cultural productivity unless the internal culture situation is ripe; however, the great number of florescences can be shown to have a direct relationship to external influences, often in the form of "stimulus importation" ("stimulus diffusion").

Ibid., p. 201.
69 Sorokin, viewing Kroeber's procedure from the standpoint of his own classification of ideational, idealistic, and sensate cultures, objects that the Kroeber results inevitably have a sensate bias. Sorokin maintains that sensate cultures are individualistic and singularistic; ideational cultures are collective and anonymous.

How shall we comment concerning Kroeber's actual conclusions? (Some may wish to say lack of conclusions.) Because he found no law of cultural growth, no inevitable pattern, nothing cyclical, nothing consistently repetitive, and no necessary order in the development of different cultural activities (painting and the rest), did he after all achieve only meager results? Some might find it easy to speak of prodigious intellectual labor—a mountain of effort—producing only a hill of substantive findings. This writer does not agree with this judgment. Negative conclusions can be both worthy and important. We suggest, for instance, that social scientists may be persuaded from this study that easy or intuitive generalization from historical data cannot be made.[70] We also believe—mainly because of the quality of Kroeber's work—that few social scientists will feel the need to go over this particular ground again. That no pattern of cultural growth is found, no necessary order of activities shown, no "must" factor divulged, is rather convincingly set forth. Social scientists will turn to other interests. No immediate reason for a repetitive study seems to be at hand. This itself indicates that the study has had value. All results cannot be positive.

Inevitably, some comparison is invited between the over-all impressions made by Sorokin, Spengler, Toynbee, and Kroeber. This writer agrees with the following estimate made by the late Clyde Kluckhohn:

> *Kroeber's study is the most modest of the four from the point of view of elaborateness of factual detail and sweep of generalization. Spengler and Sorokin are much more passionately intense. Spengler felt he knew the answers before he wrote his book, and Sorokin's data are ordered in accord with a scheme ("ideational," "idealistic," "sensate"). Kroeber lacks the brilliant apperceptive intuitions of Spengler, the creative fire and the wealth of material of Sorokin, and the original and penetrating historical insights of Toynbee. However, his methodology is surely more rigorous than that of Spengler or Toynbee and . . . sounder than that of Sorokin—for all of the latter's statistics and his care. And . . . Kroeber's book has more intellectual and emotional poise than those of the other three writers.*[71]

It must be kept in mind, however, that the preceding four writers had different things in mind and devised different explanations of

---

Hence, a greater attempt to glorify and immortalize people is alleged to occur in a sensate era. Moreover, Sorokin feels that the criteria of creativity in ideational and sensate cultures are quite different. This argument is something for the reader to consider. See Pitirim A. Sorokin, *Social Philosophies of an Age of Crisis* (Boston: The Beacon Press, 1950), pp. 260–264.

[70] For instance, Spengler's ironclad notions are clearly laid to rest.

[71] A review of A. L. Kroeber, *Configurations of Culture Growth* by Clyde Kluckhohn in *American Journal of Sociology*, Vol. 51 (January, 1946), 336–341.

human events as they ranged over the centuries of history. Their perspectives were different. It is interesting as this writer sees it that this florescence in the study of historical sociology occurred in the approximate period of 1920–1940. Moreover, other writers who are primarily less historical—MacIver, Mumford, and a host of others—should not be kept out of the picture. This writer ventures one final reflection in this section dealing with the contributions of the late Alfred L. Kroeber. This is to suggest that if another macrosociological or social science study of socio-cultural change and/or the philosophy of history should be made during coming years—and *eventually* motivations for a repetitive study are likely to arise—is it not more satisfactory to employ a group of experts who will master the purely factual aspects of changes in different departments of society and culture? In short, is not Sorokin's procedure more to be recommended in such large-scale studies? This writer, greatly admiring Kroeber's energy and zeal, suggests that the vast intellectual terrain is now too much for any one social scientist to explore. Kroeber immersed himself in the manifold details of changing sculpture, painting, literature, drama, philosophy, science, and so on. To his credit he achieved a performance of high quality. But such a vast task is more appropriate for team research, with experts dealing with parts of the subject in the light of their competencies.

MAX WEBER (1864–1920)

The theories of Max Weber present a dilemma. He is undoubtedly one of the greats of sociology of the past century. Yet, from the standpoint of social dynamics, his contribution is valued mostly for the importance of ideas as causes and for the influence of the ideology of one institution on a different institution. In *The Protestant Ethic and the Spirit of Capitalism,*[72] Weber's theme concerned the influence of Protestant ideology on the rise of the capitalist system. Thus, *ideas* are held to constitute a basic cause, not the economic means of production, as Marx declared, or something else. But Weber was careful in making his statement. Different prime movers would be possible.[73] Ideas would be the independent variable in at least some situations. This contribution conflicts with Sorokin's notion of immanent change. The social system (capitalism) is not developing from within by virtue of its inherent properties; it is being influenced from without (by

[72] Max Weber, *The Protestant Ethic and the Spirit of Capitalism,* translated by Talcott Parsons (New York: Charles Scribner's Sons, 1958).

[73] Weber declares that "my aim is not to substitute for a one-sided materialistic (interpretation) an equally one-sided spiritualistic causal interpretation of culture and of history. Each is equally possible, ..." *Ibid.,* p. 183. On this matter see also the brief but well-phrased comment in Amitai Etzioni and Eva Etzioni (eds.), *Social Change* (New York: Basic Books, Inc., 1964), p. 7.

religious factors).[74] Weber investigated the inception of capitalism, but his thesis could equally apply to any ongoing institution. His convincing demonstration of the influence of the ideology of one institution on another started an important tradition in sociology, and this possesses other applications, needless to say, that are important for sociocultural change. The influence might not be that of religion on economics but of democratic (political) ideology on education, for example; or it might be the influence of Fascist (political) ideology on education or the family system, and so on.

Weber was born in Berlin in 1864, the son of a lawyer and political leader (a member of the German Reichstag). He studied law at the University of Heidelberg. He was made a professor of economics at the University of Freiburg in 1893—he had had early interests in economics, and the shift was not as surprising as it might sound. In a few years he returned to Heidelberg as a professor of economics. Altogether he had made a brilliant beginning in his professional life. Unfortunately, he suffered a severe illness around 1897–1900 [75] that was reported as a nervous breakdown. This kept him out of work for about four years. He returned to scholarly work in about 1901, apparently producing his best work after the sickness.[76] The writing of *The Protestant Ethic* came, then, at this stage of his life. Following this he made major studies in the sociology of religion and of social and economic organization.[77] Weber died in 1920, after he had served as a member of the German Commission for the Peace Conference at Versailles (following the First World War). At this time, says Parsons, his work was showing special promise.

The Protestant Ethic.   Even though, for our present purposes, a lengthy exposition concerning this work does not seem necessary, certain significant points should be noted. It is clear, first, that Weber

[74] This exemplifies reasoning, in short, that suggests that the influence of immanent change should not be *overly* emphasized, as we have stated before. (See Chap. 5.)

[75] In citing these personal data we have chiefly followed Talcott Parsons, "Max Weber's Sociological Analysis of Capitalism and Modern Institutions," Chapter XIII in Harry Elmer Barnes (ed.), *An Introduction to the History of Sociology* (Chicago: University of Chicago Press, 1948), especially pp. 287–289; and Reinhard Bendix, *Max Weber, an Intellectual Portrait* (Garden City, N. Y.: Doubleday & Co., 1960), especially Chap. I. Parsons declares that the illness occurred in 1900, Bendix in 1897.

[76] Parsons, *op. cit.*, p. 292.

[77] Some of Weber's important volumes in these areas published in English are: *The Religion of China: Confucianism and Taoism* (Glencoe, Ill.: The Free Press, Inc., 1951); *The Religion of India: The Sociology of Hinduism and Buddhism* (Glencoe, Ill.: The Free Press, Inc., 1958); *Ancient Judaism* (Glencoe, Ill.: The Free Press, Inc., 1952); *The Theory of Social and Economic Organization* (New York: Oxford University Press, 1947); and *Max Weber on Law in Economy and Society* (Cambridge, Mass.: Harvard University Press, 1954).

described in convincing detail a new character type that was produced by the Protestant Reformation. The new, more vigorous traits affected both workers and entrepreneurs, and this in turn led to the development of industrial capitalism. Hard work and asceticism were encouraged. Protestant working girls appeared to work harder; entrepreneurs rose to the top more often in the business world despite the advantage of wealth of many Catholic families in Europe.[78]

> *The religious valuation of . . . continuous, systematic work in a worldly calling, as the highest means to asceticism, and at the same time the surest and most evident proof of rebirth and genuine faith, must have been the most powerful conceivable lever for the expansion of that attitude toward life which we have here called the spirit of capitalism.*[79]

Not only were religious beliefs important in bringing the new personality emphasis, but Calvin's statement regarding predestination brought an increased value to rationalization. Hard work and accomplishment in the here-and-now were encouraged.[80]

Moreover, the great revival of Methodism, pointed out Weber, is related to the spirit of worldly asceticism. Indeed he quotes John Wesley as follows: "We ought not to prevent people from being diligent and frugal; we must exhort all Christians to gain all they can, and to save all they can; that is, in effect, to grow rich." [81]

This, at any rate, is the over-all message of *The Protestant Ethic*. Weber's insights do not, of course, relate directly to the subject of socio-cultural change. But, applying to the social structure, they have important implications for change. This is indeed a pointed illustration of the interconnections of social structure and social change. Weber is the type of sociologist, then, who contributes to social dynamics with (so far as we are aware) little direct and avowed interest in this subfield.[82]

In the light of the present-day linking of theory and research, one may inquire as to uses of *The Protestant Ethic*. It has constituted the theoretical framework, indeed, for many a project—dozens or even scores of them. To cite a few recent examples, there are the projects

---

78 McClelland comments that such traits are, of course, linked with what would now be called the achieving type of personality. See McClelland, *op. cit.*, pp. 48–49.

79 *The Protestant Ethic and the Spirit of Capitalism, op. cit.*, p. 172.

80 Weber observes that "in practice this means that God helps those who help themselves." (Quoted by McClelland, *op. cit.*, p. 48.)

81 Weber, *op. cit.*, p. 175.

82 His prime interests, as may already be evident, lay in the fields of sociology of religion, social organization, the sociology of law, and, to some extent, methods of research.

of Murray and Rosalie Wax,[83] Benton Johnson,[84] and Robert E. Kennedy, Jr.[85]—for a beginning. But Weber has had a tremendous influence, furthermore, on other theorists. Doubtless, foremost of all, his ideas have constituted a cornerstone for Parsonian theory from the date of *The Structure of Social Action.*[86] *The Protestant Ethic* theme has been most useful to David C. McClelland as we have seen. David Riesman, Winston White, and many others have built on the thesis.

If clear propositions are to be formulated in sociology, the determinants (variables) must be stated with utmost clarity. Even the great Weber is vulnerable on this score. Zetterberg points out [87] that, even though the key position in this case is indicated in the very title of the essay—the Protestant ethic is the determinant (independent variable) and the spirit of capitalism is the result—the statement is not sufficiently precise. Thus, the following variations may occur if the italics stand for the variables that may be related: (1) the *Protestant* ethic and the spirit of *capitalism;* (2) the Protestant *ethic* and the spirit of *capitalism;* (3) the *Protestant* ethic and the *spirit* of capitalism; and (4) the Protestant *ethic* and the *spirit* of capitalism. As Zetterberg adds, all four ways of interpreting the thesis are in varying degrees present in Weber's writing. Zetterberg concludes that "much confusion could have been avoided if the determinant and the result of the proposition had been more clearly specified." [88]

Bureaucracies and Charismatic Leadership. It was pointed out at the beginning of this discussion of Weber that two of his other contributions have relevance for the field of socio-cultural change.[89]

---

[83] M. Wax, "Ancient Judaism and the Protestant Ethic," *American Journal of Sociology,* Vol. LXV, No. 5 (1960), 449–455; and R. and M. Wax, "The Vikings and the Rise of Capitalism," *American Journal of Sociology,* Vol. 61 (1955), 1–10.

[84] Benton Johnson, "Ascetic Protestantism and Political Preference in the Deep South," *American Journal of Sociology,* Vol. LXIX, No. 4 (January, 1964), 359–366; and "On Church and Sect," *American Sociological Review,* Vol. 28, No. 4 (Autumn, 1963), 539–548. The latter article is based on the ideas of Ernst Troeltsch as well as Weber.

[85] Robert E. Kennedy, Jr., "The Protestant Ethic and the Parsis," *American Journal of Sociology,* Vol. LXVIII, No. 1 (July, 1962), 11–20.

[86] Talcott Parsons, *The Structure of Social Action* (New York: McGraw-Hill Book Co., 1937).

[87] Hans L. Zetterberg, *On Theory and Verification in Sociology,* rev. ed. (Totowa, N. J.: The Bedminister Press, 1963), pp. 13–14.

[88] *Ibid.,* p. 14.

[89] For example, see Talcott Parsons, Chapter 13 in Barnes, (ed.), *op. cit.;* Parsons, *The Structure of Social Action, op. cit.;* Bendix, *op. cit.;* H. H. Gerth and C. Wright Mills (eds.), *From Max Weber: Essays in Sociology* (New York: Oxford University Press, 1946), Chap. VIII, "Bureaucracy," and Chap. IX, "The Sociology of Charismatic Authority"; P. Blau and W. R. Scott, *Formal Organizations* (San Francisco: Chandler Publishing Co., 1962); Amitai Etzioni, *Modern Organizations* (Englewood Cliffs, N. J.: Prentice-Hall, Inc., 1964), especially Chap. 5.

Bureaucracies develop in terms of the increasing emphasis on rationalism; changing Western civilization has seen a constant increase in bureaucratic organization. Because (1) official business is conducted on a continuous basis, (2) stipulated rules must be followed, (3) each official's responsibilities are part of a hierarchy of authority, and (4) business is conducted on a basis of written documents, it follows that (5) bureaucratic organization is superior to other forms of administration. It is technically superior, declares Bendix,[90] much as machine production is superior to nonmechanical methods. But the advantages of bureaucracy are relative; some obstacles and difficulties are apt to accompany this organizational form. One change to be generally expected as a society develops, at any rate, is an increase in the bureaucratic form of organization.

Charismatic leadership is in part related to bureaucracies, but, more particularly, the leader who possesses *charisma*—meaning a special gift or extraordinary power for accomplishment—often emerges as the legitimacy of an old social structure is crumbling. The new leader replaces the sagging structure with a new one. Then follows a routinization of charisma that comprises the foundation of the new structure—which eventually may become old and thus be open prey for a new charismatic leader. The charismatic leader operates on the basis of personal rule. His authority is personal; people believe in his infallibility. The importance of charismatic ongoings, as the Etzionis state,[91] is that they tend to cause drastic change. The charismatic leader tends to be against tradition, although not completely. He usually does not follow precedent; he may represent the "ideal" tradition of a people. These leaders bring the opposite of gradual change without crisis, such as the change from rural to urban residence in a nation or the change of a rising standard of living. Once in control of a situation, the charismatic leader is likely to establish a bureaucracy in order to fortify his position such as Hitler, Mussolini, and other charismatic leaders did.[92]

DON MARTINDALE (1915–   )

Professor Martindale, a sociologist at the University of Minnesota, has also sought to explain the riddle of socio-cultural change. In his

90 *Bendix, op. cit.*, p. 421.

91 A. and E. Etzioni (eds.), *op. cit.*, p. 8.

92 Ernest Manheim, "Recent Types of Charismatic Leadership," Chapter 30 in Joseph Roucek and associates, *Social Control*, 2nd ed. (Princeton, N. J.: D. Van Nostrand Co., 1956), especially p. 554. In closing this section on Weber we are mindful that the discussion could be extended. However, he was not a direct contributor to social change, as we have said, and also we are influenced by the exceedingly full discussion of the Weberian ideas in the sociological literature.

volume entitled *Social Life and Cultural Change*,[93] he approaches change from the standpoint of ideas, although with less emphasis on ideas as the cause of change. Rather, he points to the importance of the people with the ideas—namely, the intellectual class—in a civilization in promoting change. Martindale is another macroscopic thinker, maintaining a civilizational view (another Toynbee in this respect). His ideas follow well those of Weber, however, because his treatment shows a major influence at the hands of the Weberian studies of religion that he translated (sometimes with others).[94] Readers who are used to Weber are likely to feel at home with Martindale. Martindale is a thinker who has an important interest in social change, although he perhaps possesses an even more major interest in sociological theory. He has written volumes on the latter subject as well as on American society.[95]

The Martindale Thesis

Martindale holds that the *social-behavioristic* theory of change bears the greatest promise.[96] Propositions based on this view include the following: (1) That the individual and only the individual is the source of all innovation; (2) that no single form of social behavior is ultimate or basic; (3) that a society must solve basic problems in the three areas of socialization, the mastery of nature, and social control; (4) that these areas are equally important; (5) that institutional forms define the circumstances of significant innovations in a society and also resistances to the innovations; (6) that the institutions must adjust to each other; and (7) that unsolved problems may be transferred to ideal and artistic spheres on the basis of the process of sublimation.[97] Martindale's main idea based on the preceding material is that change, which is concerned with the formation and destruction of social forms and systems, is significantly related to the creative activities of individuals. Even though any individual is a potential innovator, he holds that the core innovators are the intellectuals of the society or civilization; he concedes

93 (Princeton, N.J.: D. Van Nostrand and Co., 1962.)

94 Max Weber, *Ancient Judaism,* translated by Hans Gerth and Don Martindale (Glencoe, Ill.: The Free Press, Inc., 1952); Max Weber, *The Religions of India,* translated by Hans Gerth and Don Martindale (Glencoe, Ill.: The Free Press, Inc., 1958); and Max Weber, *The City,* translated by Don Martindale and Gertrud Neuwirth (Glencoe, Ill.: The Free Press, Inc., 1958).

95 See Martindale, *The Nature and Types of Sociological Theory* (Boston: Houghton Mifflin Co., 1966); *American Society* (Princeton, N. J.: D. Van Nostrand Co., 1960); and *American Social Structure* (New York: Appleton-Century-Crofts, Inc., 1960).

96 *Social Life and Cultural Change, op. cit.,* pp. 31–32.

97 *Ibid.,* pp. 38–54.

that change is not the exclusive problem of intellectuals.[98] He tests his idea of the importance of the activities of intellectuals in five civilizations: Ancient China, Ancient India, Ancient Israel, Ancient Greece, and Western society since the Renaissance.[99] The intellectuals in the preceding cases are the Chinese mandarin, the Indian guru, the priest and prophet, the Grecian philosophers, and Western humanists and scientists. They are held to be the *system innovators*—the representatives and justifiers of the whole.

Martindale's treatment is guided by the following four hypotheses: (1) Creative epochs of mankind are the periods of formation of new communities; at these times the free expression of ideas is permitted and rewarded. (2) The quality and quantity of creativity are related to the type of community in which they occur. (3) As the community matures and cultural syntheses are completed, the encouragement of free creativity tends to come to an end. (4) During the creative epochs the truth is determined in terms of criteria of thought processes, whereas during conformist epochs truth is judged on the basis of institutional procedures (that is, authority).[100]

Comment and Criticisms

We note, initially, that Martindale's macrocosmic emphasis even affects his definitions of such terms as *social change* and *culture change*. The former is defined as "the formation and destruction of groups and societies," and the latter as "the formation and destruction of particular items of culture and of civilizations." [101] Words such as *modification* and *alteration* are not mentioned. Thus he is interested in major changes on the civilizational plane—not such lesser changes as those due to racial demonstrations, changes ensuing from the passage of a new law, or changes due to the effects of an invention. A further note may be made that, whereas Martindale is particularly interested in the role and functioning of intellectuals as basic changes are made, he does not appear to have precisely defined an intellectual. Who or what is an intellectual? His designated examples, to be sure, are the Chinese mandarin, the India guru, the Western humanist and scientist, and so on; but is this the end of the list? Is an editor an intellectual? A novelist? A columnist? A writer of stories or journal

---

98 *Ibid.*, pp. 54–55.

99 In the case of the first four, attention is centered on the time period of from 900 B. C. to 200 B. C. This is called the Axial period of human history. Martindale takes the term from Karl Jaspers, and it means that contemporary civilization in those respective areas is believed to have developed from the institutional forms of this period. *Ibid.*, pp. 66–69 and 90.

100 *Ibid.*, p. 91.

101 *Ibid.*, p. 33

articles? A city planner who conceives the idea of building a turnpike or new shopping area? The roots of the intellectual, declares Martindale, are in the area of socialization, for "he is fundamentally a teacher, philosopher, artist, and moral counsellor." [102] Yet the special functions of intellectuals lie in "innovating or conserving activities in communities and civilizations. They are key persons of the reconstitution of the basic institutions into such more comprehensive systems." [103] These are Martindale's general ideas of the intellectual, whether they are entirely clear or not.[104]

Our most important query as to the Martindale theory centers on his main point: In system innovations of the sort that he describes (in Ancient China, India, and so on), is the role of the intellectual as important in causing changes as he declares? His point, it appears to us, is difficult to establish. He has ably stated that intellectuals are the key or core innovators, the strategic reference point in the study of change. The thesis is fascinating and important. Has he *proved* it? Events in past or other epochs are so complicated that proof can be difficult. Intellectuals may function in relation to leadership as Martindale notes.[105] How powerful is the role of advisor to the prince (or member of the "brain trust," if you will)? How influential was Rexford Tugwell or Raymond Moley with President Franklin D. Roosevelt; Walt W. Rostow or Arthur M. Schlesinger, Jr. with John F. Kennedy; Lord Cherwell with recent British governments; or X shaman with Y tribal chief? In general, one does not know. In order to be able to answer the question one would need to know the number of times that advice was taken, that advice was *not* heeded, and that advice was partially taken, and relative to what kind of issues. Martindale declares:

> The intellectual in the role of advisor to a prince may not be in the lead position, but, in terms of the entire operation of the social order, he may be even more significant. As formulator of policy, he may even determine the fate of the prince. Or again, the intellectual

---

102 *Ibid.*, p. 56.

103 *Ibid.*, p. 71.

104 Winston White has interpreted intellectual ideology in contemporary America on the basis of articles in the following five periodicals: *American Scholar, The Atlantic Monthly, Commentary, Dissent,* and *Partisan Review.* See White, *Beyond Conformity* (New York: The Free Press of Glencoe, Inc., A Division of The Macmillan Company, 1961), p. 5. Writers for such publications are likely to deal with "reconstituting basic institutions in comprehensive systems," although the extent of their final influence will surely be debated. Whether modern scientists are just as much core innovators is open to question. The physicist who invents a new infrared process or application of lasers or the chemist who makes a new glass or plastic composition would seem to be of a different order, but the collective influence in such journals as *Science* and the *Bulletin of the Atomic Scientists* may be along the lines of Martindale's thinking. We suggest that further clarification is in order.

105 Martindale, *op. cit.*, p. 80.

> *in the position of teacher of the young may have more long-range*
> *influence on the social order than many persons wielding more direct*
> *forms of power.*[106]

This statement may be correct. The present view is neither to accept nor reject it. We simply do not know whether such influence is extensive or not. It needs to be *proven* if possible. No doubt all teachers at times wonder as to the extent of their influence, as probably do ministers and priests. We suspect that editors, writers, and media commentators (if they are to be classed as intellectuals) do the same. At any rate, Martindale's statement of the power of intellectuals does not constitute proof.

Does this discussion mean, then, that we are totally unmoved and unconvinced by Martindale's theory? No. In our view, Martindale may overemphasize the influence of intellectuals, but they undoubtedly have *some* influence. At the least, he has called attention to a variable in socio-cultural change that is not ordinarily mentioned. This is, then, another variable to be considered. Martindale makes clear that the intellectual is not the sole source of change, in case anyone has the notion of carrying this to an extreme. Different intellectuals may, however, disagree in their advice. What then? If the elite administrator chooses from among the ideas offered, does that not indicate that *he* is the "top man"? Do not intellectuals generally constitute an adjunct to leadership? [107] It also may be worthwhile to recall that in Brinton's study of four revolutions [108] one of the important uniformities found was the transfer of allegiance by the intellectuals. However we may interpret these points, it seems in any case that Martindale does not demonstrate the *processes* by which intellectuals bring about change. On the other hand, he presents well his ideas in the context of science (a happy contrast from Spengler and Toynbee), and his *Social Life and Culture Change* is indeed impressive in its all-around erudition.

DISCUSSION REGARDING THE VARIOUS THEORIES OF CHANGE

As we reflect on the various theories of change presented in Chapters 5–8, some over-all, if exceedingly brief, comments should be stated. We

---

106 *Loc. cit.*

107 Since writing this, this sociologist has seen Clagett's statement along the same line. It suggests that it is the power elite—the policy makers of any given group—rather than the intellectuals who are more likely to determine social and cultural changes. See A. F. Clagett, Jr., "Neo-Behaviorist Principles of Social and Cultural Change: Revision and Synthesis of Martindale's Propositions," *International Journal of Comparative Sociology*, Vol. 5 (March, 1964), 107.

108 Crane Brinton, *The Anatomy of Revolution,* revised and expanded edition (New York: Vintage Books, 1965), p. 251.

have two in mind: First, let us make positively clear that by no means have all worthwhile theoretical orientations toward socio-cultural change been examined in these chapters.[109] Our objective has been to select some of the better-known and more influential theories for the reader's consideration, ones that, in short, are thought to be of marked importance for one reason or another (in one case for *negative,* although still important, reasons). These formulations can be collectively regarded as minimum theoretical knowledge with which the student of change should be familiar. None of them constitutes strict theory in Merton's sense. Some students or others may elect in the future to attempt to develop sets of interdependent and verifiable statements of relationships between the variables emphasized in these orientations (and, hence, construct strict theory). Still others may wish to construct new theories that emphasize different variables or perspectives. In either case, some knowledge of existing theory will be helpful if not sometimes necessary. The new often grows out of the old. Constructing new theories, however, can be perilous if one is unfamiliar with results already achieved. This includes, of course, profiting from past mistakes.

Secondly, what are the prospects of eventually formulating a *total theory* of socio-cultural change? If nearly all the theories contain some measure of truth and often explain change in some aspect of living, can they finally be consolidated? Difficult, even impossible, as such consolidation would appear to be at this time, nevertheless it may be that an "it is darkest before the dawn" element is present. Moore [110] has expressed the belief that sociology is closer to attaining an integrated theory of change than many believe. Parsons [111] has declared that a fully developed theory of social change will be inseparable from one of society itself. The need for integration and synthesis has been

109 Indeed we have qualms of conscience as we realize the many omissions that have had to be made. The latter include (in random order) Howard Becker's orientation emphasizing the sacred-secular scheme of analysis; Florian Znaniecki's ideas relative to creativity; Alvin Boskoff's social-system ideas; Amitai Etzioni's explorations of changes in international relations and in elements of Israeli society; Julian Steward's theory of multilinear evolution; Hornell Hart's contributions with respect to technology and to graphic representations of change (often taking the form of the logistic curve); F. Stuart Chapin's endeavors relating to inventions and to synchronous cycles; Walter Goldschmidt's contributions concerning technology; the energy theories of W. Fred Cottrell and of Leslie A. White; and Godfrey and Monica Wilson's anthropological contributions emphasizing the *scale* of change and relating to notions of disequilibrium and lag, among others. However, certain theories will be discussed in later chapters: H. G. Barnett's theory of innovation in Chapter 10, and the David McClelland, Everett Hagen, John H. Kunkel, and Walt W. Rostow theories relating to developing societies in Chapter 14.

110 Wilbert E. Moore, "A Reconsideration of Theories of Social Change," *American Sociological Review,* Vol. 25, No. 6 (December, 1960), 810–818, especially p. 818.

111 Talcott Parsons, *The Social System* (New York: The Free Press of Glencoe, Inc., A Division of The Macmillan Company, 1951), Chap. XI.

expressed by Kroeber [112] and Sorokin.[113] Kroeber declares that "there is no reason why this integration should not be envisaged and begun now, ..." Sorokin maintains that the macroscopic and microscopic social and cultural systems will take their proper place in the totality, the smaller systems fitting into the larger. The dyads, triads, and other small units (especially families) would constitute building blocks for neighborhood and community systems; and larger systems would be joined to form national and, eventually, world systems. Moore [114] has already argued for the conception of a single-world supersystem. Sorokin holds that existing theories are mutually exclusive or contradictory only where they are wrong.[115]

Methodological advances involving the growing use of the computer may aid such an integration of theories. As we have mentioned earlier, simulation and other techniques hold great promise. The possibility can be entertained, at any rate, that the various theories of socio-cultural change will someday be integrated into a totality—undoubtedly joined, as Parsons declares, to an integrated theory of society itself. This is the time for an open mind. At least we hope that some will not insist on saying—at a time when man has walked on the moon—that one just cannot make a theoretical *sociological* accomplishment of this nature within, say, one, two, or three decades.

ANNOTATED BIBLIOGRAPHY

Kroeber, A. L., *Configurations of Culture Growth* (Berkeley: University of California Press, 1944). See also Kroeber, *An Anthropologist Looks at History* (Berkeley: University of California Press, 1963).

> Kroeber found no law of cultural growth, nothing cyclical or regularly repetitive, but he did find that cultural florescences tended to occur; geniuses clustered in time and space. An important, carefully done, and confidence-inspiring work, even if the results cannot be called startling. In *An Anthropologist Looks at History* this leading social scientist, during his later years, provides fascinating and quite valuable explorations of civilizations and history.

Martindale, Don, *Social Life and Cultural Change* (Princeton, N. J.: D. Van Nostrand Co., 1962).

> Martindale maintains that the intellectual class, as system innovators, has special importance in promoting major changes; he illustrates

---

[112] A. L. Kroeber, *An Anthropologist Looks at History* (Berkeley: University of California Press, 1963), Chap. 8, "Integration of the Knowledge of Man," pp. 129–130.

[113] Pitirim A. Sorokin, "Sociology of Yesterday, Today, and Tomorrow," *American Sociológical Review*, Vol. 30, No. 6 (December, 1965), 833–843, especially 838–843.

[114] Wilbert E. Moore, "Global Sociology," *American Journal of Sociology*, Vol. LXXI, No. 5 (March, 1966), 475–482.

[115] Sorokin, *op. cit.*, 842.

with the Chinese mandarin, the Indian guru, and other intellectuals. He may have exaggerated the influence of intellectuals. Nevertheless this is a hypothesis to be examined further. As with the other thinkers covered in this chapter, Martindale has a broad, historical perspective.

Sorokin, Pitirim A., *Sociological Theories of Today* (New York: Harper & Row, 1966).

Sorokin comments on the ideas of Toynbee, Kroeber, Martindale, and many others. He favors Toynbee more than most.

Spengler, Oswald, *Untergang des Abendlandes,* translated by Charles F. Atkinson as *The Decline of the West* (New York: Alfred A. Knopf, 1926; Modern Library edition, 1965).

A work of great erudition—also one, unfortunately, showing much inflexibility and mysticism. Based largely on intuition rather than on facts, it is interesting to read but highly dogmatic.

Toynbee, Arnold J., *A Study of History,* 12 vols. (London and New York: Oxford University Press, 1934–1961).

A great thinker ranges over world history, concerning himself with the growth of civilizations. A notable series that occupied the author for forty years. The challenge-and-response theory, stimulating as it is, is rooted in classical mythology, not in scientific fact. Toynbee's writing has appeal, stresses religious ideas. In Vol. XII (1961) he cheerfully meets his critics.

Weber, Max, *The Protestant Ethic and the Spirit of Capitalism,* translated by Talcott Parsons (New York: Charles Scribner's Sons, 1930; new paperback edition, 1958). See also Reinhard Bendix, *Max Weber: An Intellectual Portrait* (Garden City, N. Y.: Doubleday & Co., 1960); see also, *American Sociological Review,* Vol. 30, No. 2 (April, 1965), "Papers on Max Weber," by Talcott Parsons, Reinhard Bendix, Paul Lazarsfeld and Anthony Oberschall, Edward Shils, and Guenther Roth; *International Social Science Journal,* Vol. XVII, No. I (1965), "Max Weber Today," articles by R. Bendix, W. Mommsen, T. Parsons, and P. Rossi.

This "sociological great" is famous for the views proclaiming ideas as a basic force in history and establishing that ideas of one institution may have crucial significance for another one. Weber seemingly did not have a direct interest in social change. Nevertheless his thesis in *The Protestant Ethic and the Spirit of Capitalism* and his work concerning bureaucracy and charismatic leadership add up to a worthy contribution.

Samuelsson, Kurt, *Religion and Economic Action: A Critique of Max Weber,* translated from the Swedish by E. Geoffrey French (New York: Harper Torchbook, 1964; original Swedish publication, 1957).

A Swedish economic historian disputes the Protestant ethic thesis. Samuelsson's main view is that the spirit of capitalism as exemplified by Benjamin Franklin and many captains of industry did not flow from Puritanism and its teachings; it was on the contrary different in kind.

Measuring Socio-cultural Change

"The conceptual and other difficulties of measurement do not justify the refusal to measure . . . ." (Stated with reference to measurement of economic growth.)

SIMON KUZNETS (1959)

Social scientists and others frequently speak of socio-cultural change in the United States during the present era as the most rapid that the world has ever had. An anthropologist, referring to unusually rapid change in a certain primitive society, describes the natives as "people who have moved faster than any [primitive] people of whom we have records." [1] On what basis are such statements made? The answer is that it is on the basis of general (subjective) impression, for actual objective measurements with which to prove such allegations are, for the most part, lacking. *Measuring* socio-cultural change is, unfortunately, one of the least-developed phases of this entire subject. It is currently a frontier area—an area of challenge—in the field of sociology. But we must add that it is an area of intense interest. Concern with social accounts, social indicators, and "monitoring" social change currently represents virtually a *social movement* within social science and within certain governmental circles. Out of this abundant interest and intellectual activity a scientifically valid measure of change is quite likely to come. Some dilemmas need to be resolved (as we shall see), and new data along certain lines may be sought.

However, before probing the interests of this subject on the current frontier we should examine certain fundamental points. We should also indicate why the measurement of change constitutes a problem area—again, an area of challenge. Let us begin with the challenge aspect. It seems that the study of social change itself experienced some slippage of interest during the approximate 1940–1960 period. As was stated in Chapter 1, sociological attention at this time was centered on social theory (emphasizing the social system [2]), methods of research

[1] Margaret Mead, *New Lives for Old, Cultural Transformation—Manus, 1928–1953* (New York: William Morrow and Co., Inc., 1956; paperback edition, New York: Mentor Books, 1961).

[2] Even more, the theory of the social system at this time largely emphasized the

(some of which, it is true, had application to socio-cultural change), and other substantive areas. If some slackening of interest occurred concerning the total subject of change, it would be unlikely that *measuring* the phenomenon would provoke much zest; at any rate, little was accomplished. But the tendency is often found—which Joseph Spengler noted with reference to economics [3]—to develop qualitative conceptualization of a subject first, with the quantitative measurement coming later. In the instance of social change, sizeable accomplishments with regard to measurement, expecially measuring social trends, were made by Professor Ogburn (see Chapter 7) during the 1930s and 1940s. Some contributions were also made by Professor Hornell Hart [4] during the same approximate period and by others, even extending into the 1950s. But, by and large, work in measurement tapered off during the 1950s and early 1960s as major attention was focused on Parsonian theory. It seemed that further work regarding measurement had to wait for this refined theory of the social system.

During recent years, when considerable interest in socio-cultural change *has* been aroused, certain troublesome issues have arisen concerning the philosophy of measurement itself. These issues are not confined to social change alone, nor even to the field of sociology alone; rather they concern measurement in all the social sciences and even, in a general way, in all scientific subjects. They center on the over-all subject of quantification, including the relation between qualitative and quantitative data. In recent times a reaction has set in opposing the earlier emphasis on quantification as represented by Lord Kelvin's statement to the effect that you know something about a subject when you can measure it; but when you cannot express it in numbers, your knowledge is of a meagre and unsatisfactory kind. Rosenblith [5] has declared that the view underscoring the maturity of a science in terms of the number of quantitative concepts it uses, is passé; it reflects an image of a world, he contends, perceived according to nineteenth-century physics. This is more than an issue of "to count or not to count." Leontief, pointing out that the quality-quantity dispute has

---

(static) social structure, as was maintained in Chapter 6 in discussing the contributions of Professor Parsons.

[3] Joseph J. Spengler, "On the Progress of Quantification in Economics," in Harry Woolf (ed.), *Quantification: A History of the Meaning of Measurement in the Natural and Social Sciences* (Indianapolis, Ind.: The Bobbs-Merrill Co., 1961), p. 139.

[4] See Hart, "Social Theory and Social Change," Chapter 7 in Llewellyn Gross (ed.), *Symposium on Sociological Theory* (Evanston, Ill.: Row, Peterson and Co., 1959); all of Hart's chapters in F. R. Allen, *et al.*, *Technology and Social Change* (New York: Appleton-Century-Crofts, 1957); and Hart, "Logistic Social Trends," *American Journal of Sociology*, Vol. 50 (March, 1945), 337–352.

[5] Walter A. Rosenblith, "The Quantification of the Electrical Activity of the Nervous System," in Daniel Lerner (ed.), *Quantity and Quality* (New York: The Free Press, Division of The Macmillan Company, 1961), p. 98.

been the *leitmotiv* of a running methodological controversy in social science, maintains that "it represents only one facet, one stage, of the wider contest between the proponents of concise analytical methods and the defenders of the descriptive individualizing approach." [6] The reader may recall Robert M. MacIver's strictures (see Chapter 6) against too strong a reliance on the quantitative, stressing the view that counting and measuring constitute only the first step in social investigation. Sorokin, who also had "combat experience" in the qualitative-quantitative wars, similarly cautioned against an undue emphasis on the quantitative as well as (in some cases) the improper use of it (see Chapter 5). At any rate, a modern appreciation of the qualitative, coupled with a wary feeling that theories might be constructed based on some incomplete but readily quantified data, has manifested itself. Many scientists today would grant equal status, in terms of scientific validity, to qualitative classifications and to quantitative measurements.[7] This matter, then, needs to be given due consideration by many scientists, including those interested in the measurement of socio-cultural change.

Another line of thought that needs to be considered amounts to an extension of Spengler's observation that scientific endeavor tends to begin with qualitative thought, with quantitative measurement coming later. Examples of this phenomenon are widely known, but the subject is consequential for our present purposes. Thus, many concepts begin in the qualitative realm, but gradually find expression in quantitative language. Lerner writes:

> From animal experiments, psychologists made the great leap to "quantified" propositions about basic human "qualities": intelligence (Binet), memory (Ebbinghaus), conditioning (Pavlov), learning (Thorndike), training (Woodworth), perception (Cannon). Sociologists, starting from the statistical analysis of "social qualities" such as class poverty (Booth) and household budgets (LePlay), soon demonstrated, through aggregative studies of suicide (Durkheim), accidents (Yule), and unhappiness (Jahoda-Zeisl), that the most "qualitative" private decisions could be illuminated by quantifying their public distribution.[8]

[6] Wassily Leontief, "The Problem of Quality and Quantity in Economics," in Lerner (ed.), *op. cit.*, p. 117.

[7] In Lerner's words,

> Contemporary scientists tend to be less concerned with causes than with consequences, investigate wholes which are "more than" (cannot be expressed adequately as) the sum of their parts, and accord equal status, as valid knowledge, to qualitative classifications . . . and to quantitative measurements.

In Lerner (ed.), Introduction, *op. cit.*, p. 33.

[8] *Ibid.*, p. 13

These are mere illustrations. Attitude research, studies of work, industry, leisure, health, and such apparently unlikely subjects as mental hygiene and sex behavior, as well as many others, have gradually received quantitative expression. It may be that all, or perhaps nearly all, subjects—given sufficient time—are potentially amenable to quantitative treatment.[9] Some subjects, such as population study, lend themselves to numerical expression with ease; others, as religion or the psychological study of sensation, provide more difficulties in this respect. Concerning the latter, Professor S. S. Stevens declares that ". . . the eminent scholars who have said that sensation cannot be measured comprise a long and distinguished list. Some have asserted it flatly, as a truth too obvious for argument." [10] In the same way, Lazarsfeld [11] has noted that Gabriel Tarde declared in his day that measuring attitudes was impossible and that Zizek felt the same way about occupational prestige—which today has become a research routine. Other examples could be given. However skeptical statements were in advance, the eventual change to quantitative form of many "qualitative" subjects has not been deterred. This is likely to be the case with the measurement of socio-cultural change. Eventually social scientists will probably refer, not to *"rapid* socio-cultural change" in some area, but to change having a rate of —— (numerical expression).

Comparisons between economics and sociology are of interest concerning the measurement of their basic data. Among the social sciences, economics is generally considered the quantitative science par excellence. It is usually conceded that economic behavior is quite amenable to the use of quantitative methods, granting that all branches of the subject are not equal in this respect.[12] Yet, sociology has also adopted quantitative methods to an impressive degree, even though the development came later than in economics. If economists have taken important strides in measuring (economic) change,[13] one inevitably poses the question as to why sociologists have not accomplished more in developing measures of the change of socio-cultural systems. We have already volunteered some explanation as to why this has occurred—or why significant accomplishments have *not* occurred—but it appears

9 George A. Lundberg declares that, "The assumed conflict between qualitative and quantitative methods must, then, be abandoned in favor of the view that these terms merely represent different stages of refinement and objectivity in our technique of description." Lundberg, *Social Research,* 2nd ed. (New York: Longmans, Green and Co., 1942), p. 23.

10 S. S. Stevens, "The Quantification of Sensation," in Lerner (ed.), *op. cit.,* p. 71.

11 Paul F. Lazarsfeld, "Notes on the History of Quantification in Sociology," in H. Woolf (ed.), *op. cit.,* p. 199, footnote 104.

12 Joseph J. Spengler, *op. cit.,* pp. 131, 135, 144.

13 One has only to consult volumes in economic statistics to be aware of the vast amount of work that has gone into the study of index numbers (of prices, pro-

that the economists have shown that this kind of measurement can be made.[14] Dilemmas and obstacles to achievement exist in both cases; we have not fully dealt with the qualitative-quantitative issue. At any rate, we see no reason to believe that either discipline has more measurement problems than the other.

The objective of this chapter, then, is to explore the possibilities of measuring changes in socio-cultural systems (or some subsystem) over some period of time. It is assumed that these changes have been brought by such influences as have been indicated in the chapters on approaches and theories: immanent factors; economic, technological, ideological, political, religious, leadership, and similar influences; socio-cultural strains; or X, Y, or Z factors (singly or in combination)— changes that may have been planned or that were quite unanticipated.

Because changes can be macroscopic or microscopic or something in-between, measurement needs to be appropriate for the scope and nature of the data. Different kinds of measurement may be used in varying studies. In order to illustrate some different ways of measuring change we shall point to studies that have already been performed. This will require a review of the literature in which *examples* rather than an exhaustive listing of studies will be stressed. Then, we shall consider some criteria regarding measurement studies of change.

REVIEW OF SELECTED STUDIES OF CHANGE

Macroscopic Studies [15]

Since we have already discussed Sorokin's study [16] of fluctuations in various departments of culture in Graeco-Roman and Western civiliza-

---

ductivity, and the like) and the analysis of time series. See, for example, Frederick C. Mills, *Statistical Methods*, 3rd ed. (New York: Henry Holt, 1955); and Frederick E. Croxton and Dudley J. Cowden, *Applied General Statistics*, 3rd ed. (Englewood Cliffs, N. J.: Prentice-Hall, Inc., 1967); Karl A. Fox, *Intermediate Economic Statistics* (New York: John Wiley & Sons, 1968); and Alpha C. Chiang, *Fundamental Methods of Mathematical Economics* (New York: McGraw-Hill Book Company, 1967). We are not asserting, however, that no criticisms have been made of index construction. We shall discuss this subject before long.

[14] Lazarsfeld and Rosenberg (with a frown at their fellow sociologists) declare: "For the past fifty years economists have given careful attention to the logic of index formation; sociometrists often put together any index which happens to come to their minds." Paul F. Lazarsfeld and Morris Rosenberg (eds.), *The Language of Social Research* (Glencoe, Ill.: The Free Press, Inc., 1955), p. 10.

[15] We find the classification of (1) macroscopic, (2) intermediate, and (3) microscopic studies useful for present purposes even though we do not believe that all studies will fit neatly into these divisions. We use this as a rough characterization only.

[16] Pitirim A. Sorokin, *Social and Cultural Dynamics*, 4 Vols. (New York: American Book Company, 1937 and 1941).

tions from 600 B. C. to approximately A. D. 1935 and A. L. Kroeber's as lengthy investigation of patterns of culture growth [17] in some detail (see Chapters 5 and 8, respectively), we will comment briefly on the measurement aspects of the two studies. They may serve to represent, and in some respects to indicate some of the problems of, the large-scale type of investigation. Sorokin, it will be recalled, measured fluctuations in painting, sculpture, architecture, music, literature, systems of truth, ethics, the law, systems of social relationships, war, and internal disturbances over the stated period of years. His method of doing this was to have selected experts make a qualitative and then a quantitative assessment of change in these various activities. Then he drew up a series of tables and charts that portrayed the various quantitative changes. These voluminous data were related, in turn, to three over-all systems of culture—the ideational, sensate, and idealistic—each with its own mentality, philosophy, and *weltanschauung*. Sorokin's measurement of cultural fluctuations was widely criticized, as was noted in Chapter 5, on the grounds that his quantification of some of the data (especially involving art forms and ethical systems) was unconvincing. His use of experts in that vast enterprise was regarded as quite proper (and surely helpful) and also unobjectionable was the making of the qualitative and quantitative assessments by them. Critics did not contend, moreover, that quantitative expression of such data could not be done. But the inference was that, at the time Sorokin made the study, the data concerning some of the departments of culture would have been better left in qualitative form. Sorokin was also criticized for failing to use certain statistical checks to ensure the reliability of the data.[18] Criticisms along this line, however, should probably be tempered to some extent (as in fact several of the critics did do) because not all current statistical techniques were available at the time Sorokin made his study; some were. Sorokin makes clear that he was not interested in detailed statistical procedures himself. Whether he had any methodological advisors (aside from the substantive experts) is not known.

Professor Kroeber, in his *Configurations of Culture Growth,* measured efflorescences or bursts of culture by means of the production of superior people (geniuses). This impresses us as an ingenious and basically correct methodology designed to fit his precise interest. As-

---

17 A. L. Kroeber, *Configurations of Culture Growth* (Berkeley: University of California Press, 1944).

18 A discussion of Sorokin's methodology is still of value. See Robert K. Merton and Bernard Barber, "Sorokin's Formulations in the Sociology of Science," in Phillip J. Allen (ed.), *Pitirim A. Sorokin in Review* (Durham, N. C.: Duke University Press, 1963). Regarding the use of various statistical checks, see Matilda White Riley and Mary E. Moore's chapter entitled "Sorokin's Use of Sociological Measurement," in Allen, (ed.), *op. cit.*

suming heredity to be a constant type of influence in the production of superior people (that is to say, each generation supposedly has a constant number of highly endowed people based on the genes and chromosomes), actual variations in the number of geniuses, then, can be presumed to represent fluctuations in the cultural environment. Some reservations may be held with respect to Kroeber's choice of superior persons in various fields on the basis of textbook judgments and encyclopaedia articles, but it may be that this procedure does not involve major difficulties. A listing in *Who's Who* might be used during recent years, but it must be remembered that some of Kroeber's data applied to the time before Christ. All in all, we suggest that Kroeber's measurement was almost brilliantly devised for the problem at hand.

Intermediate-Scope Studies

Many studies of socio-cultural change may be classified as in intermediate-scope category. One example of this group would undoubtedly be the Report of the President's Research Committee on Social Trends entitled, *Recent Social Trends in the United States*.[19] In this report the committee was interested in setting forth social trends that occurred during the first third of the twentieth century in this nation. Two dozen or more experts (nearly all were social scientists) participated in the project. The twenty-nine chapters comprising the report discussed trends in population, natural resources, invention and discovery, communication, economic organization, occupational patterns, education, social attitudes, metropolitan communities, rural life, health, family life, activities of women, and other subjects. The study emphasized the quantitative statement of trends although its Director of Research, Professor William F. Ogburn, observed elsewhere that both quantitative and qualitative data had been used.[20] Ogburn pointed out that trend studies do not have to adhere to the language of mathematics even if the word *trend* suggests objective measurement. He did caution that if the measurement of data was unsure and inadequate (and this, in his context, doubtless *did* mean unquantified, because he emphasized the use of statistical methods), one would need to be more careful in making generalizations.[21]

[19] Report of the President's Research Committee on Social Trends, *Recent Social Trends in the United States,* 2 Vols. (New York: McGraw-Hill Book Co., 1933).

[20] William F. Ogburn, "Social Trends," in Louis Wirth (ed.), *Eleven Twenty-Six: A Decade of Social Science Research* (Chicago: University of Chicago Press, 1940), pp. 64–65.

[21] *Ibid.,* p. 67.

Another intermediate-scope study is the report of the President's Commission on National Goals, which bears the title, *Goals for Americans*.[22] This has certain resemblances to the preceding report, and, at the time of the inception of the *Goals* project, word circulated informally that it was to be "another *Recent Social Trends*-type study" a generation later. But there are significant differences between the two reports: (1) *Goals for Americans* contained much quantitative information, but was probably not as quantitative a total product as the *Trends* work; (2) the participants in *Goals* comprised a distinguished group,[23] but they were not as concentrated in social science as were the *Trends* authors; and (3) most important of all with respect to methodology, the intent and design of the *Goals* venture did not call for a neutral study of change; rather, a list of national goals was to be set forth as the authors saw them. In all, 82 goals were outlined in 11 domestic areas. National progress was then assessed in relation to these goals. In short, the goals were not objectively determined; they were the formulations of a group of distinguished Americans, each of whom had the advice of a small panel. If the study was less objective than *Trends* (read "scientific" if you wish), this writer would add that the statement of goals appeared reasonable. The generally favorable reception of the volume appeared to mean that a preponderant concurrence with the authors' ideas had developed.

A third—and recent—study of trends of change in American society was sponsored by the Russell Sage Foundation and supervised by Eleanor Bernert Sheldon and Wilbert E. Moore.[24] A distinguished group of authors was recruited, including Conrad Taeuber writing on population trends, Daniel Bell discussing the measurement of knowledge and technology, William J. Goode writing on family change, Iwao Moriyama discussing measurement of health status, and Otis Dudley Duncan discussing trends in social stratification and mobility. Many of the authors (as is evident) are sociologists, some are United States government officials. This volume is similar in type to both the *Recent*

---

[22] Report of the President's Commission on National Goals, *Goals for Americans* (Englewood Cliffs, N. J.: Prentice-Hall, Inc., A Spectrum Book, 1960).

[23] Authors of chapters in *Goals* are Henry M. Wriston, Clinton Rossiter, John W. Gardner, Warren Weaver, August Heckscher, Clark Kerr, Herbert Stein and E. F. Denison, Thomas J. Watson, Jr., Lauren K. Soth, Catherine B. Wurster, James P. Dixon, Jr., Morton Grodzins, Wallace S. Sayre, William L. Langer, John J. McCloy, and William P. Bundy.

[24] Eleanor Bernert Sheldon and Wilbert E. Moore (eds.), *Indicators of Social Change: Concepts and Measurements* (New York: Russell Sage Foundation, 1968). Authors of chapters, in addition to the editors, are Conrad Taeuber, A. W. Sametz, Stanley Lebergott, Daniel Bell, Joyce and William C. Mitchell, William J. Goode, N. J. Demerath, III, Milton Moss, Philip H. Ennis, Iwao Moriyama, Beverley Duncan, Otis Dudley Duncan, and Ida C. Merriam.

Social Trends and *Goals for Americans* projects, although Sheldon and Moore have organized it in terms of four structural rubrics: (1) the demographic base, (2) major structural components of American society (as production of goods, organization of knowledge and technology, and family life), (3) distributive features (as the distribution of schooling, of health attributes, and of leisure), and (4) aggregative features of the society (such as its stratification and mobility and its condition of welfare). These are felt to be component parts of the functional system.[25] The *Indicators of Social Change* is also characterized by a discussion on the part of many authors of the problems of measurement in their respective spheres. The idea of monitoring social change grew out of the interest in social indicators. This volume is notable in many ways, and we shall make further references to it.

Microscopic Studies

Finally, we turn to several examples of microscopic studies. Characteristically, the latter are studies of communities, neighborhoods, or social subsystems (families, schools, churches, corporations, hospitals, and the like) as they have changed during a relatively short period of time. Many community, neighborhood, and subsystem surveys are one-shot appraisals; they are studies of one point in time. The study may have a historical introduction, but this is not sufficient to make it a *change* study. For a valid change study the researcher must have restudied or revisited the area with the primary objective of assessing what has happened since the prior (benchmark) study.[26]

We cite two examples. One is Robert Redfield's study, *A Village That Chose Progress.*[27] Redfield and a co-worker (A. V. Rojas) had made an early study of a Mayan village in Mexico called Chan Kom.[28] Because the village was undergoing some interesting changes at the time of the first study (1931), the authors wanted to return to see how things had worked out. Redfield found the opportunity to do this in 1948. *A Village That Chose Progress* is, then, a story of what happened in Chan Kom during the seventeen years. The village had taken some early actions that brought progress; [29] Chan Kom had

25 *Ibid.*, p. 4.

26 We venture the comment that, although examples of this type are available, not enough revisiting studies of communities and subsystems have been made after benchmark assessments.

27 *A Village That Chose Progress: Chan Kom Re-visited* (Chicago: University of Chicago Press, 1950).

28 Robert Redfield and A. V. Rojas, *Chan Kom: A Mayan Village,* Carnegie Institution of Washington Publication No. 448 (Washington, D. C.: 1934).

29 Leaders of the village (at the time a frontier settlement) made the decision "to convert the settlement into a pueblo, which meant to adopt many of the ways and

progressed economically and politically much faster than did the sur-
rounding Mexican communities. Thus it was a kind of community
success story. Redfield describes—qualitatively for the most part—the
changes in social institutions that took place. Aside from economic
and political factors, religion, taste and manners, and even speech
(more people spoke Spanish, which was regarded as a sign of progress)
were affected. To a considerable extent Chan Kom took on the ways
of civilization. Redfield suggests that the Chan Kom story tells us
something about civilization that is relevant elsewhere.[30] Perhaps an
American or other village might—comparably—decide to solicit industry, also (hopefully) with desirable aftereffects. Or an underdeveloped
area might make the decision to modernize, with consequences gradually unfolding. At any rate, the change in this Yucatan village was
small in scale; Chan Kom's population in 1931 was only 251, and in
1948 it was only 437. The subtitle of the volume is *Chan Kom Re-
visited;* it might have been "Progress in the Microcosm."

A second example of a microscopic study of change is the Lynds'
Middletown in Transition.[31] The authors performed the field work for
the original Middletown [32] study in 1924–1925; Dr. Lynd and his staff
returned for the restudy in 1935. The main reason for the return in
this case concerned economic factors. The first study had been under-
taken during times of prosperity. Because the severe (United States)
national business depression began late in 1929 and was at its peak
during approximately 1931–1933, it had presumably produced effects
by 1935. There was interest, then, in determining how this small supposedly typical, Midwestern city had been affected by the depression.
What had changed during the decade? What had not changed? Here
the community's population was considerably larger than in Chan
Kom. In this instance economic factors constitute the independent
variable, and other community institutions the dependent variables.
After discussing "getting a living" in Middletown and the dominance
of the X family (a leading family), the Lynds systematically describe
changes in family life, education, government, religion, leisure-time
activities, the press, and other institutions.

In these various studies—roughly selected as examples of macro-

---

political forms of townspeople. . . . [The people] wished to make their settlement
not only a pueblo but the most important and powerful community in this part of
the frontier region." Redfield, *A Village That Chose Progress, op. cit.*, pp. 1 and 7.

30 *Ibid.*, p. 24.

31 Robert S. and Helen Merrell Lynd, *Middletown in Transition* (New York:
Harcourt, Brace and Co., 1937).

32 Robert S. and Helen M. Lynd, *Middletown* (New York: Harcourt, Brace and
Co., 1929).

scopic, intermediate, and microscopic researches on change—it is clear that considerably different approaches and procedures have been used. The Sorokin and Kroeber studies explored long-term changes in departments of culture. The Sorokin, *Recent Social Trends, Goals for Americans,* and *Indicators of Social Change* studies all place considerable reliance on quantitative data, more so than the others. The latter three projects assessed changes in major social institutions, as did the community studies of Robert Redfield and the Lynds. However, *Recent Social Trends* emphasized lead and lagging factors in change, *Goals for Americans* emphasized change in relation to formulated goals, and *Indicators of Social Change* discussed trends of change in relation to functioning components of the society. The type of data found in the Redfield and Lynd (community) projects was chiefly qualitative. At this point we return to the central question of the chapter—the possibilities of measuring changes of social systems and their cultures.

TENTATIVE SUGGESTIONS CONCERNING THE MEASUREMENT OF CHANGE

The issue of measuring socio-cultural change consists of two parts: (1) Can sociologists and anthropologists perform measurement satisfactorily (in the judgment of their peers and other interested persons) that will show change with respect to social systems and cultural activities? (2) Should social scientists and others concentrate on change in the components of a system, perhaps relating the changes to desired goals, functional entities, or should they concentrate on something else? Or is there the possibility that an index of socio-cultural change might eventually be formulated that would command general approval? The second question is without doubt the more difficult one.

The Possibilities of Satisfactory and Valid Measurement

There is likely to be little argument with regard to the first question. Sociologists and other social scientists can measure socio-cultural phenomena *in general;* they have done so and will continue to do so. More and more subjects in the process of change can be stated in quantitative terms. Even the increasing content of the volumes of the United States Census (or similar compendia) or the censuses of other nations indicate this. Many changes in a society and its culture can be shown on the basis of this data viewed historically. *Recent Social Trends, Goals for Americans,* and *Indicators of Social Change* give ample evidence of this. We do not believe that any serious debate exists concerning this initial point.[33] Some subjects may be especially difficult to measure objectively, and some researchers may not perform the measurement convincingly in terms of their precise subject and other circumstances. But the principle is largely unargued at the present time.

Nevertheless, there are some principles that need to be followed in performing quantitative measurement. Professor S. S. Wilks calls them "requirements of measurement."

> *The first requirement about measurement . . . is that making a measurement must be an* operationally definable *process. That is, a measurement process must be defined by specifying a set of realizable experimental conditions and a sequence of operations to be made under these conditions which will yield the measurement. The basic reason for such a requirement is to make the measurement process as objective as possible so that different competent scientists operating the process can obtain comparable results.*
>
> . . .
>
> *The second basic requirement of a measurement process is that of* reproducability *of the outcome. Once a measurement process has been defined as objectively as possible, repeating the process should yield measurements in "reasonable agreement" with each other.*
>
> . . .
>
> *The third requirement of basic importance for a measurement process is that of the* validity *or the* accuracy *of the process: that is, the extent to which the process yields "true" measurements of the object being measured.*[34] *(italics in original)*

These points have been widely followed. On the other hand, many studies are highly regarded but are not markedly quantitative in nature: for example, the Redfield and Lynd researches. Some might hold, of course, that greater quantitative emphasis would have improved these and other studies.

Measuring Components of Change or Constructing a Total Index

Whatever our views concerning quantitative and qualitative examples of research, it is obvious that an index (whether of change or

[33] Our earlier comments relative to the quantitative-qualitative issue do not negate this conclusion. Qualitative considerations should not be forgotten; they clearly exist. The influence of qualitative classifications can often be treated statistically, as by the use of the analysis of variance procedures (which analyze the relationship between one quantitative and one qualitative variable). At any rate, the quantitative measurement of changes may increasingly be achieved.

[34] S. S. Wilks, "Some Aspects of Quantification in Science," in H. Woolf (ed.), *op. cit.*, pp. 5–7.

anything else) is 100 per cent quantified. To construct an index is difficult, remembering that it is expected to represent a variety of quantitative and qualitative factors and bearing in mind Professor Wilks' third requirement that the index must yield true measurements of the total panorama. Constructing such an index is apt to be arduous —a task that needs to be performed with great care. The theory of constructing such an index—any index—has been stated in some detail, with illustrations from the literature, by Lazarsfeld and Rosenberg.[35] Defining the process operationally includes the major steps of (1) conceptualizing the elements in society and culture that are changing; and (2) selecting appropriate indicators that will satisfactorily represent the elements conceptualized.

Even though a total index would be useful and it has appeal (if generally approved), most social scientists are not inclined to press for a general index of change at present. Efforts along this line may be premature.

The *Indicators of Social Change* doubtless sets the tone for present perspectives on the subject. The current emphasis is to find answers to devising a satisfactory measurement of components: obtaining valid and meaningful indicators and the like. A helpful step forward may be to devise an index that will represent changes in one component only (as health or education). Thus, Moriyama [36] comments on the need for an over-all health index; a number of disparate factors would be brought into the one index. The index might not fit all purposes, he concedes, but it might at least be useful for one stated purpose. He outlines desirable properties for an index of health. Similar indexes for other components might be devised.

Improvement may be needed in selecting proper and meaningful indicators in general. What would comprise valid indicators to measure changes in *technology* in a nation such as the United States? Dr. H. E. Hoelscher,[37] Dean of the School of Engineering of the University of Pittsburgh, is among those who suggest that energy production and consumption comprise desirable indicators. A decade before, Professor Ogburn and this writer,[38] who were interested in comparing the states of the United States and many foreign nations relative to technological development and standard of living, experimented with different mea-

35 Paul F. Lazarsfeld and Morris Rosenberg (eds.), *The Language of Social Research* (Glencoe, Ill.: The Free Press, Inc., 1955), especially Sec. I.

36 I. M. Moriyama, "Problems in the Measurement of Health Status," Chapter 11 in Sheldon and Moore (eds.), *op. cit.*, especially pp. 591–592.

37 H. E. Hoelscher, "Technology and Social Change," *Science*, Vol. 166 (October 3, 1969), 68–72.

38 William F. Ogburn and Francis R. Allen, "Technological Development and Per Capita Income," *American Journal of Sociology*, Vol. LXV, No. 2 (September, 1959), 127–131.

sures. We felt that the phenomenon of technological development is complex. We experimented with various measures including the value of capital goods (that is, of plant and equipment),[39] capital investment in new plant and equipment, and the consumption of inanimate energy. The results were regarded by the authors as generally satisfactory; all measures were used in one way or another. Qualitative differences in technology present a problem in measurement. Bell, for example, asks "How does one distinguish the change wrought by electricity from that created by atomic energy? We cannot. Both are 'revolutionary' innovations. But there is no way of matching their effects in a comparable way." [40] If such a matter cannot be resolved in the future, it may be that we shall have to be content with approximations in the measurement of entities. The qualities of reasonableness and the extent to which the selection is convincing to other competent observers may have to largely determine the use of specific indicators as measures of some larger socio-cultural factor as, in this case, technology.

The improvement in the development of meaningful indicators for various purposes is illustrated by Sametz's modifications of the Gross National Product (GNP) figure as a measure of economic growth.[41] Sametz contends that the unmodified GNP is *not* a good measure of economic growth. An adjustment is first needed to correct for price change and population increase or decrease (thus converting to per capita form), as is generally agreed. Then an allowance should be made for increasing leisure time, housewives' services and other "domestic" production (which is currently excluded from the GNP), and the various governmental and nongovernmental "costs" of industrialization. Modification is also made to correct for the quality of goods. Sametz's final measure, which he calls the "Welfare GNP per capita" (expressed in dollars), is regarded as a much improved representation of economic growth and welfare.[42]

In finding representation for nonquantifiable socio-cultural ideas, indirect and inferential material may sometimes be used. Lazarsfeld [43] points out that in some American towns families do not lock their doors when they leave the house; this, if still practiced, may be an

39 Because the value of capital goods was not available for American states (which we wanted to compare), we made special calculations of the earnings attributable to plant and equipment (manufacturing) from which the total valuation of capital goods could be estimated. This was, however, somewhat laborious.

40 Daniel Bell, "The Measurement of Knowledge and Technology," Chapter 5 in Sheldon and Moore (eds.), *op. cit.*, especially p. 177.

41 A. W. Sametz, "Production of Goods and Services," Chapter 3 in *ibid*.

42 *Ibid*. See Table 4, p. 89.

43 Lazarsfeld, "Notes on the History of Quantification in Sociology," in H. Woolf (ed.), *op. cit.*, p. 199.

indicator of mutual trust. In the large city, on the other hand, the installation of extra locks in recent years no doubt connotes the opposite feeling.[44] Or the number of highway ride seekers (hitchhikers) may also indicate to some degree the feeling of security along the highways—although it may also have an economic connection. What indicator may validly represent such a phenomenon as less dicipline for children in the typical American family? Another example would be Lipset's [45] usage of the number of individuals securing higher education as a measure of the achievement emphasis in the four major English-speaking nations (England, the United States, Canada, and Australia). He gives reasons for discounting the effects of wealth and occupational factors in the higher-education enrollment figures, at least so far as comparing the four nations is concerned. In devising measures of this sort considerable ingenuity is often needed.

In any event, out of the total welter of quantitative and qualitative factors that may be changing in a society and its culture, the person attempting to develop valid indicators or perhaps to construct an index of change necessarily has to select quantitative indicators regarded as significant in the light of the socio-cultural content. If some changes are significant but qualitative in nature (and are nonconvertible to numerical terms), they presumably have to be omitted from an index at least. The more significant the items of change that are included in the index, the more valid the index is likely to be.[46] However, due to data-unavailability problems, if nothing else, perfection can hardly be expected in this matter.

The problems associated with academic examinations and grades are similar. From a large, theoretically almost-limitless number of possible examination questions—objective and subjective—that could be given relative to subject X, let us assume that an instructor Y decides to administer an examination composed of 75 objective questions. The assumptions would be (1) that these particular questions will fairly represent the panoramic totality of possible questions, and (2) that objective questions will serve as satisfactorily for given purposes as essay or other types of questions. Based on the assumptions, the results can then be expressed in quantitative form; one's grade is a 78 or 94.

---

44 One extreme case is reported of a lady who had eight locks installed on her apartment door. See "Outwitting Burglars Is Now A Universal Pastime," *The New York Times* (April 23, 1970).

45 Seymour M. Lipset, *The First New Nation* (New York: Basic Books, Inc., 1963), pp. 259–261, including Table VI.

46 It will present a "truer" measure (in Wilks' sense) of the changes that have taken place. This is perhaps an appropriate time to underscore the fact that an index does not constitute a direct measure of some phenomenon; it is an indirect measure (an index of it).

A few years ago Clyde Kluckhohn [47] reminded us that Americans like to grade examinations quantitatively on the zero-to-100 scale, whereas Europeans, for instance, usually do not. The latter prefer such qualitative scores as "high honors," "honors," or "pass" for the student or governmental applicant. Measuring change is similar. One can make a generalized, qualitative, subjective assessment, because change is rapid in a certain area, much more so than in a different area. But, as Merton and Barber suggest, these can be in gross error due to the temporary feelings of the person and other factors.[48] On the other hand, quantitative measurement implies such considerations as mentioned with respect to the examinations. One must select quantitative indicators that comprise, it is assumed, a fair representation of the total qualitative-quantitative factors of change. In the instance of the examinations the instructor, in the nature of the case, decides the matter. Concerning a measure of change the researcher selects; however, professional peers will carefully scrutinize the indicators chosen, and will have ideas as to whether or not a convincing representation has been achieved.

Following the Lead of the Economists?

To return to an earlier theme, sociologists are aware of the considerable progress of the economists in quantitative measurement. Assuming that problems in the two fields are roughly similar, is it reasonable to ask: *If* the economists can develop reliable indexes of business activity, productivity, and other significant conceptualized factors in the economy, can sociologists do the same in the socio-cultural realm? Are the economic indexes reliable? The field of economics, it is true, has its own critics within the fold. Leontief,[49] for example, conceding the work of Wesley C. Mitchell and others in developing descriptive economic statistics, calls into question some of the assumptions of constructing an index. An index showing the output of consumers' goods averages various items all used by consumers (bread, shoes, suits, TV sets, and so on), ". . . but they differ from one another in many of their qualities too. In no case does there exist a common unit which can be unambiguously used to measure the magnitude of all the individual members of each group before one proceeds to sum them up

47 *Mirror for Man* (New York: McGraw-Hill Book Co., 1949), p. 243.
48 Error, at any rate, may manifest itself with respect to the use *either* of quantitative or qualitative treatment. As Merton and Barber put it, "That quantitative methods in sociology can be, and have been, abused is surely not in question, any more than that qualitative methods, based on ill-devised and ill-confirmed impressions, can be and have been abused." In Allen (ed.), *op. cit.,* p. 354.
49 In Lerner (ed.), *loc. cit.*

or to average them out." [50] Thus, pounds or tons of steel are added to yards or meters of cloth. "As one summarizes the various items in an over-all index," says Leontief, "one reduces the qualitative variety at the cost of ever increasing quantitative indeterminacy." [51] The more general the contents of an index number, the more arbitrary its measure will be.

On the other hand, the economic statisticians would contend that aggregate index numbers measure the changing value of a fixed aggregate of items, and that, as carefully computed, this does bring valid results for the purposes at hand. The statisticians recommend careful scrutiny of the accuracy of the data; comparability of the items (that is, insuring that over the years each item has not undergone a change in condition such that its nature is different at the end of the period than at the beginning); representativeness of the data used; and all-around adequacy of the data.[52] Certainly the economists have had much experience in devising unweighted and weighted index numbers relative to many subjects. However one reacts to the criticisms of a Leontief, it is clear that no letup has occurred in the official (and unofficial) use of such indices as the Federal Reserve Index of Industrial Production and the GNP—granted that Sametz has modified the latter as a measure of economic growth or welfare. It would seem that sociologists, like economists, have to make up their own minds regarding the validity of the indices and the importance of the criticisms of the index concept.[53] It seems reasonable here to consider the over-all judgment of peers, recognizing that some criticisms will be made in any event.[54] One should also bear in mind the alternative, namely: That imperfect as indices may be, both economics and sociology are likely

[50] *Ibid.*, p. 126.

[51] *Ibid.*, p. 127.

[52] See, for example, Mills, *op. cit.*, Chaps. 13–14; Croxton and Cowden, *op. cit.*, Chaps. 17–18; and other volumes of economic statistics.

[53] It is no doubt apparent, incidentally, that a criticism such as Leontief's bears application to *many* indices—whether in economics, sociology, psychology, or other fields. Croxton and Cowden and other authors provide further detail concerning such indexes as the Federal Reserve Index of Industrial Production, the American Telephone and Telegraph Company Index of Industrial Activity, and the New York Times Weekly Index of Business Activity. It is obvious, moreover, that sociologists have devised many indexes relating to socio-economic status, social mobility, and other subjects.

[54] Our view in emphasizing the factors of reasonableness and of being convincing to qualified peers in this chapter is regarded as similar to the comment expressed by Frederick C. Mills concerning the testing of hypotheses. Mills states:

> If we are to have confidence in a hypothesis it must have support beyond the statistical evidence. It must have a rational basis. . . . It must be "reasonable." . . . Secondly, the hypothesis must fit logically into the relevant body of established knowledge.

Op. Cit., p. 244.

to be in far worse shape if they have no indices at all. A reliance on qualitative and subjective impressions would probably lead to greater error still.

Summarizing this discussion of devising indicators, including the possibility of constructing an over-all index of socio-cultural change, considerable emphasis is currently placed on developing proper indicators. The development of a system of social accounts—concerning which we shall comment presently—is also much favored. The over-all measurement of change by an index is not a high-priority item at present. A minority view may be said to favor efforts to construct an aggregative index.[55] Those holding this view are likely to believe that (1) an imperfect index is better than none at all and (2) such an index, which is a social invention, will probably be steadily improved. If it meets a significant need, it will doubtless receive further attention. After all, such inventions as the electric light and automobile were very imperfect in their original form. For the development of indicators or an index the use of theory should be helpful, even though it does not appear that strict theory is necessary. The use of a model of society, such as the one set forth by Robin Williams, Jr.,[56] should indeed be helpful.

At the same time it should be recognized that for some purposes the use of components of change may be preferable to the use of an over-all index. An aggregative index *averages out* the influence of individual factors or components involved; yet for some purposes it may be important to know these individual quantities. This is as true of an index of business activity or of individual intelligence (the IQ) as of an index of change.

Assessing Approximate Trends by Inference

Another approach toward measuring socio-cultural change is, briefly, that of approximating by inference. The late Professor Hornell Hart,[57] among others, followed this approach. He hypothesizes an increasing acceleration of change (in culture especially) by demonstrating it with reference to certain *elements* of culture, namely: in cutting-tool effi-

[55] This writer favors such efforts, and, hence, in this case espouses the minority view. In fact, with a co-worker (W. Kenneth Bentz) he has constructed an over-all index designed to measure change in the states of the United States, 1940–1960. See Allen and Bentz, "Toward the Measurement of Socio-Cultural Change," *Social Forces*, Vol. 43, No. 4 (May, 1965), 522–532.

[56] Robin M. Williams, Jr., "A Model of Society—The American Case," Chapter 2 in Bertram M. Gross (ed.), *A Great Society?* (New York: Basic Books, Inc., 1966, 1968).

[57] Hornell Hart, "Acceleration in Social Change," Chapter 3 in F. R. Allen, *et al.*, *op. cit.*

ciency, speed-up in modes of transportation, an increased expectation of life, and increased powers of military destruction. He then provides a rationale that seeks to explain why the preceding have occurred. Because these elements have experienced accelerating change as his data show, he infers that a more general acceleration has taken place.

We are discussing this neutrally at this time, our chief purpose being to point out that this is an alternate approach that can be used. It bears similarity to the use of components. It appears that the usefulness of the inferential procedure largely relates to the validity of the particular elements chosen and to the detailed treatment that is provided.

Comparing the Rate of Change in Different Nations

Our final challenge is that of comparing the rate of change, using some kind of an index, in different nations. Perhaps we should phrase this negatively: Is it at all possible that sociologists will be able to make such comparisons? This is the most difficult challenge of all relative to measuring change, and the reader has probably guessed some of the reasons why. The main reason, at any rate, is that the cultural context in different areas varies so greatly. A second reason—applying particularly to macroscopic studies—is that the entire philosophy and outlook of even the same culture over long periods of time may change. Hence, cultural meanings are different. Quantitative assessments of phenomena may appear to remain at a certain level, yet changing socio-cultural contexts may bring numerical error.[58]

Does this mean that the entire subject of measuring change in international perspective is not even worth discussing? This writer at least would not come to such an extreme conclusion. In the first place, the historical record teaches us again and again that what seems difficult or impossible today may be accomplished in another few years. With memories of those earlier sociologists who declared that attitudes and other subjects could *never* be quantitatively measured, we point out that people who say, "It can't be done" often are forced to retract the statement. Then, too, modern sociologists *are* interested in comparative organizational and processual study. This subject is in vogue today. This already-manifested interest may easily be carried over to the study of comparative change. Indeed it is in strong evidence even now in application to underdeveloped areas. Rostow [59] and others have set forth

---

[58] Hans Speier comments on the use of an economic index in relation to a changing historical context in Sorokin's *Social and Cultural Dynamics*, Vol. III. Sorokin had experts express judgments of economic well-being in various areas, using a scale from 1 to 10. Speier's point is that in France, for instance, between the years 1100 and 1925 the cultural context itself had changed. See Hans Speier, "Review of Sorokin, *Dynamics*, Vol. III," *American Sociological Review*, Vol. II (1937), 928.

[59] Walt W. Rostow, *The Stages of Economic Growth* (Cambridge, England: Cambridge University Press, 1960).

stages of economic growth. Certain quantitative indicators as the GNP, expectation of life at birth, and many others present an approximate gauge of the extent of modernization in a society. Is it possible that such indicators, with some experimentation, can be used to gauge the rate of change? We can similarly observe that much international (comparable) data derived from the United Nations and other sources are available.[60] Thus, one has more to work with than some may realize. Extreme care must of course be used in undertaking international comparisons.[61] Moreover, one can hardly be a perfectionist in this kind of endeavor.[62] Yet, attempts to compare different nations with regard to their over-all rate of change may well be made, beginning no doubt with societies having similar cultural patterns and encompassing medium to short periods of time.[63]

Social-Systems Accounting

We close this chapter with a discussion of an innovation that is widely favored at this time: social-systems accounting. This, it must be emphasized, is, however, considerably different from measuring change as it has been discussed up to this point. Social-systems accounting seeks to answer such questions as: What is the progress of a system or subsystem? What is the state of affairs of the system? Or, merely, "How is it doing?"

At various times we have referred to *Social Indicators,* which was

60 See, for example, Bruce M. Russett, *World Handbook of Political and Social Indicators* (New Haven: Yale University Press, 1964); B. Berry, "Geography and Economic Development," *University of Chicago Department of Geography,* Research Paper No. 62 (1960); relative to measuring science see Stevan Dediger, "Measuring the Growth of Science," *Science,* Vol. 138, No. 3542 (November 16, 1962), 781–788; for a valuable collection of charts based on such data see Norton Ginsburg, *Atlas of Economic Development* (Chicago: University of Chicago Press, 1961).

61 For a helpful discussion, see Norman S. Buchanan and Howard S. Ellis, *Approaches to Economic Development* (New York: The Twentieth Century Fund, 1955), Chap. I, especially pp. 5–9.

62 It is not only that data may be missing or unreliable, but every index, as Leibenstein points out, is an approximation. If one must be a perfectionist, he would probably do well to avoid these problems entirely. See Harvey Leibenstein, *Economic Backwardness and Economic Growth* (New York: John Wiley & Sons, Inc., 1957; paper edition, 1963), pp. 8–9.

63 Ronald C. Engle has made such a study in his "Value Differences and Comparative Rates of Socio-Cultural Change in Four English-Speaking Democracies," Unpublished Doctoral dissertation, Florida State University, 1966. Relating his theme to Professor Seymour M. Lipset's previous analysis of value differences in Great Britain, Canada, Australia, and the United States, Engle has measured the rate of change in these nations, 1930–1960, by the use of an index composed of thirty indicators. He found that the United States had the highest gross rate of change, followed by Canada, the United Kingdom, and Australia (in that order). This is explained on the basis of the differing value orientations.

edited by Raymond A. Bauer [64] and includes contributions by Bertram M. Gross, Albert D. Biderman, and others. Chapter 3 of the *Social Indicators* constitutes, in particular, a major contribution toward social-systems accounting. Written by Professor Gross, it outlines an over-all societal information system of indicators. These indicators assess the present and anticipate the future; yardsticks are provided by use of which one can ascertain the state of the system. The Gross system of social statistics relates to a model of a social system at the national level; it contains two main interrelated elements—system structure and system performance. [65] It presents, in short, a descriptive social accounting system.

System Structure.   This consists of: "(1) people and (2) non-human resources, (3) grouped together into subsystems that (4) interrelate among themselves and (5) with the external environment, and are subject to (6) certain values and (7) a central guidance system that may help provide the capacity for future performance." [66] Gross comments that the *people* constitute the basic element of system structure; they are the basis of the entire system. Subsystems (families, communities, organizations, associations, and other groupings) are often of major relevance. External relations are likely to be of major import because "no nation is a closed system." [67] Any external nation may try to influence a given system through persuasion and pressure as well as internal penetration.

System Performance.   "Information relating to system performance," says Gross, "plays a more vital social role than that bearing on system structure." [68] The elements of system performance are (1) satisfying interests, (2) producing output, (3) investing in systems, (4) using inputs efficiently, (5) acquiring resources, (6) observing codes, and (7) behaving rationally. Gross discusses each of these elements in turn. However, he has more to say about the first one than the others, because social systems exist to serve human interests or needs; he observes that interests are both simple and complex, objective and subjective, private and public. Concerning the other elements, Gross points out that producing output is instrumental in satisfying interests; one can invest in "hard goods" but also in people (their education and

[64] R. A. Bauer (ed.), *Social Indicators* (Cambridge, Mass.: The MIT Press, 1966).

[65] Gross writes: "This model, or any part thereof, may be flexibly applied to describe the unique characteristics of any country whatsoever, no matter what the level of industrial development or the type of political regime." *Ibid.*, p. 155.

[66] *Ibid.*, p. 183.

[67] *Ibid.*, p. 204.

[68] *Ibid.*, p. 213.

health); efficiency is measured both by the ratio of actual to potential output and by total productivity; behavioral codes vary throughout the world, but a hard inner core can probably be found in all societies that promote law and order, honesty, loyalty, and justice; and the rationality of a given course of action can be assumed if it satisfies human interests. Furthermore, rational social behavior requires the sustained promotion of pure and applied science and of many technologies that will bring the scientific results into contact with the lives of people. Gross then compares the seven performance elements as today's advanced nations recorded them in their developing years and as today's poor or underdeveloped countries desire them.[69] He also cites the performance elements that are currently changing in the United States and other advanced nations as they move from the industrial to postindustrial conditions.[70] Gross' view is that the advanced nations have not arrived at a final destination, in which further change will be negligible; rather, they are moving—rapidly in fact—toward a post-industrial era in which the quality of life will receive more emphasis. A life expectancy above 70–75 years, a highly educated population, a decreased percentage of the labor force working in both agriculture and manufacturing, and an increased development of transnational and humanistic values, are among the experiences that will be more characteristic of people in this era.

Many will agree that Professor Gross has explored some new vistas in his writing, and that, in general, social-systems accounting bears much promise. He, thus, does not *execute* an example of such accounting, he feels that spade work is necessary before it is tried. He is content to outline such a system and show the need for it.[71]

ANNOTATED BIBLIOGRAPHY

Lave, Lester B., *Technological Change: Its Conception and Measurement* (Englewood Cliffs, N. J.: Prentice-Hall, Inc., 1966).

> Example of modern measurement performed by an economist. Highly mathematical. Agricultural data are emphasized.

---

[69] *Ibid.*, p. 252 (note Table 3.11 on p. 253).

[70] *Ibid.*, pp. 254–255. It is also helpful to refer back to Table 3.6 on pp. 214–215.

[71] Another contribution to *Social Indicators* is a methodological exploration by Albert Biderman who, in part, discusses mechanisms for gathering data on new developments falling outside the regular trend series. Also, Robert A. Rosenthal and Robert S. Weiss discuss methods and problems of reporting information back to organizations—in short, the feedback problem—including the effects of such feedback on policy. We should point out, furthermore, that two volumes of *The Annals of the American Academy of Political and Social Science* entitled, "Social Goals and Indicators for American Society" were issued, respectively, in May, 1967, and September, 1967. Both volumes were edited by Professor Gross. And a third *Annals* volume on indicators, emphasizing political aspects, was issued in March, 1970.

Lazarsfeld, Paul F., and Rosenberg, Morris, (eds.), *The Language of Social Research* (Glencoe, Ill.: The Free Press, Inc., 1955).

Invaluable general reference on conceptualization and measurement.

Lerner, Daniel (ed.), *Quantity and Quality* (New York: The Free Press, Division of The Macmillan Company, 1961).

Helpful discussion. In addition to Lerner's Introduction, the chapters by Stevens, Rosenblith, and Leontief are especially recommended.

Merritt, Richard L., and Rokkan, Stein (eds.), *Comparing Nations: The Use of Quantitative Data in Cross-National Research* (New Haven: Yale University Press, 1966).

Worthwhile reading. Comprises papers presented at a conference dealing with the cross-national use of quantitative political, social, and cultural data held at Yale University in 1963.

Russett, Bruce, and others, *World Handbook of Political and Social Indicators* (New Haven: Yale University Press, 1964).

Extremely helpful handbook that compares nations using political-economic-social indicators (75 tables in all). A mine of useful information.

Sheldon, Eleanor Bernert, and Moore, Wilbert E. (eds.), *Indicators of Social Change: Concepts and Measurement* (New York: Russell Sage Foundation, 1968).

A rewarding volume, the product of distinguished social scientists and others. It summarizes well sociology's current status and dominant viewpoints with respect to measuring change.

Woolf, Harry (ed.), *Quantification,* A History of the Meaning of Measurement in the Natural and Social Sciences (Indianapolis, Ind.: The Bobbs-Merrill Co., 1961).

Lazarsfeld's chapter, entitled "Notes on the History of Quantification in Sociology" is especially valuable. Also recommended are the chapters by S. S. Wilks and Joseph J. Spengler.

Concerning Social Indicators

Bauer, Raymond A. (ed.), *Social Indicators* (Cambridge, Mass.: The MIT Press, 1966).

Begun as an effort to assess the social impact of space exploration, this volume outlines social indicators with which to evaluate the "progress" of any social system or subsystem. A promising development—perhaps a major breakthrough—of the late 1960s.

"Social Goals and Indicators for American Society," Vols. I and II, *The Annals of the American Academy of Political and Social Science,* Vols. 371 and 373, May, 1967, and September, 1967.

Both of these issues of *The Annals,* which were edited by Professor Bertram M. Gross, are very rewarding. In Volume I notable articles include Gross and Springer's stage-setting article, Williams' on values, Duncan's on discrimination against Negroes, Glaser's on crime and delinquency, and Moynihan's on urban conditions. Of the many worthwhile articles in Volume II, one should especially single out Gross' on new goals for social information, Miller's on poverty, and Bauer's on societal feedback.

"Political Intelligence for America's Future," *The Annals of the American Academy of Political and Social Science*, Vol. 388, March, 1970.

    A third issue of *The Annals* is devoted to social indicators and social reports, with Bertram M. Gross and Michael Springer serving as editors. Especially recommended are Springer's introductory article, Etzioni's on societal guidance, Long's on political institutions, and Mancur Olson's on social reporting.

10 Innovation

> *Social changes of today are connected with inventions of the past and inventions of today will no doubt foreshadow the social changes of the future.*
>
> WILLIAM F. OGBURN (1933)

> *The most incisive form of cultural addition is invention.*
>
> ALFRED L. KROEBER (1948)

> *In the ever-renewing society what matures is a system or framework within which continuous innovation, renewal and rebirth can occur.*
>
> JOHN W. GARDNER (1964)

To Professor William F. Ogburn, who (as was noted in Chapter 7) emphasized invention as the central factor in cultural evolution, an *invention* is "any new element in culture." [1] He grouped inventions and scientific discoveries together. Stressing that inventions did not have to be mechanical in nature (the popular connotation of the word), he pointed out that they could be social, legal, religious, or aesthetic.

Professor A. L. Kroeber defined an *invention* similarly. It produces "something new." [2] He also pointed out that inventions did not have to be mechanical or technological; they could be new family organizations, new types of government, or new written constitutions. He thought of a *scientific discovery* as an intellectual invention or a philosophical idea. He appeared not to make a strong distinction between an invention and a discovery.

Ralph Linton defined "a discovery as any addition to knowledge, an invention as a new application of knowledge." [3] He had certain inter-

1 William F. Ogburn, "Change, Social," an article in the *Encyclopaedia of the Social Sciences,* Vol. III (New York: The Macmillan Company, 1930), pp. 330–334, especially p. 331; Ogburn, *Social Change* (New York: The Viking Press, 1950), pp. 80–83.

2 A. L. Kroeber, *Anthropology,* rev. ed. (New York: Harcourt, Brace and Co., 1948), p. 352.

3 Ralph Linton, *The Study of Man* (New York: D. Appleton-Century Co., 1936), p. 306.

ests concerning discoveries and inventions, as we shall see, and he pointed to the importance of such inventions as the use of fire, food raising (domestication of plants and animals), the art of writing, and the wheel for the long-term development of mankind.[4]

H. G. Barnett defines the term *innovation*—the others do not seem to have used this term extensively—as follows:

> *An* invention *is an alteration in or a synthesis of preexisting because it is qualitatively different from existing forms. Strictly speaking, every innovation is an idea, or a constellation of ideas; . . . .* "Innovation" *is therefore a comprehensive term covering all kinds of mental constructs, ...*[5]

Barnett states that an *invention* is more or less synonymous with an *innovation* except that, for most people, the former is "a thing." He does not distinguish between an *invention* and a discovery.[6]

Another anthropologist, E. A. Hoebel, makes the following distinction between an invention and a discovery:

> *An* invention *is an alteration in or a synthesis of preexisting materials, conditions, or practices so as to produce a new form of material or action. It may be technical or social. A* discovery *is the process of becoming aware of something which has been existing but which has not been previously perceived. Vitamins and sunspots were discovered, not invented.*[7] *(italics in original)*

A sociologist, Bernard Barber,[8] declares that the terms *scientific invention* and *scientific discovery* are analytically the same; hence, he uses them interchangeably. He criticizes the view that inventions refer to a machine or other physical thing while discoveries relate to new ideas; both, he observes, are understood in terms of ideas.

Another sociologist, Richard T. LaPiere,[9] does distinguish between inventions and discoveries—in the Hoebel manner. He cites Newton's law of gravity as an example of something that previously existed but was not previously identified (a discovery). LaPiere states that the overall term *innovation* may be either an invention or a discovery.

Finally, we turn to the definitions of some economists. Simon Kuz-

[4] Ralph Linton, *The Tree of Culture* (New York: Vintage Books, 1959), Chap. 2.

[5] H. G. Barnett, *Innovation: The Basis of Cultural Change* (New York: McGraw-Hill Book Co., 1953), pp. 7–8.

[6] "It is fruitless to try to establish a rigorous and meaningful distinction between 'discovery' and 'invention!' " *Ibid.*, p. 8.

[7] E. A. Hoebel, *Man in the Primitive World*, 2nd ed. (New York: McGraw-Hill Book Co., 1958), p. 593.

[8] *Science and the Social Order* (Glencoe, Ill.: The Free Press, Inc., 1952), pp. 193–194.

[9] *Social Change* (New York: McGraw-Hill Book Co., 1965), p. 112.

nets [10] distinguishes between inventions and scientific discoveries, although he adds that the distinction is not always sharp. His general distinction is the same as Hoebel's and LaPiere's. He points out that inventions tend to be practical and useful, a product of superior mentality, and are a combination of available and existing knowledge. But Kuznets limits inventions to technical products; social inventions and aesthetic and other creations are excluded. Technological invention is his sphere of interest.

Irving H. Siegel defines scientific discovery and invention along the lines of Hoebel, LaPiere, and Kuznets: The former ". . . is the act of wrestling a secret from nature; more specifically, a *discovery* may be a 'new' fact, principle, hypothesis, theory, or law concerning natural [including human] phenomena . . . . *Invention* may be regarded as purposeful and practical contriving based on existing knowledge (theoretical and applied) and uncommon insight or skill." [11] Siegel seems to equate the term *invention* with technological products (as Kuznets did), but a careful reading of his statement does not disclose that he positively states that. Siegel suggests that sociological and anthropological theories might take note of the distinction between a scientific discovery and an invention.

Perhaps a sufficient number of definitions have been sampled to provide a sense of the varied meanings assigned by reputable social scientists to these different terms. It is incumbent on us to state how these terms will be used in this textbook. First, the term *innovation* is assumed to be all-inclusive, denoting any new element in society and culture; thus, both inventions and discoveries are subsumed under this heading. An *invention* is defined as a purposeful alteration in, or synthesis of, existing materials, conditions, or practices so that a new form of material or action is produced. It generally results from a superior ability or skill. An invention may be mechanical, social, religious, or artistic—such as television, the computer, the space capsule, the Peace Corps, a school having a new type of program, a new religion, or a new scientific "game" (such as Coleman's "Ghetto" or Gamson's SIMSOC). A *scientific discovery,* on the other hand, is the act of bringing to light (wresting from nature if you will) knowledge or other phenomena that has previously existed but that has been unknown or unrecognized. Examples range from primitives discovering a root that

10 Simon Kuznets, "Inventive Activity: Problems of Definition and Measurement," in National Bureau of Economic Research, *The Rate and Direction of Inventive Activity: Economic and Social Factors* (Princeton, N. J.: Princeton University Press, 1962), pp. 19–22.

11 Irving Siegel, "Scientific Discovery and the Rate of Invention," in National Bureau of Economic Research, *op. cit.,* pp. 441–442. The underlining is by Siegel.

serves as an effective remedy for some ailment, geologists discovering that oil or mineral deposits are found in a certain area, Pasteur discovering that germs cause people to come down with certain diseases (as expressed in the germ theory of disease), Einstein discovering a new relationship between mass and energy in 1905 represented by the equation $E = mc^2$ (which indicated the potential of atomic energy), Rutherford and others discovering the phenomena of radioactivity, and several psychologists discovering that differences in Negro-white intelligence test scores may be fully explained by environment factors (especially schooling), to the discovery by Katz, Lazarsfeld, and perhaps other associated sociologists of the role of the "opinion leader" or "influential" in the flow of communication.[12]

The distinction between inventions and scientific discoveries has value, as we see it, even though we agree with Kuznets that the distinction is not always sharp; the latter may especially be the case at the present time. Rosenblith [13] points out that as the gap between science and technological application narrows, which is characteristic of the present, it is difficult (especially for the nonspecialist) to tell where science leaves off and where technology begins. To make the distinction is desirable, however, because the two processes are fundamentally different. In some instances the distinction will be most significant; one may wish to explore interconnections between the two processes and their achievements. We grant that in other cases the distinction will have less relevance; certainly in primitive society and in other areas where the development of formal science is nonexistent the main interest may be to see how invention has developed given this situation. As we shall see, however, this does not mean in such cases that the rational spirit is entirely lacking.

Permeating this volume has been the theme of equal emphasis on social and cultural change. Perhaps it is unnecessary to state that this

[12] Since Columbus is said to have *discovered* America, is this to be included too? The answer is "Yes"; the idea of such exploration is the same (and America as a continent existed before Columbus arrived). Here we are emphasizing *scientific* discovery, it is true. Discoveries in the scientific realm are ordinarily the ones that are contrasted with inventions. But some explorations, such as those of Admiral Richard E. Byrd in the Antarctic and especially those connected with the International Geophysical Year of 1957–1958 in that area, were largely scientific in nature. We may also take this occasion to point out that, sociologically and anthropologically, discoveries and inventions are not considered as such *unless* they are known in the society-culture to a reasonable extent. If a person discovers or invents something and does not make it known, it exists only for that individual; it is not an innovation from the standpoint of social science. See Kroeber's discussion on that matter, *op. cit.*, 2nd ed., p. 362. Linton's observations regarding what he calls "individual peculiarities" are also germane. *The Study of Man, op. cit.*, pp. 274–275.

[13] Walter A. Rosenblith, "On Some Social Consequences of Scientific and Technological Change," *Daedalus*, Vol. 90, No. 3 (Summer, 1961), 502–503.

holds specifically for the subject of innovation. That the latter may relate to either culture or social system may be obvious to many, yet most anthropologists and some sociologists have tended to link innovation with *cultural* change.[14] The traditional list of inventions—from motor vehicle to computer and space capsule—relates to culture to be sure. Yet, innovations in social systems from earliest times to the present often assume immense importance. Mumford [15] calls attention to the importance of the university as a social invention, beginning with the one in Bologna (Italy) in 1100, which was followed by others in Paris, Cambridge, and elsewhere. Or one may consider the social importance of the factory, the laboratory, and its modern sequel, the research organization. Then there is the corporation and many allied and subinstitutions in the economic realm such as the holding company, the chain store, the department store, and the mail-order house. There are, similarly, subinnovations in the school and college sphere, such as specialized schools, summer schools, new divisions, new institutes, year-around operations, and others. There are conferences for special groups of people such as the "Pugwash" conference for scientists.[16] Hundreds of professional and scientific organizations (for example, the National Science Foundation, the Social Science Research Council, and a long list of others) have great social value and impact, as do the many foundations (from Carnegie and Ford to Rockefeller and Rosenwald). In the political area many inventions have been made, the long list including the creation of the TVA, Social Security, and Civilian Conservation Corps (CCC) during New Deal days and the Peace Corps and many others since; nor should we forget the European Common Market and, of course, the United Nations Organization itself.

At the same time, many inventions have restricted application, and their social impact is often slight. Records of the United States Patent Office and similar offices of other nations disclose that the vast majority of patents relate to small parts of some machine or gadget. Yet, small inventions accumulate and are intertwined with the major ones. Many inventions, moreover, are hardly of supreme moment. Consider the *cafeteria* as a self-service restaurant offering lower cost and speedier service. It seems to have been inaugurated in 1885 both in New York (as a speedier service for businessmen in the stock exchange area) and in

14 As witness the title of Barnett's book.

15 Lewis Mumford, *Technics and Civilization* (New York: Harcourt, Brace & Co., 1934), p. 137.

16 These conferences among scientists from the East and West are properly called Conferences on Science and World Affairs. The first conference was held during July, 1957 at Pugwash, Nova Scotia, and the name "Pugwash" stuck. See Eugene Rabinowitch, "About Pugwash," *Bulletin of the Atomic Scientists*, Vol. XXI, No. 4 (April, 1965), 9–15.

Chicago.[17] It spread to business clubs, to YWCA's and YMCA's, and eventually to colleges and to communities generally. It had certain allied innovations such as the Horn & Hardart Automat, which began in Philadelphia after 1900 (following a previous trial in Germany) and became prominent in New York and other cities. The point to be made is that the cafeteria may exemplify thousands of other business, political, educational, and other innovations that offer new services and may bring advantages of various sorts. But few would claim that the world has been greatly influenced by this type of innovation. Whether one eats in a regular restaurant, a cafeteria, an automat, or in a drive-in restaurant (another innovation) is hardly of much consequence.

Some method is needed to separate the truly momentous innovations (seen from the standpoint of all humanity or from that of a single society and its culture) from the detailed, minor, and perhaps even trivial ones. Certainly over the long span of years the invention of glass, or of printing, or of the wheel, or of nuclear energy is not in the same class as that of a "new look" toothbrush, or a new-style camera, or perhaps a new film (such as Kodachrome).

One answer to this problem may be the classification of *basic* and *improving* inventions that was suggested some years ago by Linton. A basic invention, said Linton, is one "which involves the application of a new principle or a new combination of principles." [18] It is basic in that it opens up new potentialities and is likely to be the forerunner of other inventions. In current terminology, this would often be called a breakthrough. One thinks of the transistor,[19] the computer,[20] and the nuclear reactor. An improving invention, on the other hand, is as the name implies: It consists of the modification of an existing element such that its efficiency is increased, it meets new uses, or other improvement is made. Some improving inventions have considerable importance. The IBM computer System/360 is no doubt vastly superior

---

[17] "Cafeterias," an article in the *Encyclopaedia Americana*, Vol. 5 (New York: Americana Corporation, 1963), 1963 ed., p. 142.

[18] Linton, *The Study of Man, op. cit.*, pp. 316–317.

[19] This has been called by Nelson "one of the most important inventions of the twentieth century." He points out that it is not just that the transistor replaces the vacuum tube in established products, but it stimulates growth in other products (including the making of new inventions) that were uneconomical before the development of the transistor. Richard R. Nelson, "The Link Between Science and Invention: The Case of the Transistor," National Bureau of Economic Research, *op. cit.*, pp. 553–554.

[20] Among the scores of people who have noted the importance and promise of the computer, Rosenblith observes that the computer "is likely to become one of humanity's most important scientific and social tools." Not only is it a tremendous labor-saving device, but it is revolutionary in that it provides a tool that amplifies the capacities of the human brain. Rosenblith, *op. cit.*, pp. 506–507. See also, John Diebold, *Man and the Computer* (New York: Frederick A. Praeger, 1969).

to its predecessors. The Chemcor glass product introduced by the Corning Glass Works in 1962 appears to be a durable (indeed extremely strong) type of glassware as compared with the common glassware used over the centuries.[21] Amazing improvements have obviously been made over the years in the telephone (self-dialing, direct long-distance dialing, and the rest), the automobile, airplane, and countless other inventions. It is true that all inventions have antecedents.[22] Yet, one measure of the importance of both inventions and scientific discoveries is this factor of whether they are opening up a new field (whether they involve a new principle) or whether they merely seek to improve on a previous product or idea.[23] A three-way classification, moreover, might have value.[24]

A second method of separating the extremely important from the less important or trivial is to consider the social effects of the discovery or invention. How many people are affected? How major has been the effect? What is the influence upon social institutions? Here one might develop a functional theory of discoveries and inventions. Comparison of the society and/or selected institutions *before* and several decades *after* the introduction of the invention (automobile, computer, other) could be made. What functions does the discovery or invention have for the society? The impact of Darwin's discovery of evolution was sufficiently great in Europe and America for the century after it to be called "Darwin's century." Similarly, Freud's discovery of the unconscious mind and allied contributions have had a considerable impact on psychology, psychiatry, sex education, and other fields.

Assessments of the social importance of both discoveries and inventions may, however, present some difficulties. For one thing, a discovery or invention may appear to be minor in importance at first but later warrant a higher ranking. Siegel [25] illustrates this with Goddard's early

21 One of Corning's research goals is said to be to invent a composition of glass that will be unbreakable. Pamphlet, courtesy of Corning Glass Works, Corning, New York.

22 This is sometimes given as an objection to trying to decide if an invention is *basic* or *improving* (or derived). Barnett thinks that rendering such decision is apt to be a subjective process. For his discussion see Barnett, *op. cit.*, pp. 8–9.

23 Kuznets has elsewhere proposed that *improvements,* defined as "minor beneficial change in a known invention or process," be distinguished from major inventions. Simon Kuznets, *Six Lectures on Economic Growth* (Glencoe, Ill.: The Free Press, Inc., 1959), p. 30. The situation is not a black and white one, however, because in some cases an invention is not denoted as major (certainly in its social use) until improvements are made.

24 Thus Bennett proposes the classification of (1) basic or extensive inventions that satisfy intense wants of a large number of people; (2) developmental or intensive inventions that may be important for the inventor and other inventors; and (3) minor inventions. William B. Bennett, *The American Patent System* (Baton Rouge: Louisiana State University Press, 1943).

25 Irving H. Siegel, in Natural Bureau of Economic Research, *op. cit.*, p. 444, including footnote 7.

work in rocketry and the endeavors of various people concerning stereo-phonic recording. Other distinctions may be noted. Inventions may relate to a specific subject or have a more generalized application. Among social inventions, the travelers' check was invented by the American Express Company in 1891 as an aid to the traveling public; checks could be cashed on the basis of a double-signature device rather than on personal knowledge or being vouched for, as might be possible in one's home community.[26] The withholding tax was invented by Mr. Beardsley Ruml [27] during the Second World War as a means of pay-ing-as-you-go for the income tax; this social invention was joined to another social invention, the income tax itself. The travelers' check and withholding tax apply to specific situations. But other inventions that are more generalized have even broader application. The *lock* was invented as a security measure many generations ago. Originally a crude device—both lock and key were made of wood—it was steadily improved.[28] Eventually many types of locks were made, and almost endless combinations of individual locks are now produced. Another generalized invention is the *paperback* book. The principle can be used with any book; hence, the social effects tend to fan out. Begun in the early 1940s,[29] the number of scientific paperbacks available at the end of the first decade was estimated to have been only about fifty.[30] By 1960, more than fifteen hundred titles had been published, and the number has accelerated since then. The educational impact of the paperback, although virtually impossible to measure, is considered to be important.

Assessing the social importance of inventions tends to involve sub-jective judgments. But, as we saw in the preceding chapter, techniques for making more objective appraisals can gradually be developed. Even at the present time a panel of experts in a certain field (such as educa-tion or medicine) might make a decision regarding the most important

[26] *The New York Times* (October 20, 1957).

[27] *The New York Times* (April 19, 1960). During earlier years Mr. Ruml was a social scientist and also a professor of education at the University of Chicago. Known for the originality of his ideas he later became a government adviser, chair-man of R. H. Macy & Co. (New York department store), and chairman of the Federal Reserve Board of New York.

[28] Siegfried Giedion, *Mechanization Takes Command* (New York: Oxford Uni-versity Press, 1948), pp. 51–76.

[29] A forerunner of the current paperback were the Haldeman-Julius "Little Blue Books" that were published in Girard, Kansas, beginning in 1919. Mr. Haldeman-Julius decided to settle in Kansas, moving from Philadelphia, holding the dream of "good literature for the masses." It has been estimated that before his death in 1951, "hundreds of millions of these forerunners of today's paperbacks were sold." *The New York Times* (June 14, 1964).

[30] Hayward Cirker, "The Scientific Paperback Revolution," *Science,* Vol. 140 (May 10, 1963), 591–594, especially p. 592. The author is president of Dover Publications, Inc., New York.

inventions made during a specified time interval in that field. If so, they would be using another social invention, the "Delphi technique," which was developed by Olaf Helmer of the Rand Corporation.[31] The latter "technique" has been used in forecasting important inventions of the future.

Kuznets[32] suggests that the magnitude of an invention can also be assessed in terms of the nature of the technical problem solved. Concerning mechanical inventions, it is to be noted that patent statistics of the U. S. Patent Office or those of other nations are not of much help in this matter. In the first place, not all inventions are patented. Even if they were, secondly, the magnitude of the invention would not necessarily be indicated. The social-importance factor may have some delayed reactions too. Sometimes a worthy invention is made, but its use has to wait until valid concepts relating to it have been formulated. An early invention, the *microscope*, affords a good illustration.[33] This invention was available but neglected during the eighteenth and much of the nineteenth centuries (an early microscope had been invented by Leewenhoek in 1674), and it was not until the germ theory of disease had been established and the need arose to identify microorganisms, that its value in medicine was established.

PROCESSES OF INNOVATION

We need to distinguish between *processes of scientific discovery* and *processes of invention*. Both develop in relation to the existing society and culture, but in their details the two processes have significant differences.

Processes of Scientific Discovery

We can be brief in summarizing the processes of making scientific discoveries because the principles of scientific method are, and certainly should be, part of the basic knowledge of all college students.[34]

31 See Olaf Helmer, *Social Technology* (New York: Basic Books, 1966).

32 Kuznets, in National Bureau of Economic Research, *op. cit.*, pp. 25–27.

33 See this writer's "Technology and the Practice of Medicine," Chapter 16 in F. R. Allen, *et al.*, *Technology and Social Change* (New York: Appleton-Century-Crofts, 1957), p. 389. Also see Bernard J. Stern, *American Medical Practice in the Perspectives of a Century* (New York: Commonwealth Fund, 1945), p. 41.

34 Mumford regarded the invention of the experimental method of science as "without doubt the greatest achievement of the eotechnic (early) phase of the machine age." He dates the eotechnic period roughly from A.D. 1000 to 1750. He compares this achievement with other inventions of the period such as mechanical clocks, the telescope, inexpensive paper, the printing press, and the magnetic compass. However, the scientific method was a social invention that led to thousands of discoveries. It is perhaps a supreme example of the invention from which social effects fan out. See Mumford, *op. cit.*, pp. 131–132.

Thus, the quest for proven knowledge involves the observation and accurate measurement of phenomena; the collection and classification of facts and the rendering of proper conclusions based on them; and the testing of hypotheses. The major goal of science, then, is to produce tested, and hence valid, generalizations—generalizations thus rooted in empirical evidence.

The socio-cultural influences that may impinge on the development of science in different areas comprise a fascinating and important story, one told by Merton,[35] Barber,[36] and other researchers involved in the sociology of science. Illustrative of this theme was the perversion of science into "Aryan science" in Nazi Germany, the modern "coloring" of science in Communist Russia with the doctrines of Karl Marx, and the distinctive emphases of science among such peoples as the Greeks and Arabs. Suffice it to say that in all societies a reciprocal influence tends to exist between science and other components of the society. This is not the place, however, for an extended pursuance of this subject, and we shall have to refer the reader to treatises in the sociology of science.

The modern researcher (the "pure scientist") has different motivations from the practical inventor; one can, however, exaggerate the differences. "Knowledge for knowledge's sake," or abstract scientific endeavor with no thought of application whatever, appeals to many scientists. At the same time many "pure" scientists are interested in practical accomplishments that include inventions.[37] They may not live in the ivory tower as much as some may think; in recent times some have established corporations or other businesses. Needless to say, additions to theory are often made during the course of seeking solution to practical problems. But this is a complicated problem that is not a main concern at the moment.

Processes of Invention

Some of the factors in making inventions—whether mechanical, social, or otherwise—are similar to those involved in achieving scientific discoveries. For one thing, both processes take place in a socio-cultural setting. The pure scientist may deliberately ignore some factors in the setting, but not all scientists are interested in pure research. Even pure scientists may have practical interests involving applications of knowledge. Furthermore, research grants and other incentives may spur activity in the direction of practical projects. For the

[35] Robert K. Merton, "Science and the Social Order," Chapter XV in Merton, *Social Theory and Social Structure,* rev. ed. (New York: The Free Press of Glencoe, 1957).

[36] Barber, *op. cit.,* Chaps. II–III.

[37] See the comment by Nelson, *op. cit.,* pp 580–581.

inventor, the practical interest and socio-cultural awareness are greater still. He is impelled to improve on some communication, transportation, or perhaps military device. The cold war has increased the value of such inventions as the missile, antimissile, and helicopter. Even extremely generalized (almost vague) factors, such as the presence of marked achievement orientation among people in contrast to an emphasis on ascribed characteristics, will affect the making of inventions. Such broad emphases in a culture as expecting change to occur (or the reverse) will have an impact on the process of invention. Barnett [38] for instance, observes that the Zuni people of New Mexico do not expect change in any area of their life, whereas the nearby Navajos welcome change. Changes can sometimes be expected in some parts of a culture but not in others. In American society, indeed, change is more or less expected in technology, whereas it is not so cordially welcomed in religion, family life, or political structure. Change may be accepted—usually within certain limits.

The Culture Base. The total accumulation of available knowledge has much to do with the number (and sometimes also the type) of inventions that will be made. When the total stock is abundant, a relatively high rate of change can be expected; and the reverse. New ideas are suggested from the old; the inventor thinks up new ideas in terms of the sum total of existing ones. This suggests that a principle of continuity operates.[39] This is true of both mechanical and social inventions. The invention of television in the United States was a logical sequel to that of the radio, and the computer was a most impressive, although reasonable, recombining of such devices as the calculator, transistors, and other electronic elements. Both showed continuity from the old. To have had either develop in Ghana or even in the United States fifty years earlier would have been utterly unbelievable.

Sometimes, in the recombining process, elements are taken from an entirely different field, as a principle or an element of physics being applied to something in psychology. This is the principle of *cross-fertilization*.[40]

Because the existing accumulation of elements at any given time— the culture base—is shared by many, it is inevitable that various inventors will think up gadgets or ideas at about the same time. This common culture base factor explains the oft-repeated occurrence of

38 Barnett, *op. cit.*, pp. 56–57.

39 W. F. Ogburn and M. F. Nimkoff, *Sociology,* 4th ed. (Boston: Houghton Mifflin Company, 1964), p. 661.

40 *Ibid.,* p. 662.

simultaneous inventions.[41] The virtually simultaneous statement of the theory of natural selection by Darwin and Wallace is often noted. Similarly, television was developed independently by Vladimir Zworykin and Philo Farnsworth (both in the United States), and indeed many other mechanical and social inventions have occurred simultaneously; and this will continue.

Improving inventions also is apt to come in bunches. If the basic invention is shown to meet a need and seems to have promise, many corporations (and sometimes individuals) are likely to develop models —especially if the market appears to be lucrative. Frequently the models are quite similar. Perhaps the most conspicuous example of this at the present time is in the computer business. Competition here is especially keen due to the unusually profitable market. One model after another pours forth from IBM, Control Data, Burroughs, Radio Corporation of America, General Electric, Honeywell, National Cash Register, Sperry Rand, and other corporations.

The Factor of Need and Demand. It has often been alleged that "necessity is the mother of invention." If so, who is the father? The paternal element is clearly the existing culture base. However, the latter is important enough that we must revamp the entire analogy because, whether giving birth to inventions or human offspring, it will not do to have the father more important than the mother.

It is more correct to say that the existing culture gives birth to inventions. The father, to continue the analogy, is the hard-working, imaginative, sometimes-frustrated inventor. He is the one likely to pace up and down, perspire, lose weight, and worry greatly that the event may not come off as anticipated. The *need factor* is more of a helpful, associated element, such as both parents badly wanting the child or seeking to have an expert physician in attendance.[42]

The need (or demand) factor merely helps to capture and focalize the attention of inventors. It motivates the invention process. This can be seen in countless instances. Need, however, has a socio-cultural as well as an individual dimension. There is great need for a cancer cure and for other medical solutions; during the Second World War American shipping losses caused by German submarines brought a sharp demand for antisubmarine devices; the same war brought a critical demand for an answer to the V-1 buzz bomb and the V-2 rocket used by

[41] We have earlier noted the work of Ogburn and Dorothy Thomas on this subject. These authors listed approximately 150 such cases. (Ogburn, *Social Change, op. cit.*, pp. 90–102.)

[42] Professor Ogburn stated the matter more simply. After discussing the maxim he declared: "It is nearer the truth to say that the existing culture is the mother of inventions." *Social Change, op. cit.*, p. 83.

Nazi Germany near the end of the war;[43] possible nuclear war also brought demand for a plan of attack that could effectively damage the enemy without drawing return fire to one's homeland;[44] the population increase has introduced a demand for postal innovations to effectively handle the tremendous modern volume of mail—hence, the zip code, the motor cart for mail carriers, and experimentation with automated processes; population and industrial advance have brought greater demands on water supply, and innovative efforts have turned to conversion of sea water and other measures; the early automobile needed a self-starter, which Charles F. Kettering of General Motors was able to invent in 1912;[45] and the problem of air and water pollution has brought strong demands for corrective measures that are spurring innovative efforts at the present time (including the steam and electric cars). It is often stated that there is an answer to every problem. This *may* be true, if enough time is allowed. Sometimes the demand brings forth needed mechanical or social inventions quickly, as some of the illustrations indicate. In other cases—the cancer problem is a prime illustration—existing cultural elements are *not* yet sufficient such that the needed invention can be developed. Pollution is probably not in this category.

The *individual component* in relation to need can be described more briefly. Broad socio-cultural needs may not themselves bring sufficient motivation for invention. Problems associated with goal attainment, pattern maintenance, and the like of the social system may not impel individuals to sustained activity without some personal linkage or special sensitivity. Friends and relatives afflicted with a disease rather than countless hospital cases often have served to sharpen the motivation of medical researchers. Mr. Kettering, inventor of the (automobile) self-starter, tells us that the general manager of the Cadillac Motor Company "sensitized" his interest after a close friend had broken his jaw while cranking an automobile.[46] The American Express Company

43 See this writer's, "The Influence of Technology on War," Chapter 15 in Allen, *et al., op. cit.*, especially p. 369.

44 Oskar Morgenstern ingeniously devised a plan that would accomplish this. He called it the "Oceanic System." The United States would have an invulnerable retaliatory force in the form of roaming nuclear-powered submarines armed with Polaris missiles having hydrogen warheads. This has advantages over fixed bases located within the continental United States. Oskar Morgenstern, *The Question of National Defense* (New York: Random House, 1959), Chap. 4.

45 "Charles F. Kettering, Prophet of Progress," *Science,* Vol. 129 (January 30, 1959), 255–256.

46 "Charles F. Kettering: Inventor," *The New York Times* (November 26, 1958). Also, many people were reported to have suffered a broken arm as the crank would often snap back (during the cranking process). But one cannot be so naive as to believe that such incidents, distressing as they were, constituted the full story. Undoubtedly the General Motors Corporation (and other automotive concerns) were

developed the travelers' check after its president, J. C. Fargo, returned from a trip to Europe fuming because "even letters of credit of a leading American businessman weren't readily accepted there." [47] The innovation of placing telephone booths on street corners and at other accessible places during the late 1940s seems to have developed from frustrations developed by individuals seeking to telephone, yet unable to find a booth.[48] These examples can be multiplied, but they add up to the influence of *personal* motivation in the arduous task of invention.

The Individual Factor: The Inventor and his Characteristics. Individual sensitivities and special awarenesses, then, often impel some people to try to remedy a difficult or undesired situation if they can do so. Extra motivation to find a solution may be needed when, as Mr. Kettering puts it, "all initial efforts have ended in failure. [But] The one time you don't want to fail is the last time you try." [49] At this point, however, we wish to explore more fully some of the usual characteristics of inventors.

Rossman's data indicate that the most common motivation of inventors is simply a "love of inventing," with a "desire to improve" [50] coming a close second. In other words, they *like to create,* much as some people might like to play baseball, be actors, or enjoy the game of politics. Ordinarily their motivations do not seem to run to the financial (reward) aspect of their work, although Thomas Edison had a secondary interest along this line.[51] Secondly, inventors tend to be skilled people of high ability for the most part. The reader may recall that several of our definitions of inventions given at the beginning of this chapter mentioned that they were products of superior mentality and products of uncommon insight and skill. The average invention is difficult to make (we shall examine the accident factor presently).

---

fully aware that sales would greatly increase if the hand-crank operation could be replaced by a self-starter. Many women, in particular, did not buy cars until the self-starter was invented.

47 *The New York Times* (October 20, 1957). It was reported that a company clerk, Marcellus F. Berry, conceived of the double-signature system.

48 Again (as with the self-starter invention) one cannot believe that a few cases of frustration or even injury in the former case told the full story. Obviously, American Telephone and Telegraph Company officials were fully aware of the likelihood of income increase for the company if booths were made easily accessible.

49 *The New York Times* (Nov. 26, 1958).

50 Joseph Rossman, *The Psychology of the Inventor* (Washington, D. C.: Inventor's Publishing Co., 1931), p. 152.

51 "His [Edison's] social thinking was of the dollars-and-cents kind. . . . An invention that could not be sold was to him a commercial and therefore a social failure." Waldemar Kaempffert, "Scientist-Magician Who Reshaped a World," *The New York Times Magazine* (February 9, 1947).

However, the special ability is apt to be different from that, say, of the pure scientist. The inventor is usually practical, not an abstract thinker. Many inventors have been tinkerers. Kettering was probably in character when he declared: "I'm a pliers and screwdriver man, not a theory man." [52] This is undoubtedly less true of the modern research-organization worker. Furthermore, theoretical knowledge, rather than tinkering, will probably become more and more important as society steadily moves in the direction of the post-industrial society.[53]

The inventor's mental processes run to the *unconventional*. Many inventors have scoffed at conventional theory.[54] His mind may take a different path, almost as if by nature. To be unconventional does not mean that one cannot be educated and, hence, "habituated to the established ways of thinking in a field." [55] It does mean that the creative, innovative person will respond in a more flexible, unpredictable manner than the ordinary individual with a high IQ (but who is less innovative).[56]

Other traits can be inferred from the nature of the inventor's situation. He needs to have above-average confidence in his own judgment. He may develop this if he remains an inventor, because he will be continually pitting his own explanation of things against the generally accepted (traditional) version. He necessarily holds the deviant view; it does not follow, however, that all mental deviants are inventors.[57] The inventor must have, or develop, persistence. This is an occupational requirement, because inventions are often time consuming. Even if he has successfully made an invention, he must interest others in it—and other people generally have the conventional views regard-

[52] Source is same as in footnote 46.

[53] Indeed, theoretical knowledge is likely to be a central factor in the innovation process, says Bell. Daniel Bell, "The Measurement of Knowledge and Technology," Chapter 5 in Eleanor B. Sheldon and Wilbert E. Moore (eds.), *Indicators of Social Change* (New York: Russell Sage Foundation, 1968), pp. 152–153.

[54] Again the worker in the large research organization is not so likely to be anti-theory. Kettering gleefully pointed out that his diesel engine invention operated in a way not sanctioned by the prevailing theory. "According to the theory," said Kettering, "our Diesels still don't work." (Same source as footnote 46.)

[55] LaPiere declares that the informed person is indoctrinated to the established ways. "This is the reason why highly trained and recognized experts in any field of endeavor rarely innovate . . . and why innovations so often come from . . . talented amateurs." LaPiere, *op. cit.*, p. 119. It could be, however, that (1) the average innovator *is* well informed—an expert if you will, and (2) that some well-informed people in a field are of the inventive turn of mind although others are not. We are not persuaded that the typical inventor is an amateur.

[56] See Jacob Getzels and Philip Jackson, *Creativity and Intelligence* (New York: John Wiley & Sons, Inc., 1962). The subjects of the study are gifted children.

[57] Following Merton's typology—which is noted by LaPiere, *op. cit.*, p. 127—only one of the four types of deviant behavior involves innovation. Merton, *op. cit.*, p. 140 ff.

ing the subject.[58] All in all, inventors are supposed to have a difficult life, granting that some, on the other hand, will eventually be famous as great benefactors of the human race. Edison himself declared:

> *The inventor tries to meet the demand of a crazy civilization. Society is never prepared to receive any invention. . . . it takes years for the inventor to get people to listen to him and years more before it can be introduced, and when it is introduced our laws and court procedure are used by predatory commercialism to ruin the inventor. They don't leave him even enough to start a new invention.*[59]

Some inventors become affluent. Edison, as suggested, was one. Some will experience difficult times but end up a notable success, like Chester Carlson the inventor of the Xerox copying machine.[60] Many modern inventors, however, are not the solitary, "worker-in-the-garret" sort. They are employed by a large research organization in which the inventor's situation is vastly different. Technical aids, library facilities, and equipment are likely to be of the best. The run-of-the-mill financial problems that the lone inventor may have are likely to be minimal. Based on gradually developing studies of the modern research laboratory, it appears that much of the "romance" is now taken out of inventing.[61]

Many have been concerned lest the large industrial laboratory dominate the field of invention. It appears, however, that the private in-

---

[58] The story of George Westinghouse trying to interest American railroads in his air-brake invention is a classic. After many leading railroads scorned the new device, officials of a small branch-line agreed to try it. The air-brake was a major success, and was eventually adopted by all railroads.

[59] D. D. Runes (ed.), *The Diary and Sundry Observations of Thomas Alva Edison* (New York: The Philosophical Library, 1948), p. 179.

[60] After graduating from the California Institute of Technology with a degree in physics, Mr. Carlson came East. He became interested in the possibilities of a copying machine, and in 1938 invented the world's first dry, electrostatic machine. He approached a score of companies as potential backers, but all turned him down with what he called "an enthusiastic lack of interest." Finally, the research director of the Haloid Company, Rochester, New York, heard about Carlson's invention. Haloid and Mr. Carlson joined forces in 1948 to form Haloid Xerox Inc. (later changed to The Xerox Corporation). But the machine was steadily improved, and in 1960 the Xerox 914 copier "revolutionized the industry." Xerox's steady growth became a "rocket-like ascent." See "The Story of Xerox and Xerography" (pamphlet), courtesy of The Xerox Corporation.

[61] For a discussion of the advantages and disadvantages of the large research organization, see John Jewkes, David Sawers, and Richard Stillerman, *The Sources of Invention* (London: Collier-Macmillan Limited, 1958), pp. 164–165. The authors' generalizations are based on case histories of about fifty inventions, which are given in Part II. The list includes Automatic transmissions, Bakelite, ball-point pen, cellophane, cinerama, mechanical cotton picker, cyclotron, DDT, fluorescent lighting, helicopter, insulin, jet engine, Kodachrome, long-playing record, magnetic recording, neoprene, nylon, penicillin, power steering, radar, radio, rockets, safety razor, silicones, streptomycin, television, titanium, transistor, zerography, and zip fastener.

ventor still plays an important role. This is the conclusion of Jewkes, Sawers, and Stillerman,[62] for instance, who suggest that the eclectic approach seems best for the making of innovations. The various conditions all aid the process in different ways, and no one source of inventions should dominate the others. Nelson, discussing the subject with special reference to Bell Telephone Laboratories' invention of the transistor, reaches a similar conclusion. He admits that the distinction between basic and applied research is not clear-cut. Some inventions, he concludes, are best made in a large organization like Bell and some by the lone inventor. As for scientists, the pure-science type like Einstein would be generally unhappy at Bell, and "Bell would be most unhappy if most of its research scientists were as intellectually pure as Einstein." [63]

We have now explored, albeit briefly, the influences of the cultural base, of need or demand, and of the inventor himself in the *invention* process. We have observed that some of the components of the process are socio-cultural and some individual. Another factor must now be considered, that of accidents.

Accidents and the Serendipity Pattern

The serendipity pattern, which applies to both discoveries and inventions, refers to that happy situation where one is searching for one result and, by chance and with surprise, comes upon entirely different findings or results not being sought. One often stumbles upon the unexpected because of some accident. The word *serendipity* is derived from a Persian fairy tale called *The Three Princes of Serendip;* [64] in the story the princes were always making discoveries, by accidents and sagacity, of things of which they were not in quest. It is like attending a meeting or a social gathering with some purpose in mind, and having an illuminating time because of unexpectedly finding out some very *different* and *valuable* things.

Discoveries and inventions are quite commonly made on this basis. Professor Walter B. Cannon [65] emphasized it, as have Ernst Mach, James Bryant Conant, and others.[66] But the serendipity achievement

62 *Ibid.*, pp. 242–246.

63 Nelson, National Bureau of Economic Research, *op. cit.*, p. 583.

64 The word appears to have been coined by Horace Walpole, in about 1754, who had read a translation of the fairy tale. See the editorial on "Serendipity" in *Science*, Vol. 140 (June 14, 1963), 1177, and the fascinating "Letter to the Editor" written by S. S. West, H. J. Adler, Kathleen Lonsdale, Millard Zeisberg, Philip Bard, and Walter C. Alvarez in *Science*, Vol. 141 (September 6, 1963), 862; and Vol. 142 (November 8, 1963), 621.

65 *The Way of An Investigator* (New York: W. W. Norton, 1945), Chapter 6, "Gains from Serendipity."

66 See discussion in Barber, *op. cit.*, pp. 203–206.

comes to the investigator who is prepared; a chance event often occurs, but most people would not catch its significance. However, the scientist or inventor who is more familiar with the material or the situation is more aware of the significance of the occurrence. Sometimes he sees this in a flash, sometimes he explains it later. Examples of serendipity include Cannon's discovery of sympathin, Roentgen's discovery of X-rays, Sir Alexander Fleming's discovery of penicillin, Goodyear's vulcanization of rubber, Nobel's invention of dynamite, and others. A recent example was reported by Dr. S. Donald Stookey, Manager of Research at the Corning Glass Works in New York State.[67] He was experimenting with substances used in glass making when an electric furnace went out of control and the temperature rose five hundred degrees higher than was planned. An unknown hard crystalline substance was created that was later slightly modified and given the now well-known trade name *pyroceram*. This unexpected result of the furnace difficulty, coupled with acute observation by an expert, is regarded as a major invention in glass making. In social science Merton has commented on several examples of serendipity.[68] One such case concerns an unexpected finding in a suburban housing research project (Craftown) in which parents claimed they could often go out during the evenings "because there are many teen-agers here who can look after the kids." But from the data of the study it was clear that Craftown did *not* have a large adolescent population. What brought the illusion among the parents? The researchers were made aware quite by surprise, that close cohesion in the community had brought a feeling of confidence. In short, parents felt that the children were in safe hands whether the number of teen-agers was large (as they thought) or not. The researchers, at any rate, discovered the close social cohesion in Craftown, which was not their initial point of interest.[69] Merton summarizes that the serendipity pattern, involving unanticipated, anomalous, and strategic findings, exerts pressure on the investigator toward a new direction of inquiry. As related to innovation it tends to bring a new, unanticipated discovery or invention.

Effect of Science on Invention

The impact of science on invention is important. It contrasts the situation in preliterate and underdeveloped areas (where science is only slightly developed and rationalism shows itself in empirical ref-

---

67 See "Profitable Mistake at Corning Glass," *Fortune* (July, 1957), 68.

68 Merton, *op. cit.*, 2nd ed., pp. 105–108.

69 Other examples by Merton relate to disparate data from *The American Soldier* that were finally explained by the concept of relative deprivation—which was *not* the original focus of the inquiry. *Ibid.*, pp. 227–229 and 241–242.

erence) and in highly industrialized areas. It is significant that practically all (or perhaps all) of the British and American inventions described by Jewkes and his co-workers were based on science. Primitives have invented new hunting and fishing implements and tools, devised new types of shelter (lean-to, tipi), and new religious ceremonies. But inventions based on rudimentary science are of a different order from the cyclotron, fluorescent lighting, the helicopter, the jet engine, radar, rockets, the space vehicle, television, the computer, and so on. This indeed is one of the basic reasons why we wished to distinguish between scientific discoveries and inventions in the first place: to underscore the varying impact of meagerly developed versus highly developed science on inventions in different societies.

We commented earlier on the modern tendency of pure science and technological application to merge together; it is sometimes difficult, as we pointed out, to separate the two processes distinctly. Several other factors in the modern scientific age in advanced nations include the vast resources of materials and equipment that are products of science and that are available for the use of inventors. The scientific equipment available in such an institution as Bell Telephone Laboratories is staggering to contemplate.[70] Another present-day tendency is that of closing the gap between new scientific knowledge and its application to invention. Thomas J. Watson, Jr., President of the IBM Corporation, states the following:

> *The next ten years may well bring about technological changes which will make past progress seem small indeed. This will result from the rapidly closing gap between new knowledge and its direct application to our life. The principle of the vacuum tube was understood around the turn of the century; but it was not used in any major way until after World War I. On the other hand, the transistor was discovered in 1948. Within five years, it was being widely used in many types of equipment. The solar battery was hardly born before it was flying in our satellites.*[71]

On the other hand, a recent study [72] of key research events (including pure science work, applied research, and developmental studies)

[70] In addition to previous references, see Francis Bello, "The World's Greatest Industrial Laboratory," *Fortune* (November, 1958), 148–157.

[71] Thomas J. Watson, Jr., "Technological Change," Chapter 8 in Report of the President's Commission on National Goals, *Goals for Americans* (Englewood Cliffs, N. J.: Prentice-Hall, Inc., 1960), p. 195.

[72] See a report of this study in *Technology Review*, Vol. 71, No. 5 (March, 1969), 52–53, under the heading "The Importance of Being Aimless." The study was performed by a team studying the history of research, under a National Science Foundation contract, at the Illinois Institute of Technology Research Institute. The selected technological developments were the video tape recorder, the oral contraceptive pill, magnetic ferrites, the electron microscope, and the matrix isolation technique used in observing chemical reactions.

involved in the accomplishment of five selected technological developments indicates the role that *nonmission* (or *pure*) research plays in
over-all development. In each of these developments pure science provided the origins that could later be advanced and applied. Of all the
key research events taken together, 70 per cent were nonmission (pure)
science, and three quarters of them were performed in universities. Of
the mission-oriented research (as distinct from actual development) 54
per cent was done by industry and most of the rest by universities. Industry of course took over at the development stage. "The number of
nonmission [pure science] events peaks significantly between the 20th
and 30th year prior to an innovation. In other words, today's technological innovations spring very largely from purely scientific work that
was done that long ago." [73]

These are some of the factors related to the scientific impact on invention.[74] One may reflect that the discussion emphasizes *physical*
science and *technological* application. What can we say about the effects of *social* science on the making of *social* inventions? This subject
—something of an underdeveloped area itself—deserves far more attention than it usually receives.

ORGANIZING FOR INVENTION

One thesis of this chapter emphasizes the tremendous social importance of innovation. It is frequently affirmed. Perhaps it is enough to
observe, with John W. Gardner,[75] that "a society decays when its institutions and individuals lose their vitality." Innovations are needed to
bring social renewal. Every need potentially has an answer, although
one cannot always expect the answer immediately. The control of war,
a solution to the pollution problem, a complete answer to water short-
age problems, a reduction in crime in cities—these are gigantic, complicated problems. What is needed in the quest for answers to
problems, declares Gardner,[76] is a system that provides for continuous
innovations. Often, further technological invention is needed in order
to make our environment more humane and fulfilling, although complementary social inventions may be required too.[77]

[73] The article concludes that "The main lesson is, clearly, that to cut back on all
current research that is not aimed at specific payoffs would be to deprive the next
generation of the scientific ground on which it will build." *Ibid.*, p. 53.

[74] See also Aaron W. Warner, D. Morse, and A. S. Eichner (eds.), *The Impact of
Science on Technology* (New York: Columbia University Press, 1965).

[75] Gardner, *op. cit.*, p. 2.

[76] *Ibid.*, p. 7 and Chap. 8. Man is now, says Gardner, beginning to pursue innovation systematically.

[77] Donald N. Michael, *The Unprepared Society* (New York: Basic Books, Inc.,
1968), p. 39.

This chapter has distinguished between *scientific discovery* and *invention,* a matter that is useful at this point. It may be suggested that the major problems, for the most part, do not lie with the former. Science is well established in the educational and research systems, and scientific endeavor has been, and is, highly productive. We would not be so bold as to declare that no problems at all exist with regard to the organization and functioning of science, but we do think that the notable lack—the most pressing problems—are not to be found in this realm.

Need for Social Inventions

We shall discuss mechanical (technological) invention and social invention separately. Although the first is an area of enormous productivity in Western civilization, the greatest need is for various keys to social inventions. The whole situation is vastly different from that of technological invention. It is not that the scientific discovery element is in a deplorable state because, on the contrary, social science research has been exceedingly productive during recent decades. But there has not been a systematic effort in social technology. It is not that social technology and social engineering [78] are entirely lacking; they are not. But they are not emphasized enough. Where are the MIT's and Cal Techs of *social* technology? Where are the organized groups of people —in bureaus or centers—working on socio-economic-political needs and possible solutions to meet them? [79] Where are the experts studying the processes involved in making *social* inventions? It appears that on this front man's larger task lies ahead. The social sciences, of course, developed later than the physical. Nevertheless, casting explanations and rationalizations aside, this is the area of greatest need. It is not enough to have a few social scientists here and there, harried and pressed for time, to suggest haphazardly an occasional social invention. A proper organization for continuous social invention is required. The

---

[78] Michael defines social engineering as "the systematic application of knowledge and theory about men and institutions to the guidance-transformation-manipulation of men and institutions." *Op. cit.,* p. 51.

[79] We have, of course, centers where research is conducted relative to *specific* subjects (such as population, underdeveloped areas, the Soviet Union). Perhaps the nearest thing to a *general,* social science research center is the Rand Corporation, which is operated by the United States Air Force. The Hudson Institute and the Committee for the Year 2000 of the American Academy of Arts and Sciences are currently engaged in prediction studies. Scores of conferences are organized to discuss individual problems. The need is for an organized, sustained effort by trained social scientists whose *main business* would be to meet problems. The focus of the group would be on making social inventions and on the *process* of making social inventions. Preferably, the group would be located in a university setting.

demands of nation and world are too great. The more social inventions that are produced, the better (in all probability) will be the practice. A proper organization for making social inventions should be a cardinal element in the actively oriented society that is responsive to the needs of its citizens. We shall note this further in Chapter 13.

ANNOTATED BIBLIOGRAPHY

Anderson, Harold, (ed.), *Creativity and Its Cultivation* (New York: Harper & Brothers, 1959).
> A high quality symposium on creativity. Contributors (besides Anderson) include Erich Fromm, Harold Lasswell, Rollo May, Margaret Mead, Henry A. Murray, and Carl R. Rogers.

Barnett, H. G., *Innovation: The Basis of Cultural Change* (New York: McGraw-Hill Book Co., 1953; paperback edition is undated).
> Study of the setting, incentives for, processes, and acceptance of innovation. The data are largely anthropological. Psychological factors are emphasized.

Bell, Daniel, "The Measurement of Knowledge and Technology," Chapter 5 in Eleanor B. Sheldon and Wilbert E. Moore (eds.), *Indicators of Social Change* (New York: Russell Sage Foundation, 1968).
> Much is found in this lengthy and eminently valuable chapter. Bell's discussion of the modern knowledge base, the social results of technological change, and the developing field of technological forecasting is especially worthwhile.

Gardner, John W., *Self-Renewal,* The Individual and the Innovative Society (New York: Harper & Row, 1964).
> Perceptive discussion of the need for creative, innovating persons in modern society.

Machlup, Fritz, *The Production and Distribution of Knowledge in the United States* (Princeton, N .J.: Princeton University Press, 1962).
> Machlup canvasses the entire information base of American society: education in school and home; research and development; the mass media; information machines and information services.

National Bureau of Economic Research, *The Rate and Direction of Inventive Ability* (Princeton, N. J.: Princeton University Press, 1962).
> A superior contribution by the economists.

Ogburn, William F., *The Social Effects of Aviation* (Boston: Houghton Mifflin Co., 1946).
> Ogburn, a sociologist who emphasized the influence of inventions in social change, here systematically describes the social effects of a modern invention.

Price, George R., "How to Speed Up Invention," *Fortune* (November, 1956), 150–153 and 218–220.
> Price proposes six methods of stimulating technological invention that range from rewarding engineers and others more handsomely and encouraging radical thinking and new designs to performing research on the research process itself. Indeed he urges that improvements be made on the entire research and development process.

Rossman, Joseph, *The Psychology of the Inventor* (Washington, D. C.: Inventor's Publishing Co., 1931).

Study of the motivations and dilemmas of inventors.

Runes, Dagobert D. (ed.), *The Diary and Sundry Observations of Thomas Alva Edison* (New York: Philosophical Library, 1948).

Interesting and significant ideas on inventing—also on education, the machine, war and peace—coming from one of the greatest inventors of all.

Schon, Donald A., *Technology and Change* (New York: Delacorte Press, 1967).

Schon, a former research consultant with Arthur D. Little, Inc., writes of innovation from the standpoint of the American corporation. Most corporation executives *say* that industry must engage in product innovation; but the latter is often disruptive and Schon maintains that many corporations actually resist innovation.

11 *Resistance to Innovation*

This chapter begins with the assumption that a scientific discovery or an invention has been made. When it is given to the world, or the world hears about it, the idea or the gadget may be resisted. Discoveries and inventions that have encountered virtually no resistance are few. Even if one tries to imagine innovations that would provoke little or no resistance—for instance, the electric light, pain-killing drugs or other medical inventions, or possibly the food invention of ice cream —it is nevertheless likely that some people, somewhere, have objected to even these products. The cost factor, quality of a product, or related phenomena (side-effects if you will) may constitute points of resistance for the most constructive and eagerly awaited developments. Many types of resistance are offered to discoveries and inventions as we shall see. Resistance may be made to either social and cultural innovations and directed to scientific discoveries or to inventions (mechanical or social).[1] At any rate, unqualified acceptance of innovations can in no wise be guaranteed, regardless of how socially beneficial an innovation may seem.

Resistances stem from several sources: (1) cultural, (2) psychological, (3) economic, (4) ideological, (5) dislocations and complexities, and (6) vested interests. We shall also note the irrational nature of certain resistances; people may verbalize resistance to an innovation on the basis of X factor, but evidence may be disclosed to indicate that the real objection relates to Y or Z factors.

TYPES AND FORMS OF RESISTANCE

Cultural Resistance

Resistances to innovation that are broadly cultural in nature often take one of two forms: (1) *general cultural inertia* or (2) *clashing of the innovation with existing cultural values or other elements*.

The norms of every culture define different types of behavior as right, essential, tabooed, and so forth. There is an accepted and an ex-

[1] Most of the resistances apply to discoveries *and* inventions (mechanical and social), though, as we shall see, there are some differences.

pected way to do almost everything. These norms are sanctioned and have much social force behind them. When some one proposes an innovation—a different way—he must not anticipate that members of the society will be overjoyed and avid to consider and try the idea *as a general thing*. Their characteristic response, on the other hand, is likely to be that of a frown. "Who is this 'queer bird' who thinks that we should depart from the ways of our fathers (or our corporation leaders, or our club leaders, or our fraternity)?" In this situation the old hand is apt to say (in the words of John Gardner): " 'You just have to understand how we do things around here,' and what he means is that 'how we do things' is Sound and Respectable and the Best Way." [2] This attitude is common. Inventions—at least many inventions—are hardly given the welcome mat.[3]

In addition to the general inertia that every innovation has to overcome, some discoveries or inventions may specifically clash with existing cultural values or a significant cultural element. If the conflict is major, the innovation may actually be stopped in its tracks. Often the conflict exists with reference to only one institution. The Darwinian theory of evolution (as a scientific discovery) clashed, for example, with the religious explanation of the creation of man. Intense, widespread argument followed. For many years millions of people refused to accept the biological (scientific) explanation, and many do not today; but doubtless the percentage of "refusers" is becoming smaller as scientific knowledge spreads. In an earlier year, Nicolaus Copernicus published his full thesis that the sun, not the earth, was the center of the universe. Copernicus (who seems to have been of timorous nature) waited until the end of his life to make his view known, so certain was he that a storm of disapproval and vilification would follow.[4] The storm did develop—primarily from religious sources because the Copernican theory, proclaiming a plurality of universes, conflicted directly with religious beliefs—but Copernicus was already dead. His German friend, Rheticus, had to withstand the furor. The Italian philosopher, Bruno,

---

2 John W. Gardner, *Self-Renewal* (New York: Harper & Row, 1964) p. 45.

3 We shall discuss from time to time the difference between technological and social inventions in this respect. Often the invention in technology pays off. The main test concerns its efficiency. How well does the new typewriter, fountain pen, or electric shaver work? On the other hand, the innovation in social structure is sometimes resented even though it would obviously be an improvement over the old. See Margaret Mead's discussion in *Continuities in Cultural Evolution* (New Haven: Yale University Press, 1964).

4 The story of Copernicus and the related experiences of Bruno and Galileo have been told in scores of books. We have followed A. R. Hall, *The Scientific Revolution, 1500–1800* (Boston: The Beacon Press, 1954), Chapter 3, "The Attack on Tradition: Mechanics," and Chapter 4, "The Attack on Tradition: Astronomy." For a brief treatment see Lynn and Gray Poole, *Scientists Who Changed the World* (New York: Dodd Mead & Co., 1960), "Copernicus," pp. 13–26.

who taught the new theory of the solar system, was condemned to death and burned at the stake. Furthermore, Galileo, the great Italian astronomer, who taught the Copernican view, was condemned by the Church. In order to escape Bruno's fate, he recanted what he knew to be true. In such cases involving conflicts with major values and the existing mores, the volume and intensity of resistance are almost guaranteed to be strong. It is unnecessary to cite details concerning other instances such as the conflict of Freudian theory (a discovery) with the existing Puritannical code of the early twentieth century wherein the word *sex* was hardly to be mentioned. In cases of this kind it has to be acknowledged that if the resistance is so strong as to overpower the force of the innovation itself, then no change will occur. This sometimes takes place, especially in local situations and in the perspective of a short time. If the innovation basically has merit or is factually substantiated (although still resisted), it will more likely be delayed for a while and accepted later. This type of resistance may develop, furthermore, on a regional basis, such as the resistance of the white South (especially in the Deep South) to the United States Supreme Court desegregation decision of 1954 and to the ensuing legal moves and actions. Also, to cite resistance to an *invention*—because many of our examples have concerned scientific discoveries—consider the resistance to the adoption of birth control measures in various underdeveloped nations. Reducing the high birth rate in these areas is regarded as a virtual necessity, if living standards are to be raised. However, resistance often develops in these poverty-ridden areas based on religious beliefs or on the view that abundant progeny is a sign of the father's manliness, a high prestige value for men who, in these areas, have little other source of status. As a result, one author declares that "birth control programs are among the most difficult of social changes to inaugurate." [5]

Psychological Resistance

An initial impediment to change from the psychological standpoint is the matter of *habit*. This is the personal equivalent to cultural inertia. We become accustomed to behaving in a certain manner; that is, our habit patterns are formed, and we do not easily change—without some good reason. We feel comfortable with the old. What has stood us well in past years we are inclined to keep. This can be linked in some people with an intellectual syndrome of over-all conservatism. Some people are far more attached to the status quo than others. It

[5] Robert L. Heilbroner, *The Great Ascent*, The Struggle for Economic Development in Our Time (New York: Harper & Row, 1963), p. 114.

may take much influence to induce them to change. This is true even for expedient changes, such as (on college campus) from a quarter system to a semester or trimester system. Almost any suggestion to try something new meets with instantaneous disapproval.

Fear of the new is another psychological trait that serves as a point of resistance to new things. This viewpoint is presumed to have been a restraining influence on civilian air travel during the early period of aviation. Taking the first flight was an adventuresome experience for many people because they were not used to three-dimensional travel; many were squeamish about getting their feet off *terra firma* for the first time.[6] The average person seems to be anxious about his first flight; but at the present time this initial anxiety toward flying has mostly been overcome. Space travel will doubtless experience similar resistance during the years ahead. Citizens are quite used to their own planet just as in preaviation days they felt more comfortable with ground underfoot. When, in a few years, the cry of "All aboard for Mars and Jupiter" is heard, many of us will hold back. Fear of the new also occurs in less dramatic situations. This is one element in many controversies concerning fluoridation of community water supplies.[7] It has been stated that the typical person who resists fluoridation tends to be older than average, to have less education than average, to have a lower income, and to have fewer children.

This writer and Charles M. Grigg[8] investigated the resistance toward the development of nuclear industries during the early 1960s and found that this resistance took the motif of fear of the new often as fear of radioactivity. A total of 28 per cent of the population sampled believed that working in a nuclear plant would be more dangerous than working in other industrial plants. In answer to the question "If a nuclear plant were built in your county, would you be especially worried about dangers due to radioactivity," 27 per cent of the urban respondents and 24 per cent of the rural respondents said

6 This is of some interest in view of the fact that the safety record of aviation (measured by passenger fatalities per 100 million passenger-miles flown in scheduled airline operations in the United States) is impressive. Indeed the airline fatality rate is less than one-half that of passenger automobiles and taxis. For one account of aviation's safety record see F. R. Allen, "Aviation," Ch. 9 in Allen *et al., Technology and Social Change* (New York: Appleton-Century-Crofts, 1957), esp. pp. 191–192. The latest fatality figures are found in *Air Transport Facts and Figures,* published by the Air Transport Association of America.

7 Some conflict of view exists even among physicians and dentists, although a substantial majority seem to favor fluoridation. For samplings from the vast literature, see Morris Davis, "Community Attitudes Toward Fluoridation," *The Public Opinion Quarterly,* Vol. XXIII, No. 4 (Winter, 1959–1960), 474–482; and Thomas F. A. Plaut, "Analysis of Voting Behavior on a Fluoridation Referendum," *The Public Opinion Quarterly,* Vol. XXIII, No. 2 (Summer, 1959), 213–222.

8 F. R. Allen and Charles M. Grigg, "Public Knowledge-of and Attitudes-Toward the Use of Nuclear Energy." Unpublished study.

that they *would* be worried about this hazard. Women were typically more worried about the radiation hazard than men; persons with more than average schooling (defined as more than a high school education) were less worried than those with less education; and those who had higher scores on a test of nuclear knowledge were less worried about radioactivity than those who had lower scores on the test.[9]

Ignorance is another psychological trait associated with resistance to innovations, as already noted concerning fluoridation and the radiation hazard. It is sometimes coupled with fear of the new. This has often concerned new foods. Not too many years ago some individuals thought that citrus fruit brought an acid condition to the digestive tract; however, modern advertising has so extolled the benefits of vitamin C found in this fruit that probably the old-time resistance based on the acid matter has faded. At any rate, ignorance lies at the base of many instances of resistance. A comparison of attitudes toward the United Nations Organization held by (1) a sampling of persons having only a grammer school education or less and (2) a sampling of political scientists or even (3) a sampling of college graduates is revealing as to the effect of ignorance.

Economic Resistance

This is one form of resistance that mostly relates to technological inventions, machines, and gadgets, although it can apply to social inventions and scientific discoveries too. Resistance to the purchase of automobiles, TV sets, air conditioning, airplanes, and helicopters, often relates to economic factors. The cost exceeds our budget.

In many cases the cost factor is related to the efficiency of the article. The latter may serve its function efficiently or it may be crude in operation. Most articles and machines are crude at first. The early automobile chugged along with fits and starts. The first airplanes, flimsy contraptions, barely got off the ground on their first, most unimpressive flights. The first moving pictures frequently had breaks in the film; the operator would have to stop the show, turn on the lights, and patch up the film—after which the movie would be resumed, usually with another break imminent. The first TV shows had many "snow storms." Indeed imperfections are to be expected at first.[10]

[9] Also see Vincent H. Whitney, "Resistance to Innovation: The Case of Atomic Power," *American Journal of Sociology*, Vol. LVI, No. 3 (November, 1950), 247–254; and Lillian Wald Kay, "Education for the Atomic Age—A Psychological View," *Nucleonics* (April, 1950), 5–13.

[10] LaPiere declares that ". . . innovations in organization are often very crude to begin with and must go through a longer period of developmental refinement than is necessary with most innovations in technology and ideology." Richard T. LaPiere, *Social Change* (New York: McGraw-Hill Book Co., 1965), p. 109. One may say that *all* innovations tend to be crude in the beginning.

If the invention meets a need and persists, however, it tends to be steadily improved. Hence the present-day automobile, a smoothly functioning machine, bears little resemblance to the cars of 1900, just as modern jet planes are a far cry from the Wright Brothers' flying machine of 1903. So it is with social inventions such as the income tax and Social Security.

However, during the early stages of nearly all inventions (we are primarily thinking of mechanical inventions) the machine is crude and at the same time it is expensive. As a source of resistance, this economic combination is formidable. Eventually the mechanical imperfections are likely to be removed, and the article will be mass-produced—hence the cost will decline. To assess correctly the ultimate development of an invention during its early stages of development is often difficult. It is on the order of trying to appraise the potentialities of a five-year-old boy or girl. Nevertheless, sometimes the early crudities will be totally removed, and the final impact of an invention will be so great that we speak of the "automobile age," "air age," or "age of the computer."

One other type of resistance, that of *vested interests,* often relates to economic matters. However, in many cases it is noneconomic in nature; and because vested interests comprise such a major and common type of resistance, we shall defer discussion of this and deal with it under a heading of its own.

Ideological Resistance

Ideological resistances to innovations are also often found. One that easily comes to mind in American society is the opposition by the Catholic Church to birth control. It is true that this resistance has by now receded on the part of many individual Catholics.[11] Although the Pope's position has not changed, the opposition of liberal Catholics to the Pope is significant. The Roman Catholic opposition to abortion is included in this too, because to Roman Catholics, life begins with the fertilized egg and the pill is regarded as an abortive agent. Another

---

[11] A growing number of Catholic priests, it is stated, are advising parishioners to follow their own consciences regarding pill use. *The New York Times* (May 31, 1966). Other types of "liberalization" have also taken place; for instance, adopting new experiments relative to convent life. These experiments include wearing regular clothing in the convent and outside, instead of religious habits; using maiden names instead of religious names (thus, Sister Simon Stock now becomes Sister Joan Smith); the regulation of prayer life by each individual, rather than by uniform community rule; and permission to telephone or write letters at will (in some convents outgoing and incoming letters were inspected). *The New York Times* (February 20, 1968).

ideological form of resistance is that by the medical profession to anything suggesting socialized medicine, including the enactment of the Medicare Law of 1965.

A less consequential but interesting form of resistance in the United States has been directed toward the increasing numerical expression of life showing itself in all-number telephone designations, license-plate numbers, postal zip-code numbers, social-security numbers, student numbers, faculty numbers, and the like. Does a person lose his identity in this sea of numbers? [12] Are we no longer John Smiths and Mary Joneses, but only a sum of perforations on an IBM card? The Anti-Digit-Dialing League of San Francisco has called this phenomenon creeping numeralism, and the foundation of the resistance seems to lie in our *individualistic* ideology. Do we no longer value the unique individualistic qualities? Is life increasingly a matter of mathematics? Do communities also lose their identity? Are Mansfield, Ohio and Hartford, Connecticut no longer Mansfield and Hartford, respectively, but 44903 and 06115 (zip code numbers)?

Similarly, the former telephone exchanges have passed with the coming of the digit-dialing system. No longer do we use the former exchanges: "Magnolia 4," "Sweetbriar 9," "Aphrodite 7," and the like.[13] Again, some may resist the passing of the earlier qualitative usages. Nevertheless, the vast increase in the number of telephones, the volume of mail, and similar concerns—reflecting population growth itself—has necessitated some quantitative types of treatment. At any rate, resistances have arisen, whatever we may think of them.

Social Dislocation

The late Professor Nimkoff [14] called attention to resistances involving innovations that bring about major dislocations. Some discoveries and inventions may be socially beneficial yet dislocating; because society requires a certain harmony and equilibrium among its parts, those developments that threaten to bring much dislocation are often resisted. He cites the example of calendar reform: Two different plans for a new and better calendar—the Cotsworth Calendar and the World

[12] Richard Gehman, "Number, Please!" *This Week* (March 29, 1964).

[13] The editors of *The New York Times* comment: "Why can't we have romance in the telephone business the way we used to have? What's wrong with Magnolia 4, or Sweetbriar 9, or Cantaloupe 6, or Aphrodite 7? . . . Where are the beautiful exchanges of yesterday? Where is the 'voice with a smile'? Gone or going perhaps with the buffalo and the steam locomotive. We wish they wouldn't." Editorial, "Magnolia 4, Farewell," *The New York Times* (June 27, 1962).

[14] M. F. Nimkoff, "Obstacles to Innovation," Chapter 4 in Allen, *et al., op. cit.,* pp. 65–67.

Calendar [15]—have been suggested. They are desirable in various ways, but probably will not be used due to the dislocation that would be entailed. Professor Nimkoff notes that not all innovations that bring social dislocations are resisted. Sometimes the amount of the dislocation is not appreciated immediately.

Over-all Complexity of Ideas

This writer suggests that one type of resistance not ordinarily mentioned is due to the over-all complexity associated with a discovery or invention. Consider the social invention, civil defense. This invention has encountered much apathy—one type of resistance—for some years. It appears that the apathy has resulted largely from the uncertainty related to a highly complex situation: the alternative actions of foreign leaders as well as leaders in one's own nation, uncertainties related to using different war agents and weapons (nuclear, biological, chemical, and more conventional ones), uncertainties relating to radioactive hazards (direction of wind currents and meteorological elements), uncertainties related to warning the population, problems concerning shelters, and other factors are all involved. Even though civil defense has experienced resistances of other kinds, the complexity of the problem and its solution seem to have been the main causes of the resistance.[16]

Vested Interests

Innovations affect people and groups differently. Some gain, some lose by the change. Thorstein Veblen, the social economist whose theories were discussed in Chapter 7, coined the term *vested interests* to denote those who lose in the event of some change. These persons have a vested interest in the status quo. They may exert much pressure and resist some anticipated change determinedly. Often the matter is economic. A businessman or corporation may find that a rival is starting a new type of business that promises to cut into his sales and profits. A ready example was the announcement in April, 1970, that IBM would enter the office copier field, an area in which The Xerox

15 The World Calendar Movement was started by Miss Elizabeth Achelis in 1929, believing that "life should be simplified." Quarters of the year would be divided equally. One day is left over, which would be called "Worldsday" and would be an international New Year's holiday. *The New York Times* (September 26, 1966).

16 For a discussion of resistances to civil defense, see George W. Wallis, *Some Social Dimensions of Attitudes Toward Civil Defense.* Unpublished Doctoral dissertation, Florida State University, August, 1963, especially Chap. VII. The population sample interviewed resided in the Cape Kennedy area of Florida.

Corporation had been preeminent.[17] Xerox immediately filed a lawsuit against IBM charging infringement of patents, hoping to stop or slow down the IBM move. Those who would like to hold to the status quo are likely to do all they can to thwart the new enterprise. Many mechanical inventions bring new competition for old activities and concerns. The automobile of around 1900 threatened the business of the wagon and buggy manufacturers. The marketing of TV after the Second World War promised to undercut both radio and the motion picture. The motel (having its beginning in the United States around 1925) gradually posed a threat to the established hotel and inn. Transoceanic aviation gradually cut into the business of the established shipping lines. One of the uncertainties for any established enterprise is indeed that at any time an innovation may be made that will cut into the ongoing business. Moreover, the resistance of vested interests may relate to *processes* adopted by business or industry. The laboring class has often resisted the mechanization of industry with much vigor. As far back as 1811–1812 in England, the Luddites smashed new machinery and rioted generally.[18] At various times in American history workers have protested mechanization, the latest outcropping being directed against automation. Mr. George Meany, President of the AFL-CIO Convention, called automation a "curse" in early 1964.[19] Also, resistance by specific categories of workers may develop.[20] It is significant, however, that not all labor leaders issue protests against automation. The late Walter Reuther,[21] for instance, did not oppose it; indeed he pointed out that labor gains in the long run, conceding that automation may bring difficulties for workers in the short run.

But vested interests pertain to many activities, not just business concerns. Residents in a community develop vested interests in their neighborhood. When zoning changes are proposed, residents often band together to resist the proposal. Or, if a new interstate highway is routed close to one's residential area, objections on the basis of neigh-

17 *The New York Times* (April 22, 1970).

18 See Neil J. Smelser, *Social Change in the Industrial Revolution* (Chicago: University of Chicago Press, 1959), pp. 249, 330, and 357.

19 *The New York Times* (January 3, 1964).

20 Ida R. Hoos, in her study of *office automation*, found that the greatest resistance was shown by the tabulating personnel. The latter knew that the computer is a threat to their job; the "big brain" computers take over much of the tabulating work. To some workers automation offers a path to monotony-free work, but to the tabulators "it represents a grim future with no job at all." Hoos, *Automation in the Office* (Washington, D. C.: Public Affairs Press, 1961), p. 52.

21 Walter P. Reuther, "Policies for Automation: A Labor Viewpoint," *Annals of the American Academy of Political and Social Science,* Vol. 340 (March, 1962), 100–109; and Walter P. Reuther, "Congressional Testimony," in Morris Philipson (ed.), *Automation, Implications for the Future* (New York: Vintage Books, 1962), pp. 267–315.

borhood vested interests are voiced. Or parents may resist the bussing of school children, which may be necessary if racial integration is to be attained.

In colleges and universities proposals for curriculum changes may be considered disinterestedly by many people, but the departments that are to be affected adversely by the proposed changes are quite likely to resist as strongly as they can. In recent years state governments in the United States have been acutely concerned with the apportionment problem: developing an equitable formula for selecting governmental representatives from the counties. The vested interests factor enters the problem in that during past years the rural counties have had a large representation in nearly all of the states. These rural interests and their leaders usually dislike relinquishing some of their political power, preferring the status quo. As many states have urbanized in recent years, however, the urban counties have become underrepresented in the state legislatures—making an adjustment necessary. So successful has been the rural resistance to adjustment in the composition of state legislatures that the United States Supreme Court finally had to render a decision on the issue. On June 15, 1964, it decided, in a major decision, that state legislatures must apportion its members on the basis of equal population.[22] It was believed that only about ten states in 1964 apportioned according to the recommended plan of the Supreme Court and that about forty would have their governmental districts upset. The big gainers from the redistricting would be, of course, the cities and the fast-growing suburban areas.

Various organizations, however, do not always perceive that their interests are in jeopardy as a change is being made. The new apportionment formula for state legislatures, which was just discussed, was not in this category. The threat was quickly perceived by the rural interests. But some developments—especially mechanical inventions— do not seem much of a threat to anything in the beginning. One must remember that the typical invention is quite crude when first made. The early automobile was not impressive in looks or performance; but as it was improved more and more railroads were driven into bankruptcy—although competition by the motor vehicle was perhaps not the sole cause. The first airplanes barely rose off the ground. Yet, several decades later, the shipping interests were having severe difficulties because of airline competition. Many economic, educational, medical, and other innovations may be deceptive in this regard— before they are fully developed. The motel, it is stated,[23] was initially scorned by the hotel interests who failed to sense the coming competi-

22 *The New York Times* (June 16, 1964).
23 Gardner, *op. cit.*, p. 46.

tion. So we must amend our generalization to the effect that vested interests are often a powerful resisting force to innovations, *provided* they are surely aware that their interests are being jeopardized by the change. Man often underestimates in such situations.

Groups and communities in their manifestations of vested interest opposition do not, of course, always win. The change may still be made. In one oft-noted study, W. F. Cottrell [24] describes the threat posed to a railroad town in the American West. The town (called Caliente for study purposes) was the site of a water and service stop on the main line of the railroad. However, the inauguration of Diesel locomotives meant that this service point on the railroad line was no longer needed; diesels can travel a longer distance before requiring service. The decision of the railroad to use diesels spelled the end of Caliente, therefore; vested interest opposition lost out to technological change. Town leaders tried to attract new industries, but were unsuccessful. Since the Diesels destroyed the *raison d'être* of Caliente, it is apparent that even though vested interests resist determinedly, they do not always win. Caliente had to accept its fate in the name of progress.

A similar situation concerned a managerial decision of the U. S. Steel Corporation to move one of its plants from the community of Ellwood, Pennsylvania, to Gary, Indiana. The corporate decision was announced during August, 1946. What followed has been set forth by Charles R. Walker.[25] Many workers were promised jobs in the new location, but most wanted to stay in Ellwood; they had a vested interest in the present community—in its schools, churches, and other institutions. An emergency mass meeting was held. Businessmen launched a campaign to bring other companies (as Caliente had done). Union delegates conferred with the president of U. S. Steel; the latter promised to restudy the plans. However, the net result was the same as in Caliente. Corporation economics had won. The vested interests in Ellwood did not affect the company decision. The vested interest resistance was of no avail.

IRRATIONAL AND COVERT RESISTANCE

LaPiere [26] has wisely called attention to the fact that resistance to innovations may be irrational, devious, and covert in nature. People

---

24 W. F. Cottrell, "Death by Dieselization: A Case Study in the Reaction to Technological Change," *American Sociological Review*, Vol. 16 (June, 1951), 358–365.

25 Charles R. Walker, *Steel Town* (New York: Harper & Bros., 1959), especially Chaps. V–VII.

26 LaPiere, *op. cit.*, p. 175 ff.

may mask their *real* objection to an innovation (mechanical or social). A common stratagem in doing this, observes Gardner,[27] is to stand on high moral ground. They will hold that the "old way" of behavior (prior to innovation) follows high moral and spiritual principles that are being threatened. Contraception may be resisted on the grounds that it "violates the sanctity of life." [28] Objections have been raised in relation of the divine right of kings, the right of the individual to pursue his own interests, and the purity of the race. When the political (voting) franchise was proposed for women in this nation, strong resistance developed on the basis that "the sanctity of the home would be destroyed, the innate purity of women would be sullied, and children would be neglected and let run wild should women leave hearth and home for voting booth." [29] Often patriotism and the current opposition to Communism have been invoked. Fluoridation of water supplies has been held to be a Communist plot to poison our water supplies.[30] Among uninformed people the volume and stridency of such arguments may overwhelm the logic on the other side.[31]

At any rate, the *real objection* to the innovation is likely to involve a different factor, although this may not always be the case. People who are determined to defeat a new proposal will usually invoke all possible objections. The real points of resistance are likely to be those that have been described earlier, of which the opposition of vested interests is often a strong one. The objection will almost surely *not* be couched in terms of "If this new proposal is adopted, I (John Jones) and my interests will lose prestige or income." Rather, it will be stated with reference to lofty principles and objective generalizations (sometimes of world significance) and in high-sounding phrases. As is observed in Freudian psychology, the verbalized statements and the real motivations may be at wide variance, although this is not so in every instance.

INDIVIDUAL AND ORGANIZATIONAL RESISTANCE

At this point we should briefly call attention to the fact that virtually all the resistances to innovation that have been described—from those

---

27 Gardner, *op. cit.*, p. 49.

28 LaPiere, *op. cit.*, p. 179.

29 *Ibid.*, p. 180. LaPiere also refers to Eleanor Flexner, *Century of Struggle: The Women's Rights Movement in the United States* (Cambridge, Mass.: Harvard University Press, 1959).

30 William Atwood, "Fluoridation: Why All the Controversy?" *Look*, Vol. 22, No. 13 (June 24, 1958), 19–21. The author examines many "unreasonable" objections to fluoridation that have been advanced.

31 *Ibid.*, p. 20. A more difficult problem develops, moreover, when public relations firms are employed to phrase and publicize "unreasonable" objections in highly convincing manner.

based on habit, cost, and imperfections of the article to vested interests —can apply to individual persons *and* to decision-making officials of organizations. We may have the image of the individual citizen resisting the TV invention or the United Nations as a social invention. But we must not forget that the person in some circumstances may be a General of the Army or Admiral of the Navy who is reacting as a procurement official to a new missile or airplane; the consequences of the decision to accept or reject may be major.[32] Or the person reacting to an innovation may be a high official in an insurance company whose corporation is considering the purchase of computers. Again, the consequences of the decision may be considerable for the corporation. Or the decision-making person may be a university president, or even the President of the United States, who is considering the possibilities of a social invention. Acceptance or rejection in these cases is certainly no individual matter.

Professor Alvin Boskoff [33] has described the sources of innovative values. The crucial part of the process, he declares, lies in the trial and evaluation of the innovation by people; the institutional level and its groups are especially important in this. The *making* of innovations, then, provides only the *possibilities* for socio-cultural change; the control (trial and evaluation) phase determines the facilitation or suppression of the innovation or innovative behavior. Top leaders and power elites can bring changes in receptivity to innovation. Boskoff derives certain hypotheses from these ideas, but these more-detailed considerations cannot be discussed here.[34] It can be observed in general that social systems tend to resist innovations that interfere with, or are dysfunctional to, their basic needs: (1) pattern maintenance and tension management, (2) adaptation, (3) goal attainment, and (4) integration. Sometimes an innovation brings results that are, on the whole, beneficial for the social system (hence, the innovation is adopted) and yet some problems accrue. Effort will then be made to deal with the problems.

[32] This writer has elsewhere described how the outcome of battles and entire wars may depend on the weapons that have been selected, developed, and provided. Near the end of the First World War, the use of the improved tank finally brought the German defeat; the use of radar by the British in 1940 was a basic factor in winning the Battle of Britain; The German V-1 and V-2 missiles threatened to knock out England during the latter part of the Second World War; and the use of the A-bomb in 1945 brought Japan to her knees (she was gradually losing). See this writer's "The Influence of Technology on War," Chapter 15 in F. R. Allen, *et al., op. cit.,* especially pp. 384–385.

[33] Alvin Boskoff, "Functional Analysis As a Source of a Theoretical Repertory and Research Tasks in the Study of Social Change," Chapter 8 in George K. Zollschan and Walter Hirsch (eds.), *Explorations in Social Change* (Boston: Houghton Mifflin Co., 1964).

[34] *Ibid.,* pp. 231–233.

THEORY AND EMPIRICAL RESEARCH
CONCERNING RESISTANCES

At various points in this volume we have referred to Merton's [35] emphasis on the interrelations between theory and research. In an exceedingly brief statement we may say that theory defines concepts, establishes the pertinence of uniformities, permits derivation of hypotheses, and guides empirical research. Empirical research, for its part, does more than confirm or refute hypotheses. It initiates, reformulates, deflects, and clarifies theory.

The subject of resistance to innovation offers many suggestive ideas in simple form. It lacks strict theory, as Merton has defined the term. But the needs for empirical data are, in this instance, even more pressing. The reader may have noticed how few empirical researches have been cited in this chapter. We would like to know, for example, *how many* and *what* resistances seem to be found relative to all important innovations? Are there preponderant resistances that relate to mechanical inventions that do not seem to develop regarding social inventions and vice versa? What type of resistances toward various innovations relate to social-class variables? What resistances are affected by racial factors? What are the differential resistances found with respect to the two sexes? What types of resistances especially relate to the different educational levels? Then, on the global scene, what typical resistances are likely to be made to ideas and material equipment in relation to the universalistic-achievement, universalistic-ascriptive, particularistic-achievement, and particularistic-ascriptive patterns of social structure?

Activism and Resistance.   We conclude this chapter by musing over an entirely different matter. The resistances to innovation that we have discussed are all found in various situations. They are all potentially important and sometimes are empirically important in slowing down change. The pace of change, in short, would be considerably greater but for these resistances. However, in our present active-oriented society, these resistances do not represent the spirit of the times. Quite the reverse. *Change* is the leitmotif of the present, not resistance. If anything, the modern activist is impatient with resistances, particularly if he sees the latter as institutional inertia or footdragging in relation to needed developments (lags) that ought to be taken up.[36]

---

35 Robert K. Merton, *Social Theory and Social Structure*, rev. ed. (Glencoe, Ill.: The Free Press, Inc., 1957), Chaps. II and III.

36 A significant issue emerges from this situation, which we shall discuss in Chapter 13.

Resistances can be irrational, as we have pointed out, but they are indeed rational and warranted in some circumstances; man is wise not to rush headlong into all new activities. The modern activist will himself want to resist actions that run contrary to the social values that he holds. For those espousing the active perspective toward change, removing resistances and lags that have taken form in various situations may require much ingenuity. But the preliminary question to be decided, then, is whether resistance in some situations is proper and advisable or not; in the latter event it might be resolved by persuasion, a social invention, or other positive action.

ANNOTATED BIBLIOGRAPHY

Barnett, H. G., *Innovation: The Basis of Cultural Change* (New York: McGraw-Hill Book Co., 1953; paper edition, undated).

> A helpful discussion of resistances to innovation is found in Part IV (especially Chapter XIII); the factors of lack of compatibility with customs, inefficiency, and cost are emphasized.

LaPiere, Richard T., *Social Change* (New York: McGraw-Hill Book Co., 1965).

> LaPiere discusses both rational and irrational types of resistance. Discussion of the covert type of resistance is especially interesting.

Nimkoff, M. F., "Obstacles to Innovation," Chapter 4 in F. R. Allen, *et al.*, *Technology and Social Change* (New York: Appleton-Century-Crofts, 1957).

> Obstacles to innovation are shown to include (1) difficulties in adding to knowledge and (2) resistances to knowledge and innovations that have been added. Social, psychological, and other resistances are considered. Recommended.

Ogburn, William F., *Social Change* (New York: B. W. Huebsch, Inc., 1922; The Viking Press, 1950), Part III.

> Pioneering sociological consideration of resistances to innovation based on tradition, habit, social pressures, vested interests, and other factors.

Stern, Bernhard J., *Social Factors in Medical Progress* (New York: Columbia University Press, 1927).

> Early study of resistances to medical discoveries. Some discoveries now regarded as great blessings were bitterly resisted at the time.

Veblen, Thorstein, *The Vested Interests and The State of the Industrial Arts* (New York: B. W. Huebsch, Inc., 1919).

> This book introduced the concept of *vested interests,* seen as an important factor in resisting economic change. Resistance on the part of those who lose in the event of change has been shown in many (noneconomic) areas too. A most useful concept.

12 Diffusion

If we know what a society's culture is, including its particular system of values and attitudes, we can predict with a fairly high degree of probability whether the bulk of its members will welcome or resist a particular innovation.

RALPH LINTON (1952)

Most social change . . . proceeds less from giant new innovations than from diffusions of existing techniques or, more importantly, of privileges. In effect, what has often been the property of the few becomes the claim of the many.

DANIEL BELL (1967)

The first quotation here from the late Professor Ralph Linton indicates the general relationship between what is *diffused* and existing social values and attitudes. If one were to broaden such a statement in order to characterize the entire diffusion process as it is visualized at the present time, one could say that diffusion involves the "(1) *acceptance*, (2) over *time*, (3) of some specific *item*—an idea or practice, (4) by individuals, groups or other *adopting units*, linked (5) to specific channels of communication, (6) to a *social structure*, and (7) to a given system of values, or culture." [1] (italics in original statement)

Anthropologists have made diffusion studies for many years, and in earlier times placed great emphasis on diffusion. Although there has been some reaction to the early overemphasis, all anthropologists appear to be impressed with the importance of diffusion in bringing change.[2] Linton's description of the "average day of an average Ameri-

[1] Elihu Katz, Martin L. Levin, and Herbert Hamilton, "Traditions of Research on the Diffusion of Innovation," *American Sociological Review*, Vol. 28, No. 2 (April, 1963), 240.

[2] See, for example, Ralph Linton, *The Study of Man* (New York: D. Appleton-Century Co., 1936), Chap. 19; A. L. Kroeber, *Anthropology*, 2nd ed. (New York: Harcourt, Brace, 1948), Chap. 10 (especially pp. 411–418); and E. A. Hoebel, *Man in the Primitive World*, 2nd ed. (New York: McGraw-Hill Book. Co., 1958), Chap. 34. Hoebel declares:

> *It is clear that cultures grow more through cross-fertilization and diffusion than in isolation through independent invention. There is no surer way to destroy the vigor of a culture than to attempt to keep it "pure." (P. 607)*

can"—which emphasized the importance of diffusion—has become a classic.[3] His intent was not to proclaim diffusion as a more important process of change than innovation itself. Culture elements must be invented or discovered somewhere; innovation is thus basic. Linton's thesis was that within any one area far more elements are derived from diffusion than from invention within that area. Even in American society—an unusually inventive one—he maintained that more than 90 per cent of the socio-cultural elements had been diffused from other areas, and only about 10 per cent had been invented by Americans.[4] Regarding other societies his view was that more than 90 per cent of the cultural elements were products of other societies.

The literature on diffusion can be compared to a river with several sources. Among sociologists, F. Stuart Chapin[5] in 1928 studied the diffusion of the city manager form of government. Rural sociologists, led by Herbert F. Lionberger, Eugene A. Wilkening, and Everett M. Rogers, have been especially active.[6] The diffusion of farm implements, innovations such as hybrid corn, soil conservation practices, and similar objects or ideas have become subjects of lively interest. Recently, medical sociology, centering originally at Columbia University and led by Elihu Katz, Herbert Menzel, and James Coleman,[7] has produced diffusion studies concerned with (1) drugs or medical techniques in

3 Linton, *op. cit.*, pp. 326–327.

4 *Ibid.*, p. 325.

5 F. Stuart Chapin, *Cultural Change* (New York: The Century Co., 1928). See also Raymond V. Bowers, "The Direction of Intra-Societal Diffusion," *American Sociological Review*, Vol. II (1937), 826–836; and Bowers, "Differential Intensity of Intra-Societal Diffusion," *American Sociological Review*, Vol. III (1938), 21–31.

6 As samples from a considerable literature, see Herbert F. Lionberger, "The Diffusion of Farm and Home Information As an Area of Sociological Research," *Rural Sociology*, Vol. 17 (1952), 132–140; Lionberger, *Adoption of New Ideas and Practices* (Ames: Iowa State University Press, 1960); Bryce Ryan and Neal C. Gross, "The Diffusion of Hybrid Seed Corn in Two Iowa Communities," *Rural Sociology*, Vol. 8 (1943), 15–24; Eugene A. Wilkening, "Change in Farm Technology As Related to Familism, Family Decision Making, and Family Integration," *American Sociological Review*, Vol. 19 (1954), 29–37; C. Paul Marsh and A. Lee Coleman, "Group Influences and Agricultural Innovations," *American Journal of Sociology*, Vol. 61 (1956), 588–594; and Everett M. Rogers, *Diffusion of Innovations* (New York: The Free Press of Glencoe, Division of The Macmillan Company, 1962). The latter provides an extensive, over-all bibliography.

7 As samples from this literature, see James S. Coleman, Elihu Katz, and Herbert Menzel, *Medical Innovation: A Diffusion Study* (Indianapolis, Ind.: Bobbs-Merrill, 1966); Elihu Katz, "Communication Research and the Image of Society: Convergence of Two Traditions," *American Journal of Sociology*, Vol. 65 (1960), 435–440; Elihu Katz, "The Social Itinerary of Technical Change," *Human Organization*, Vol. 20 (1961), 70–82; Herbert Menzel, "Innovation, Integration, and Marginality: A Survey of Physicians," *American Sociological Review*, Vol. 25, No. 5 (October, 1960), 704–713; James S. Coleman, Elihu Katz, and Herbert Menzel, "The Diffusion of an Innovation Among Physicians," *Sociometry*, Vol. 20 (December, 1957), 253–270; and Elihu Katz, Martin L. Levin, and Herbert Hamilton, "Research on the Diffusion of Innovation," *American Sociological Review*, Vol. 28, No. 2 (April, 1963), 237–252.

which the adopters are physicians and (2) vaccines, chest X-rays or other medical ideas, where the adopters are ordinary citizens. Education diffusion studies have been abundant too; many were guided by Professor Paul Mort of Columbia.[8]

Two different over-all perspectives regarding diffusion, then, can be discerned if one surveys the total anthropological-sociological realm: (1) The broad, international interest that, for the most part, has been held by the anthropologists has been concerned with such diffusion analyses as the practice of coffee drinking, use of tobacco, use of gunpowder, and the diffusion of myths as these have spread from believed points of origin. (2) The second focus is more local and detailed, comprising such studies as the diffusion of farm implements or of medical innovations within a county or city. Both macroscopic and microscopic interests, then, are represented.

A marked contrast exists between the early and the modern focus on diffusion. First, the old-time study of the process manifests little interest in the actual dynamics of diffusion. As of 1936, for instance, Linton[9] observed that the dynamics of diffusion can be understood only by studying the process in actual operation; little of this had been done at that time. Diffusion requires a donor as well as a recipient. If an article or idea is to spread, it must be presented to some group of people by some one or some group, and it must be accepted. Only then will it be integrated into the society and its culture. This process needs to be traced in detail for different kinds of inventions and discoveries because the diffusion rate and resistances vary greatly. Secondly, modern media of communication and contact are, of course, vastly different from earlier times. We now have what could be called the new diffusion.[10] A phenomenal acceleration of the speed of diffusion has occurred. If one takes Kroeber's[11] description of the spreading of the use of bronze from western Asia to central and northwestern Europe around 3500 B. C. as an illustration of the early process, it is clear that it was exceedingly slow. It required approximately 1,700 years for the use of bronze to spread to Europe. In the modern, mass-media age a new product or idea, if important, is known over a wide area in a matter of hours. A third difference has been the advent of planned diffusion. Ordinarily the spread of products and ideas as it

8 Rogers, *op. cit.*, pp. 39–42.

9 Linton, *op. cit.*, pp. 328 and 334.

10 Then, too, many other (noncommunication) socio-cultural elements have changed due to increased urbanization, industrialization, differentiation, education, and the like, so that one is faced with the new diffusion in the new society and culture.

11 A. L. Kroeber, *Anthropology*, rev. ed. (New York: Harcourt, Brace & Co., 1948), p. 700.

has occurred over the centuries has not been especially planned.[12] Articles have tended to spread along trade and travel routes. Occasionally the spreading has been promoted by business interests who hoped to derive a profit thereby. American products—from cigarettes and Coca Cola to the computer—illustrate this. Even this is comparatively recent, is partly related to the development of the mass media themselves, and has flourished with the inauguration of global perspectives (which is itself largely due, of course, to the communications inventions). Also, many underdeveloped areas are interested in modernizing, which involves the exporting of new basic ideas (as industrialization) and new attitudes to these areas. Again, the process needs to be planned in order that new ideas can have a greater chance of being accepted.

THE ADOPTION PROCESS

Stages

Rogers [13] has listed five stages that tend to occur in the adoption process, namely: (1) *Awareness:* The individual is exposed to the innovation but lacks full information about it; becoming aware of it (the necessary first step) is usually a random occurrence. (2) *Interest:* When the individual has developed interest, he seeks further information about the innovation; he tends to favor it in a general way. (3) *Evaluation:* At this stage the individual considers the innovation in relation to his present and anticipated future situation and decides whether to try it or not; if the advantages outweigh the disadvantages, he will decide to try it; the actual trial is, however, conceptually distinct from this *decision* to try the idea.[14] (4) *Trial:* At this stage the individual uses the innovation on a small scale. This is a test or "dry run" to see if complete adoption will be decided. (5) *Adoption:* At this stage the individual decides to continue the *full use* of the innovation. Motivational aspects of the individual personality will be involved in this decision. An innovation can be rejected at any stage in the process. Sometimes the results of the *trial* stage are misinterpreted. Some associated factor may bring poor results, and the person may conclude that the innovation is inferior or undesirable in some

---

12 Conrad M. Arensberg and Arthur H. Niehoff, *Introducing Social Change* (Chicago: Aldine Publishing Co., 1964), p. 2.

13 Rogers, *op. cit.*, pp. 81–86.

14 Rogers suggests that the *evaluation* stage is the least distinct of the five and empirically the most difficult about which to question respondents. *Ibid.*, p. 83.

respect. Rogers [15] maintains that these theoretically postulated stages are verified by empirical data.

These five stages appear to be useful, although it may be that empirical studies of the adoption of different kinds of inventions or discoveries (as mechanical and social) may later require some modification of the statement.

Characteristics of the Innovation

It is clear that some innovations are adopted quickly, some slowly, and some not at all; the nature of the innovation itself has much to do with the adoption and its rate. Some characteristics will stimulate the adoption of an innovation, others may retard it. Rogers [16] provides a helpful summary of five major characteristics of innovations that are important in this regard: (1) relative advantage, (2) compatibility, (3) complexity, (4) divisibility, and (5) communicability.

Relative advantage refers to the degree to which an innovation is superior to the ideas or products it supersedes. Some items function more efficiently than others; some have higher economic cost; and [17] some have novelty or other value. Sometimes an idea itself is regarded as advantageous, but it has an influence on another subject where difficulties may be encountered. At any rate, the relative advantage of an idea or article means *advantage as perceived by members of a social system. Compatibility* is the degree to which an innovation is consistent with the existing cultural values and past experiences of the adopters. Birth control techniques, however much needed in underdeveloped areas, may conflict with religious beliefs or family mores; examples of incompatibility are common in underdeveloped societies. People do not accept ideas indiscriminately; they borrow what will best fit the pattern of their culture.[18] Compatibility, then, is important; again this means *compatibility of a new idea as perceived by members of a social system. Complexity* refers to the degree to which an innovation is relatively difficult to understand and use. Any new idea can be placed on the complexity-simplicity continuum. In general, the adoption rate of an innovation is slowed down as it is deemed complex by members of a social system. *Divisibility* is the degree to which an innovation can be tried on a limited basis. Some ideas or articles can be tried on a small scale; others cannot. Such inventions as the radio and air-

15 *Ibid.*, p. 95.

16 *Ibid.*, pp. 124–134.

17 See also H. G. Barnett, *Innovation: The Basis of Cultural Change* (New York: McGraw-Hill Book Co., 1953), Chap. XIII. This writer has, of course, discussed some of these factors—crudity of innovations, their economic cost, possibilities of bringing dislocations, necessity of changing habits, and so on—in the preceding chapter.

18 Arensberg and Niehoff, *op. cit.*, p. 63.

conditioner have to be accepted *in toto;* it helps the adoption rate of an innovation if it can be tried in a limited way first.[19] Lastly, *communicability* is the degree to which innovations can be easily observed, communicated to others, and, hence, diffused over an area.

Adopter Categories

The concept of adopter categories illustrates a modern emphasis in diffusion research. Once again Rogers [20] has provided a helpful summary of adopters based on evidence found in many empirical studies. He mentions five categories, which are regarded as ideal types: (1) *Innovators:* These are venturesome people who are eager to try out new ideas; these are the rash, the daring, the risking people; they must be willing to absorb an occasional debacle when some idea proves to be unsuccessful. (2) *Early Adopters:* These individuals are more integrated in the local system than are innovators. Early adopters tend to be prominent localites; they are respected for their embodiment of the successful and discrete use of new ideas; hence, these are the people to check with before trying a new idea; if they approve, the diffusion process will be aided. (3) *Early Majority:* These persons adopt new ideas just before the average member of the social system; their characteristic trait is deliberation; these individuals aid in legitimizing innovations, although they are seldom leaders. (4) *Late Majority:* These individuals follow after the average social-system members; sometimes adoption results from social pressures or economic necessity; public opinion must favor an innovation before this group is convinced. (5) *Laggards:* Their point of reference lies in the past; they are the last to adopt; they have almost no opinion leadership; they have traditional values and generally are suspicious of innovators and change agents.

Various corollaries ensue from these categories. Early adopters tend to be younger than later adopters; [21] earlier adopters tend to have a higher social status than later adopters; [22] earlier adopters tend to have a more favorable financial position than later adopters; [23] earlier adopters usually have greater ability to deal with abstractions than do later adopters; [24] and impersonal sources of information are more important for early adopters of innovations than for later adopters.[25]

[19] Perhaps the temporary trial of a new tooth powder or new razor blade is an illustration. Rogers adds that widespread evidence does not exist to validate this generalization. Rogers, *op. cit.,* p. 131.

[20] Rogers, *ibid.,* pp. 168–171.

[21] *Ibid.,* pp. 172–174.

[22] *Ibid.,* pp. 174–175.

[23] *Ibid.,* pp. 175–176.

[24] *Ibid.,* pp. 177–178.

[25] *Ibid.,* p. 179.

Opinion Leaders and the Flow of Ideas

The opinion leader is defined as a person who is influential in approving or disapproving new ideas. Merton [26] has used the term *influential* to denote this kind of person; Lionberger has called him a "key communicator," [27] and other designations have been followed. Opinion leaders appear to be distributed in all occupational groups, and on every social and economic level. If the opinion leader or influential has extra importance in the flow of ideas, one wonders what are the major influences on the influential himself? The hypothesis of the two-step flow of communication emerged from this, namely: Ideas seem to flow from the mass media to opinion leaders, and then *from them* to the less active members of the population.[28]

Personal influence has been found to be an essential factor in decision making. It appears to be especially important in the *evaluation* stage in the adoption process. It seems, moreover, that it is more important for the later adopters than for the earlier adopters. Personal influence from peers is more important, furthermore, in uncertain (not clear-cut) situations.[29]

Certain characteristics of opinion leaders, as compared with their followers, have been discerned.[30] Opinion leaders tend to conform to social system norms more closely than do the followers or average members. There is, moreover, little overlapping among different types of opinion leaders. The fact that John X is a leader in one area has little bearing on the likelihood that he will be a leader in another; the hypothesis of the generalized leader does not seem to be well supported. Furthermore, opinion leaders use more impersonal and cosmopolitan sources of information than do their followers. Indeed, the former are more cosmopolitan people generally than are their followers. Opinion leaders enjoy more social participation than their followers, although they are not necessarily the formal leaders (power holders) in their communities. Opinion leaders tend to be more innovative than their followers.

Social status in general can act as a barrier to the flow of ideas in a system, however. Persons of high prestige and reputation—as apart

---

26 Robert K. Merton, *Social Theory and Social Structure,* rev. ed. (Glencoe, Ill.: The Free Press, Inc., 1957), Chapter X.

27 Lionberger, *Adoption of New Ideas and Practices, op. cit.,* p. 55.

28 This is summarized in Elihu Katz and Paul F. Lazarsfeld, *Personal Influence* (New York: The Free Press of Glencoe, Division of The Macmillan Company, 1955; paperback edition, 1964), Chap. II. The authors illustrate this in Sect. III with respect to marketing leaders, leaders in women's fashions, public affairs leaders, and "movie" leaders.

29 For further ideas in this regard, see Rogers, *op. cit.,* pp. 219–223.

30 *Ibid.,* pp. 233–240.

from opinion leaders—usually do not advocate radical innovations; they have to be careful relative to their status.[31] The eminent man is constrained by the expectations of his admirers. He has some obligation to conform to the norms of the group; his freedom to advocate novel ideas is restricted. Indeed, radical departures may often be advocated at the risk of prestige loss. For this reason Barnett suggests that the elite are seldom in the vanguard of cultural change.[32]

Yet, the situation is not clear-cut. Various innovations have diffused from the upper class downward.[33] These innovations, however, tend to meet important needs, and they do not conflict with approved norms. Class, rather than individual, acceptance is gradually emphasized. Men, for the most part, appear to ape their superiors. On the other hand, when some idea or device is linked with the lower class, it seems to acquire negative value so far as diffusion is concerned. Many innovations, from the use of the automobile to the use of contraception, began as upper-class behavior. But some—for instance, cigarette smoking—have spread from a lower or marginal class.[34]

Role of the Change Agent

The change agent or "professional advocate" is a professional person who attempts to influence adoption decisions in a direction that he feels is desirable. Usually this means seeking to secure the adoption of new ideas, but sometimes it is attempting to slow the diffusion process and prevent the adoption of certain innovations. A new idea may perhaps compete with an old one sponsored by the change agent. Examples of such agents include technical assistance workers in underdeveloped areas (including members of the Peace Corps), county extension agents, promoters of drugs for medical use, salesmen and dealers of new products, public health officials, and school administrators.

The change agent largely works directly with people. He is the agricultural county agent who is trying to induce farmer X to try out

---

31 H. G. Barnett, *Innovation: The Basis of Cultural Change* (New York: McGraw-Hill Book Co., 1953), p. 319.

32 This, however, may not *always* be true. The Putneys, in a study of a Mexican community, noted an instance in which prestige leaders were radical innovators and yet suffered no loss of prestige. But this seems to be in the nature of an exception to the general rule. Snell and Gladys J. Putney, "Radical Innovation and Prestige," *American Sociological Review*, Vol. 27, No. 4 (August, 1962), 548–551.

33 This has been called the trickle effect, because goods and services trickle down to the lower classes. See Lloyd Fallers, "A Note on the Trickle Effect," *Public Opinion Quarterly*, Vol. 18, No. 3 (Fall, 1954), 314–321.

34 Richard T. LaPiere, *Social Change* (New York: McGraw-Hill Book Co., 1965), p. 205.

a new seed or method of cultivation. She is the county nurse endeavoring to persuade ignorant patients to consult the trained physician instead of the local midwife. He is the businessman who wrangles with bankers, trying to launch a new product on the market. He is the political reformer who pleads with his unaroused fellows in the effort to have a new law enacted. Persuading people to abandon familiar endeavors and to replace them with something new involves many different techniques. Different agents operate along different lines. At any rate, the hold of the old must be weakened, and the new must be made interesting and attractive. The arts of propaganda and advertising have a place.[35] Certain generalizations, moreover, seem to have been validated by research. For instance, commercial change agents appear to be more important at the trial stage than at any other time in the adoption process. It similarly seems that commercial change agents are more important for earlier adopters than for later adopters at the trial stage.[36] In general, a successful program of change needs to be tailored to fit cultural values and past experiences. The clients should be made to perceive a need for the innovation. Change agents should concentrate their efforts on opinion leaders in the early stages of the diffusion of an innovation.[37]

Before coming to any firm conclusions concerning the ingredients of the adoption process, we wish to consider the special situation of adoption in underdeveloped areas.

ADOPTION OF IDEAS AND PRODUCTS IN UNDERDEVELOPED AREAS [38]

Some special features pertain to diffusion in the underdeveloped areas of the world. First of all, the diffusion of ideas and products in these areas is desired in a relatively short period of time—usually within a few years. The actual time may turn out to be much longer than peasant leaders anticipate, but demonstrable results are sought in fairly short order. Secondly, diffusion in this context applies to a considerable extent to borrowing *scientific knowledge* and allied matters and behavior; this occurs, moreover, in areas where this kind of knowledge either has existed in slight measure or not at all.[39] Thirdly, this

35 The preceding few sentences have been adapted from LaPiere, *ibid.*, pp. 151–153.

36 Rogers, *op. cit.*, p. 263.

37 *Ibid.*, pp. 278–282.

38 In this section the writer has relied rather heavily on George M. Foster, *Traditional Cultures: And the Impact of Technological Change* (New York: Harper & Row, 1962) and Arensberg and Niehoff, *loc. cit.*

39 G. M. Foster, *op. cit.*, p. 9

is a cross-cultural type of diffusion, hence *cultural* stimulants and resistances will count heavily in determining the degree of success
achieved. Finally, this is an instance of *planned change;* yet it must
come voluntarily. However much leaders in underdeveloped areas may,
for example, desire industrialization, the peasants themselves must be
willing to adopt various new ideas and practices.

Conditions in the Typical Underdeveloped Community: The Setting

It is worthwhile to have a preliminary picture of the type of environment in which the change agent in the underdeveloped country works.
Briefly the picture is one in which a high percentage of people are
employed in agriculture, the tools and techniques used are primitive,
per capita income is low, the volume of trade is low, the illiteracy rate
is usually high, existing education is rudimentary, nutrition is inadequate, public health and sanitation are rudimentary, the rural areas
are overcrowded, much child labor exists, the status of women is low,
the middle class is generally weak or nonexistent, birth rates and death
rates are both high, and the over-all state of technological development
is low.[40] Despite differences in language, religion, political organization
and other elements, it is remarkable, says Foster, how the cultural
forms are so similar.[41] Against this backdrop the peasant (whether in
Mexico, India, Peru, or Egypt) tends to be fatalistic—and no wonder!
He has little or no control over the basic decisions made concerning
his life, and, worse yet, he usually does not know how and why they
are made.[42] The villager believes that the outside world is dangerous
and unpredictable; he does not understand actual conditions, and he
often believes the wildest rumors.[43] With the outside world regarded
as a constant threat, one might expect that common adversity would
draw the peasants together in a spirit of unity. Unfortunately, it usually does not work that way. With meager resources in the community,
the people are suspicious and distrustful of each other; tensions, envy,
and schisms are often severe. Gossip is harsh; and neighbors seem

[40] We shall discuss this subject more fully in Chapter 14, but for present purposes
we have followed the characteristics as listed in Harvey Leibenstein, *Economic Backwardness and Economic Growth* (New York: John Wiley & Sons, Inc., 1957; paperback edition, 1963), pp. 40–41.

[41] Foster, *op. cit.,* pp. 47–48.

[42] *Loc. cit.*

[43] For example, Jane Phillips, working in an antihookworm campaign in Ceylon
sponsored by the Rockefeller Foundation, reports how natives distributed medicine
in capsule form. An extensive whispering campaign warned them that the capsules
were time bombs that would explode after several months or years. (This is cited
in Foster, *op. cit.,* p. 50).

ready to believe the worst about each other. Because the productivity in these areas is small, peasants believe that if someone gets ahead, it must be at the expense of someone else. If a technical aid program assumes the existence of a high degree of village cooperation, it is clearly headed for trouble. The extended family prevails, and frictions and conflicts often abound. This is the usual setting in which the change agent operates. A planned diffusion of ideas and products will indeed need to be carefully planned, if it is to avoid many pitfalls and achieve its ends.

It is important that change agents (as program planners and technical specialists) be aware of the struggle between the forces of change in underdeveloped areas and the forces for stability. The strength of the status quo forces must be weakened, or their results neutralized, while the change forces are built up. Both barriers and stimulants to change may be cultural, social, or psychological in nature. Effective strategy is often for the change agent to begin with projects that represent the problems and needs of the peasants themselves.[44]

Cultural Barriers and Stimulants to Change

Among the cultural barriers to change are *traditional values and attitudes,* which may be extremely important. People with novel ideas come under the suspicious eye of the group. Fatalism is reinforcing. When an infant dies, for example, the peasant often will not acknowledge the absence of medical care or public sanitation; he will reason that it was the destiny of the baby not to grow up. Beliefs about the supernatural also set limits on the adoption of ideas. If the peasants believe that animal life is sacred, setting up a system of slaughterhouses and meat-processing plants is likely to be doomed.[45] *Ethnocentrism* often constitutes a sizeable bulwark against change. Western people may feel that democratic ideas, a high standard of living, and technological progress clearly stamp their culture as vastly superior to many others. It may come as a rude shock to some persons that many peasants—indeed people the world over—tend to view their basic cultural ideas, beliefs, and social forms as natural and best. True, they will easily grant the superiority of a steel knife over a stone knife. But, as Foster declares, this sort of thing is not the *essence* of culture; it is beliefs and values.[46] It is difficult to prove superiority in these things. One may assert that if the state of enlightenment in some society is

44 Probably one of the least successful viewpoints is that of "If you people will learn to do more things the way we do them, you will be better off." In addition to being ethnocentric, this is hardly flattering. *Ibid.,* p. 261.

45 Arensberg and Niehoff, *op. cit.,* p. 67.

46 Foster, *op. cit.,* p. 68.

much greater than in another and if the average person lives twice as long in one society than in another, this indicates the superiority of the former—if one is aware of the differences. But the average peasant is not so aware. He is simply attached to the cultural ideas of his area; they have made him in considerable part as he is.[47]

Pride and dignity also may constitute barriers to change. Natives will acknowledge poor economic conditions in many areas or will acknowledge a need for more education, but they will not concede that their area is deficient in all ways. Often adults feel that they will "lose face" if, at their time of life, they go back to school. Often older women resist maternal and child health programs on the grounds that, if young pregnant women attend clinics (for instance), such reflects on the ability and judgment of the older ones.[48] Norms of modesty may bring a resistance point to adopting ideas. Medical examination and treatment may be resisted by native women when it is done by a male physician; or the husband may object to the treatment. This resistance may be overcome by having it done by female physicians, except that there are usually few of the latter in these areas.[49]

Another major barrier to adopting new ideas or products derives from an incompatibility of culture traits, as we have discussed before.[50] Sometimes unforeseen (to the change agent) consequences of planned innovation will bring difficulties. As an illustration of this Foster cites the case of Eskimos in Alaska who acquired a certain disease from their sled dogs.[51] Yet if they exterminated the dogs (which would be required to control the disease), what would they do for transportation?

Social Barriers and Stimulants to Change

Social barriers are not as numerous as cultural ones. New ideas are frequently resisted, however, on the score of bringing undesirable effects upon family, kinship, and friendship patterns. The mutual obligations and reciprocal patterns of the extended family often affect

[47] One field worker in Colombia (Mrs. Virginia Pineda) reported the following incident while working with some cattle-raising Indians: She was talking with an Indian woman of high social class who mentioned that her husband had purchased her with some cattle. Mrs. Pineda felt sad that the Colombian women could be sold like a cow. Suddenly the tenor of the conversation changed. The Indian woman asked, "And how many cows did you cost *your* husband?" When the reply was that she had not been sold at all, the Indian woman abruptly declared that she (Mrs. Pineda) must not be worth anything if her husband had not given a single cow. She thereupon lost all respect for Mrs. Pineda and would not talk further. (Incident reported in *Ibid.*, p. 69.)

[48] *Ibid.*, p. 71.

[49] *Ibid.*, p. 74.

[50] For examples of this see Arensberg and Niehoff, *op. cit.*, p. 79.

[51] Foster. *op. cit.*, p. 80.

many types of behavior. These patterns are often incompatible with the individualization that accompanies the processes of urbanization and industrialization, and so they often comprise a considerable brake on change. Innovations may be resisted, moreover, on the grounds that they interfere with the pleasurable meetings of friends or cooperative work groups.[52] The innovation itself may be both rational and desirable, but the peasants may not want their pleasant contacts disrupted. *Vested interests* are an important factor of resistance in underdeveloped, as well as developed, nations. Innovations, for example, may affect authority patterns adversely. Finally, resistance to the adoption of new ideas or practices may rest with class or caste barriers. Innovations may bring new or aggravated problems to persons having high status.

Psychological Barriers and Stimulants to Change

Different cross-cultural perceptions may result concerning innovations. Gifts, for instance, may be viewed differently in different areas. In some localities gifts are thought to be worthless; the argument is that if someone gives something away it *must* be without value, otherwise he would keep it. Then, there are different role perceptions of behavior. Peasants may have unique conceptions of the role of a physician and may not wish to tell him about their symptoms. They may say that the folk healer brings cures without the patient telling things. Can't this Westernized physician do as well? Their opinion of the latter may then decline. Language problems may constitute barriers to change, as can be widely illustrated.

Inducements for change may be much in evidence too.[53] The perceived utility of the new idea or practice is of major importance. Indeed, the intrinsic appeal or lack of appeal will count heavily in the adoption process. If the appeal is linked with perceived economic gain, the stimulant force will be heightened. Compatibility with the existing culture pattern is also a major factor. Another stimulant factor is the prestige of the donor group. This is often not an all-inclusive type of influence, however. For instance, American society has high prestige in the realm of technological advancement, and French society has high prestige with regard to women's fashions. But other peoples may not necessarily admire either society in an all-around way. Any trait coming from an admired source, however, will generally be given serious consideration.[54] Another factor that influences the acceptance

---

[52] See *ibid.*, pp. 96–99 for examples.

[53] See the discussion in Linton, *op. cit.*, pp. 340–346; and in Barnett, *op. cit.*, Chaps. XI and XIII.

[54] This is also true of industrial products. When the IBM Corporation announced

of the innovation is the prestige of the persons under whose auspices the new idea or element is presented. Finally, sheer faddism may have influence. Some ideas or products may have neither important utility nor high prestige, yet they are a fad of the moment. Some type of behavior or trait is simply the "rage." Large numbers of people may eagerly adopt the new item even though, as they calmly reflect on it later, the adoption may seem foolish. The adoption process has its irrational, as well as rational, elements.

OTHER INSTANCES OF PLANNED DIFFUSION

Not only have underdeveloped nations planned the spreading of ideas or elements, but the United States government—and perhaps other governments—has also espoused programs of planned diffusion. The United States Atomic Energy Commission programs serve as an illustration. Under the auspices of the Atoms-for-Peace program and others, grants have been given to various nations for nuclear reactor research projects. Scientists have been sent from many nations to the Oak Ridge Institute of Nuclear Studies for medical and radiological training in the safe and efficient use of radioisotopes. Moreover, scientists and engineers from many nations have been sent to the (U. S.) School of Nuclear Science and Engineering located at the Argonne National Laboratory near Chicago where courses have been given on the design, construction, and operation of nuclear reactors and the handling of irradiated materials. Considerable financial sums have been contributed by the United States government toward the cost of nuclear research reactors to be established in various foreign nations. This was also a part of the Atoms-for-Peace program.[55] This, again, is planned and guided diffusion. In short, knowledge of nuclear subjects does not merely inch its way to other nations. The United States government has actively sought out qualified scientists, engineers, and medical personnel and invited them here; it has then provided instructional programs relative to the preceding subjects.[56] This was done in the ultimate interest of world peace.

We shall not enter into an extended discussion of the Peace Corps

---

in 1970 that it would enter the office copier field, a common reaction was, "Coming from IBM, this new copier will be of top quality."

[55] These examples of planned and supervised diffusion have been noted in numerous news releases of the United States Atomic Energy Commission, Washington, D. C.

[56] For further information concerning the theory and practice of planned change, see Warren G. Bennis, Kenneth D. Benne, and Robert Chin (eds.), *The Planning of Change,* 2nd ed. (New York: Holt, Rinehart and Winston, 1969); and Ronald Lippitt, Jeanne Watson, and Bruce Westley, *The Dynamics of Planned Change* (New York: Harcourt, Brace & World, 1958).

and related problems, but, once again, this program involves the planned diffusion of selected practices (health, agricultural, educational, and the like) as they are needed in foreign situations. Peace Corps volunteers act as change agents in introducing the needed elements.

Leads for Future Research

It may be suggested that the research on diffusion as performed up to the present time has merely sampled a vast territory. As we have seen, valuable studies have been made in rural sociology, medical sociology, and education; able projects have related to "personal influence" and other subjects. Spreading fashions have been studied from time to time.[57] However, empirical observations suggest that, the human breed being as it is, people frequently compare their own behavior and practices in *many* sectors of life: corporate life, schools, hospitals, clubs, state governments, even national governments, and many others. They see how others deal with some subject; if the others have more successful results than they do, they are likely to adopt the others' practices. Corporations keep an eye not only on their competitors but also on others in the quest for new and better policies. As colleges, or departments within a college, consider curriculum and other changes, they are sooner or later likely to have a look at the program of X, Y, or Z college (which they respect or consider their kind of college). State governments often carefully inspect the practices or laws of other states. Delegations of United States senators may visit other nations to scrutinize policies for controlling crime, dealing with urban problems, or coping with the dilemmas of civil defense; leaders from other nations in turn visit this nation in order to see if America has answers for some of their problems. The diffusion of ideas and behavior, then, is likely to occur regarding scores of subjects—not just the three or four that have interested sociological researchers up to this time. The rise of education and the development of the mass media have enormously expanded the significance of the diffusion process. Millions of people who live many miles away from some development are aware of it; awareness may quickly change to interest, interest to evaluation, and finally evaluation to adoption. Moreover, the content of education itself can be diffused to other nations: Theories and viewpoints in chemistry or sociology can be exported from Europe to America and vice versa (or to and from other areas).[58]

---

[57] Kroeber, *op. cit.*, 2nd ed., pp. 245–247.

[58] In sociology, for example, the "European ideas" of Durkheim, Weber, and others were exported to the United States approximately one generation ago (with

Also, traditional societies who elect to modernize are adopting the program of industrialization with its attendant changes. In the modern closely knit world the significance of diffusion is greater than ever before.

Internal Diffusion.   Professor Daniel Bell has called attention to the importance of the diffusion of goods and privileges within the United States.[59] Just as many people want automobiles and television sets, so they may desire a good education or decent housing. Goods and services diffuse from the few to the many. Bell notes, as an example, that 14 per cent of American youth went to college in 1939, whereas in 1966–1967 the figure reached 42 per cent.[60] The diffusion of goods and services *within* a nation is, then, another important aspect of the subject. Many subjects could well be studied in this context in addition to the wish for a college education mentioned by Bell: diffusion of the contraceptive pill, of the urban renewal idea, of the wish for fluoridated community water supplies, of the wish for a home fallout shelter, and of the use of computers may be of current interest. It appears, at any rate, that diffusion is an exceedingly important process of change both within a nation and between nations. We suggest that research on this subject may be considerably expanded.

Demonstrating Diffusion by Mapping Techniques.   One comparatively new lead for diffusion research places emphasis upon the methodological, namely: it shows the diffusion of innovations by the use of mapping techniques performed at successive time periods. Torsten Hägerstrand [61] has pioneered in this work. One can measure the spatial distributions of many features that have been introduced in an area—for example, agricultural items, the automobile, or the telephone. These distributions are then shown in cartographic form. Hägerstrand shows maps of population distribution in his native Sweden first; then he shows the spatial distributions of agricultural items, the telephone, and the automobile. He develops a series of models to express the diffusion of these items, which take note of these

Parsons and others acting as change agents); and, during more recent decades, the theories of Parsons, Sorokin, and others have diffused to other parts of the world. This is so commonplace that many people may not specifically identify it as the diffusion of ideas it obviously is.

59 Commission on the Year 2000, American Academy of Arts and Sciences, "Toward the Year 2000: Work in Progress," *Daedalus* (Summer, 1967), 643. Professor Bell is chairman of the commission.

60 *Ibid.*, p. 657.

61 Torsten Hägerstrand, *Innovation Diffusion As a Spatial Process,* translated from from the Swedish (Chicago: University of Chicago Press, 1967). The original Swedish publication occurred in 1953.

factors: (1) awareness of the innovation, (2) the role of market influences, and (3) amount and source of information received. The diffusion of innovation is seen as a learning (persuasion) process, and networks of social communication are regarded as important. Hägerstrand also proposes that a hierarchy of such networks exists—one operating on the local plane, another on the regional plane, and a third on the international level. Hägerstrand has, in addition, developed the Monte Carlo simulation models of spatial diffusion. Although Monte Carlo simulations have been used in physical science, in systems analysis, and in gaming, Hägerstrand appears to be the first social scientist to put them to extensive use. Predicting future distributions of social factors may be possible through the use of the Monte Carlo techniques, and this technique will probably be used by increasing numbers of sociologists, geographers, and other social scientists.[62] Then, Brown [63] has used Hägerstrand's techniques to measure the diffusion of television receivers in southern Sweden as a further empirical test of the earlier conceptualization. Again, the presentation is characterized by many charts and tables; Brown concludes with a mathematical model of the diffusion of innovation.

Another mathematical treatment of the diffusion of innovations has been presented by Mason and Halter.[64] Again, a model of diffusion is formulated and tested. This project applies the Theil-Basmann method (involving two-stage least squares) to a system of simultaneous equations dealing with the sociological variables. The factors of adoption of the innovation, the social structure, and production are built into the model. Agricultural items constitute the innovations diffused. The effect of "influentials," as emphasized in the Katz-Lazarsfeld two-step hypothesis, is recognized in the adoptions. The authors conclude that the Theil-Basmann procedure (methodology) is useful for such a diffusion study and holds promise for other studies.

62 The reader should also note the important Postscript in this Hägerstrand volume written by Professor Allan Pred of the University of California at Berkeley. See other publications by Hägerstrand such as, "On the Monte Carlo Simulation of Diffusion," *European Journal of Sociology*, Vol. 6 (1965), 43–67; and "Quantitative Techniques for the Analysis of the Spread of Information and Technology," in C. Arnold Anderson and Mary Jean Bowman (eds.), *Education and Economic Development* (Chicago: Aldine Publishing Co., 1965), pp. 244–281. See also William L. Garrison and D. F. Markle (eds.), *Quantitative Geography*, Part I, Economic and Cultural Topics (Evanston, Ill.: Northwestern University Studies in Geography, 1967), pp. 1–33.

63 Lawrence A. Brown, "Diffusion of Innovation: A Macroview," *Economic Development and Cultural Change*, Vol. 17, No 2 (January, 1969), 189–211.

64 Robert Mason and Albert N. Halter, "The Application of a System of Simultaneous Equations to an Innovation Diffusion Model," *Social Forces*, Vol. 47, No. 2 (December, 1968), 182–195.

SOME CONCLUSIONS

Certain conclusions appear warranted by the material presented in this chapter. First, it is evident that considerable empirical data are available regarding the adoption process. Much of this is quantitative and hypothesis-related, although it chiefly relates to certain special fields and subjects such as the diffusion of farming and medical innovations within the United States.[65] Material concerning the diffusion of ideas and practices in underdeveloped nations is more likely to be qualitative in nature.

Another conclusion is that advances in the theory of diffusion are needed. Rogers [66] has made a significant beginning in this regard, however. The theory of diffusion requires incorporation at the higher level of the total theory of socio-cultural change. In general, the theory of diffusion is virtually the opposite of that of immanent change: most of the time at least, changes originate from outside the system. Diffusion of the type suggested by Professor Bell relates to the individual in contact with the total society or culture.

We have expressed the view that diffusion is a subject for investigation that virtually has only been sampled thus far. Social scientists, however, have almost always proclaimed the importance of this process of change. As a subject for further research it has great potential. Methodological advances, often with elaborate mathematical treatment, are steadily being made. Hägerstrand's work in Sweden, including his use of the Monte Carlo simulation techniques, is especially to be noted.

ANNOTATED BIBLIOGRAPHY

Barnett, H. G., *Innovation: The Basis of Cultural Change* (New York: McGraw-Hill Book Co., 1953; paperback edition is undated).

> The acceptance or rejection of innovations is discussed in Part Four. Generally worthwhile reading. Barnett's conclusions are given in Chapter XIV.

Coleman, James S., Katz, Elihu, and Menzel, Herbert, *Medical Innovation: A Diffusion Study* (Indianapolis, Ind.: Bobbs-Merrill, 1966).

> A well-done study of the adoption of a new drug by practicing physicians in four Midwestern cities. Pharmacists' prescription files were used to trace the adoption of the drug, and more than one half of the physicians were interviewed. The social-friendship networks among physicians were significantly related to the adoptions.

---

[65] We have not emphasized the empirical data in this chapter. However, the Rogers volume closely assesses the empirical findings in stating generalizations; other volumes such as the Katz-Lazarsfeld, *Personal Influence, op. cit.*, are helpful.

[66] Rogers, *op. cit.*, Chap. XI.

Foster, George M., *Traditional Cultures: And the Impact of Technological Change* (New York: Harper & Row, 1962).
> Foster follows the "applied anthropological" perspective; much evidence relates to Central and South America, India, and Pakistan. Reflecting experiences on his part, the volume emphasizes cultural, social, and psychological factors in diffusion.

Katz, Elihu, and Lazarsfeld, Paul F., *Personal Influence* (New York: The Free Press of Glencoe, Division of The Macmillan Company, 1955; paperback edition, 1964).
> A study of the flow of influence in the differing areas of marketing, public affairs, fashions, and movie attendance. The two-step hypothesis is developed. Exceedingly well done.

Katz, Elihu, Levin, Martin L., and Hamilton, Herbert, "Traditions of Research on the Diffusion of Innovation," *American Sociological Review*, Vol. 28, No. 2 (April, 1963), 237–252.
> An overview of elements in the diffusion process, assessing the contributions made by anthropologists, rural sociologists, educators, public health workers, and others.

Linton, Ralph, *The Study of Man* (New York: D. Appleton-Century Co., 1936), Chap. 19.
> A valuable, early statement. Contributions of this sort provided a base from which more recent diffusion research has been launched.

Rogers, Everett M., *Diffusion of Innovations* (New York: The Free Press of Glencoe, Division of The Macmillan Co., 1962).
> The best, single, all-around summary and synthesis of the diffusion process that this writer has seen: traditions of research, stages in adoption, characteristics of the innovation, adopter categories, opinion leaders, and change agents. Rogers ends by listing 52 generalizations concerning diffusion.

Concerning Demonstration of Diffusion by Mapping Techniques:

Hägerstrand, Torsten, *Innovation Diffusion As a Spatial Process,* translated from the Swedish (Chicago: University of Chicago Press, 1967).
> A pioneering study that measures the spread and adoption of innovations, using the technique of mapping distribution at successive times. Models are painstakingly developed. Of note is Hägerstrand's development of the Monte Carlo simulation models of spatial diffusion.

Brown, Lawrence, A., "Diffusion of Innovation: A Macroview," *Economic Development and Cultural Change,* Vol. 17, No. 2 (January, 1969), 189–211.
> Follows the Hägerstrand thesis, demonstrating it with respect to the diffusion of television receivers in an area of southern Sweden. An abundance of empirical data is provided. A worthy study.

13 | *Activism*

It is evident that an active orientation toward socio-cultural change has been on the rapid rise in many parts of the world during recent years, including the Western nations and most definitely the United States. The deliberate effort to anticipate and direct change—to determine one's wants for the future and vigorously seek to attain them—may be, as Daniel Bell has declared, "the most important social change of our time."[1] In a preliminary discussion of this development (see Chapter 4) it was observed that the active or self-determinative approach to change is actually a *master approach;* it gathers others, such as the economic, political, technological, leadership, educational, and collective behavior, under its folds. At the same time activism is an approach that reflects an attitude toward *change* itself.

The assumption is made in the present chapter that the activist perspective is no transient or fleeting phenomenon. It will be with us during the foreseeable future. We suggest, on the other hand, that it is a *crescive* type of development on the order of industrialization or urbanization. It is true that the current version of activism in American society rose suddenly and rather dramatically during the mid-1960s, resulting mostly from active dissent relative to racial injustice, ghetto conditions, and the Vietnam war. But the active perspective represents more of a generalized accompaniment to the advanced development of society. Inkeles and associates,[2] in setting forth characteristics of modern man, point to the active orientation toward society and occurrences in general as one element of a syndrome of attributes. The syndrome relates to attitudes, values, and ways of feeling and of acting. In short, exposure to the modern setting of increased urbanization, industrialization, high levels of education, extensive mechaniza-

[1] Daniel Bell, "Notes on the Post-Industrial Society (I)," *The Public Interest,* No. 6 (Winter, 1967), 25.

[2] Alex Inkeles, "The Modernization of Man," Chapter 10 in Myron Weiner (ed.), *Modernization: The Dynamics of Growth* (New York: Basic Books, Inc., 1966); Inkeles, "Making Men Modern: On the Causes and Consequences of Individual Change in Six Developing Countries," *American Journal of Sociology,* Vol. 75, No. 2 (September, 1969), 208–225; and David Horton Smith and Alex Inkeles, "The OM Scale: A Comparative Socio-Psychological Measure of Individual Modernity," *Sociometry,* Vol. 29 (1969), 353–377.

tion, high rates of social mobility, and the like tends to produce various characteristics among modern people.[3] Modern man, summarizes Inkeles,[4] has the attitude of *efficacy*. In his words, "The modern man is the one who believes that man can learn, in substantial degree, to dominate his environment in order to advance his own purposes and goals, rather than being dominated entirely by that environment." Again [Central to the syndrome of modern man is the] "belief in the efficacy of science and medicine and a general abandonment of passivity and fatalism in the face of life's difficulties. . . . [Also modern man wishes] to take an active part in civic and community affairs and local politics." [5]

In discussing activism in relation to social change we shall largely focus attention on American society, recognizing that Inkeles' research sees the active perspective in broader context; it is necessary, however, to delimit the present area of discussion. Assuming the American setting, then, we shall primarily seek an answer in this chapter to the following question: Precisely what kind of activism, incorporating what policies and what practices, is regarded as appropriate for this society at the present time and in the near future? For, as we shall see, alternatives *are* available. However, before approaching this central question, let us briefly review what kind of active programs and thinking American society has already had. A condensed historical introduction to the subject is likely to be helpful.

Development of the Activist Sentiment

It is true that the activist sentiment in the American nation has waxed and waned. But, if we begin with *thinking* on the subject, we see at once that this perspective is not confined to recent years and the present. In fact, active-oriented thinking characterized some of the founding fathers of the science of sociology. Auguste Comte (1798–1857),[6] the French sociologist-philosopher whose ideas were known in intellectual circles in the United States, stated the general view that

[3] This fact is of considerable interest, as Smith and Inkeles themselves declare. Despite the ample cultural diversity found in the six nations they studied and an even greater number of human groups (because some of the nations had ethnic and other subdivisions), finding the same general results seems to suggest something like a "psychic unity of mankind"—which the authors believe is increasing. See *ibid.*, p. 377.

[4] Inkeles, in Weiner (ed.), *op. cit.*, p. 143.

[5] Inkeles, "Making Men Modern: . . . ," *op. cit.*, p. 210.

[6] Auguste Comte, *Positive Philosophy*, translated by H. Martineau (New York: Blanchord, 1855); see also H. E. Barnes, "The Social and Political Philosophy of Auguste Comte," Chapter III in Barnes (ed.), *An Introduction to the History of Sociology* (Chicago: University of Chicago Press, 1948).

the social process might be modified and advances brought by "intelligent activities of mankind." In such modification he saw the influence of public opinion as considerable. These Comtean beginnings were much extended by the pioneering American sociologist, Lester F. Ward (1841–1913). Ward was a leader in advocating the overthrow of the laissez-faire perspective; he favored the conscious control and direction of social forces in the interests of human welfare. His views were known as societal self-direction. He summarized his ideas in a series of theorems, which are perhaps remarkable if one recalls that they were published in 1883. The theorems are [7] (1) Happiness is the ultimate end of conation. (2) Progress is the direct means to Happiness. (3) Dynamic action is the direct means to Progress. (4) Dynamic Opinion is the direct means to Dynamic Action. (5) Knowledge is the direct means to Dynamic Opinion. (6) Education is the direct means to Knowledge. Ward devotes a chapter in his volume to a discussion of each theorem.

A detailed recounting of other actively oriented sociological thought during this century is not possible here.[8] Undoubtedly the list of sociologists over the years who have been actively interested in bringing improvement to the total society or to its various subareas is quite lengthy. One would very likely want to include Robert S. Lynd, C. Wright Mills, William F. Ogburn, Louis Wirth, the regionalists Howard W. Odum and Rupert B. Vance, W. Lloyd Warner and Robert Havighurst (concerning education), Elton Mayo (concerning the industrial system), Gunnar Myrdal, the late Arnold Rose, and many others relative to race relations. It was pointed out in Chapter 7 that Thorstein Veblen's criticisms of the business system led to many improvements. The work of Austin MacCormick, Donald R. Cressey, and many others concerning prison reform should be mentioned. This list is a mere beginning that only suggests the full list that could be compiled. With some sociologists, efforts designed to bring social improvement might comprise a major, conscious interest; with others such an effort might be less in the forefront of their minds, but nevertheless it would be real and important. We leave attempts to compile a full list of active-minded sociologists and their ideas to others because such a historical chronicle is not our main interest here. We suggest, however, that even a brief survey of the record justifies the statement that many sociologists have held an active interest in social happenings. A general,

[7] Lester F. Ward, *Dynamic Sociology*, Vol. II (New York: Appleton, 1883), pp. 108–109. See also Ward, *Psychic Factors of Civilization* (Boston: Ginn & Co., 1893) and *Applied Sociology* (Boston: Ginn & Co., 1906).

[8] For an earlier exploration of this subject, see this writer's "Social Action and Social Problems," Chapter 25 in M. G. Caldwell and L. Foster (eds.), *Analysis of Social Problems* (Harrisburg, Pa.: The Stackpole Co., 1954).

long-term interest is indicated. Undoubtedly, interest in racial, urban, pollution, war, and other problems has brought a marked rise in active sentiment at the present time. Attention has also been directed in recent years to facilitating social science contributions to the society. Then, there is a sizeable number of sociologists at present who wish to emphasize the active solution of problems as the prime interest of the field.[9]

The trends of development of American society gradually brought new conditions in which the need for social actions was more evident. And increasingly the effective regulation of social forces could be achieved. In this sense Auguste Comte and Lester F. Ward were much ahead of their time. The condition of education, of the communication arts, and of other social elements was so rudimentary that prospects for *attaining* societal self-direction in their day were poor. Their ideas were notable, but the *public will* that would bring dynamic action to remedy social problems was quite lacking in those laissez-faire times. However, the many value and other changes over the years in American society were to modify this. In Chapter 1 such changes were surveyed, emphasizing socio-cultural conditions as of 1870, 1910, 1940, and the present. (The reader may wish to refer back to Table 1 on page 16).

Some of the changes shown are that the population increased more than five-fold between 1870 and the present (it is now steadily advancing beyond the 200 million mark); living patterns became increasingly more urbanized (more than 70 per cent of the people now live in the more impersonal and complex urban communities); national productivity advanced to a truly colossal figure (the GNP now exceeding the the figure of $865 billions annually); the Federal government gradually developed into a bureaucratic giant (the increase in the number of civilian employees and in total expenditures tells another amazing story); also business corporations, universities, hospitals, and other organizations often became huge bureaucracies; the people, being healthier on the average, now live more than twenty years longer than they did in 1910; this means that the total national population now includes a much larger percentage of older citizens than it did in 1870 and in 1910. Before pointing to other significant trends, we pause to

[9] See, for example, *Knowledge into Action: Improving the Nation's Use of the Social Sciences,* Report of the Special Commission on the Social Sciences of the National Science Board, National Science Foundation (Washington, D. C.: Government Printing Office, 1969). As representative of sociologists who take exception to the Weberian dictum that social science should be *value-free*—rather they hold that sociologists should stress the solution of problems and should espouse value positions in so doing—see Alvin W. Gouldner, *The Coming Crisis of Western Sociology* (New York: Basic Books, 1970); and T. S. Simey, *Social Science and Social Purpose* (New York: Schocken Books, 1969).

observe that the *needs* of societal self-direction were made greater by these population, urban, bureaucratic, and other trends. Certainly the active outlook is required to a far greater degree with the newer conditions than it was during the earlier, less-populated, more rural, simpler times. Laissez faire became increasingly dysfunctional for the advancing society.[10] Needs of the contemporary period are more pressing; they literally demand attention.

Some of the developments of modern American society are especially relevant for the activist view in the sense that they brought the probabilities that societal control could be much more adequately achieved. As the reader may suspect, these trends relate to the education-communication-public-opinion sectors. The following changes can be singled out for specific mention: (1) A vast increase occurred in school attendance in general and college training in particular. Hence, the horizons of millions of people were broadened; they steadily developed cosmopolitan (rather than only local) interests; they were "generally grounded" in a diversity of subjects in addition to being prepared for some occupation; their communications ability (oral and written) was made adequate; and *college* training brought the aftereffect that many graduates would keep up their reading and studying in later years; doubtless some high school graduates would also continue to read quality books and magazines. (2) Major strides were taken regarding the development of the mass media of communications. The advent of television, combining the visual with the audio capability, was notable; the combination of formal schooling with media learning brought a far more informed public opinion than America had had before. (3) The significant development of other technologies, such as the computer and nuclear energy, was notable, too, the computer enabling man to accomplish objectives that were previously impossible. Further strides are being made concerning automation and cybernetics. (4) The immense development of the research and development industry, allied with education itself, has effected a knowledge explosion; thus, huge storehouses of knowledge can be readily used and data retrieved instantaneously; specific mention should be made moreover of the development of *social science* knowledge, which is particularly relevant for our present purposes. This may still not be as abundant as many would desire, yet all the social sciences have moved ahead rapidly during the past generation. Available knowledge as of the present time *is* impressive. Certainly the state of American society

[10] Faulkner's thesis is that the twenty-year period 1897–1917 was crucial in the decline of laissez-faire values. See Harold U. Faulkner, *The Decline of Laissez Faire, 1897–1917* (New York: Harper & Row, 1968, Harper Torchbook edition), especially Chap. XV.

(including the nature and criticalness of social problems) is better known today than at any time during the past.

Nevertheless, these developments, important as they are, did not in themselves produce a marked rise in the activist movement. People may have been *better prepared* to deal with social problems, thanks to the increase in knowledge and in technical resources, but they were not acutely motivated to act in the interests of the common weal. The average citizen, including the average college student, was quite apathetic regarding social and political questions during the late 1940s and 1950s. As was pointed out in Chapter 4, current activism arose in connection with the protest movement of the 1960s. Active dissent was stimulated by continued racial injustice, ghetto conditions, the Vietnam war, and several lesser conditions. The perspective of dissenters was gradually broadened in about the mid-1960s, so that after this it included positive ideas of what these individuals *did* want. The same type of person who had engaged in the protests now stated his *positive* wants—goals toward which he would energetically strive. Thus, the protest activities constitute the "precipitant" (MacIver's term) of the present-day activist movement. The broad increase in education, more elaborate media programs, acceleration of research, impressive computer achievements, and the like meant that American society was better prepared to execute action programs; the latter would be more likely to succeed. One could say that the day of the active society was approaching.

The advent of activism, moreover, would have a considerable impact upon the social sciences. In these sciences, to be sure, some accept and some do not accept the new perspective and its various tenets. Differences of opinion do not seem to reflect age levels, however; this does not appear to be a generation-gap phenomenon. In the main it can be said that proponents of the active view have an interest in putting knowledge to work. Research and teaching would be expected to be relevant (that overworked but necessary word) to actual conditions and to the needs of mankind; but this does not imply a widespread abandonment of basic research. Some would have it that organizations of intellectuals—such as, specifically, the various professional associations—can no longer stand apart from the struggles of the day. Thus, as interpreted by various social scientists, politicization of the professions is involved.[11]

11 For a clear cut statement by an eminent political scientist of a credo that is close to what has been described here, see David Easton, "The New Revolution in Political Science," *The American Political Science Review*, Vol. LXIII, No. 4 (December, 1969), 1051–1061. This article comprises the presidential address of Professor Easton at the 65th annual meeting of the American Political Science Association,

In essence, then, activism represents a point of view. Still, one can have different kinds of programs to carry out the active outlook. A crucial question is, "What brand of activism, in specifics, would seem to be most desirable for American society?" What options are possible? What alternative forms can be stated? Various individuals, in short, may have different conceptions of an active society. We attempt to answer this line of questioning by first presenting the views of a well-known contemporary sociologist on the subject. After summarizing this conception we shall then state what are, in our judgment, some of its commendable and less-commendable features. Then, we shall consider variations and alternatives of the active-society model as deemed appropriate for this society. The latter ideas may have to be expressed in more abbreviated form than we would have liked.

THE ETZIONI CONCEPTION OF THE ACTIVE SOCIETY

The fullest, most elaborate exposition of the active society as of the present time is undoubtedly that found in Professor Amitai Etzioni's volume bearing that title.[12] This society has certain basic components, in Etzioni's view, namely: self-conscious and knowing actors; one or more goals that they are committed to realize; and access to levers (or power) that will allow them to reset the social code. It is expected that this society will respond more fully to the needs of its actors. Man is held to be better able to attain this responsive society, one that is master of itself, in the present, "post-modern" era; this is due to the advantages and benefits of the new technologies of communication, knowledge, and energy that were developed after the Second World War. Thus, such inventions as television, the computer (a basic element in automation and cybernetics), and nuclear energy have ushered in new opportunities and options, one being the option of the active society itself. An active society, as Etzioni envisions it, does not exist anywhere at this time; but he thinks that Israel and the Scandinavian nations come closer to the concept than other nations.

If the active society presumably lies ahead of us (and many nations are moving in its direction), what are other conditions of this society?

September 2–6, 1969. His remarks would apply equally well to sociology. However, many social scientists oppose the specific point that professional associations should take stands on social, economic, and political issues beyond those directly affecting their discipline. For an able explanation of this viewpoint, see Philip M. Hauser, "On Actionism in the Craft of Sociology," *Sociological Inquiry*, Vol. 39, No. 2 (Spring, 1969), 139–147.

12 Amitai Etzioni, *The Active Society: A Theory of Societal and Political Processes* (New York: The Free Press, Division of The Macmillan Company, 1968).

The active society has active publics, citizens who are politically informed and who act politically. Responding to the needs of its citizens, this society is in a state of constant transformation. It pursues its major values more determinedly and tends to realize them. *Constant transformation* is so much the heart of Etzioni's basic message that it merits closer inspection. It implies a more active orientation, he declares, than the system concept of homeostasis or the ultrastability one in cybernetics.

> *A societal unit has* transformability *if it also is able to set—in response to external challenges, in anticipation of them, or as a result of internal developments—a new self-image which includes a new kind and level of homeostasis and ultrastability, and is able to change its parts and their combinations as well as its boundaries to create a new unit. This is not a higher-order ultrastability but an ability to design and move toward a* new *system even if the old one has not* become unstable. *It is an ability not only to generate adaptive changes or to restore new stability to an old unit, but also to bring about a new pattern, new parts, and, hence, a new society.*[13] *(Underlining is by Etzioni)*
>
> *The full measure of transformability is not realized until a unit can transform its internal structure and its boundary-relations with other units in response to its internal needs, searching for a more effective way of meeting them under the given environmental conditions and seeking to move toward a greater realization of the values to which it subscribed or of new values to which it has become committed. Such* self-triggered *transformability is a "higher" and less common level of activeness than* environmentally-triggered *transformation. The more it is achieved, the more societal actors may be considered their own masters.*[14] *(Underlining is by Etzioni)*

"Self-triggered" transformability, then, is especially regarded as a mark of the active society. Transformation in general frequently requires dissolving a unit's old structure and building a new one. "In this sense, the unit may be said to have been rejuvenated." [15] The fact that some societal units can be transformed more easily than others is accounted for, says Etzioni, by differences in control and in consensus. He then proceeds to discuss the factors of societal knowledge, the relations of knowledge and power, and societal consciousness in relation to action. In this over-all dynamic process he assumes that passivity is the more natural and expected condition; "it is activeness that requires effort and explanation." [16]

The subject of *mobilization* is also worthy of note. This concept is defined as "the process by which a unit gains significantly in the con-

13 *Ibid.,* p. 121.
14 *Ibid.*
15 *Ibid.*
16 *Ibid.,* p. 122.

trol of assets it previously did not control." [17] Mobilization is the source of energy for societal action. As with decision making and social planning, it implies a collective actor who is capable of controlling societal processes. Mobilization is deliberately initiated, directed, and terminated in the active society; it is not a mere by-product or outgrowth of social interaction. It may, Etzioni concedes, have unanticipated consequences. It makes societal units less private, more public.[18] Mobilization brings potentials closer to actualization. If Marx claimed that history is most affected by interclass struggle, Etzioni holds that collectivities are affected by both conflict and cooperation—and "the most important struggle is the one to mobilize under the given conditions and for the purpose of changing them." [19] Mobilization drives are of course affected by external conditions. Finally, Etzioni calls attention to the "surprising" increase in the capacity for societal action when the level of mobilization is sharply increased, as in crisis situations.[20]

Etzioni's theory of social guidance declares that when a society is *not* responsive to the wishes and needs of its citizens, this inevitably leads to alienation. Alienation, when it develops, tends to encompass most (if not all) social relationships. Moreover, highly alienating structures generally rely on coercion to a significant degree. One subcategory of alienation that he implies [21] is characteristic of American society, is denoted by the term *inauthenticity*. A relationship, institution, or society is inauthentic "if it provides the appearance of responsiveness while the underlying condition is alienating." [22] The alienated person feels that he does not belong; his efforts are without meaning. The individual involved in inauthentic relationships, on the other hand, feels cheated and manipulated. In any society outright alienation occurs when both the appearances and social conditions are nonresponsive; and inauthenticity occurs when appearances are responsive while reality is not.[23]

These are some of the major emphases in Etzioni's *The Active Society*. The book teems with ideas; many of his more detailed points are interesting and of value. It seems clear that this volume presents

[17] *Ibid.*, p. 388.

[18] *Ibid.*, p. 393.

[19] *Ibid.*, p. 394.

[20] *Ibid.*, p. 397.

[21] Etzioni indicates this although this writer does not see a direct statement to that effect.

[22] *Ibid.*, p. 619.

[23] *Ibid.*, p. 621. Further detailed comments are not practical here. In general, we would suggest that several of the chapters in the body of the book are especially important for the Etzioni thesis—for instance, Chapter 15, "Societal Mobilization and Societal Change"; Chapter 17, "The Mechanisms of Consensus"; and Chapter 18, "Unresponsive Societies and Their Transformation."

a picture of a (mostly) "future-type society"; the active society could be regarded as one type of utopia. Nevertheless, many current trends of developing American society are moving in the direction of the pictured society. Because of this fact, because Etzioni's ideas are of basic interest and importance, and because questions are likely to exist as to whether he has gone too far or perhaps not far enough, it is here predicted that this volume will receive continued attention in the field of sociology for some years. To be sure, Etzioni's projection of trends is discontinuous insofar as the concept of *transformability* and the notion of constant transformations are concerned (more about this later). However, his conception of this future society does not constitute a real theory (as he suggests in the subtitle). Even though his concepts and processes appear to be generally clear in substance, often an illusion of precision is attached to the processes that does not in fact exist.[24] At certain points one is inclined to raise questions, which, under these circumstances, may be difficult to answer.

DISCUSSION AND EVALUATION OF
THE ETZIONI IDEAS

Beginning with points that are favorable to Professor Etzioni's conception of the active society, we comment first of all that he has aligned himself well with the spirit of the modern age. Applying his discussion to American society, it appears that man may indeed increase his active control over the ongoing social order—and for much the sort of reasons that he gives. Such modern advantages as the notable accumulation of knowledge, marked development of the mass media, the high development of secondary school attendance, the rising tide of university enrollment, and the aid of such technological inventions as he mentions (especially the computer)—do make a considerable difference. The impact of these factors on public opinion, for instance, is of great moment. The vast penetration of the communications media and, furthermore, the ability to assess accurately the state of public opinion through the increasingly reliable polling arts (and then to inform leaders and citizens of it) are crucial for social-action programs. All segments of society go a considerable distance in developing a collective state of information and awareness concerning points of interest (which includes problems). Differences of opinion will almost surely exist; but even then the degree of consensus and the divergent viewpoints of different groups are indicated. Such a situation may or may

[24] For making us aware of this we are indebted to Professor Anatol Rapoport's excellent review of "The Active Society" in the *American Sociological Review*, Vol. 33, No. 6 (December, 1968), 982.

not constitute the mass-society equivalent of the early town meeting; nevertheless, it is functional for the ethic of social action.

Etzioni also writes in the spirit of the age insofar as public support is concerned. By this we mean that a substantial portion of the American public is interested in—even presses for—this very active control of social processes. Many would say that Etzioni is just one step ahead of actual trends. Relating his ideas to developing sociological thought, moreover, Etzioni is in fact the latest in a long line of distinguished predecessors (that goes back, as we have said, to Comte and Ward) who have advocated efforts to control the ongoing social processes for the betterment of man. Thus he is no maverick or "against-the-current" swimmer or "sideshow performer outside the main tent." Rather, he is a modern leader in a continuing and widely approved perspective. To make these expansive statements, however, does not mean that all or even a majority of sociologists would necessarily accept all the specific ideas—certainly the total package—of the active society.

Secondly, Etzioni's characterized active society would, if translated into an actual operating system, deal effectively with many socio-cultural lags that today are often stubborn and socially dysfunctional; or so it seems to us. We do not wish to become embroiled in detailed cases of this, but institutional and organizational lags resulting often from a failure to adjust based on vested-interest positions, personal intransigence, gross individualism, and other attitudes are likely to be effectively removed by the active-minded publics and the mobilization for change.[25] Catching up on such institutional and other lags is a matter of no little importance.

Turning to questioning and critical points, we wonder if Etzioni's description of the more activized and mobilized publics tells the complete story. It appears that only the "transformation-minded" publics and collectivities will be so mobilized. Will not the conservative, "status-quo" publics and groups then be motivated to mobilize *too* in defense of *their* positions? In that event, would the result be the same kind of power struggles—perhaps intensified—that now occupy the political-economic-social scene? This seems a reasonable probability. Would much be gained if it occurred? One may point out, moreover, that many publics are notably active at the *present* time. If the mobilizations and demonstrations were to be increased and if countermo-

[25] Some would say that provisions for medical care in the United States at this time comprise an excellent example of such a lag (based on a conceived vested-interest position). A prominent physician (Dr. John H. Knowles, director of the Massachusetts General Hospital) has, for example, charged that "The American medical profession has [maintained] a fifty-year history of negativism and resistance to change." *The New York Times* (February 23, 1970). However, we are not rigorously documenting this as a lag, as should be done.

bilizations and demonstrations followed—with students taking to the streets, followed by Blacks, followed by construction workers, followed by the "silent majority," succeeded in turn by antiwar groups, "hawkish" devotees, labor organizations, then antilabor organizations, and so on—how much turmoil and confusion would the nation stand before it became weary of activism itself? America has already been called "the chaotic society." [26] In brief, might the accelerated and conflicting expression of views finally provoke a reaction? Such does not seem likely at the time of this writing. Yet the social climate may change in future years. The *direction of change* could turn. Sorokin's theory of limits (see Chapter 5) is, after all, not without application. Any trend can be pushed to a marked degree and finally reach its limit. That the pendulum might swing in this particular case is at least something to be kept in mind, unlikely as it seems at the moment.

Questions of uncertainty and of the likelihood of success of the social transformations also arise. The principle of transformations is central and fundamental, as Etzioni makes clear, to his entire enterprise. Yet, lack of clarity as well as much uncertainty exists relative to this principle; indeed, this is an apt illustration of a process that sounds quite precise but is in fact extremely vague. It is evident that all societies are in the process of *some* socio-cultural change, but Etzioni clearly means much more than this. Are any limits set or assumptions made with regard to these human-directed transformations? Would he hold for American society that the United States Constitution, Bill of Rights, and the like are guaranteed? To what extent are the past order and its practices weighed in making the transformations, or do the current wants of the mobilized publics entirely determine the actions taken? The Etzioni statement does not make these matters clear. It is abundantly clear, on the other hand, that the principle of transformability is no trivial item. Both the public and social scientists would want to scrutinize carefully exactly how it would be applied. Nor is it easy to assess to what extent an adoption of the policy of social transformations would result in an exchange of admitted problems (including inequities) for perpetual turmoil. This is not necessarily a *negative* criticism. We simply suggest that Etzioni has not devoted enough explanation to a principle of the active society that is indeed crucial.

Some persons might maintain that, even apart from the preceding, uncertainties are likely to accrue to the social transformations in any case. After publics had decided to adopt certain programs is it likely that elites would modify or extend the activities once the program was

26 See Professor Philip Hauser's presidential address before the American Sociological Association bearing that title, which was published in the *American Sociological Review*, Vol. 34, No. 1 (February, 1969), 1–19.

started? Fallibilities and corruptions of elites might occur as in present-day society except that, in the more fluid transformation-minded order, they might involve greater risks. Some conjecture is necessarily involved in these comments.

A practical question is: Would the general public be willing to adopt such a program of social transformations? Unless much more information is provided and assurances of stability are built into the program, we would be skeptical of public adoption as of the present time. (Others may elect, of course, to come to a different answer.)

The main objection to the policy of social transformations as the majority of American citizens would interpret it would be that—whatever the possible benefits—this is a "blank-check" policy or (to change the metaphor) one constituting a veritable leap in the dark. And we suggest that the majority of Americans would want none of it. Nor would many be mollified by the argument that the people themselves, in the form of their mobilized publics, would be in the driver's seat; hence, the actions taken would be of their own making. Many would hold that, either different kinds of publics will clash, with the result that the situation will not differ greatly from the present, or special and unwanted manipulations of policy will likely take place. In either case a sizeable percentage of the people would reject the policy of social transformations.[27] We remind the reader that we are referring to the *predominant* attitude of the American public in this matter. Some segments of that public would undoubtedly subscribe to perpetual transformations at this time, regarding which we shall comment presently. We venture to suggest that sociologists and other social scientists would be more attracted to the Etzioni thesis than the predominant adult public. Many possible reasons might relate to this, but we think that Glazer [28] is essentially correct in observing that contemporary sociologists generally favor change and only slightly defend the status quo. The Bauers make the interesting point that "among intellectuals social pessimism is more often and more readily approved than is social optimism." [29] The optimist runs the risk of being regarded as uncritical, possibly of having sold out. The critical-pessimistic syndrome favors change. Then, of course, a significant number of social scientists are members of minority groups, and hence might be ex-

[27] Some will have memories, from their own experiences or from the study of history, of cliques grasping power. It is no exaggeration to say that some will think of the Hitler experience in Germany during the 1930s, ridiculous as this might seem to others. Here, too, the people appeared to approve of the "transformations."

[28] Nathan Glazer, "The Ideological Use of Sociology," Chapter 3 in Paul F. Lazarsfeld, *et al.*, (eds.), *The Uses of Sociology* (New York: Basic Books, Inc., 1967), especially p. 69.

[29] Raymond A. and Alice H. Bauer, "America, 'Mass Society,' and Mass Media," *The Journal of Social Issues*, Vol. XVI, No. 3 (1960), 59.

pected to be cordial to transformations. Finally, radicals who have completely rejected the existing system would obviously tend to favor social transformations.[30]

The reluctance of the *general public* to support the active program of Professor Etzioni (particularly the element of social transformations) would center on, we suggest, two points. First, the public would hold that American society would lose much if—despite the high hopes of this system of societal guidance—the results were to be grossly disappointing or even catastrophic. Small cliques might gain control of the new, more fluid system or other problems might develop. It is not as though this nation would start from a poverty, disease-ridden, mostly illiterate, politically uninformed, and unstable condition as, for instance, characterizes many underdeveloped nations. Proponents of the Etzioni conception would no doubt retort that activized publics pursuing wanted social goals would not be likely to bring forth catastrophic results. However convincing this might be to some people, we suggest that the general public would not be impressed with this; the latter would emphasize the "runaway" possibilities of a system that deliberately attempts to alter social structures and processes unless positive containments were built into the system. *If* unfortunate results were to occur, the public would see American society as much the loser. The majority of individuals would have in mind the various strengths of this nation—economic, industrial, scientific, technological, political, educational, medical, and so on—admitting the presence of consequential problems. Nevertheless, they would point to the United States as a leading nation of the world in many respects and would insist that proper emphasis be placed upon the strengths as well as the problems.[31] They might contrast this nation with its high standard of living and advanced institutions and political strengths (as well as problems), with, say, India or Russia or, if one wishes, with Nigeria or Ghana. The public, we venture to predict, would see the policy of constant transformations as highly risky involving real possibilities for social loss.

The second point is that the public, considering that America might have much to lose with constant social transformations, appears to

[30] See Richard Flacks, "Social and Cultural Meanings of Student Revolt: Some Informal Comparative Observations,"*Social Problems,* Vol. 17, No. 3 (Winter, 1970), 353.

[31] Radicals, of course, would not agree with this emphasis. If one believes that the past is a colossal, unintelligible failure or that the only salvation for this country is to burn everything down and start again, this view does not admit of a large number of "strengths." These two perspectives obviously do not square with each other. The general public considers the dissident ("the past is a failure") view to be emotional and immature, factually incorrect, and extremist. The dissidents emphasize the various national problems—racial, urban, pollution, and other—and the necessity of much change.

doubt that such transformations are needed anyway. Because the public has never (to our knowledge) expressed its view on this question *directly,* we shall have to discuss this inferentially. Nevertheless, we propose to present reasonably solid data (at any rate, the best available) showing the reactions of the public or special groups to related questions. Ideally we should like to point to data concerning such a question as: How many American citizens think that their society is inauthentic? In this instance, however, even an approximate estimate seems to be difficult, if not impossible, because Etzioni tells us that (1) people may have a feeling of inauthenticity but may be unaware of it (p. 633); (2) people may have inauthenticity feelings of varying depths (p. 634); and (3) a person's acceptance, rejection, or even ambivalance in regard to a particular social structure does not allow us to judge whether or not his commitment is inauthentic. (p. 634) It seems, then, that as one gets down to particulars the concept has a jelly-like and obscure (hence nonmeasurable, certainly as of this time) nature. No doubt each person's feeling would vary in time too. Granted the intangible nature of the concept, it does seem probable that a sizeable number of Americans may feel (to varying degrees of depth) that their society gives the appearance of being responsive while the underlying condition is alienating. But how large is a "sizeable number" and what percentage would it be of the total 200-million-plus population? Apparently one has no way of knowing. Making a volume assessment of inauthenticity feelings under the circumstances apparently has to be written off.

Etzioni himself concludes: "(a) that post-modern society is inauthentic to a significant degree, though the scope and depth of its inauthenticity has not yet been established; (b) that this condition of post-modern society seems to be more the result of the inauthenticity of political processes than of the disintegration of cohesive units or technological-economic factors; and (c) that inauthenticity in one institution nourishes it in others. . . ."[32]

We may generally agree with these sentiments, but, again, what is being inauthentic "to a significant degree?" But if our original question has to remain unanswered, we at least wish to probe further, for example, relative to (1) contentment with the society, (2) the wish for change, and (3) the desire for constant or continuous transformations (if possible).

Is it likely that various public opinion polls would shed light on the extent of inauthenticity and related matters not through direct questioning but via probings of related concepts or similar ideas? We shall

---

[32] Etzioni, *op. cit.,* p. 635.

examine a series of pollings endeavoring to keep as close to the present time as is possible.

A Gallup Poll of March, 1968, asks: "On the whole, would you say that you are satisfied or dissatisfied with the future facing you and your family?" [33] Of the total national (United States) sample, 48 per cent said that they were satisfied; 46 per cent said that they were dissatisfied; and 6 per cent had no opinion. However, one can be satisfied or dissatisfied for a variety of reasons, many of which might have nothing to do with inauthenticity. The per cent dissatisfied was slightly higher for women than for men; higher for the less educated than for college educated; higher for farmers than for white-collar and professional occupations; higher for older people than for those of age 21–29 and 30–49; and sizeably higher for those having an income under $3,000 (54 per cent) than for those having an income of $10,000 or more (40 per cent).

A Gallup Poll of August, 1968, probes with respect to the "sick society" question: "Some people are calling this country a 'sick society.' Do you agree or disagree with them?" [34] Of the total United States sample, 36 per cent agreed that this nation is a "sick society"; 58 per cent disagreed; and 6 per cent had no opinion. Of those affirming, Negroes had a higher percentage than whites (48 to 35); grade school educated were sizeably higher than college educated (39 per cent and 30 per cent); and Protestants were higher than Roman Catholics (38 per cent and 32 per cent). The sex and age categories showed little disparity in their reactions. Again, one could consider a society "ailing" for diverse reasons.

A series of Gallup pollings during July, 1968, delving into "Is Life Getting Better?" brought the following results: A high percentage of the United States Sample (80 per cent) believed that, "Life in the United States is getting better in terms of intelligence"; [35] an extremely high percentage of people (88 per cent) believed that, "Life is getting better in terms of knowledge"; [36] only about one quarter of the sample (26 per cent) believed that, "Life is getting better in terms of happiness"; [37] and only about one sixth of the sample (15 per cent) believed that, "Life is getting better in terms of peace of mind." [38] Here the

[33] *Gallup Opinion Index,* Report No. 34, April, 1968 (Princeton, N. J.: Gallup International, Inc., 1968), p. 28.

[34] *Gallup Opinion Index,* Report No. 38, August, 1968 (Princeton, N.J.: Gallup International, Inc., 1968), p. 18.

[35] *Gallup Opinion Index,* Report No. 41, November, 1968 (Princeton, N. J.: Gallup International, Inc., 1968), p. 22.

[36] *Ibid.,* p. 21.

[37] *Ibid.,* p. 19.

[38] *Ibid.,* p. 20.

results, although of interest, are probably to be viewed as mixed and uncertain insofar as inauthenticity is concerned.

A Harris Poll during December, 1968, probed the liberalism-conservatism of the respondents: "What do you consider yourself—conservative, middle-of-the-road, liberal, or radical?" [39] White people were divided as follows: conservative 39 per cent; middle-of-the-road 33 per cent; liberal 15 per cent; and radical 2 per cent (and 11 per cent "not sure"). The Black distribution was conservative 30 per cent; middle-of-the-road 21 per cent; liberal 30 per cent; and none radical (with 19 per cent "not sure"). If the usual identification of conservatives with those advocating little change, middle-of-the-road with those desiring moderate change, liberals with those espousing substantial (but not drastic) change, and radicals advocating drastic change is presumed, this bears implications for individuals' degrees of satisfaction with prevailing conditions. Again, one's degree of satisfaction is not necessarily related to inauthenticity.

A Gallup Poll during March, 1970,[40] involving a national adult sample, inquired whether people identified themselves as liberal or conservative (the expressions radical and middle-of-the-road are ignored here). It is of interest that Americans on this sample by a ratio of 3-to-2 preferred to be labeled conservative rather than liberal.

A Harris poll concerning *alienation* was administered during April, 1968.[41] A "Total Alienation Score" was computed on the basis of seven reactions, and the total national sample score was 30 per cent; the score for Negroes was 54 per cent as of this date. In 1966, the total score had been 24 per cent, with 34 per cent for Negroes. Some of the statements (to which the sample responded) were: "What I personally think doesn't count very much; People running the country don't really care what happens to people like me; and I feel left out of things."

These pollings provided findings that are not necessarily easy either to interrelate or to apply to the extent-of-inauthenticity estimate in the United States. Different readers may draw different conclusions from them. Here we attempt to make one very general conclusion only, namely: the feelings of satisfaction (or the opposite), the views regarding the "sick society," the self-placements as to conservatism, liberal, and so forth, and the alienation scores suggest, in a general way, that the motivation for continued social transformations is *not strong*. If the "Total Alienation Score" is to be accepted at face value, 30 per cent of the total American society is disclosed to be alienated—and 70

[39] Hazel Erskine, "The Polls," *Public Opinion Quarterly*, Vol. XXXIII, No. 1 (Spring, 1969), 157–158.

[40] *The New York Times* (April 16, 1970).

[41] Same as footnote 39, p. 152, Hazel Erskine, "The Polls."

per cent is *not*.[42] Again, we concede that others may wish to conclude differently; pollings such as these undoubtedly deliver different messages, which conceivably might be interpreted in different ways. All persons reflecting over this evidence, furthermore, have to admit that the information is at best tangential to the concept of inauthenticity and allied subjects. It would seem to us, however, that for a society to desire intensive and perpetual social transformations, the feeling of dissatisfaction, of alienation, of the society being "sick," of desiring considerable (probably drastic) change would indeed need to be strong. For the two reasons given, then, we suggest that the application of Etzioni's principle of social transformation would not be accepted by the American people at the present time. In outlining the elements and operations of the active society, if they are to be applied to this society, Etzioni has moved in the right direction; however, if our perspectives are correct, it seems that he has gone too far.[43]

Generational Variations

Our interpretation of the preceding evidence indicates that American adults would not accept Professor Etzioni's principle of social transformation and allied considerations of societal guidance, at least at this time. But the reactions of American youth could well be a different matter. If youth is defined as "men and women aged 18 through 24," it is clear that one segment of this category of people at least holds at this time radically different perspectives; we shall presently comment on this segment. Youth culture, to be sure, has a distinctive thrust of its own.[44] Adolescence is a period during which a series of largely irrevocable decisions have to be made; it is also one during which the socialization process is making its mark on personality development. Youths, then, approach the adult world with diverse attitudes and experiences, depending on the detailed occurrences of socialization. The "silent majority of the young," says Grinder,[45] find that their

[42] Of course, 46 per cent of the respondents replied that they were dissatisfied with the future facing them and their families. We have noted, however, that many factors may be associated with such a feeling, often having nothing to do with inauthenticity; purely *individual* elements could relate to this, such as some family member having made a poor occupational choice.

[43] On the other hand, from the standpoint of certain radical groups, it could be that he has not gone far enough.

[44] From the vast literature on this subject, the following are suggested: Talcott Parsons, "Youth in the Context of American Society," *Daedalus,* Vol. 91 (1962), 97–123; R. E. Grinder, "Distinctiveness and Thrust in the American Youth Culture," *Journal of Social Issues,* Vol. XXV, No. 2 (April, 1969), 7–20; and Edgar Z. Friedenberg, *Coming of Age in America* (New York: Vintage Books, 1967).

[45] Grinder, *op. cit.,* p. 7.

social relations satisfactorily prepare them for the transition from play groups and youth activities to adult roles; but many others are not in this contented category. The traditional issue of generational conflict has revolved around the issue of "Who should be in the driver's seat?" (with confident and ambitious youth alligned against experienced adults). This phenomenon occasions no surprise. An ample minority of youth, however, goes beyond this. It largely rejects the adult world itself. Continuing the earlier analogy, they do not wish to "drive the car" and "call the signals." They don't even want to go where the car is going; they want to get out and have nothing to do with the journey.[46] Friedenberg may or may not be correct in labeling this segment as "loosely the hippy group." These people are likely to welcome with open arms the active society—social transformations and all. In fact, mostly rejecting the social structure of the adult world, this segment of youth is likely to say: "The more transformations the better."

A survey of American youth conducted for *Fortune* magazine in 1968, by Daniel Yankelovich, Inc.,[47] arrives at a similar conclusion in distinguishing between these two divisions of youth. This survey provides in-depth interviews with a total of 718 young men and women from this 18–24 age range—with the sample made representative regarding race, sex, marital status, family income, and geographic region. The sample was divided into those attending college (or who *had* attended college) and noncollege youth; college youth were found to significantly differ as to (1) those who were interested in college as a springboard for a better career and a better position in society—regarded as the traditional motivation for attending college; and (2) those who assumed these practical benefits and, on the other hand, were especially interested in "making changes in existing society." The *Fortune* study labeled the former as the "practical-minded group" (it comprised 58 per cent of the college attenders); it called the second, change-minded students the "forerunner group" (which, then, comprised 42 per cent of the college people). *Fortune* believes, however,

---

[46] Actually Friedenberg's language is more colorful than ours in describing this. He writes:

> *"Instead of arguing about who should be in the driver's seat?, young people loosely identified as hippy (continuing this metaphor) feel as if they were locked in the back of a vehicle that had been built to corrupt specifications, was unsafe at any speed, and was being driven by a middle-aged drunk. . . . What they want is to get out while they are still alive."*

E. Z. Friedenberg, "Current Patterns of Generational Conflict," *Journal of Social Issues*, Vol. XXV, No. 2 (April, 1969), 22–23.

[47] *Fortune*, Vol. LXXIX, No. 1 (January, 1969), *American Youth: Its Outlook Is Changing the World*, "What They Believe: A Fortune Survey," pp. 70–71 and 179–180.

that the forerunners will become more prevalent in the years ahead.[48] Again, a reasonable conclusion seems to be that the forerunners would generally embrace the active society—with its many social transformations. Another conclusion, indeed an assertion of the *Fortune*-Yankelovich survey, is that the problem of the generation gap is centered (on the youth side) on this forerunner group.

The forerunners, constituting 42 per cent of the *Fortune* sample who attended college, would comprise an estimated 2,300,000 persons when projected to the entire national population. They are (says *Fortune*) "among the most privileged members of the most affluent society in history," [49] yet they directly challenge the institutions of that society. Their attitudes and values as revealed in the survey probing are exemplified by the following: (1) One half of the forerunner group agrees with those who have called ours a sick society; this compares with 32 per cent maintaining this belief from the "practical-minded" (college) group and 44 per cent holding this belief from the noncollege group. (It also compares, as the reader will recall, with the 36 per cent having this belief in the Gallup *adult* polling of that same year, 1968. In short, the Gallup poll percentage averages out as an approximate figure if the practical-minded college and the noncollege percentages are combined). (2) *Fortune* asked: "What values do you believe are always worth fighting for?" (aside from the particular issue of the Vietnam war)—listing various possibilities. The value of *protecting our national interest* was checked by 40 per cent of the forerunner group (as compared with 73 per cent of the noncollege and 65 per cent of the practical-minded people). *Containing the Communists* was checked by 28 per cent of the forerunners (as compared with 68 per cent of the noncollege group and 59 per cent of the practical-minded group). *Maintaining our position of power in the world* was checked by 22 per cent of the forerunners (in contrast to 54 per cent of the noncollege group and 46 per cent of the practical-minded group). And *fighting for our honor* was checked by 20 per cent of the forerunners (in contrast to 64 per cent of the noncollege group and 44 per cent of the practical-minded college group). Then (3) the *Fortune* survey asked if civil disobedience is justified under any circumstances. To this 66 per cent of the forerunners answered "Yes" (as compared with 18 per cent of the noncollege group and 32 per cent of the practical-minded college group).[50]

The number of those holding the forerunner views may well increase during coming years as the *Fortune* staff believes, although this should

48 *Ibid.,* p. 70.
49 *Ibid.,* p. 68.
50 *Ibid.,* pp. 70–71.

not be accepted as a foregone conclusion. For one thing, this segment of the college population will soon join the adult labor force. It may be that we shall have to wait to see the impact of occupational experience on this group. In short, they will soon attain adulthood themselves, and then look back at the "new youth." The crucial issue of these maturing years (which usually include occupational and often include parental experience—which can be sobering) is: Will these Americans that were "change-minded" in college *continue* to maintain these views (or possibly even intensify them) such that a relentless wave of change will sweep over the society, *or* will they gradually adjust to the prevailing norms of the majority and finally become "pillars of society" as has often occurred in the past? [51] So often the "college radical" has settled down with the attainment of a position of power to become the arch conservative. Physiological and socio-psychological attributes of periods in the life cycle as well as other influences, of course, relate to this. Still, the present age is different in some respects, and we may have to wait to see the future developments of the present-day cohort of change-minded, 18-to-24-year-olds.

Our interest in the forerunner college group does not stop here. Because the existence of a generation gap—or, for that matter, a gap between the sexes or between the races—is socially dysfunctional, an effort might be made to reduce the gap. Careful attention to the criticisms and complaints of the forerunners might be worthwhile; mature America might consider if any (and how many) complaints are indeed valid and should constitute a basis for change. The forerunner group undoubtedly includes many and varied types of individuals. Many of the latter are serious and responsible. Individuals of this sort merit the attention, even the gratitude, of mature America, regardless of whether or not one finally concludes that their views are "right" or "wrong." The early *family life* of the forerunner type, as indicated by a number of studies,[52] is of interest. Many of the parents are in the high-income, highly educated, and high occupational-status categories. The parents typically have a strong commitment to intellectuality, are politically aware, and tend to be skeptical about conventional middle-class values and life-styles (such as the materialistic emphasis, status

[51] Flacks, maintaining a radical position, holds that the current college revolutionaries comprise the vanguard of a new social and cultural era that is struggling to emerge. Flacks, *op. cit.,* pp. 354 and 356.

[52] Kenneth Keniston, *Young Radicals* (New York: Harcourt, Brace and World, 1968); Richard Flacks, "Who Protests: The Social Bases of the Student Movement," in J. Foster and D. Long (ed.), *Protest: Student Activism in America* (New York: William Morrow and Co., 1970), pp. 134–157; and D. Westby and R. G. Braungart, "Class and Politics in the Family Backgrounds of Student Political Activists," *American Sociological Review,* Vol. 31 (October, 1966), 690–692.

striving, strict methods of rearing children, and sex repression). The socialization of their sons and daughters, then, took note of these attitudes. It is not that these parents were usually permissive or over-indulgent, but (in the words of Flacks) "they rather consciously or-ganized family life to support antiauthoritarian and self-assertive im-pulses on the part of their children." [53] As these children moved on to further socialization in school, they frequently encountered repres-sive and arbitrary authority; with further transitions to the larger society they were no doubt especially sensitive to hypocrisies, rigidities, and injustices of institutions (and tended to question fundamental premises of institutions). Meeting kindred spirits in college and else-where, they tended to create a kind of counterculture.

However, this cannot be assumed to tell the full story of the per-spectives and early family life of change-minded youth. Steven Kel-man,[54] Harvard '70 (valedictorian of his class), offers different ideas in his participant-observer account of the Harvard confrontation and strike of April, 1969. His statement is noteworthy for a number of reasons, not the least of which is that it provides an inside reckoning of events as seen by participating students. Kelman, to be sure, writes as a socialist (he is currently national president of the Young People's Socialist League). He is highly critical of the Harvard radicals, espe-cially the Students for a Democratic Society (SDS) group. The diversity of the change-minded (or, as *Fortune* called them, the "forerunner") students is clearly indicated. Some dissidents do have the psychological outlook and family upbringing described by Flacks, Keniston, and others; Kelman refers to them as the "hereditary radicals" and they do not comprise a large number. But at Harvard they lost control to the New Left. Also, one has to consider the cultural radicals who are generally alienated students and, finally, the moderates who eventually joined forces with the SDS faction in control, the New Left. This coalition brought on the Harvard confrontation. In short, the change-minded group at Harvard was quite pluralistic.

Many of those in this coalition (especially the moderates) were not change-minded even in their freshman year, never mind the conditions of their early family life. What is strikingly told by Kelman is the process by which the SDS gradually won over the moderates to its side during the years 1966–1969. The former gained control of the mass media (in this case the Harvard *Crimson*). The latter spread the word that the New Left was "where the action is" and the monopoly outlet for youthful idealism; the SDS was placed in the limelight, other

---

53 Flacks, "Social and Cultural Meanings . . ." , *Social Problems, op. cit.,* p. 348.
54 Steven Kelman, *Push Comes to Shove, The Escalation of Student Protest* (Bos-ton: Houghton Mifflin Co., 1970).

groups in the shadows. The SDS was able to establish a university course given with credit (Social Relations 148/9) that indoctrinated students along radical lines and prepared for the confrontation. Little by little the Harvard scene approached a "dream world." Kelman is eloquent on this point:

> *Where else but in this dreamworld could socialists be denounced as reactionaries? Where else but in this dreamworld could it be argued that a "course" which presented primarily a diet of SDS pamphlets as its reading list and taught by section men whose only qualification was adherence to the SDS ideology was no more biased than the typical course given at Harvard? Where else but in this dreamworld could the statement oft-repeated during the strike that "we've learned more during this week than in all our courses at Harvard" be viewed as anything but a pathetic admission of how little serious work or study one previously had done? Where else but in this dreamworld could "liberated" files refer to stolen documents, a "liberated" university refer to one where none of the academic functions for which a university is set up in the first place are going on, and a "liberated" student refer to one who, on the verge of exhaustion from prolonged sleeplessness and endless mind-dulling meetings, participates catatonically in a series of robot chants and parades?* [55]

The SDS view was at any rate put over at Harvard for a brief period. A leading university, which might be assumed to harbor only a small amount of alienation (Kelman thinks the latter was small), succumbed to clever manipulation. Kelman's view is that the SDS brand of activism is highly suspect. In his words, "SDS is deeply sick today. . . . The current leadership of SDS has subverted the noble ideas of a just and humane society by making SDS into an organization for the propagandization of barbarism." [56]

Others who were at Harvard during 1969 may dispute Kelman's account—and his conclusions. We shall not attempt to say, moreover, how typical the Harvard events were of other campus disruptions. Many Americans will disapprove of the ideology of the SDS. [57] Also democratic society, many will insist, has to protect itself from the archdestroyer, nihilistic type that has no interest in constructive ideas. But the change-minded types include sincere, idealistic, and responsible

[55] *Ibid.*, pp. 238–239.
[56] *Ibid.*, p. 115.
[57] *At its June, 1969, convention the right wing of SDS, in expelling the Progressive Labor party from SDS, set up . . . the following "principle" as a condition for SDS membership. According to their official statement, those who do not "support the Democratic Republic of (North) Vietnam, as well as the Democratic Republic of China, the Peoples' Republic of Korea and Albania, and the Republic of Cuba" are "no longer members of SDS."*

Ibid., p. 112. (Italics are Kelman's)

people, too. Their views, it will be asserted, should be heard. Whether very much of the generation gap will be closed as the result of examining the views of the latter, we cannot say. The effort should be made. Even some modest reduction will be worthwhile.

Tentative Conclusions

This discussion has carried us beyond the consideration of Etzioni's ideas of social transformations and other elements of his theory of societal guidance. However, our first conclusion is that the majority of the American people would *not* accept his principle of social transformations but that the forerunner (dissident) type of American youth (including some "converted moderates," based on the Harvard experience) probably *would* accept it. An exceedingly important question at this point, therefore, is whether the forerunner group is indeed a *forerunner group* (that is to say, it will increase in number and lead the way to a new era) or whether it will be a gradually receding group. If the former is to occur, it will have to impress the American people with the soundness of its ideas as well as by its methods of operation. It will have to convince and satisfy its own adherents in these respects.

From the standpoint of the forerunners, then, developing sound programs and carrying them out acceptably (certainly nonviolently) has to be regarded as important. Taking over buildings on college campuses and like activities during recent years has not been assuring in this connection. American public opinion has moved in the conservative direction in recent years, although we shall not attribute this solely to youth and campus activities. Even more telling, perhaps, are the results of a large sampling of reactions of (United States) university and college faculty members. College faculty often have perspectives similar to the students' in many regards. Yet a survey of 60,447 faculty members sponsored by the Carnegie Commission on Higher Education shows that more than 80 per cent of the respondents believed that "campus demonstrations by militant students are a threat to academic freedom." Furthermore, over 76 per cent agreed either strongly or with reservations that "students who disrupt the functioning of a college should be expelled or suspended." [58] It seems that college faculties, whom the study describes as more liberal than the general population on most issues,[59] have become more conservative with respect to these

[58] Reported in *The New York Times* (April 23, 1970). The survey was taken during the 1968–1969 academic year.

[59] We have earlier noted that social scientists as a group often show more liberal responses to issues than the average faculty member. For example, in this Carnegie survey, 35.3 per cent of the sociologists favored immediate withdrawal of United States troops from Vietnam, as compared with 15.7 per cent of members of chemistry departments. *Ibid.*

campus matters. The respondents opposed suggestions that students exercise control over faculty appointments and promotions, undergraduate admissions policies, content of courses, and requirements for a bachelor's degree. The avoidance of excesses is a significant item with respect to any social movement, although we are not dwelling on the specific matters just mentioned.

A second tentative conclusion is that activism as a process of sociocultural change is itself under some assessment, more so than we may realize. As stated at the beginning of this chapter, this outlook, which seeks to anticipate and direct change—to determine one's wants and vigorously try to attain them—is, we believe, important and generally promising. The American people, in our judgment, generally favor this view. But it may be that excesses can develop here, too, and people should not expect to attain *everything* that they want—partly because other goals have to be considered in addition.

Stability, for instance, is another such goal. In the light of this reasoning some observers may indeed see the forerunner individuals as correct in some respects, mistaken in others. Although often they are products of superior background, their socialization experience has hardly helped them to adjust to the existing order—quite the reverse. With their self-assertive yet counterculture orientation, some will maintain that they are simply asking for *too much*. Does any citizen have the right, some will ask, to expect perfection (and on one's own terms) with regard to any and all institutions? And then, if society is not as they want it, the pronouncement of a minority may be: "The only salvation for this country is to burn everything down and start again." The socialization experience of this minority has stressed *their* wishes, not so much adjusting to others or seeking improvements steadily within the system. It could be that benefit would be obtained both for society and for themselves if (1) society paid attention to their ideas and (2) they made an effort to adjust to an admittedly imperfect society, all the while pressing for the improvements in which they believe. At any rate, some modesty may need to be linked with the activist approach. Desirable as we believe the latter is, people may not be able to obtain *everything* that they want. At least the latter is a large order.

SOME ALTERNATIVE VIEWS CONCERNING ACTIVISM: AN OUTLINE

In suggesting some alternative views relative to activism we make two affirmations at the outset: First, let us make clear once again that we favor some brand of the active orientation, and we have declared that, in our judgment, the American public is also generally cordial to this perspective. Secondly, we favor *many* of the ideas of Professor Etzioni, even if we have cast doubt on his policy of continued social transformations for the reasons that have been given. We have, at the same time, concluded that a majority of the American public would find the policy unacceptable, certainly at this time. It is possible that this particular policy might be modified in some manner to make it acceptable for American society; for example, limits might be built into the transformations. This policy without modification might be appropriate, it is conceded, for a smaller nation such as Israel or one of the Scandinavian nations.[60] The transformations might be more manageable in a smaller setting, involving a smaller number of people.

The alternative conception to the active society that we are about to propose, albeit in outline form, provides for (1) most of the elements of Professor Etzioni's conception with, however, the social-transformation principle omitted, and (2) the addition of several new factors. Among the elements of Etzioni's that we find attractive and valuable (hence to be retained) are fostering better-informed and more active publics, which is a trend of American socio-political life in any case; [61] making a greater effort to be responsive to the needs of citizens; mobilizing resources of various kinds in order to meet problems; increasing the use of all knowledge, including social science knowledge; using the principles and processes of cybernetics insofar as the application of that science to social data permits; and following the practice of social planning. The ideal with regard to the latter, it seems to us, is not to have a planned society but to emphasize what Rupert B. Vance has called the "continuously planning society." [62] Let us discuss several of these elements briefly before considering the newer ones that we would add.

Government is undoubtedly the social institution that is prominent in taking actions that would improve the life of citizens. We assume, therefore, that in an active society government will make an extra effort to initiate such measures. However, to better respond to the needs of citizens is to make a decision with respect to a fundamental issue. Often efforts in behalf of citizens encounter institutional lags and inertias. Should society *compel* institutions to change policies in

---

[60] It would not be appropriate for traditional (underdeveloped) societies, however, because of the factors of illiteracy and rudimentary education; the latter would prevent the effective participation of publics.

[61] We discount the factor of *too much* activity and participation of publics—hence the occurrence of undue turmoil and uproar—at this time. Only a few years ago the public was very apathetic. But this could become an acute problem and perhaps soon.

[62] Rupert B. Vance, "The Place of Planning in Social Dynamics," in H. W. Odum and Katherine Jocher (eds.), *In Search of the Regional Balance of America* (Chapel Hill, N. C.: University of North Carolina Press, 1945).

order to take up lags? The policy of social transformations, if accepted and followed, would do exactly that—if the informed publics mobilized their resources along that line. This is a policy, a *method* of accomplishing things, that we do not believe Americans would sanction; they would accept this only as a matter of last resort. To transform or rejuvenate an institution in such a manner means running roughshod over the institutional or organizational leaders and overseers. Even though a large number of people might wish to correct a lag, the majority would not approve of this procedure. Organizational leaders and others in proper authority have the right to decide policies. But other methods can be used to induce change. Publics can be mobilized. The pressure of public opinion can be strong and unrelenting. Social inventions can be devised that will facilitate change. In short, desired, orderly change can be achieved in various ways. Much as many Americans might wish to see certain institutional lags corrected, the establishment of a policy of social transformations introduces the factor of continuous instability. And this is a price that many would not like to pay for the correction of certain lags, if other methods of dealing with situations can be devised. "Is there a rate of social change so rapid and so general as to be inconsistent with stable behavior?" is a question posed by Levy.[63] The question merits study and reflection. Just as a lower limit exists in the rate of change compatible with a relatively modernized society, so could it be said that an upper limit exists beyond which proper human adjustment is impaired. As Levy also observes,[64] instabilities that do develop tend to spread easily. The active society bespeaks the active pursuit of change. With this principle we are in accord. However, societies also have needs of stability. It appears to us that Etzioni has overdone the transformation factor and insufficiently provided for reasonable stability.

One feature of the modern era is the enormous increase of knowledge (including social science knowledge). Bell has with impressive elaboration set forth the structure of "the knowledge society." [65] Concerning social science, the great increase of knowledge coupled with the will of many social scientists to use that knowledge practically marks the present scene. Etzioni has himself called attention to the exponential growth of social science, which means that "society has much more information about itself, a development that generates a whole new set of options for societal control, new decisions to be made, and a new

[63] Marion J. Levy, Jr., *Modernization and the Structure of Societies,* Vol. II (Princeton, N. J.: Princeton University Press, 1966), p. 789.

[64] *Ibid.*

[65] Daniel Bell, "The Measurement of Knowledge and Technology," Chapter 5 in Eleanor B. Sheldon and Wilbert E. Moore (eds.), *Indicators of Social Change* (New York: Russell Sage Foundations, 1968), pp. 198–240.

range of processes to be guided." [66] Moreover, the projected increase in the number of scientists, as well as the projected increase of undergraduate college attendance as a per cent of the 18–21 age group up to the year 2000 [67] (which would affect the future state of public opinion), is expected to aid the attainment of an active society. These various knowledge factors would seem to favor the gradual attainment of an active society, although the actual participation of sociologists and/or the use of sociological knowledge appears to be somewhat disillusioning as of this time. At least Gans, in summarizing the work of sociologists in antipoverty and community action programs of the 1960s, declares that their role was "all too minor" in these projects; [68] and Pettigrew and Back, in considering the uses of sociology in the desegregation process (thus since 1954), conclude that "the disuse here is more immediately apparent than the use." [69] Nevertheless, sociologists have been used to some extent in predicting racial trends, in interpreting specific events, and in consulting with respect to desegregation. Glazer, in discussing the ideological uses of sociology, makes the disconcerting point (for the present theme) that sociologists more often seem "to attack society and its arrangements than to figure out how they might be improved." They usually do not "prop up the facade of society." [70] Daniel Patrick Moynihan, social scientist and former adviser to President Nixon, has made a similar charge: Admitting that during past years he has been optimistic as to the use of social science knowledge in the management of public affairs, he now asserts that social scientists are better at "analyzing social ills without at the same time displaying a similar competence at offering solutions." [71] Perhaps, a bit sobered by such examples, we may conclude that social science knowledge is itself impressively increasing and we *hope* that social scientists will be able to contribute actively and effectively in the guidance of social processes.

We have earlier discussed general principles of cybernetics (see

[66] Etzioni, *op. cit.*, pp. 9–10.

[67] Bell, *op. cit.*, Table 17 on p. 217. Original source of data was Allan M. Cartter and Robert Farrell, "Higher Education in the Last Third of the Century," *The Educational Record* (Spring, 1965), 121.

[68] Herbert J. Gans, "Urban Poverty and Social Planning," Chapter 16 in Paul F. Lazarsfeld, W. H. Sewell, and H. Wilensky (eds.), *The Uses of Sociology* (New York: Basic Books, Inc., 1967), especially p. 437.

[69] Thomas F. Pettigrew and Kurt W. Back, "Sociology in the Desegregation Process: Its Use and Disuse," Chapter 25 in Lazarsfeld, Sewell, and Wilensky (eds.), *ibid.*

[70] Nathan Glazer, "The Ideological Uses of Sociology," Chapter 3 in *ibid*, p. 75–76 and 699.

[71] As reported in *The New York Times* (May 16, 1970).

Chapter 3). Although we hold out promise for the use of cybernetics, partly because the feedback mechanism is very useful for social relationships (also major advances will undoubtedly be made during coming years concerning the computer itself), nevertheless *social* communication is extremely complicated. Undoubtedly a greater recognition of social-system complexity will need to be made, as Gross [72] observed in connection with the use of cybernetics (he is receptive to it) regarding social-systems accounting. Cybernetics should be useful in relation to steering mechanisms of ongoing systems, although one must realize that it is still comparatively untried with reference to socio-cultural systems. In short, we are hopeful relative to the use of cybernetics, tempered however with a note of caution.

Some New Elements

We now propose to discuss new factors that we believe may well be added in the effort to attain an active society. These factors have been previously described in earlier chapters, but they may constitute worthy additions to the capabilities of a society that attempts to be responsive to its citizens and, in general, to the meeting of needs. The discussion here will have to be brief.

The Active Facilitation of Inventions. Inventions constitute a major form of socio-cultural addition; yet, in practically all societies they are made only on the basis of individual whim and interest. The latter is likely to be spasmodic and intermittent. For the society that is actively formulating goals and making an effort to reach them—in short, seeking to control change for specific ends [73]—this procedure is inadequate. Innovations are of too much consequence for that. Individual inventors may perceive needs and endeavor to meet them; and some inventions, as was noted in Chapter 10, come from serendipity. However, the active society would establish a bureau or department that would constantly assess needed inventions, set priorities, and take measures that would facilitate or speed up specific inventions or even the invention process itself. The United States is an inventive-minded country; it experiences no dearth of inventions. Yet, its inventive in-

---

[72] Bertram M. Gross, "The State of the Nation: Social Systems Accounting," Chapter 3 in Raymond A. Bauer (ed.), *Social Indicators* (Cambridge, Mass.: The MIT Press, 1966), p. 178.

[73] Daniel Bell, Introduction to Herman Kahn and Anthony J. Wiener, *The Year 2000: A Framework for Speculation on the Next Thirty-Three Years* (New York: The Macmillan Company, 1967), p. xxvi.

terests seem to largely relate to mechanical inventions.[74] Many inventions in this realm could, however, be speeded up, thus bringing improvements to American citizens sooner.[75] The greater need lies with reference to social inventions. The devising of *social* technology lags considerably behind the physical. It was observed in Chapter 10 that society needs to organize for inventions—and especially social invention. It is just that an active society would surely do this. It would maintain a constant, running inventory of major problems, with a competent, imaginative staff on the lookout for mechanical and social inventions that would alleviate if not solve the problems. The demands of a fast-moving world are too consequential. The actively oriented society would not permit the important process of invention to proceed in the uncertain and haphazard manner it does now. This society would, furthermore, provide training for making inventions; again we have to emphasize that the United States is a technologically advanced nation, but it is underdeveloped in the production of *social* technology. We may ask again: Where are the MIT's and Cal Techs of *social* technology? An active society would have them. It would also have some bureaus attached to the social science departments of selected universities in which imaginative-minded and alert staff members would be devising social inventions designed to meet various state, national, and world problems.

The Active Interest in Diffusion.   Diffusion is like innovation in that it is much too important and potentially valuable a process to be permitted to take place in its current meandering, haphazard fashion. Corporations may actively, even aggressively, plan to diffuse the use of their products (in the quest of larger profits) and to adopt new products developed in other areas or even special features of those products; creators of fashions necessarily have an interest in diffusion. But, apart from this, diffusion is usually not organized and systematized. However, the answer to many a problem may be found in some other nation or region; thus, one does not always need to invent the

---

[74] It is of interest, for example, that of the one hundred scientific and technological innovations that Kahn and Wiener list as "almost certain" to be made before the year 2000, practically all are mechanical inventions. Twenty-five of them are innovations "that most people would consider unambiguous examples of progress"; another twenty-five are "clearly controversial innovations" (some would maintain that government policy might restrain or discourage their development or diffusion); and the remaining fifty are simply "interesting innovations." See *Ibid.*, Table XVIII, pp. 51–55.

[75] Taking them as an example, the twenty-five inventions listed by Kahn and Wiener "regarded by most people as unambiguous examples of progress" could be speeded up. *Ibid.* Similar lists of social inventions could be compiled, as well as problem situations in which social inventions are needed.

solution to a problem. Often it is helpful to merely look around. The active society will not have a laissez-faire attitude toward diffusion. In emphasizing responsiveness to its citizens it will have a keen interest in both the diffusion of goods and ideas between nations and internal (domestic) diffusion. After all, such problems as crime, delinquency, drug addiction, pollution, and racial difficulties are not confined to American society; other peoples may have developed ingenious answers to such problems. *Within* the United States problems of X university or Y hospital, similarly, are usually not limited to that one institution. Again, it may be helpful to look about to see if improvements or solutions have been devised by others. As mentioned in Chapter 12, it may be helpful to compare behavior and practices in *many* sectors of living. We do not believe that the full advantage of this procedure has been derived by any means, even though much informal comparing is done. Without belaboring the point, we simply state that the active society will *of course* have an interest in this important process. Many gains can accrue from this source. It will have one or more bureaus in which competent staff members will be constantly on the alert for new ideas developed in other areas that may be useful in American society. Even the humblest or most exotic people may have superb ideas or practices concerning some subject. On occasion the germ of an excellent idea or solution to a problem may be found, although an addition to, or modification of, the idea may be required before it would be appropriate for American conditions; in such cases, the staff of such a bureau would work on the adaptation. The bureau devoting its energies to diffusion would, furthermore, be drawing up plans by means of which articles or privileges might be extended from some favored groups to all segments of the American population. Finally, bureaus of diffusion would seek to bring improvements to the process of diffusion itself. Indeed, if various nations established the pattern of the active society itself, individual nations might borrow from each other practices or elements that had proven to be especially successful. If the total program worked out successfully, it would undoubtedly spread itself—much as did the city manager form of government or the fluoridation of community water supplies.

We have only briefly set forth these ideas. This is not the place for the lengthy statement.

ANNOTATED BIBLIOGRAPHY

Etzioni, Amitai, *The Active Society: A Theory of Societal and Political Processes* (New York: The Free Press, Collier-Macmillan Limited, Division of The Macmillan Company, 1968).

In addition to our comments given on page 119, this work impresses us as one of the major, provocative volumes of the present. It may comprise the focus of social science discussion for a decade or more, regardless of the extent of one's agreement with the author.

Bell, Daniel, and Kristol, Irving (eds.), *Confrontation. The Student Rebellion and the Universities* (New York: Basic Books, Inc., 1969).

Seymour Lipset provides a general profile on campus activists, and Samuel Lubell discusses the generation gap. Campus activism as manifest at Berkeley, San Francisco State, Columbia, and Cornell is described respectively by Nathan Glazer, J. Bunzel, Daniel Bell and R. Starr (writing separately on Columbia), and N. Tarcov. Kristol explores a restructure of the university, and Talcott Parsons discusses the academic system generally. This is very worthwhile, recommended reading. Most articles were previously published in *The Public Interest* (Fall, 1968).

Bendix, Reinhard, "Sociology and the Distrust of Reason," *American Sociological Review*, Vol. 35, No. 5 (October, 1970), 831–843.

A pointed warning that sociology is currently endangered by a widespread distrust of reason. Scholarly work is belittled by modern dissenters when it is not directed to problems considered "relevant." This needed, well-considered warning is found in Bendix's presidential address before the 65th Annual Meeting of the American Sociological Association, August, 1970.

Easton, David, "The New Revolution in Political Science," *The American Political Science Review*, Vol. LXIII, No. 4 (December, 1969), 1051–1061.

Contains a credo of activism that is of interest to political scientists but to sociologists and other social scientists as well. Proponents of the active view have an interest in putting knowledge to work. This article comprised the presidential address of Professor Easton before the American Political Science Association.

Flacks, Richard, "Social and Cultural Meanings of Student Revolt: Some Informal Comparative Observations," *Social Problems*, Vol. 17, No. 3 (Winter, 1970), 340–357.

Informative and revealing discussion of the current student revolt and the rise of campus radicalism. A worthwhile article, written from the radical position.

Hauser, Philip M., "On Actionism in the Craft of Sociology," *Sociological Inquiry*, Vol. 39, No. 2 (Spring, 1969), 139–147.

Professor Hauser takes the stand that actionist ideology and behavior have no place in sociology except concerning matters that pertain to the craft itself. The sociologist is advised not to turn activist at the expense of his functions as a scientist.

Kelman, Steven, *Push Comes to Shove: The Escalation of Student Protest* (Boston: Houghton Mifflin Co., 1970).

An illuminating analysis of the Harvard confrontation of 1969, which is critical of the SDS radical position. Kelman's account is fast-moving, youthful, and often brilliant. Much recommended whether or not one agrees with the author's perspectives (some readers might object to the dormitory-style language in which four-letter words are no rarity).

Lazarsfeld, Paul F., Sewell, W. H., and Wilensky, Harold (eds.), *The Uses of Sociology* (New York: Basic Books, Inc., 1967).

> Helpful on many counts. Much recommended. Chapters include Nathan Glaser on "The Ideological Uses of Sociology," Herbert Gans on "Urban Poverty and Social Planning," Thomas Pettigrew and Kurt Back on "Sociology in the Desegregation Process," and Philip M. Hauser on "Social Accounting."

Denzin, Norman K., "Who Leads: Sociology or Society?" *The American Sociologist,* Vol. 5, No. 2 (May, 1970), 125–127.

> Discussion of fundamental points relative to problems of pure versus applied sociology in contemporary context. A brief but worthwhile article. Recommended.

14 Modernizing Nations: Industrialization and Beyond

A major interest in the contemporary world relates to socio-cultural change in modernizing nations. Indeed, a universal pattern of modernity is developing from the marked diversity of traditional values and institutions. *Change* to many millions of people today means this revolutionary transition in man's way of life from the more closed and rigid structures of traditional societies to the differentiated, relatively open structures of advanced nations. Thus, to the peoples of Asia, Africa, and Central and South America, as well as to specialists in international relations and diplomats, this is the image of the word *change* that in all likelihood will be held.

Discussion of modernizing nations is not, however, a subject apart from the content of the previous chapters. Previously stated ideas will often apply. The changes associated with modernization affect both society and culture. Both social structure and way of life are basically transformed as the transition proceeds from the underdeveloped (traditional) to the advanced (modernized) condition. Many of the approaches to change that were described in Chapters 3 and 4 are relevant; some are necessary for the adequate study of this special type of change. It is true that economic change is central. To develop or modernize a society means to place considerable emphasis upon the economic sphere. Industrialization is a key process. Yet virtually all the social institutions will sooner or later be involved. Moreover, economic growth will not occur to a significant degree if certain social and cultural prerequisites are not fulfilled. Hence, in the actual or contemplated development of an area one needs to pay careful attention to cultural values and to technological, political, demographic, educational, psychological, and other factors. The interweaving of these influences is real if complicated. It is of interest, moreover, that as traditional nations reflect over the appeals of modernization, they cannot select piecemeal some individual element that attracts them and graft this onto their existing structure (and leave the rest); this is quite impossible. They must experience the entire transformation.[1]

[1] This is especially noted by Levy. See Marion J. Levy, Jr., *Modernization and the Structure of Societies*, Vol. II (Princeton, N. J.: Princeton University Press, 1966), p. 748.

Turning to theories of change, it is clear that theories especially relevant for the modernization process focus on values as well as the more obvious economic, technological, and demographic factors. More specifically, the theories of Ferdinand Tönnies and Robert Redfield suggest themselves as a possible framework. The changes undergone as a society develops are similar to those involved in the transition from *gemeinschaft* (small community emphasis) to *gesellschaft* (larger society having a more formal, contractual system)—following Tönnies' conceptions.[2] Indeed, if the modernization cycle of a present-day nation is completed, such a change will have been made. Similarly, Redfield's folk-urban dichotomy is pertinent. The folk society has a certain style of life; it maintains distinctive values. As the people adopt the ways of civilization their society and culture are transformed to emphasize literacy, urban living, more advanced technology, and other factors.[3] In the folk society and culture the people have multiple-interest actions; change is usually minimal. In the urban life actions are generally of the single-interest variety, reflecting the division of labor that is found. The rate of change is higher here. Moreover, greater emphasis is placed on rationalism.[4] The heart of the underdeveloped-modernized contrast, as many see it, lies between the society where the traditional forms of action predominate and the one where rationalistic modes of thought prevail. By the word *traditional* one does not mean ideas and social behavior taken over from ancestors and forebearers, because all societies have a sense of their historical past and a need for continuity of norms. One refers, rather, to a deliberate affirmation of traditional norms alleging that their merit derives from a sacred orientation; one thinks of a "past glorious age" or a past sacred lore.[5] Another way to look at the traditional-rationalistic dichotomy is to describe it in terms of Talcott Parsons' pattern variables. Indeed this tends to divide the over-all qualities into components.[6] Three of Parsons' five pairs of pattern alternatives are useful here: the emphasis on achievement versus ascription, on universalistic value orientation versus particularism, and

[2] Tönnies saw the "community" and "society" systems as ideal types. Ferdinand Tönnies, *Gemeinschaft and Gesellschaft* (Leipzig: 1887), 8th ed., 1935; *Fundamental Concepts of Sociology: Gemeinschaft and Gesellschaft*, English translation, translated by Charles P. Loomis (New York: Harper & Row, 1963). Harper Torchbook Ed.

[3] Robert Redfield, *The Primitive World and its Transformations* (Ithaca, N. Y.: Cornell University Press, 1953; Great Seal Books, 1957), Chaps. 1–3.

[4] Bert F. Hoselitz, "Main Concepts in the Analysis of the Social Implications of Technical Change," Chapter 1 in Hoselitz and Wilbert E. Moore (eds.), *Industrialization and Society* (The Hague: Unesco, Mouton, 1963), p. 12.

[5] *Ibid.*, pp. 14–15.

[6] For a full discussion see Bert F. Hoselitz, *Sociological Aspects of Economic Growth* (Glencoe, Ill.: The Free Press, Inc., 1960), Chap. II. Also see David C. McClelland, *The Achieving Society* (Princeton, N. J.: D. Van Nostrand Co., 1961), Chap. 5.

on the specificity versus diffuseness of interest. It is clear that achievement as a generalized emphasis is linked with the modernized society even though some ascriptive elements can be found; the ascriptive emphasis—allotting economic roles on the basis of who a person is rather than what he can do—is typically found in the underdeveloped society. Similarly, whether roles are allotted according to impersonal rules applying to every one (universalism) or whether special groups or individuals are favored (particularism) is relevant. The former occurrence is usual in advanced (modernized) societies, the latter in underdeveloped ones. Again, highly specific roles, which follow from an increasing division of labor, are characteristic of the advanced society; on the other hand, diffused roles—where the person tends a crop, makes his clothes, builds his house, and so on—are generally found in the simple peasant society. A logical linkage of the latter two characteristics is found in modernized society: If universalistic criteria prevail—the same rules apply to all—it is almost inevitable that the rules be specific. Hoselitz [7] observes that in the change from traditional to modernized society, universalistic norms do not necessarily have to replace particularistic ones; yet he points out that in all cases of successful modernization the allocation of economic roles has changed from the ascriptive to the achievement basis, and functionally diffuse norms are replaced by functionally specific ones.

It is time that we specify in a formal statement what we mean by modernizing an underdeveloped society. Wilbert E. Moore has phrased it lucidly:

> *What is involved in modernization is a "total" transformation of a traditional or pre-modern society into the type of technology and associated social organization that characterize the "advanced," economically prosperous, and relatively politically stable nations of the Western World. . . . [It is] a general transformation of the conditions of life and the way life is socially organized.*[8]

Bearing in mind that economic factors assume a more-than-average importance in assessing how developed or underdeveloped an area is, we agree with Kuznets [9] on the point that economic growth is perceived (and evaluated) from the standpoint of the advanced nations. The latter furnish the criteria of growth. The underdeveloped nations aspire to the levels of the advanced, not vice versa. But in the lands of rising expectations it may not be realized that the political and social changes required for economic development are drastic. Moreover, the

[7] Hoselitz, in Hoselitz and Moore (ed.), *op. cit.,* pp. 18–19.

[8] Wilbert E. Moore, *Social Change* (Englewood Cliffs, N. J.: Prentice-Hall, Inc., 1963), pp. 89–90.

[9] Simon Kuznets, *Six Lectures on Economic Growth* (Glencoe, Ill.: The Free Press, Inc., 1959), p. 17.

process is slower than many will realize; numerous frustrations may be expected. Finally—and this will be discussed later—the desired goal of economic development may not be achieved in all areas. Many pitfalls and potential snags lie along the route.

In the remainder of this chapter we shall discuss the over-all process of modernization, dealing first with the central economic factors and later with allied social, political, educational, demographic, psychological, and other elements. Then, we shall summarize some of the hazards and impedimenta of the process. Finally, we shall state some ideas relative to *the planning of change.* It is obvious that the changes in underdeveloped areas are not haphazard or unanticipated but are generally planned. Although the growth of social institutions and other forms may also be planned, this is a convenient place for the discussion of the subject.

PROCESSES OF MODERNIZATION

The Core Economic Processes

Assuming that many economies (or nations) began several centuries ago with an equally low standard of living, why is it that by the present time some of these countries have increased their productivity per person tremendously and now enjoy a high standard of living where others have not? [10] Moreover, the gap between the two groups in per capita output is steadily increasing. The answer to the question is usually that, despite differences in climate and resources, the main factor responsible for the huge gap in productivity and living standards is that some nations some generations back adopted the policy of industrialization; the others did not. However, this is far from a simple matter. Many important related factors and preconditions are involved,[11] for a nation does not industrialize if its values and other conditions preclude it. At any rate, some nations such as the United States, Great Britain, France, Germany, Denmark, Norway, Russia, have developed economically; others, such as Italy and Spain have shown intermediate development; and many others, especially in Africa and Southeast Asia, remain largely underdeveloped. *Per capita output of goods* or *per capita income* are often used as an index of economic

[10] Harvey Leibenstein, *Economic Backwardness and Economic Growth* (New York: John Wiley & Sons, Inc., 1957; paperback printing, 1963), Chap. 1.

[11] As Hunter phrases it, "economic development is a pervasive process of change involving political, sociological, psychological, and other cultural dimensions at least as important as the purely economic ones." Holland Hunter, "Optimum Tautness in Developmental Planning," *Economic Development and Cultural Change,* Vol. IX, No. 4, Part I (July, 1961), 562.

development, although many other elements are involved in the concept and doubtless no perfect measure of it exists.[12]

The economic characteristics of underdeveloped areas are, however, quite clear: (1) A high proportion of the population is engaged in agriculture, usually from 70 to 90 per cent; (2) a low productivity occurs in agriculture despite the many workers, largely because farm implements and agricultural technology are usually rudimentary; (3) the agricultural output generally is composed of cereals and raw materials; (4) the average person has very little capital; (5) per capita income is low, often near the subsistence level; (6) most of the people have little or no savings; and (7) whatever savings do exist are usually achieved by a landholding class.

The process of modernizing a society with such economic characteristics is indeed complicated. In general, three parts of the process can be distinguished: (1) Prerequisites for industrialization must be present or attained; (2) the industrialization itself becomes achieved and concomitant changes are observed; (3) long-run and broader results of industrialization are noted. The associated political, demographic, and other elements show an influence in complex ways. For example, if several societies have reached a certain stage of industrialization, it does not follow that the necessary next step for each will be the same. The model of change will clearly be different depending, for example, on whether capitalist or communist programs are followed; but many other influences will also manifest themselves. It is the kind of process, moreover, where at one time a technological change in a society will be needed, at another a political move, at still another an educational change, or some combination of these. Let us now describe the parts

---

[12] This writer follows Kuznets, Leibenstein, and other economists in believing that *per capita output of goods* and *per capita income* are generally satisfactory as measures of economic development, even though they are not perfect. Leibenstein points out that "It must be taken for granted that an index of any sort is only a bench mark or a sign of something and not a substitute for the complete vision and understanding of everything that may interest us." (Leibenstein, *op. cit.*, pp. 8–9.) One may also consider that these two measures are conceptually distinct and not *always* perfectly associated in fact. David C. McClelland, *The Achieving Society* (Princeton, N. J.: D. Van Nostrand Co., 1961), p. 84. On the other hand, Professor Ogburn and this writer found *per capita consumption of energy from nonamimal sources* and *per capita income* in 53 nations (using United Nations figures) to be highly correlated ($r = 0.9$). William F. Ogburn and Francis R. Allen, "Technological Development and Per Capita Income," *American Journal of Sociology*, Vol. LXV, No. 2 (September, 1959), 127–131. Pool chooses to define economic development, not in terms of a productivity figure (he cites GNP per capita), but in relation to certain values as high achievement motivation and secularism. Ithiel de Sola Pool, "The Role of Communication in the Process of Modernization and Technological Change," Chapter 14 in Hoselitz and Moore (eds.), *op. cit.*, p. 281.

of the process in a compressed, approximate, and admittedly rudimentary form.[13]

Prerequisites to Modernization

In order to modernize, a society must have, or learn to develop, certain value emphases and translate them into behavioral characteristics. These include the allotting (and performance) of tasks on the basis of merit and ability (the core meaning of Parsons' term *universalism*); the development of high achievement motivation; the institutionalizing of rationalistic thought; the willingness to be residentially mobile; and certain underlying economic factors such as the institutionalizing of property, labor, and an exchange system. Capital formation, moreover, is a necessity. The spirit of entrepreneurship has to be fostered.[14] Political authority, and some nationalistic emphasis, is a further requirement. It is evident, then, that much is involved in the traditional-to-modern transformation. It is not that these traits or values have to be "full blown" in order that the process begin. For one thing, the new values will be mixed for some years with the prevailing traditional ones. Nevertheless, some beginnings with the new emphases must show themselves. The over-all transformation will be gradual and will undoubtedly take a long time. Problems are almost sure to develop. One thing is amply clear: The simple wish for a higher standard of living and better life generally is not enough to achieve the conditions of the modernized society. The wish alone will not "automatically lead to its own fulfillment" (Moore's phrasing [15]).

A brief listing of traits or values which are prerequisite for modernization belies the wealth of ideas accumulated relative to their roles in the overall process. Before proceeding further, let us consider somewhat more fully two of these factors, namely: the political factor and the achievement motivation. Concerning the former, Parsons [16] ob-

[13] We shall follow the treatment in such volumes as Hoselitz and Moore (eds.), *op. cit.*; Kuznets, *op. cit.*; Leibenstein, *op. cit.*; Moore, *Social Change,* Chap. 5; Myron Weiner (ed.), *Modernization* (New York: Basic Books, Inc., 1966); Levy, *op. cit.* (2 Vols.); Robert L. Heilbroner, *The Great Ascent* (New York: Harper & Row, 1963).

[14] See W. Thomas Easterbrook, "The Entrepreneurial Function in Relation to Technological and Economic Change," Chapter 3 in Hoselitz and Moore (eds.), *op. cit.* Hoselitz relates the development of entrepreneurs to the concept of deviance. That is to say, early entrepreneurs deviated from the existing social norms. Often their behavior was marginal to a given culture. *Ibid.*, Chap. 1, especially pp. 25–27.

[15] Moore, *Social Change, op. cit.*, p. 96.

[16] Talcott Parsons, *Structure and Process in Modern Societies* (Glencoe, Ill.: The Free Press, Inc., 1960), Chap. 3, especially pp. 116–131.

serves that underdeveloped nations tend to have strong commitments to political independence as well as to economic development itself—whatever their other value commitments to religion, philosophy, and family life. Political authority, he argues, is a necessary agency to aid industrialization. This is related to the class structure in which a two-class system is usually found. The upper group has the political power and will need to favor the change toward industrialization; otherwise the vested-interest viewpoint may cause them to oppose the change. This is also likely to be related to the granting of independence and other colonialism issues. Leadership must be found, in short, to counteract the restorationist conservative trend and guide the industrial trend. This is where education is important. Some citizens may have been educated in the West, or educated under Western auspices at home, and so may see the great need for modernization. This is important in order that social change be effectively deflected from the older traditions. Leadership is also important in order that a stable political system be achieved; the risk of a Communist takeover always exists in such a change. One factor here is that the two-class system that is commonly found often favors a Marxist definition of events. The role of the intellectuals thus assumes much importance. The upper classes in underdeveloped areas tend to be interested in political power and religion, and hence may fear the symbol of Western materialism. Parsons observes that leadership for specialized bureaucratic organizations must be provided: a strong, highly educated, technically trained group. A stable political system, yet favorable to the change, is almost indispensable.

However, the relations of political factors to economic growth are complicated in that different kinds of political systems have different needs. The new traditional nations vary in their authority bases. This approach is emphasized by Apter,[17] who divides the over-all political systems into three categories: *a mobilization system, a reconciliation system,* and *a modernizing autocracy.* Each type has its own (1) patterns of legitimacy, (2) loyalty, (3) decisional autonomy, (4) distribution of authority, and (5) ideological expression.[18] Apter lists the characteristics of each system.[19] We cannot go into his detailed discussion, but the

[17] David E. Apter, "System, Process, and Politics of Economic Development," Chapter 7 in Hoselitz and Moore (eds.), *op. cit.*

[18] Guinea and Ghana are cited as examples of the mobilization system, whereas the Soviet Union and Communist China are examples "in a more extreme form"; Nigeria and the United States are given as examples of the reconciliation system; and Buganda, Morocco, and Ethiopia are examples of the modernizing autocracy. Apter, *op. cit.*, p. 139.

[19] *Ibid.*, p. 140.

main point is that economic development brings different effects to the varying types of political system.[20]

Turning to the achievement motivation, McClelland's [21] notable volume has made the most convincing case of any for this as an element to be included in explanations of economic development. He brings much evidence to bear on the hypothesis that this particular motivation is in part responsible for economic growth. Being impressed with Weber's thesis of the Protestant Reformation producing a character type that ultimately resulted in the development of modern industrial capitalism, he introduces psychological reasoning to show how the inner dynamics of this came about. McClelland interprets the connection between Protestantism and the rise of capitalism in terms of a revolution in the family; the latter leads to more sons having strong internalized achievement drives.[22] But McClelland relates the need of achievement (abbreviated as n Achievement) to the presence of entrepreneurical activity and economic development in both preliterate and modern societies. For example, for many modern nations he relates n Achievement (measured by the content of children's readers) to economic development (measured by national income per capita and electricity produced per capita) during the period 1925–1950. The factor of n Achievement is indeed impressively correlated with the latter, using these figures.[23] Noting the importance of technological innovation for economic growth, moreover, he again introduces data that indicate that n Achievement is a kind of basic introductory element that leads to constructional activities, technological innovations, and thence to rapid economic growth.[24]

Then McClelland considers sources of n Achievement. Why are some people more highly motivated along the achievement line than others? Taking the cue from Winterbottom's and Rosen's studies of motivation,[25] he observes that mothers of sons showing high n Achievement

[20] See also, for an over-all theoretical discussion of the political factor, Gabriel Almond and James S. Coleman (eds.) *The Politics of the Developing Areas* (Princeton, N. J.: Princeton University Press, 1960).

[21] David C. McClelland, *The Achieving Society* (Princeton, N. J.: D. Van Nostrand Co., 1961).

[22] *Ibid.*, p. 49.

[23] *Ibid.*, pp. 90–92 (Note Table 3.4). McClelland adds that n Achievement is positively correlated with *subsequent* economic growth for the electrical output measure, or for both measures combined. On the other hand, the n Achievement level is not related to *previous* economic growth. In brief, the increased achievement-mindedness of the influence during childhood will show itself in the years following.

[24] *Ibid.*, p. 151.

[25] M. R. Winterbottom, "The Relation of Need for Achievement to Learning and Experience in Independence and Mastery," in J. W. Atkinson (ed.), *Motives in Fantasy, Action, and Society* (Princeton, N. J.: D. Van Nostrand Co., 1958); and

tended to expect "self-reliant mastery" at earlier ages than mothers of sons with low n Achievement. Also the fathers of the "highs" show less dominating behavior than do the fathers of the "lows." Thus child-rearing pressures on several dimensions bear a significant influence in producing n Achievement. Certain influences—not only father dominance (which tends to bring low self-reliance in the son) but having low standards of excellence in the first place—do not lead to developing n Achievement.[26] McClelland illustrates the thesis with various groups: Jewish people, Negroes, French-Canadians, and others.[27] Jewish boys tend to be strong in n Achievement. Although this may be partly due to the nature of their religious beliefs, McClelland thinks it is even more brought about by Jewish family life in which high levels of aspiration for children tend to be set, the mother is usually warm toward her son, and the father is generally not a stern authoritarian (for instance, not as compared with other ethnic peoples).[28]

Another psychological theory should be considered—that of Hagen.[29] Again, it concerns the *beginnings* of economic development. Hagen believes that the change from traditional to modern society will not occur without a change in personalities. The authoritarian and innovational personality types are typical, respectively, of traditional and modern societies. After explaining the nature and process of formation of the two types,[30] he poses the key question: If the change from authoritarian to innovational personality type is needed in the modernizing process, and if the traditional society is ordinarily very stable, what forces will cause such major change in values and personality characteristics to take place?

Hagen's answer is that such personality changes follow "the perception on the part of the members of some social group that their purposes and values in life are not respected by groups in the society whom they admire and whose esteem they value." [31] Hagen shortens this to the phrase, the *withdrawal of status respect*. Different influences—changes in the power structure, nonacceptance of expected status on migrating to a new society, and others—may cause such withdrawal of respect. Hagen adds that such a withdrawal does not merely imply

---

B. C. Rosen, "Race, Ethnicity, and Achievement Syndrome," *American Sociological Review*, Vol. XXIV (1959), 47–60.

26 *Ibid.*, p. 356.

27 *Ibid.*, p. 362 ff (note Table 9.7).

28 The methodology used in this book is sophisticated and elaborate. McClelland gives a summary of the total content, incidentally, in "The Achievement Motive in Economic Growth," Chapter 4 in Hoselitz and Moore (eds.), *op. cit.*

29 Everett E. Hagen, *On the Theory of Social Change, How Economic Growth Begins* (Homewood, Ill.: The Dorsey Press, Inc., 1962).

30 *Ibid.*, Chs. 5–7.

31 *Ibid.*, p. 185.

feeling inferior; in a traditional society the peasant will feel inferior to elites, yet no frustration or humiliation will occur. Moreover, if one is a member of a minority group or is an outsider, this is different because he may not have previously received respect in the society at all. Professor Hagen believes that this withdrawal of respect is at the root of many social revolutions occurring in underdeveloped nations today. He cites examples. He concedes that popular resentment may also be due to *new aspirations,* but declares that erosion of the traditional sense of respected status is the main cause of current turbulence. Furthermore, contact with the West is held to be the principal (if indirect) cause of the loss of respect. Native elites, who find themselves disdained by powerful European groups, attribute the condescension to the peasant class and its poor living conditions. Thus, they blame it on the lower class. Reactions of the lower classes in turn to the lack of sympathetic understanding from above bring the explosive force in the underdeveloped areas.

What follows is *retreatist* behavior (following Merton's typology). The historical sequence, then, tends to be: authoritarianism, withdrawal of status respect, retreatism, and creativity.[32] The processes by which the final stage (creativity) is reached may be somewhat fanciful. The explanation takes a psychoanalytic turn at this point. The general idea, however, is that as the retreatism deepens in successive generations, it creates circumstances of home life and social environment that are conducive to the development of innovational personality. The behavior of both fathers and mothers is related to this. In Hagen's words,

> Because of her husband's erratic or weak behavior (following loss of status respect and retreatist reaction), the mother is less controlled by his expectations than was true in the traditional case and has somewhat more autonomy in her relations to her baby. . . . This sort of care is conducive to the sprouting early in life of high need autonomy and high need achievement.[33]

The final point concerns how the feeling for initiative and achievement is influenced to take the form of *technological* innovation—which would affect economic development. But the model of technological progress and resulting power will be attractive to some individuals; and such will grow. As creative and reformist personalities emerge out of retreatism, then, "technological process is seen as a promising path to satisfaction of the individual's needs." The values of the new generation will turn in this direction. Such, in brief, is Hagen's explanation. A change in social structure has led to a change in personality

[32] *Ibid.*, p. 217.
[33] *Ibid.*, p. 220.

(from authoritarian to innovational), which "has been treated as the prime mover in social change." [34]

It is not easy to give a generalized reaction to this. Hagen provides a wealth of material as does McClelland. His knowledge of various developing nations, especially Burma, Java, Colombia, and Japan, is considerable. Yet there are difficulties. First of all, the explanation of the sequence from withdrawal-of-status-respect leading to retreatist behavior, which gives rise in turn to creativity, seems fanciful; the final change from retreatism to creativity is especially shaky in the opinion of this observer. It is, for instance, difficult to imagine *predictions* based on this reasoning. Of course, parts of McClelland's explanation are not entirely convincing either, but in most respects McClelland backs up his ideas with impressive statistical evidence, whereas Hagen's theory seems to stand or fall on the historical record. Unfortunately, some questions exist with respect to the historical evidence and its interpretation.[35] All in all, Hagen's theory does not appear to be as convincing as McClelland's. This writer wonders, incidentally, if the withdrawal-of-status-respect factor is so much weightier an influence in bringing the change toward modernization than the development of new aspirations; but it may be that, particularly in some areas, the former is especially important. Also, Hagen has some difficulties in treating the influence of the social structure. He recognizes the importance of this influence, but seems to think of the social structure not as a system in itself but as a resultant of the predominant personality types (authoritarian and innovative). Despite skepticism regarding Hagen's central thesis, it would be a mistake to rule out the influence of the withdrawal-of-status-respect factor in stimulating the beginning of economic growth.[36]

[34] *Ibid.*, pp. 236 and 237.

[35] Bert F. Hoselitz declares that: "He [Hagen] often summarizes historical events of great significance for his model in insufficient detail, leaving out of consideration some often very obvious factors that would permit the facts to be interpreted in a very different manner." See the Hoselitz review of the Hagen book in *The American Journal of Sociology*, Vol. LXVIII, No. 5 (March, 1963), 599–600. It could be that Hagen's statement of historical events reflects his experiences in and study of Burma, Java, and other areas (concerning which he has expertise), but that the historical evidence tells a different story elsewhere.

[36] McClelland's comments regarding the Hagen theory are of interest. He felt that there was much logic to the withdrawal-of-status-respect idea (which Hagen had earlier called the "law of group subordination"). McClelland declares:

> *Don't people who are suppressed try to strike back, to compensate in some way for their inferiority? Hagen has used the idea explicitly in trying to account for the way economic growth begins. The idea has an element of truth in it, but . . . the response to subordination depends on the initial level of achievement motivation in the group. If it is high, as among Jews in the United States, then the response will be vigorous; if it is low,*

A third psychologically oriented theory has recently been stated by John H. Kunkel.[37] Kunkel's approach is rooted in experimental psychology, in contrast to the psychodynamic models of man's internal states (McClelland and Hagen). Kunkel espouses a behavioral model. The essence of the behavioral approach is that man's behavior is shaped (and, hence, may be changed) by means of differential reinforcement or punishment. This bears relationship, then, to the field of *social control.* If behavior is to be changed, the modifications must be made in reinforcing stimuli; furthermore, the older (undesired) behavior needs to be extinguished. Principles of learning come into play. If striving is consistently rewarded, it will tend to continue.[38] Thus, roles can be identified as supporting or detrimental in terms of their relationship to the goals of economic development. If they are helpful (functional) for industrialization or other processes, they will be reinforced as a supporting role. If the reverse (or if they are incompatible with a desired process), individuals who behave in terms of the role will be punished or certainly no longer rewarded.[39] As examples of projects that have followed the behavioral perspective, Kunkel cites the Vicos project in Peru,[40] a program of deliberate large-scale social change, and Pakistan's encouragement of entrepreneurs.[41] The latter, moreover, illustrates Kunkel's behavioral view with regard to *deviation;* entrepreneurship is an example of one type of deviant that is much desired for the purposes of economic development. Kunkel holds that both the Vicos and Pakistan programs were highly successful. He also analyzes other projects that are not regarded as successful (as the Zande Scheme in Africa), pointing out why, in his view, they failed.

Kunkel contends that the behavioral perspective is quite compatible with systems theory, and that computer studies of economic development (following this perspective) will be made more and more. Also, propositions derived from systems analysis can be tested by simula-

---

as among Negroes in the United States, the response is likely to be one of apathy and withdrawal. Degree of challenge also makes a difference.

McClelland, *op. cit.,* p. 339. Moreover, the level of achievement motivation may change from time to time. For Negroes in the United States, certainly for many Negroes, the level would be much higher today as compared with one generation ago.

[37] J. H. Kunkel, *Society and Economic Growth* (New York: Oxford University Press 1970); also see Kunkel, "Values and Behavior in Economic Development," *Economic Development and Cultural Change,* Vol. XIII, No. 3 (April, 1965), 257–277.

[38] Kunkel, *Society and Economic Growth, ibid.,* pp. 28 and 285.

[39] *Ibid.,* pp. 134–139.

[40] Allan R. Holmberg, "Changing Community Attitudes and Values in Peru: A Case Study in Guided Change," in Richard N. Adams *et al.* (eds.), *Social Change in Latin America Today* (New York: Harper and Bros., 1960).

[41] See Gustav F. Papanek, *Pakistan's Development: Social Goals and Private Incentives* (Cambridge, Mass.: Harvard University Press, 1967).

tion.[42] As was stated earlier in this volume, social systems are generally regarded as *open* ones. Kunkel makes the point, however, that under-developed (peasant) societies are quite *closed,* especially in the cultural sense; various *subsystems* in developing nations are very likely to be closed. Thus, social systems vary in their degree of openness—and the latter can be increased as in the Vicos project.[43] Open systems have feedback loops; the feedback may be positive or negative. Kunkel main-tains that the feedback loops operate much as behavioral principles do. An activity will usually be repeated when it is enforced and its opera-tion is successful.

The behavioral model is much simpler than those of McClelland and Hagen. Kunkel even concedes that, with its emphasis on rewards and punishment, it mainly follows "conventional wisdom." [44] Kunkel contends that the successes of the Vicos project cannot be explained well by the Hagen theory "which raises more questions than it an-swers." He adds that "while . . . the Vicos success could be explained more easily by McClelland than by Hagen, both explanations would require not only a modification of the original theory and its model of man, but also the introduction of additional elements, propositions, and concepts. . . ." [45] The behavioral model does not require the lengthy passage of time, as is posited by Hagen, during which new values and personalities are created. Nor was any concern with child-raising methods or the manipulation of personalities required in Vicos; only certain changes in the individuals' environment were made. In-deed the very ease of the operation is arresting. Granting that the theory seems to bear promise, one would like to see further illustrations of such changes in modernization. One wonders if the changes can *always* be made with relative ease and in a relatively short period of time.

Principal Economic Processes

We now return to economic advance itself. This assumes that per-sonality and cultural changes have taken place.[46] The more-strictly economic processes relate to (1) the volume of saving available for investment, (2) the size of markets, and (3) industrialization per se.

42 Kunkel, *Society and Economic Growth, op. cit.,* p. 216.

43 *Ibid.,* p. 196. Actually Chapter VII in its entirety is devoted to the relations between the behavioral perspective and systems analysis.

44 *Ibid.,* pp. 309–310.

45 *Ibid.,* pp. 151–153.

46 If these changes have *not* occurred, the economic processes are not likely to get very far. See, for example, Hagen, *op. cit.,* p. 47.

Volume of Saving. This economic factor is of crucial significance because underdeveloped areas are characterized by meager productive capacity and low resources in general. Clearly, if such a nation is to grow, its first economic task is to build up or find capital. In all societies this is done largely by saving. Saving in this sense, as Heilbroner explains,[47] does not mean putting money in a bank; it refers to saving energies and materials from the exclusive satisfying of current wants. Thus, some labor and resources must be freed from consumption-goods production and applied to capital-goods production. Bearing in mind that the standard of living is pitifully low in many of these nations and that many peasants eke out a painfully primitive life using backward tools and often having health and other problems, this is a severe request. Is the situation hopeless, then, for economic development? Not always; little by little some improvement can be made. Not all nations, however, successfully achieve the transitions. Yet, industrialization is the great need in order that production may be vastly increased; machines, power facilities, and the like are expensive; saving is sooner or later required. Even though external aid will help the struggling nation, the bulk of long-run savings generally has to come from within the country. Also, the rise in output must be faster than the population expansion, lest the *per capita output* be static or even falling. The "iron law" of economic growth, as Heilbroner (following H. W. Singer) calls it, is that "So long as the amount of savings, coupled with the fruitfulness of that savings, results in a rise in output is faster than the rise in population, cumulative economic growth will take place." [48]

The Size of Markets. An expanding market is essential for economic development; inadequate markets are a barrier to such growth. With expanding markets, innovational skill is not as necessary as otherwise would be the case; it means furthermore that greater profits will be secured, and thus greater earnings can be plowed back in the innovational and productive processes. The size of the market is not generally a problem if an innovative effort is being made; the latter can be expected to bring market expansion. The size of the market, however, like the mere accumulation of capital, does not seem to be a major force in causing economic growth to begin. The expansion of the market appears to have little effect in a sluggish society. In the same way, an increased supply of funds available for investment

[47] Robert L. Heilbroner, *The Great Ascent* (New York: Harper & Row, 1963), pp. 92–93.
[48] *Ibid.*, p. 104.

does not necessarily stir a traditional society to economic advancement. Such funds are quite likely to be siphoned off into the pockets of the traditional elite, if the social and psychological changes previously described have not already occurred. Again, if some development has occurred, one can expect, in the earlier stages, a pull between the desire to use the new wealth for old forms and privileges—as investing in land and adopting feudal habits—and the newer, more adventurous ways of extending the economic base of the society.[49]

Increasing Industrialization.   The real key to increased productivity lies in technology. With machines and mechanical power man can produce far more and with less effort. As clear as this is, the dilemma for the underdeveloped society is (as already mentioned) how to pay the high cost of the dams, generators, power lines, equipment, and machines. Yet, it can sometimes be done. The peasant society must break out into an upward spiral of achievement in which a certain strategy seems to perform miracles. The "impossible" can be accomplished finally by inching along the developmental path of Western civilization—by making one slow gain after another beginning with the primitive handicraft stage. But underdeveloped nations are not interested in such microscopic progress during, say, a single lifetime. Several activities need to be done more or less simultaneously. In the early stage of industrialization it is invaluable if some industrial capital can be obtained from abroad. Some can be purchased by the peasant society in exchange for output that has been saved. Some industrial capital can be secured from private investment by Western corporations or individuals. "Foreign aid" (gifts or loans from advanced nations) will help. Then, agriculture needs to be made more efficient by using modern technology and newer techniques.[50] So much emphasis is often placed on industrialization that some forget that farming is similarly transformed. Using modern machines and techniques, the agricultural output will be greater with fewer people working. Thus, a backward society develops a surplus work force on the farms that then can be used in building roads and dams. To accomplish this, however,

---

[49] Barbara Ward, *The Rich Nations and the Poor Nations* (New York: W. W. Norton, 1962), pp. 87–88.

[50] If *inexpensive* machines can be made available, all-around benefit is obtained. In March, 1970, the Ford Motor Company announced that it had built a new motorized hand tractor especially for use in developing nations. With this new "developing-nations tractor" a native can plow an entire acre, or cultivate more than three acres, in one eight-hour day. Ford engineers have been running tests with the 320-pound tractor since 1966. The tractor will sell for about $500 (without accessories), which is said to be about the price of a team of oxen. See *Newsweek* (March 2, 1970).

is no easy task.[51] Land reform of this sort will usually run counter to deep-rooted, legal and social institutions, tenant-landlord relationships, and so forth. These have to be broken. The opposition of the land-owning classes is likely to be determined. Larger farms tend to be encouraged in order that machines will be useful. Most of the capital for this has to come from the countryside. A rise in farm productivity will, however, make the farmer more prosperous. All in all, both industry and agriculture have to move forward; one cannot change the economy with agriculture remaining in its feudal, poverty-ridden, unproductive state. But agriculture is an especially difficult sector of the transition because, as Barbara Ward declares, "agricultural methods are thousands of years old and people prefer on the whole to go on in the ways of their fathers." [52] To convince the farmer of the wisdom of using new methods is usually far more difficult than it is with the urban industrial worker. Yet the existence of the previously mentioned expanding market will help. The farmer will have an incentive to increase his production. In any event, this change will likely involve a struggle, and it will take time.

It is clear that the over-all pace of industrialization, then, will depend on many factors. Unless agriculture can save some of its product in order that capital can be accumulated, unless some workers are freed from farms to be able to work on industrial and other needed projects, unless personalities have been changed from the old-time peasant type to the innovative, achievement-oriented type, and so on, the total process will not be fully successful. Most of these requirements occur in varying degrees in different societies. It is important to see that industrialization itself is only a stage in the total process of development.[53] It is actually the capstone (as Heilbroner terms it) of successful development in a society. This is one reason why the growth of industrial output is an imperfect index of modernization. Other factors should be considered too. If industry should be advanced before social capital has accumulated, or some agricultural reform has occurred or personalities have shown some re-orientation, one is likely to find only an industrial island in a generally undeveloped peasant area. Industrialization, on the other hand, should find roots in a socio-cultural environment favorable for its growth and in which personalities, furthermore, are attuned to its processes and benefits. They should be ready, in short, to participate in its development. Once established,

---

51 Heilbroner, *op. cit.*, pp. 93–98; and Clifton Wharton, Jr., "Modernizing Subsistence Agriculture," Chapter 19 in Weiner (ed.), *op. cit.*

52 Ward, *op. cit.*, pp. 105–106.

53 Heilbroner, *op. cit.*, p. 101.

industrialization should bring an impressive rise in the standard of living of the area. There is much to say here, some of which we may touch on in describing the alleged stages of economic growth. One could review main elements of the Industrial Revolution that occurred in England, the United States, and other nations—involving the use of steam power. A late stage of industrialization has been the introduction of increasingly automatic industrial processes—the processes generally known as automation. But this lengthy story we cannot discuss here.

Consequences of Industrialization

We shall briefly sketch some of the socio-cultural results of industrialization, acknowledging that a lengthy discussion of these subjects is not possible here. Moreover, as was found with many of the preceding topics, we have to bear in mind that many differences will be found between individual societies; this is partly due to diversities that existed even before the transition to modernization had begun. The consequences due to industrialization, at any rate, can be discussed under the following headings: (1) economic, (2) demographic, and (3) other effects on the social structure.

Economic Consequences.   Consequences that tend to occur in this area include a reduction in the proportion of people engaged in agriculture (this virtually always must occur); an increased demand for highly trained professional workers, especially physicians and engineers; a long-term upgrading of minimum and average-skill levels; an increased mobility of the laboring class; a marked lateral extension of jobs in addition to differentiation on the basis of income and prestige; the growth of the economy bringing much reinvestment of profits either voluntarily by investors or by intervention of the state; the extension of markets for both agricultural and consumer goods; and, as per capita income rises, the consumption of "necessities" and later comforts and luxuries tending to increase.

Demographic Consequences.   The theory of the demographic transition declares that high mortality rates (which are characteristic of underdeveloped areas) will decline before fertility rates decline. Thus a *transitional growth* occurs. The motives for family limitation have been thought to be economic in nature, including importantly the factor of aspirations; it is expected that similar motives will occur in former underdeveloped areas as they move along in modernization. Urbanization tends to be an accompaniment of industrialization, but sometimes an overurbanization occurs. Unless it is somehow corrected, this could be, and often has been, an acute problem.[54] The needs of birth limitation are great in underdeveloped areas; it is hoped that the personal aspirations associated with the revolution of rising expectations will lead to this result, as it has already occurred in the developed countries.

Effects on the Social Structure. The process of industrialization appears to have negative consequences for extended kinship systems. The latter is dysfunctional to the modernization process. The tribal-kinship emphasis is strong in Africa, for instance. Barbara Ward declares: "Why should an individual farmer work harder if a flock of his 'sisters and his cousins and his aunts'—and they can really be numbered in dozens in polygamous Africa—may come in and eat up his supplies? The 'extended family' acts as a sort of private welfare state." [55] Little by little a change to the "conjugal" or "nuclear" family type seems likely.[56] Then, considerable family disorganization is likely to accompany the peasant-to-modernized transition. This is likely to follow from the intensified interaction occurring in the small family, which contrasts from the multibond emphasis of the former peasant family. The value of individualism, which is encouraged by the modernization process, will bring effects on mate selection and parent-child relationships. Marriage by arrangement between kin groups is very likely to disappear, and it will be replaced by voluntary mate selection. Moreover, children will receive training from persons other than their parents; some of this will involve knowledge and skills that their parents do not share. Thus, some tensions coming from this source are inevitable. Women will gradually take jobs in developing industries. The developing industrial communities will bring a weakening of informal social controls (which formerly had been important) and will cause the need for more formal agencies and laws for maintaining order. For some urban dwellers the loss of close attachments that had hitherto existed in the family-tribal situation will bring symptoms of apathy and alienation—alcoholism and other deviations—especially if they have not adapted to the change in modernism. Furthermore, the need for literacy is associated with the modernization trend and upgrading of skills. Indeed, more than this, over-all education becomes of much greater value because it is manifestly functional in the modernized situation; therefore, a considerable development of the school system will tend to occur. Good universities, indeed, are necessary for

54 Kingsley Davis, "Population," in Scientific American, *Technology and Economic Development* (New York: Alfred A. Knopf, 1963), p. 35.

55 Ward, *op. cit.*, pp. 88–89.

56 William J. Goode, "Industrialization and Family Change," Chapter 15 in Hoselitz and Moore (eds.), *op. cit.*, p. 239.

the success of modernization, as Shils [57] points out. Educated people are needed for government positions, technical jobs, and medical, scientific, economic, and statistical services, and the like. Even though some students may go abroad for their education, the main burden for training rests on the universities of the modernizing nation itself. The development of mass communication is another necessary element in modernization. Pool declares that "it is the mass media—traditionally the press, but now others too—which make what would otherwise be wistful dreams of a few modernizers into the dynamic aspirations of a whole people." [58] People do not necessarily yearn for the industrial life. It has to be defined for them; they need to be persuaded to some extent. Peasants may have a general wish for the cure of diseases, but this is not the same as wanting pasteurized milk, chlorinated water, and sterile hospitals. They may have a motivation for "advancement," but this is not any demand for schooling in language, natural science, or social science. "The shape of the good life," as Pool concludes, "needs to be delineated." [59] Although the mass media help in these ways, it is of interest that they do not replace or destroy personal, face-to-face communication. Indeed, as we saw in Chapter 12, the factor of personal influence is important; a two-step communication flow seems to occur, the media disseminating information to opinion leaders (influentials), who then have an effect on the larger number of people.[60] All in all, the communication system in modern society has four qualities not present in a comparable degree in traditional society: [61] (1) It keeps accurate and permanent records; (2) it is extremely rapid, reporting the news within hours after its occurrence; (3) it extends men's comprehension far beyond the range of their direct experience; and (4) it coordinates the groups that have had the contact into a whole, capable of integrated action. Education, formal and by means of the mass media, tends to cause greater political consciousness and increased political participation.

[57] Edward Shils, "Modernization and Higher Education," Chapter 6 in Weiner (ed.), *op. cit.*, pp. 81–82.

[58] Pool, *op. cit.*, pp. 289 and 291. Pool observes that

> *The images people have of the world around them are the realities in terms of which they act. Such images have an abiding significance far greater than that which the concept "image," with its ethereal connotations, suggests.*

[59] *Ibid.*, p. 288.

[60] Elihu Katz and Paul F. Lazarsfeld, *Personal Influence* (New York: The Free Press of Glencoe, Division of The Macmillan Company, 1955; paperback edition, 1964).

[61] These are summarized in Pool, *op. cit.*, pp. 289–290. In addition to this valuable chapter see Ithiel de Sola Pool, "Communications and Development," Chapter 7 in Weiner (ed.), *op. cit.*

Effects on Man. Industrialization and allied changes affect man himself.[62] In the preceding chapter it was stated that modern man (as compared with the peasant in traditional society) tends to have the active-minded outlook; he believes that he can effectively dominate his environment in many ways, and he also has more interest in taking an active part in civic and community affairs. But there is much more to it than that. A whole syndrome of characteristics seems to be associated with modern man: As the entire society is transformed in the process of economic development, so people gradually adopt new traits or attributes. Just as the society is changed, they are changed people. What are these attributes that characterize modern man?

On the basis of a lengthy research project devoted to this subject, Inkeles and associates [63] posit the following qualities as fitting the conception of modern man:

> *(1) Openness to new experience, both with people and with new ways of doing things such as attempting to control births; (2) the assertion of increasing independence from the authority of traditional figures like parents and priests and a shift of allegiance to leaders of government, public affairs, trade unions, cooperatives, and the like; (3) belief in the efficacy of science and medicine, and a general abandonment of passivity and fatalism in the face of life's difficulties; and (4) ambition for oneself and one's children to achieve high occupational and educational goals. Men who manifest these characteristics (5) like people to be on time and show an interest in carefully planning their affairs in advance. It is also part of this syndrome to (6) show strong interest and take an active part in civic and community affairs and local politics; and (7) to strive energetically to keep up with the news, and within this effort to prefer news of national and international import over items dealing with sports, religion, or purely local affairs.*[64]

Elsewhere [65] Inkeles has identified other traits of modernity as being oriented to the present or to the future, rather than to the past; being more aware of the dignity of others and showing more respect for them; having more faith in science and technology (which is partly covered

---

[62] This is a different subject, therefore, from the personality prerequisites of man *for* economic development (such as are set forth in the theories of McClelland, Hagen, and Kunkel).

[63] See Alex Inkeles, "Making Men Modern: On the Causes and Consequences of Individual Change in Six Developing Countries," *American Journal of Sociology*, Vol. 75, No. 2 (September, 1969), 208–225; Inkeles, "The Modernization of Man," Chapter 10 in Weiner (ed.), *op. cit.;* David Horton Smith and Alex Inkeles, "The OM Scale: A Comparative Socio-Psychological Measure of Individual Modernity," *Sociometry*, Vol. 29 (1969), 353–377; and Inkeles, "Participant Citizenship in Six Developing Countries," *The American Political Science Review*, Vol. LXIII, No. 4 (December, 1969), 1120–1141.

[64] Quote from Inkeles, "Making Men Modern: . . .", *op. cit.*, p. 210.

[65] Inkeles, "The Modernization of Man," *op. cit.*, pp. 142–144.

in the preceding quotation); and having greater belief in distributive justice (that is to say, modern man believes that rewards should be related to contribution and not according to whim or to the ascribed characteristics of the person).

These ideas are the conclusions of a research project centering at Harvard University in which about 6,000 young men in six developing nations were interviewed. Approximately one thousand men were interviewed in each of the following nations: Argentina, Chile, India, Israel, Nigeria, and East Pakistan. Thus, all three of the continents containing the vast majority of developing nations were represented. Numerous research controls were exercised. The interview schedule included almost three hundred entries. The project began in 1962; field work was completed in 1964.[66]

Additional Commentary

Because most of the preceding statements have been brief, some additional comment and explanation may be advisable. Many of the preceding changes bear testimony to the potent influence of technology, given a favoring value system. In the United States, declares Wellisz,[67] more than two thirds of the increase in national income that occurred over the last ninety years is attributed to technological change and only one third to the increase in capital and in labor. With the help of new technology, a resource-poor country can overcome its natural handicaps. Technological progress is the prime mover of economic development; [68] however, management must modernize too and so keep up with production techniques. Also local adaptations need to be made. A policy that might be most appropriate for France or the United States may be of little value in India or Nigeria.[69] Then too, man, electing to live in a technological environment, has to adjust to the total situation.[70] Peace of mind—general contentment—is by no

[66] A brief summary of the research project itself is given in Inkeles, "Making Men Modern: . . .", *op. cit.*, 208–209. Much more detail is provided in the Smith and Inkeles, "The OM Scale: . . .", *op. cit.* The OM scale (measure of over-all modernity) is a general summary index that represents the degree to which a man possesses the attitudes that are thought to comprise "psychological modernity." Associates with Inkeles in the Harvard project are David H. Smith, Howard Schuman, and Edward Ryan.

[67] Stanislaw H. Wellisz, "The Modernization of Technology," Chapter 17 in Weiner (ed.), *op. cit.*, especially p. 234.

[68] *Loc. cit.*

[69] *Ibid.*, p. 239.

[70] William F. Ogburn, "Technology As Environment," *Sociology and Social Research*, Vol. XLI (September–October, 1956). This has been reprinted in Otis Dudley Duncan (ed.), *William F. Ogburn on Culture and Social Change* (Chicago: University of Chicago Press, 1964), pp. 78–85.

means guaranteed. However, if underdeveloped nations take the course of modernization, material benefit and a higher standard of living are likely to be theirs *if* they are able to surmount the various difficulties along the road. Many would call it economic advancement at a price. Many peasant societies, at any rate, have indicated their wishes, and have made a visible adjustment to the pros and cons of the change.

Since 1930, the underdeveloped nations have been growing about twice as fast in population as the industrialized nations.[71] It is further astonishing that the impoverished nations have about 69 per cent of the world's adults and about 80 per cent of the world's children (Davis' figures). The number of people affected in the modernization process provides one clue to the magnitude of the problem. The rapid increase of peoples in underdeveloped areas is also a sobering reminder of the extent of technological advance needed, because a rise in output *must exceed* population growth. The former increase similarly underscores the need of birth limitation in these areas.[72] The critical nature of the population problem can be pointed up by Pye's summary that it took all of recorded time to the present for the world to reach its current population level. Yet, the second three billion people will be reached in only thirty-five years.[73]

One of the greatest problems in underdeveloped areas is the underdevelopment of their human resources. "Education is of high importance both as an object of immediate consumption and as a form of investment for future production." [74] The new countries often point with pride to their steel mills, dams, or fertilizer factories as the manifestation of development. Education is indispensable in bringing agricultural and industrial progress.[75] Each nation, points out Harbi-

---

[71] Davis, *op. cit.*, p. 30

[72] For an attempt to operationalize the concept of overpopulation—relating population growth to dependency factors—see David R. Kamerschen, "On an Operational Index of 'Overpopulation'" *Economic Development and Cultural Change*, Vol. XIII, No. 2 (January, 1965), 169–187. For a study of the population problem in Central America—in the republics of Costa Rica, El Salvador, Guatemala, Honduras, and Nicaragua—see Robert S. Smith, "Population and Economic Growth in Central America," *Economic Development and Cultural Change*, Vol. X, No. 2 (January, 1962), 134–149.

[73] Lucian W. Pye, "The International Gap," Chapter 25 in Weiner (ed.), *op. cit.*, p. 344.

[74] John Kenneth Galbraith, *Economic Development in Perspective* (Cambridge, Mass.: Harvard University Press, 1962), p. 51.

[75] Galbraith states:

> *To rescue farmers and workers from illiteracy may certainly be a goal in itself. But it is also a first indispensable step to any form of agricultural progress. Nowhere in the world is there an illiterate peasantry that is progressive. Nowhere is there a literate peasantry that is not. Education, so viewed, becomes a highly productive form of investment.* Ibid., *p. 49.*

son,[76] needs to think out a strategy for its educational system. The latter has to be based on the character and traditions of the people, their stage of development, and economic and other opportunities. Importantly, the educational ideas and curriculum should relate to the needs of the area rather than ape what is currently fashionable in leading universities in advanced areas.[77] All of this, and more left unsaid, underscores education as a basic, high-priority ingredient in the total modernization process.[78]

Another vital element is *leadership*. Because pitfalls may be encountered at any turn, because able planning is required for guiding the entire modernizing process, because an effort should be expended in favor of birth limitation, because persuasion is essential for agricultural reform, because the proper kind of educational programs should be established to fit the needs of the nation, because bureaucratic organizations are to be capably run, and because care should be exercised lest weaknesses of this or that sort invite a Communist takeover, capable people are required at the helm to ensure that all these vexing matters are satisfactorily resolved. Top leadership has to make decisions concerning the entire complex modernization effort.[79] Societies also need leaders of secondary rank, for instance, in connection with specialized bureaucratic organizations. A strong, highly educated, technically trained class of people is required for this purpose.[80]

Finally, the basic *idea* held by leaders and others concerning improved economic conditions and allied "better things to come"—which often will amount only to a dream—must still guide the planning and the actions. This provides the spark that spurs on the entire program. The nature of the kernal idea is necessarily of great moment.[81] It may

[76] Frederick Harbison, "Education for Development," *Scientific American, op. cit.,* p. 49.

[77] Galbraith, *op. cit.,* pp. 56 and 58.

[78] Inkeles finds that the amount of formal schooling a man has had emerges as the single most important variable in determining his OM score. Inkeles, "Making Men Modern: . . .", *op. cit.,* p. 212.

[79] Heilbroner declares:

> [*Many considerations*] *point to the all-important role of political leadership in inaugurating, guiding, containing, and controlling the comprehensive process of change which development entails. Only political leadership of the most forceful kind can inspire the sacrifice, cajole or command the painful social adaptation, win the confidence—often the blind confidence—needed. . . . Heilbroner, op. cit., p. 155.*

[80] Parsons, *Structure and Process in Modern Societies, op. cit.,* especially p. 127.

[81] One example of this—concerning China—is found in Kenneth Walker, "Ideology and Economic Discussion in China: Ma Yin-Ch'u on Development Strategy and His Critics," *Economic Development and Cultural Change,* Vol. XI, No. 2 (January, 1963), 113–133. It is true that this statement reflects the views of one man. Ma tended to favor general balance in the economy, meaning growth in many sectors, and paying some attention to consumer demand. In a sense, two ideologies are linked in this—economic development and communism.

reflect the perspectives, certainly in part, of individual leaders. Economic development may mean different things to different peoples. It will bear connection with traditions, factors of the physical environment, available natural resources, and the like of each area.

PROFESSOR ROSTOW AND THE FIVE STAGES

We have discussed modernization as though it is one lengthy process, having many facets to be sure, but something that begins in an extremely primitive and poverty-ridden area (on the order of Nyasaland in central Africa) and that, if carried through to its logical end, leads to a technologically developed, high standard of living, urban type of society where people are well educated, secular-minded, achievement-oriented, occupationally mobile, and attuned to the mass media. Not all societies, we recognize, will follow through to the end of the process. If some of them do, the process will probably take many generations. Some peoples may become discouraged and perhaps impatient concerning the very slowness of the process. Some disillusionment is probably inevitable.

Professor Walt W. Rostow, in a volume entitled *The Stages of Economic Growth* [82] has introduced the thesis that the lengthy process of development can be depicted according to various stages. He emphasizes that uniformities tend to occur in the sequence of modernization, at the same time recognizing the uniqueness of each nation's experience. His book "presents an economic historian's way of generalizing the sweep of modern history." [83] Because he integrated a highly involved story having many variables, his volume has received much attention. It is granted that the theory is regarded as controversial today, but it is well worth examining for its illumination of the process of development; criticisms will also be noted. Rostow declares that the over-all process of economic growth has five stages: (1) the traditional society, (2) the preconditions for take-off, (3) the take-off, (4) the drive to maturity, and (5) the age of high mass consumption.

Stage One: The Traditional Society.[84] Rostow's picture of the traditional society is similar to that described in the early part of this chapter. A high proportion of the people are employed in agriculture, agriculture nevertheless has low productivity, the average person has very little capital, most of the people have little or no savings,

[82] (Cambridge, England: Cambridge University Press, 1960).
[83] *Ibid.*, p. 1.
[84] In summarizing these stages we shall paraphrase, and occasionally quote from, Rostow.

and illiteracy is widespread. Rostow observes that an essential feature of this society is that the structure is developed within limited production functions; the latter are based on pre-Newtonian science and technology and on pre-Newtonian attitudes toward the physical world. The traditional society is not, however, necessarily static. The central fact is "that a ceiling existed on the level of attainable output per head. This ceiling resulted from the fact that the potentialities which flow from modern science and technology were either not available or not regularly and systematically applied." [85] Some manufacturing may develop, but, as in agriculture, the level of productivity is severely limited. Family and clan groupings are emphasized in the social organization.

Stage Two: Preconditions for Take-Off.   This second stage of growth is one of transition. A traditional society does not move directly into the process of industrialization, first certain preliminaries need to take place. The idea spreads, for one thing, that economic progress is not only possible but that it is necessary in order that other desirable results be obtained. The latter are such concepts as national dignity, private profit, the general welfare, and a better life for children. Education changes to fit the broader economic outlook. Enterprising people come forward to take the lead in economic activities and government or both; they are willing to take risks in striving for modernization. Banks and other institutions are formed in order to accumulate capital. But this activity proceeds at a limited pace within the older (traditional) emphases and values for the most part. In some cases newer economic activities during this period function beside institutions that have the traditional stamp. A decisive feature of this period of transition often concerns, however, the political institution. To develop an effective centralized national state is "almost universally a necessary condition" for the take-off stage to get started. [86]

Stage Three: The Take-Off.   This is the period in which the old resistances are finally overcome. The forces making for economic progress now expand and come to dominate the society. Growth becomes the normal condition. In Britain, Canada, and the United States the proximate stimulus for take-off was mainly (although not entirely) technological. In general, this stage awaits the sufficient accumulation of capital, a surge of technological development in industry and agriculture, and the emergence of a power group that rates modernization as serious, political business of a high order. During the take-off, the rate of effective investment and savings may rise from approximately

[85] Rostow, *op. cit.* p. 4.
[86] We have previously noted Parsons' observations on this subject.

5 per cent of the national income to 10 per cent or more. During this period new industries expand rapidly, and a large proportion of profits is reinvested in a new plant. New techniques spread in agriculture as well as industry; agriculture is commercialized; and many farmers accept the new methods and resulting changes in their way of life. The take-off period began in Britain after 1783, in France and the United States in around 1840, in Russia in about 1890, and in India and China in about 1950.

Stage Four: The Drive to Maturity. In this period the growing economy drives to extend modern technology over the whole front of its economic activity. Some 10–20 per cent of the national income is steadily invested, and output regularly outstrips the increase in population. Techniques improve, new industries accelerate, and older industries level off. A place in the international economy is obtained. Rostow estimates that the mature economy is attained roughly sixty years after the beginning of take-off.[87] Technology has now been extended into more refined and complex processes. As a formal definition, *maturity* is defined as "the stage in which an economy demonstrates the capacity to move beyond the original industries which powered its take-off and to absorb and to apply efficiently over a very wide range of its resources—if not the whole range—the most advanced fruits of [then] modern technology." [88]

Stage Five: The Age of High Mass Consumption. In this last stage the leading sectors of the economy shift toward durable consumers' goods and services. Many people have sufficient income such that consumption is not confined to necessities; also, the proportion of people living in cities increases as does the proportion of people working in offices and in skilled factory jobs. In this stage, moreover, the further extension of technology as an overriding objective is no longer accepted. More and more resources are allocated to social welfare and security. The emergence of the welfare state is an example. Durable consumers' goods and services are diffused on a mass basis. A notable example—virtually a symbol—of this is the increasing ownership of the automobile, which has brought many social and economic effects. Rostow thinks that the United States entered the stage of high mass consumption in about 1920, and that Western Europe and Japan entered it fully during the 1950s; he suggests that Russia is technically ready for this stage but has not actually entered it yet.[89]

Rostow's ideas are not confined to the stages of economic growth

---

[87] Rostow, *op. cit.*, p. 9.
[88] *Ibid.*, p. 10.
[89] *Ibid.*, p. 11; also see chart across from p. 1.

themselves. He also speculates on whether spiritual stagnation will set in after an "economy of abundance" has been attained.[90] He compares economic growth in Russia and the United States. He considers war in relation to economic growth. Finally, he contrasts his theory of economic growth with Marx's theory. Significant as these matters are, we shall not be able to discuss them here.

Commentary on the Rostow Stages

It may be worthwhile to examine criticisms that may be—or have been—made to the theory of the five stages. As an effort in economic history it is inevitable, first of all, that other economic historians and economists would not see eye-to-eye with Rostow. One critic, for instance, declares that *The Stages of Economic Growth* has appeal because of its simplicity, relevance, and high sincerity, but "there are on every page bold assertions, immense claims, sweeping insights, unsubstantiated by analysis or documentation." [91] Another caustic critic delivers the following broadside: "Taken very broadly, Rostow's perspective on history does of course have a few things in common with other economic historians' way of looking at it." [92] After this, in a lengthy review, he takes issue with quite a few points relative to the take-off, drive-to-maturity, and high-mass-consumption stages; [93] with a momentary loss of vinegar he conceded that Rostow's treatment of the traditional and transitional stages is "remarkably successful." Near the end of his review he returns to his principal theme in the following words: "Few Western historians would rally around any one interpretation of history, and the tinny sound of the stage-of-growth would certainly not be their clarion call." [94]

---

[90] Does man require the perpetual spur of taking care of the essentials? When the fifth stage is reached "Will the devil make work for idle hands? Will men learn how to conduct wars with just enough violence to be good sport. . . ? . . . Will the exploration of outer space offer an adequately interesting and expensive outlet for resources and ambitions?" *Ibid.,* p. 91. In short, will man have a problem of boredom? Will he decline for want of prime challenges?

[91] W. N. Parker, a review of Rostow, *The Stages of Economic Growth,* in *American Economic Review,* Vol. 50 (December, 1960), 1058–1059.

[92] Goran Ohlin, a review of Rostow. *The Stages of Economic Growth,* in *Economic Development and Cultural Change,* Vol. IX, No. 4, Part 1 (July, 1961), 648–655.

[93] For instance, Ohlin holds that the take-off stage, "which is meant to be the central notion in the scheme," does not accelerate nearly as fast as Rostow thinks. In any case, the statistics regarding this are poor. Ohlin maintains that the take-off model is more appropriate for some nations than others, that the acceleration of growth is sometimes slow and sometimes rapid, and that the model is more likely to fit latecomers than old industrial nations. Regarding the maturity stage, Ohlin declares that it is not here defined in relation to new sectors of the economy and, hence, cannot be precisely dated. *Ibid.,* p. 650.

[94] *Ibid.,* p. 654.

On the other hand, many reviewers—perhaps most of them—reacted favorably to the Rostow thesis. One top-flight critic, Adolf A. Berle, Jr., had much praise for Rostow.

> *This is an important book. . . . It will, I think, affect action. It is the most dynamic book on economics I have read in several years.*
>
> *Walter Rostow . . . has tackled the job of constructing a theory of economic history. Therefore he considers, rightly, that he offers an alternative to Karl Marx's "Capitalism." He suggests a quite different brand of historical inevitability. This is what present-day economists and historians ought to be doing.*
>
> . . .
>
> *One can, and I do, quarrel with a great many specific statements. . . . Generalization about stages is difficult because no large society is ever entirely in any one phase, as Rostow recognizes. . . . But these are disputes within rather than against Rostow's central theme. He has done a stunning job. Here is economic generalization at its far-reaching best. Rostow is entitled to accolade for having attempted it and for brilliantly succeeding in evoking a choate usable hypothesis. From here on neither university nor popular economics can be taught or debated without taking his analysis into account.*[95]

Other reviews may be noted.[96] However, one significant achievement of Rostow's volume was that it led to the publication of a second one on the same theme. The 1960 Conference of the International Economic Association brought together theorists, historians, and statisticians with the purpose of examining the validity of the Rostow thesis.[97] Professor Simon Kuznets questioned the necessity of having a distinct "take-off" stage (his criticism was similar to Ohlin's), to which Rostow countered that it was a well-defined stage of development leading to sustained growth. Kuznets suggested the general view that economic growth is a gradual process rather than one involving a sharply delineated period of take-off. Empirical evidence cited by economic historians at the conference did not conclusively settle this dilemma. Nor did papers dealing with population growth, technical progress, and agriculture contribute decisively. The variety of national experiences was again indicated, and a general consensus emphasized the importance of technological progress in economic growth.

Finally, a *methodological* objection to the Rostow work has recently

[95] Adolf A. Berle, Jr., a review of Rostow, *The Stages of Economic Growth*, in *The Saturday Review*, Vol. 43, Part 2 (July 9, 1960), 18–19.

[96] See Wilfred Malenbaum, a review of Rostow, *The Stages of Economic Growth*, in *Annals of the American Academy of Political and Social Science*, Vol. 333 (January, 1961), 164–165; Harry Schwartz, a review of Rostow, *The Stages of Economic Growth*, in *The New York Times Book Review* (May 8, 1960). For a critical commentary not comprising a review for journal, see Hagen, *op. cit.*, pp. 514–522, Appendix II, "The Rostovian Schema."

[97] Walt W. Rostow (ed.), *The Economics of Take-Off into Sustained Growth*, Proceedings of a conference held by the International Economic Association (New York: St. Martin's Press, 1963).

been registered. Nisbet [98] contends that Rostow went astray by trying to make a *too-specific* statement of the stages of economic growth. If he had confined his statement of growth to abstractions relative to economic production for all mankind, declares Nisbet, he would have been unassailable. However, he too specifically made application to European and other nations. Thus, criticisms that in X nation development at some stage was not as Rostow predicted should be out-of-bounds. It is true that the acid test for any theory is: Does it predict? If a theory tells us what will occur under certain conditions, we say that it is good theory. Nevertheless in the social sciences, as Raser points out, "most theory does not pretend that it can predict single (discrete) events; . . . it is 'probabilistic'—it merely predicts processes or trends." [99]

As we near the conclusion of this discussion of developing nations, we again remind the reader that the journey toward modernization tends to be lengthy and uncertain. As Heilbroner says,

> *Illiterate peasants must be made into literate farmers. Defeated slum dwellers must be made into disciplined factory workers. Old and powerful social classes must be deprived of ancient privileges; new and untried social classes must be saddled with enormous responsibilities. . . . From our vantage point, in which all of these alterations of life are part of our remote history, we tend to forget how profoundly dislocating, how revolutionary, such changes are.*[100]

Eisenstadt [101] has called attention to recent examples of nations in the process of modernization that have given way to autocratic, authoritarian, or semiauthoritarian regimes; Indonesia, Burma, and Sudan are examples. In examining such breakdowns in modernization, one is interested to see that the take-off stage seems to have developed satisfactorily. Indeed, various important indices such as urbanization, diversification of occupational structure, and exposure to mass media were continuously expanding in these nations. The institutions were being "detraditionalized" (Eisenstadt's term); yet, the instructional structure—and especially the political area—was not able to cope with the problems brought by the socio-demographic and structural changes.[102] We cannot go into details here except to say that the lack of regulative mechanisms and normative injunctions was related to

[98] Robert A. Nisbet, *Social Change and History* (New York: Oxford University Press, 1969), pp. 253–255.

[99] John R. Raser, *Simulation and Society* (Boston: Allyn and Bacon, Inc., 1969), p. 85.

[100] Heilbroner, *op. cit.,* p. 151.

[101] S. N. Eisenstadt, "Breakdowns in Modernization," *Economic Development and Culture Change,* Vol. XII, No. 4 (July, 1964), 345–367.

[102] *Ibid.,* pp. 347 and 357.

the regression. Eisenstadt declares that these failures can be understood in terms of Durkheim's ideas: "In all these cases there took place a failure to establish and institutionalize new levels of solidarity, to make the transition from mechanical to organic solidarity or from a level of low organic solidarity to a higher one. . . ." [103]

The occurrences in Cuba have also been discouraging from the standpoint of the ongoing modernization process. Here is a nation that at the time of the Castro coup was relatively advanced in many respects.[104] It is clear that by this time it has been thrust back by its totally inexperienced leadership to a repressive system usually associated with a much earlier stage of development. We have previously mentioned the dangers of a Communist coup to nations in the process of development. Communism is a threat not only because of its conspiratorial activities, but because of the *seeming attractiveness* of its doctrines as underdeveloped nations are likely to interpret them. What is more, the Communists direct incessant propaganda at the underdeveloped areas of the world. The Communist blandishments may be favorably received, first of all, because they offer a *ready program* for use.[105] Then the program is administered in decisive manner: if land is needed, it is taken; if workers are wanted in some location, people are taken there, with little attention to their own wishes; if opposition to the program develops, it is "liquidated." To the West, the ruthlessness of the program is intolerable. Yet, as Heilbroner points out,[106] this is not necessarily the reaction of the Asian or African peoples. For the most part the latter are hungry people who have never known political freedom and, hence, are not likely to regret its absence. Accustomed to brutality and indifference, moreover, they tend to readily if resignedly submit to the new masters. Then, too, the Communist programs may achieve a degree of success. These considerations point up the immense challenges involved in a program to modernize.

Inevitably, however, one comes back to a basic point made by Levy. The difficulties involved in the modernization process are freely admitted, but the process itself cannot be avoided. In Levy's words,

> *Modernization is the problem par excellence for the vast majority of the world's people whether they are aware of it or not. . . . The members of relatively nonmodernized societies are not faced with a choice of whether to modernize or not. They will modernize to some*

[103] *Ibid.*, p. 358.

[104] Ward, *op. cit.*, p. 132.

[105] For example, Barbara Ward thinks that the very availability of the Soviet pattern helps to explain the unfolding paradox of Castro's regime. "Faced with the multitudinous uncertainties of responsibility, he [Castro] grabbed the only pattern which seemed likely to preserve his leadership and deal with his difficulties." *Ibid.*

[106] Heilbroner, *op. cit.*, p. 162.

extent, whether they like it or not, unless they die out or in rare cases of small-scale societies dwell in regions with no contacts save the most sporadic ones with the members of other societies. Whether and to what degree they modernize successfully from their point of view or that of anyone else is quite a different question.[107]

If modernization is *the* problem for the peoples living in underdeveloped nations, instability and the possibility of disorganization are the prime concerns of the advanced nations.[108] We turn to this subject in our final chapter.

ANNOTATED BIBLIOGRAPHY

Apter, David E., *The Politics of Modernization* (Chicago: University of Chicago Press, 1965).
> Political problems and alternatives that accompany modernization. Recommended.

Eisenstadt, S. N., *Modernization: Protest and Change* (Englewood Cliffs, N. J.: Prentice-Hall, Inc., 1966).
> Emphasizes the "problem side" of the modernization process; two phases of the latter are considered. Eisenstadt's basic conclusion is that for successful modernization a flexible institutional structure is needed that will absorb protests. Rather abstract writing.

Hagen, Everett E., *On the Theory of Social Change* (Homewood, Ill.: The Dorsey Press, Inc., 1962).
> Provides a wealth of material, is recommended in many ways; but Hagen's main thesis seems fanciful and difficult to establish.

Heilbroner, Robert L., *The Great Ascent* (New York: Harper & Row, 1963).
> Recommended general discussion of economic development.

Hoselitz, Bert F., and Moore, Wilbert E. (eds.), *Industrialization and Society* (The Hague: Unesco, Mouton, 1963).
> A valuable all-around appraisal of the "development" process as of 1960. The authors include, in addition to Hoselitz and Moore, Neil Smelser, David C. McClelland, Simon Kuznets, D. Apter, S. N. Eisenstadt, Philip Hauser, and Ithiel de Sola Pool.

Inkeles, Alex, "Making Men Modern: On the Causes and Consequences of Individual Change in Six Developing Countries," *American Journal of Sociology,* Vol. 75, No. 2 (September, 1969), 208–225; Inkeles, "Participant Citizenship in Six Developing Countries," *The American Political Science Review,* Vol. LXIII, No. 4 (December, 1969), 1120–1141.
> An important research project explores the effects of modernization on man himself. A worthwhile test of the theory of modern man. Much recommended.

Kunkel, John H., *Society and Economic Growth* (New York: Oxford University Press, 1970).

[107] Levy, *op. cit.*, p. 734.

[108] *Ibid.*, pp. 735 and 777–794. Of course, instabilities may accompany the drastic changes involved in modernization, as Levy makes clear, but instability and marked disorganization are special, built-in problems of the advanced nations.

An ably written book that espouses the behavioral model of personality change in modernization. Differential reinforcement—reward and punishment—are the basic levers of change. The "proof of the pudding" is seen in the Vicos and other programs. Kunkel's behavioral interpretation is quite convincing.

Levy, Marion J., Jr., *Modernization and the Structure of Societies,* 2 Vols. (Princeton, N. J.: Princeton University Press, 1966).

A major endeavor that seeks to provide knowledge of backgrounds of different societies relevant to the field of international affairs. Accents (1) the comparison of the structure of relatively modernized and relatively nonmodernized societies and (2) the present-day problems of modernization and of stability of the relatively modernized. Levy also stresses the contrast between *ideal* and *actual* structures as a force for change.

McClelland, David C., *The Achieving Society* (Princeton, N. J.: D. Van Nostrand Co., 1961).

A remarkable, perhaps brilliant, book. Makes the case for personality change as a prerequisite for economic development; family dynamics will produce achievement motivation. Perhaps somewhat overly psychological. High-quality writing, although McClelland's use of children's fairy tales and the like strains one's credulity in spots. See also McClelland and David Winter, *Motivating Human Behavior* (New York: The Free Press, Inc., 1969).

Rostow, Walt W., *The Stages of Economic Growth* (Cambridge, England: Cambridge University Press, 1960).

A rewarding general statement on the "stages." It is granted that fellow economic historians dispute Rostow at various points; in some cases the critics are undoubtedly correct. Nevertheless, a valuable, integrative book.

Weiner, Myron (ed.), *Modernization, the Dynamics of Growth* (New York: Basic Books, Inc., 1966).

Extremely worthwhile contributions made by such social scientists as Cyril Black, David C. McClelland, C. Arnold Anderson, Edward Shils, Ithiel de Sola Pool, Neil Smelser, Norton Ginsburg, Alex Inkeles, and of course Weiner himself. Some emphasis on political factors. Recommended.

Epilogue: Social Change and Social Disorganization

15

Before introducing the main theme of these final pages let us briefly review some of the principal emphases of this volume. We began with an empirical view of change, not only as it affected American generations as recent as one century ago, but also as it has affected the entire world today; it was hoped that in subsequent discussions the reader would keep "real-life conditions" in mind. We then discussed fundamentals in the sociological study of change, placing some emphasis upon the generally equal importance of social and cultural influences.[1] After this we examined several dozen approaches to the study of social alterations, which are important in themselves and also make evident the multifaceted and panoramic nature of the total study. Then we considered and evaluated some dozen major theories of change that have followed some of the approaches; these theories have come to us from leading thinkers of the past who have been impressed with different aspects of changing social life seen from the perspectives of a given place and time. Next, Sociology's accomplishments with regard to the measurement of change have been considered. At this juncture we turned to a more detailed discussion of selected *processes* of change that warrant special attention at this time, namely, innovation, resistances to innovation, diffusion, activism, and modernization. These important processes are global in scope and application although, for reasons of space, we mostly restricted discussion of the first four to American society; the last one, the modernization of peasant societies, clearly centers attention upon the world scene.

One crucial subject that has been almost entirely ignored in the preceding chapters is the relationship between social change and social disorganization; we would discuss certain aspects of the relationship in this Epilogue. Because the social world of the 1970's is one of fast-moving, tumultuous change in both modernizing and advanced nations,

1 We have agreed with Buckley's contention relative to systems theory that *human social systems differ significantly from non-human ones (as birds or insects) and from physical systems due to the importance of the cultural factor.* The reader is aware that because of this we prefer the use of the term "socio-cultural system" as Buckley does, too. See Walter Buckley, *Sociology and Modern Systems Theory* (Englewood Cliffs, New Jersey: Prentice-Hall, Inc., 1967), p. 1.

we hold that a gross error would be committed if no discussion whatever were rendered concerning the possibilities of marked disorganization. Having Western Civilization (and especially American society)
in mind we agree with Levy [2] that the factor of *stability* in social life
is a most difficult and continuing problem. Indeed extensive social
disorganization looms as a kind of special "Achilles heel" of the advanced and affluent nations. Our comments relative to this subject will
be partly sociological and partly philosophical in nature.

In reflecting upon the ever-present threat of disorganization we wish
to make clear at the outset that we do not necessarily place ourselves
with the "prophets of doom" school—easy as it might be to do that.
There is no dearth of problems and crises over which one can "wring
his hands," decry developments (including governmental or other solutions designed to meet them), or perhaps suggest changing to another
system. Nevertheless judgments on these matters need to be based on
a convincing analysis. We see no evidence that such-and-such threat at
a particular time *must* lead to calamity or ruin; and history over the
centuries has recorded severe trials and challenges for mankind.

In Chapter 5 we followed Sorokin's able writing concerning the
"Decline of the Sensate," but, although we grant that present-day
American and Western conditions resemble his dismal portrayal in
various respects, have nevertheless questioned whether the "Sensate"
era *has* to decline. Granting that contemporary Western Civilization
as an example of this cultural type *might* decline (because of vast
destruction of a Third World War, very damaging pollution, or in
fact a variety of reasons operating singly or in some joint fashion), we
at least do not think that such decline would occur in the manner of
Sorokin's statement. Similarly in Chapter 8 we have considered Oswald
Spengler's view of the decline of the West. Here we reject the theory—
not because it is pessimistic *per se*—because it provides no objective
explanation at all. The real causes of socio-cultural change are evaded
as Spengler concentrates on a mystical and highly inflexible accounting
of human developments; and his exposition unfortunately involves
special, subjective definitions of such concepts as "the soul of culture"
and "destiny." This treatment has to be regarded as unconvincing,
certainly from the standpoint of social *science*. In short, the Western
nations and the rest of the world *may be* in for a sharp decline or some
kind of collapse, but the evidence for it is by no means certain as these
writers appear to maintain.

Then we shall shy away from unbalanced social explanations, evaluations, and indictments of a society or type of society. We shall think of

[2] Marion J. Levy, Jr., *Modernization and the Structure of Societies*, Vol. II (Princeton, N. J.: Princeton University Press, 1966), p. 777.

Jacques Ellul's *The Technological Society*[3] as an example of this. Even though Ellul makes an able indictment of the society based on technique in many respects, he carries ideas to the extreme and errs in solely emphasizing *negative* factors. If his analysis were to motivate the reader to assess the influence of technology (or technique) both positively and negatively, the net result of his work might be worthwhile; but Ellul himself does not provide this balanced view. No doubt many writers of past years as well as on the current scene fail to have due regard for both positive and negative factors in a situation.

The Meaning of Social Disorganization

However, if we propose to discuss social change in relation to social disorganization, it is necessary to define the latter concept. Merton[4] has referred to *social disorganization* as "inadequacies or failures in a social system of interrelated statuses and roles such that the collective purposes and individual objectives of its members are less fully realized than they could be in an alternative workable system." Disorganization, he points out, can be thought of as resulting from multiple social dysfunctioning. Similarly Cohen[5] defines social disorganization as "a disruption or perhaps threatening of the constitutive order of ongoing activity." Such disruption—it is expressed as a matter of degree—may be caused by demonstrations, takeovers, riots, natural disasters, large-scale unemployment, effects of inventions, war, or other events. The contributing causes may lie in the array of approaches to change that were discussed in Chapters 3 and 4.

These definitions suggest that social disorganization often involves a failure to overcome one or more of the functional problems of a system. It is clear, then, that the terms *organization* and *disorganization* define a single field of interest that relates to the orderly functioning of a system or a disruption of that order. Any system will at times veer toward the "orderly functioning" end of the continuum, at other times toward the end of "disruption of expectations and of order" due to the impact of many social influences. The occurrence of a well-organized society (or subsystem) or a relatively disorganized one results, then, from the processes of socio-cultural change.

[3] Jacques Ellul, *The Technological Society,* translated from the French by John Wilkinson (New York: A. A. Knopf, 1964).

[4] Robert K. Merton, "Social Problems and Sociological Theory," Chap. 15 in R. K. Merton and Robert Nisbet (eds.), *Contemporary Social Problems* (New York: Harcourt, Brace and World, 1961), p. 720.

[5] Albert K. Cohen, "The Study of Social Disorganization and Deviant Behavior," Chap. 21 in Robert K. Merton, L. Broom, and L. S. Cottrell, Jr. (eds.), *Sociology Today* (New York: Basic Books, 1959), p. 479.

Recent Changes and Social Disorganization

In the opening chapter of this volume reference was made to various influences with respect to socio-cultural change that are here regarded as of special significance. This relates to American society with its given value system. At this point we would focus brief attention upon three areas of social change—population growth, scientific and technological change, and the upsurge of Activist sentiment—with interest in each concerning their effects on *social disorganization*. We begin with population growth. Hauser,[6] in a brilliant article that provides much information and many insights, has called the vast changes that have occurred in this sphere the "social morphological revolution." This is the product of three developments: (1) the remarkable increase in the rate of population growth itself, often known as the "population explosion"; (2) the increasing urbanization and metropolitanization of the people, which he designates as the "population implosion"; and (3) the increasing heterogeneity of the population, or "population diversification," composing different foreign stocks as well as the various racial groups. These demographic changes have in turn been affected by technological changes. The United States, comments Hauser,[7] constitutes the world's most dramatic examples of these population and technological developments. A prime resultant of the above changes is the transformation of the "little community" (Redfield's term) into the "mass society." Much of the chaos and disorganization of contemporary society may be understood, he declares, as frictions in this transition that is still under way; he cites governmental, racist, and other "lags" that have occurred. Certainly population growth has affected all social institutions. Many practices that served a useful purpose in the "little community" may be most inappropriate in the modern urban setting, such as the right to bear arms or any failure to resolve conflicts by an adjudicative or democratic procedure.[8] Moreover, insofar as organizations are concerned, the likelihood of conflict and disorganization increases as the size becomes greater. Mott [9] states that as organizational size increases (1) "the integration that the organization achieves from sharing common norms declines," (2) "the problems of interacting vertically in the same hierarchy or between hierarchies increase," (3) "the potential for conflict and friction among

[6] Philip M. Hauser, "The Chaotic Society: Product of the Social Morphological Revolution," *American Sociological Review*, Vol. 34, No. 1 (Feb., 1969), 1–19. This constituted Professor Hauser's presidential address before the 63rd Annual Meetings of the American Sociological Association.

[7] *Ibid.*, p. 5.

[8] *Ibid.*, p. 12.

[9] See Paul E. Mott, *The Organization of Society* (Englewood Cliffs, New Jersey: Prentice-Hall, Inc., 1965), Chap. 3, pp. 48–66.

the parts also increases," and (4) "the number of coordinative problems and the need for coordination also increase." In sum, it is much more difficult to maintain a well-organized collectivity composed of, say, 25,000 individuals than it is of one composed of one thousand. Also, if any doubt exists concerning the matter, it is far more difficult to maintain a relatively well-organized nation of about 205 million population (the approximate total of the United States in 1970) than it would be to do the same if the population numbered about 40 million (the approximate total in this nation in *1870*). However, as Hauser pointed out, it is not just the sheer numbers; the factors of "implosion" and "diversification" and their consequences carry weight, too. The demands upon leaders are necessarily much greater. Then, if disruptions do take place—owing to natural disasters, power failures, demonstrations and riots, inventions, and other influences—it is clear that the disorganization assumes a much larger scale. There are more people to riot, more people to "march on Washington," a larger number to be affected by the other causes of disorganization.

The influence of science and technology also has considerable impact upon socio-cultural change, as is widely recognized. The many changes deriving from this source are sometimes socially beneficial, sometimes give rise to concerns or even fears. Numerous dirty and servile jobs have been eliminated; hours of work have been shortened; an abundance of goods—and a generally higher standard of living—has been provided. The beneficial changes in the educational, medical, political, and other realms accruing from science and technology are too numerous to list. The pleasures related to automobile driving, to home living (TV, air-conditioning, and the rest), or to airplane travel, for example, are undoubted. But the negative part of the picture (including fear of "the bomb" itself) has to be reckoned, too. The problems of air and water pollution have reached the critical stage. Moreover, environmental degradation, ecological imbalance, and the like, will increase if no corrective measures are taken. Firm and continuing control measures simply have to be instituted, as major challenges have been dealt-with by the American and other nations before. Invasion of privacy by electronic eaves-dropping (including the development of computerized data banks that could significantly affect peoples' lives) must receive careful attention. Civil liberties and privacy have to be protected given the new technological capabilities.

Scientific and technological developments tend to disrupt the existing arrangements of social systems and subsystems. Every invention brings *some degree* of disorganization. New social adjustments often have to be made and these are frequently delayed—causing disorganization—as the "lag" theory of Professor Ogburn explained. To sum up, then, science and technology are great social benefactors but also major disorganizers.[10] It is well to keep in mind at this time, moreover, that these processes are steadily moving ahead if they are not being accentuated. As Diebold [11] expresses it, "technology has now become self-generating; it has reached the 'take-off' point." The computer, for instance, is throwing off whole new families of machines. He observes that entire new industries will increasingly develop in addition to the computer itself (which is still in its comparatively early development), namely, the data utility industry, the "inquiry industry" (which he likens to the publishing field of the future), and the industry of computer-based educational systems. He thinks it highly probable that "through the technology of learning systems, the entire world of education can be changed." [12] Then we have noted earlier that the new "intellectual technology" (meaning the techniques of linear programming, systems analysis, game theory and simulation as linked to the computer) permit us, in Bell's [13] words, "to accumulate and manipulate large aggregates of data . . . we can, through simulation, create 'controlled experiments' in the social sciences in order to trace the progressive and regressive consequences of alternative choices of action, and create models, . . ." These techniques, furthermore, will steadily be improved and extended. All these developments bear promise of impressive accomplishments in the future, and, needless to say, many other inventions in entirely different realms have been and are being made. Great benefits, though also considerable disorganization, may again be expected; the new inventions always undercut existing arrangements and outmode the earlier thinking. It would seem that this will be even more true of the future than of the past.

Some have emphasized that society must learn to cope with rapid social change itself, which has largely resulted from the influences of science and technology. Diebold [14] concedes that "the future will be change, and this change will be of unprecedented speed and variety."

[10] Thus the invention of the telephone "dial system" brought the unemployment of many human "operators"; the advent of the automobile numbered the days of the wagon and buggy industry; the development of the motor vehicle (including truck and van) and in part the airplane drove many railroads into bankruptcy; the coming of automation led to the unemployment of many coal miners as well as factory and office workers, and so on. The resulting problems may be placed in juxtaposition to the benefits.

[11] John Diebold, *Man and the Computer* (New York: Frederick A. Praeger, 1969), p. 146.

[12] *Ibid.*, pp. 12–14.

[13] Daniel Bell, "The Measurement of Knowledge and Technology," Chap. 5 in E. B. Sheldon and W. E. Moore (eds.), *Indicators of Social Change* (New York: Russell Sage Foundation, 1968), pp. 157–158.

[14] Diebold, *op. cit.*, p. 151.

Toffler [15] maintains that the "roaring current of change" will give rise to "future shock"—that is to say, mass disorientation on a grand scale. In this he casts technology in the roles of both hero and villain, "hero" because of the many benefits that it brings, "villain" because of the disorientation that he thinks it will also cause. Bennis and Slater [16] take the view that the accelerating rate of technological change (combined with other influences) has caused American and other modernized societies to become *temporary societies*. The latter are characterized by "temporary systems, nonpermanent relationships, turbulance, uprootedness, unconnectedness, mobility, and, above all, unexampled social change." [17] These contentions need to be carefully considered, although questions may be raised as to "how much truth" resides in them in application to "how many and what types of people." As previously mentioned, the Bennis-Slater thesis relates to many influences (not solely technology).

One reaction to technology and its influence, which is common at the present time, is regarded here as a mistaken one. This is the overall pessimistic and negativistic view that seems to have developed along with the emphasis upon pollution problems. Some may want to "turn off" technology, using it as a scapegoat for environmental and other problems. However, one must agree with Dr. Glenn T. Seaborg's [18] statement that it is erroneous to overemphasize everything that is "harmful, crass and ugly in our world," overlooking "the many benefits of the technology of the past (and also) what it might accomplish for us in the future, were we to direct it wisely." The "all-negative" perspective is unconvincing and is bound to fail precisely because it is so obviously unbalanced. The problem-side of technology requires attention (and in some cases immediate attention); but the positive side should receive its due, too. The task ahead is doubtless to direct technology to the fulfillment of major social goals,[19] including the mitigation of pollution and other problems. One may also observe that, as part of their way-of-life, the American and other peoples *do* want automobiles, TV sets, telephones, air-conditioners, refrigerators, air

[15] Alvin Toffler, *Future Shock* (New York: Random House, 1970).

[16] Warren G. Bennis and Philip E. Slater, *The Temporary Society* (New York: Harper & Row, 1968).

[17] *Ibid.*, p. 124.

[18] Glenn T. Seaborg, "The New Optimism," *The Futurist*, Vol. III, No. 6 (December, 1969), pp. 157–160 (esp. p. 157). The author is Chairman of the U.S. Atomic Energy Commission. This article was drawn from an address that he delivered at a Nobel Symposium in Stockholm during September, 1969.

[19] The preceding words have been paraphrased from the Report of the (U.S.) National Commission on Technology, Automation, and Economic Progress, *Technology and the American Economy*, Vol. 1 (Washington, D. C.: Government Printing Office, 1966), p. xiii. For further discussion along this line, see this able report.

travel, medical technology—and computers. It is futile to argue otherwise.

The rise of activist sentiment constitutes at this time another important source of socio-cultural change in many parts of the world, especially in the United States—a source that, we suggest, will become even more significant in future years. We have referred to activism in Chapter 13, following Daniel Bell, as an orientation that seeks to direct the process of change itself. "Men now seek to anticipate change, measure the course of its direction and its impact, control it, and even shape it for predetermined ends." [20] Activism, then, involves the deliberate effort to anticipate and direct change—to determine one's wants for the future and attempt to achieve them. Activism may also be regarded as a master approach toward change in that it gathers other approaches, such as the political, educational, collective behavior, and conflict ones, under its folds. We have discussed in Chapter 13 Amitai Etzioni's [21] conception of a society that follows the activist dictates. Alternative conceptions of such a society are, however, possible; we have ourselves expressed several alternative views in the earlier chapter.

Because the upsurge of activist interest—unlike the subjects of population and science-technology—has previously had chapter-length discussion at least in this volume, we may proceed more directly to the activist impact upon social disorganization. If programs are more and more to modify social institutions and other elements of the social structure in terms of the people's active wishes, it seems clear that ample re-structuring or disorganizing of existing social arrangements may take place. It is crucial at this point whether the activist program being followed assumes modifications "within the framework of the existing system," constant transformations along the lines suggested by Professor Etzioni, more radical programs (such as might be espoused by the Students for Democratic Society, Marxist organizations, or other groups) or some other alternative plan. Also, activist behavior on college campuses, for instance, has varied considerably with respect to the degree of militancy and tactics employed—hence, in the amount of disruption caused. Even a group such as the SDS has had divers emphases in its different chapters in composition, tone, and tactics.[22] Then, in one chapter (the Columbia one provides an example) activities may drastically change in degree-of-militancy as new leaders

[20] Daniel Bell, "Notes on the Post-Industrial Society (I)," *The Public Interest,* No. 6 (Winter, 1967), p. 25.

[21] Amitai Etzioni, *The Active Society* (New York: The Free Press, A Division of The Macmillan Co., 1968).

[22] The Cox Commission Report, *Crisis at Columbia* (New York: Random House, 1968), pp. 54–59.

assume office. Kelman,[23] moreover, noted the drastic change in activities of the Harvard SDS as a different faction of the organization gained control. Nevertheless one may make one generalization concerning these situations that pertains to social disorganization. In these campus disturbances one could see a new phenomenon taking place: Instead of the usual circumstance of social disorganization occurring as a *result* of the processes of social change, social disorganization was now employed as a *tactic* of *achieving some desired change*. Thus individuals and groups *sought* to disorganize—in short, one witnessed *willful, purposeful disorganization*—in order to attain some end (thwart the Vietnam war effort, obtain greater justice for Black students or admit more Black students to the college, and so on). The common procedure was to "take over" some building (Sproul Hall, University Hall, Fayerweather Hall, etc.) or group of buildings. The disruptions sometimes lasted many months (San Francisco State), at other times were of relatively short duration (Harvard and Cornell). Since the mass media publicize such events, the disruptive efforts spread quickly from campus to campus. A "multiplier effect" sets in. It is clear that the deliberate use of disorganization as a technique of effecting change has caused a considerable increase in disruptive behavior.[24] Students took their cues from the civil rights confrontations of the 1960's (some had participated in them); conflict had been employed there as a method of bringing change when it was felt that cooperation had not brought desired results.

Disorganization for "Good Reasons."   To some extent one could say that use of disruption in order to obtain desired changes amounted to "disorganization for good reasons." If disorganization was a "means," the "ends" were stopping the Vietnam war, increasing justice for Blacks, and so on. To favor these "ends" expresses a point of view, to be sure. Some would interject that to *state* one's views on these subjects is one thing; to seek to actively thwart the program of one's government, say, with regard to the war is, however, something different. With a number of students (the exact percentage would be difficult to determine) pure idealism for these causes was the main motivation for action. On the other hand, evidence indicates that in

23 Steven Kelman, *Push Comes to Shove* (Boston: Houghton Mifflin Co., 1970), pp. 140–144.

24 If radicals had not gained control in certain cases, the amount of disruption might have been smaller. As the Harvard SDS finally chose to attack the university itself, Kelman's comment is of interest: "The real reason for attacking the universities is that radicals have to obtain a mass base for radicalism on the campus itself. . . . This action secured the support of the alienated and the cultural radicals." *Ibid.*, pp. 229–231.

other cases "disorganization for disorganization's sake" occurred.[25] Nor can one forget Kelman's account of the manipulation of Harvard students in the escalation of protest there. One might hypothesize simply that as the radicals assumed control, the major disruptions followed; this, however, would not be the full story. Yet some of the disruption was for "good reasons." It is laudable, in any case, to show interest in public questions and to fight for one's beliefs. What could be more proper in a democracy than for groups to show how they feel about issues for the consideration of the elected representatives of the people (who will determine policy)? This may increase disorganization, however—especially if others are promoting different beliefs. Ideas must compete for acceptance in the public forum. To say this does not sanction the work of the arch nihilist who seeks to destroy with no ideas of constructive improvement.

This leads to the further reflection that, although people generally prefer social order and tend to dislike anarchy and chaos, nevertheless organization is not inevitably linked with what is "right" nor disorganization with what is "wrong." One can point out that a good example of a *well-organized* nation would be Germany under Hitler.[26] Other socio-cultural systems or sub-systems may be well organized but open to serious criticisms. Justice is just as important as "order," and other values may be of prime consideration. We are suggesting, then, that modern activism (coupled with the flowering of the mass media, some emphasis upon conflict and confrontation, and other elements) has unquestionably brought an increase in disorganization; but some of this has arisen for "good reasons." As was maintained in Chapter 13, the active-minded interest in ongoing society and concern with social problems and injustices are marks of progress. As a nation America has tried to bring improvements for Blacks during recent years. The path of progress has not been easy, and disorganization has obviously increased from the effort; further struggle is required. However, the vast majority of Americans feel that—despite the increased disorganization—the "right" course of action has been followed. Altogether it appears that under present conditions some increase in social disorganization is simply to be expected. We have to live with it. If this is

25 See, e.g., Bell's account of Columbia's alleged "gym" issue in Harlem. Daniel Bell, "Columbia and the New Left," *The Public Interest,* No. 13 (Fall, 1968), esp. pp. 70–71. Kelman states that Mark Rudd (the Columbia student leader) told a Harvard SDS audience that "the Columbia SDS demands themselves had been insignificant—that he 'didn't even know where the Morningside gym site was,' and that the Institute for Defense Analysis was 'nothing at Columbia.' There is only one 'issue' in these confrontations: whether or not American universities should be destroyed." S. Kelman, *op. cit.,* p. 224.

26 The period of marked social disorganization in post-First World War Germany took place *before* Hitler came to power, not *after.*

true, a huge number of Americans of all races, both sexes, all ages, and all regions of the nation, would deplore the use of violence in connection with any disruption as well as the philosophy of disruption for its own sake.

Final Thoughts

Three major areas of social change in Western society—population growth, advances in science and technology, and the rise of activist sentiment—have been singled out for attention, with special interests in their effects upon social disorganization. Other types of change could also be examined with an eye toward disorganization. It seems that on the basis of the three areas investigated, modern socio-cultural change gives rise to increased disorganization. Major advances have occurred and are still occurring, as most Westerns would reckon it, but disorganization is inevitable and must be accepted. In the case of activism it has even been noted that some disorganization has arisen for "good reasons"; most Americans would seemingly prefer their nation to have some disorganization if coupled with attempts to remedy injustice and other problems rather than have a well-organized but unjust and unresponsive society. Nevertheless one hopes that in the future one will see steady redressing of valid grievances and meeting of problems with a gradual decrease in social disorganization. Every age, it is clear, has its strong points and its distinctive problems—as well as some degree of disorganization.

At the same time one should call attention to the fact that, although modern problems are often critical and *stability* is a vulnerable point for advanced nations, the resources for meeting those problems and maintaining stability are greater than ever before. Nor do we mean only financial resources. A most distinctive characteristic of American society is its education; and as this nation moves to post-industrial times, this will be even more true. Drucker calls ours "the educated society."[27] Whatever problems and threats America and the Western world may have, more is known about those problems and possible ways of meeting them than ever before. The current stock of knowledge of social science is, of course, greater than ever before. Often it needs to be synthesized; indeed a pressing need exists for the synthesis of this fast-increasing knowledge.[28] In future years social scientists are

[27] Peter F. Drucker, *Landmarks of Tomorrow* (New York: Harper & Bros., 1958), esp. Chap. 5,; Drucker, "The Revolution in Higher Education," Chap. 4 in Thomas R. Ford (ed.), *The Revolutionary Theme in Contemporary America* (Lexington, Kentucky: University of Kentucky Press, 1965).

[28] Etzioni points out that, in social science research, it is much easier to acquire funds for the collection of information than for its analysis. He adds that far more

more likely to be called upon for contributions to ongoing society than at present. They will have to show readiness, willingness, and ability to contribute.[29] One contribution may be to present alternative conceptions of the "active society" from which leaders and others may select a preferred one for use as a framework in determining specific courses of action. It is unlikely that the various alternatives would be labelled and voted upon by the electorate. However, the basic notion of directing social change for the benefit of the total society is taking hold. Moreover, an actively-oriented society, which would be more responsive to the wishes of the people, may be presumed to give rise to a smaller amount of social disorganization. This conception, then, may be likened to "preventive sociology." To control population, science and technology, and other forces in democratic manner may be a considerable task. Modern society has by no means been *passive* in these matters,[30] but increased control in various aspects of such problems (such as the technological aspects of pollution) is clearly needed. The advice of social scientists will be generally sought in meeting specific social problems. Since modern advanced society is to some extent "disorganization-prone," increased active intervention in problems, increased emphasis upon making social inventions (as was described in Chapter 10), and accelerated study of the *techniques* of social engineering, are warranted. The people and their leaders may be expected to make substantial effort in order to achieve the social environment that they want.

---

information is collected by questionnaire surveys than is ever analyzed, even superficially. A. Etzioni, *op. cit.*, p. 147.

[29] We agree with Hauser's observation (made in 1969) that "it is to be hoped that the century from 1950 to 2050 will be the period during which the social sciences, especially sociology, will achieve a level of respectability and acceptance that will pave the way for social engineering to eliminate the chaos that characterizes contemporary society." Philip M. Hauser, *op. cit.*, p. 16.

[30] It has shown much concern regarding the contraceptive "pill." Society has been (and is currently) sensitive concerning technological advances that affect privacy as also alterations of personality and behavior by means of drugs, neurosurgical intervention, and the like. Then, behavior *resulting from* technological inventions (once they are made) has been regulated, often elaborately (as witness the many rules involving piloting and all-around operation of aircraft, radio, TV, auto driving, and other subjects).

Index of Names

Index of Subjects

DATE DUE

GAYLORD   PRINTED IN U.S.A.